How to Get the Most Out of

CompuServe

Fifth Edition

How to Get the Most Out of

CompuServe

Fifth Edition

Charles Bowen

David Peyton

RANDOM HOUSE
ELECTRONIC PUBLISHING

New York

How to Get the Most Out of CompuServe, Fifth Edition

Copyright © 1993 by Charles Bowen and David Peyton

Published in the United States by Random House, Inc., New York, and simultaneously in Canada by Random House of Canada, Limited.

Composed by Parker-Fields Typesetters Ltd.

Manufactured in the United States of America

Revised Edition

0   9   8   7   6   5   4   3

ISBN 0-679-79137-X

New York   Toronto   London   Sydney   Auckland

Contents

v

3 CompuServe Mail   29

4 The Forums   57

5 CB Simulator and Real-Time Conferencing 117

On-Line Survival Kit

Acknowledgments

We treasure the encouragement and support we get from the good people at CompuServe. Thanks to Doug Branstetter, Rich Baker, Kassie Rose, and Mary Mitchell.

Also thanks to the writers and other editors of *CompuServe Magazine* and the *Online Today* electronic publication for helping us to hear the voices of CompuServe, especially Cathy Conroy, John Edwards, Mike Pietruk, Holly Miller, Michael Naver, and R. Andrew Rathbone.

And, as always, thanks to our editor at Random House, Michael Roney, a just taskmaster and a great friend.

How to Get the Most Out of

CompuServe

Fifth Edition

Chapter

1

Getting Acquainted

In this chapter...

If you think of your computer as a car, then CompuServe Information Service becomes the road. And what a road it is! A connector to the outside world and so much more, this highway reaches information resources that were simply undreamed of a few years ago. By attaching a modem and a phone line to your computer, you can join nearly a million other people around the world who now use their computers to access some remarkable places.

Most personal computer owners have now heard of CompuServe. It is the industry leader in information services, the one that sets the standard for high-quality on-line systems. But, if you have not yet seen it firsthand, you may be sceptical about the remarkable things people are saying about it. What else *could* you think when they tell you of:

- Electronic mail, a fast, easy, reliable way to stay in touch with friends and relatives, as well as with businesses, clubs, and organizations. The same mail feature that lets an on-the-move business exec keep tabs on the home office also enables a mother to write instant letters to her son or daughter in the military. It has led the way in linking to electronic mail features on other information services, allowing CompuServe users to reach out even farther.

1

- On-line reference material, giving students an important edge in school. Not so long ago, few of us could have imagined even an electronic dictionary, but now CompuServe's reference library includes a 10 million word encyclopedia that is updated four times a year, as well as searchable electronic libraries with years' worth of back issues of newspapers and magazines, and much more.

- The latest news dispatches from some of the most respected wire services and newspapers; many reports available within minutes of their being written.

- Travel services, providing specific airline schedules and information on hotels and rental cars. You can even make airplane reservations through your computer.

- Weather features, giving local forecasts and summaries from all around the country, as well as special services, such as news of sports-related weather, ski reports, and more. In addition, up-to-the-minute weather maps can be drawn directly on your computer screen.

- Hassle-free shopping. An entire electronic mall operates just on the other side of your computer screen, and a classified ad section lets you become the merchant.

- Investor services, for shopping of another kind. Scores of financial features help you decipher the stock market, and enable you to buy and sell stocks through your keyboard at any hour.

- Games for after work, ranging from computer classics to a new style of real-time play, including multi-player games to pit your skills against players around the globe.

Yes, to many newcomers, these claims do sound too good to be true. However, we have trekked up and down these electronic byways for more than 10 years now and are here to tell you that they are all true. Furthermore, CompuServe, the nation's largest and oldest computer information service, is an innovator in new kinds of communications that are built around personal computers like yours.

Forums, for instance, are on-line clubs where people come together to exchange ideas and news about all kinds of subjects. Some 500 different forums operate on CompuServe, discussing topics as diverse as movies, genealogy, stamp collecting, law, medicine, journalism, political issues, pet care, soap operas, rock music, religion, and backpacking. Among the more popular forums are the ongoing computer-specific ones. They provide some of the best up-to-the-minute information available on all major hardware and software in today's computing community. Other forums serve small but dedicated groups, from court reporters to ham radio operators to model railroad enthusiasts to sailboaters.

Software exchange has always been an important part of CompuServe. Each forum has its own library where thousands of original programs and text files can be retrieved. Much of the software is public domain (read *free!*), while others are commercial "shareware" programs. In fact, the innovative shareware concept (in which programmers invite users to retrieve and try out new software before deciding whether to buy it) is native to CompuServe. Most pioneering shareware authors have been testing their imaginative marketing plans in CompuServe's on-line neighborhoods since the early 1980s.

Real-time talk is another CompuServe creation. For years now, CompuServe subscribers have been accustomed to sitting at their computers and carrying on conversations with the world, typing messages on their keyboards and reading instant replies on their screens. Real-time conferencing is so much a part of our electronic life now; not only is it a standard feature in all forums, but it also has a separate on-line "convention center" which lets subscribers electronically chat with celebrity guests from time to time. Besides that there is the famed CompuServe "CB Simulator," a freewheeling sort of nonstop, international cocktail party that is open to all.

Our Story Begins

CompuServe was not even a tenth of its current size when we took our first stumbling steps into this electronic world in the early 1980s. From the first, the idea that microcomputer owners were using their machines to *talk* to each other was fascinating to us. But we were skeptical journalists who went into our exploration expecting this much-touted "network nation" to turn out to be an interesting diversion at best. At worst, it would simply be so much hype (not exactly an unknown component in the computer industry, then as now). Sometime later, though, we emerged enthusiastic, and hooked. Both of us had daily CompuServe habits. Because of that, we also were considerably poorer. This exploration business is not for fixed incomes. You hold before you the testimonial of two on-line trackers who spent thousands of hours (and thousands of dollars) prowling the back roads of CompuServe, always looking for the "good stuff."

We found it and, along the way, discovered better roads. Being stubborn sorts, we always had to learn our lessons the hard way. What we have come up with is a good, reliable way to teach people about CompuServe. Since 1983, we have been writing about this remarkable on-line world, always with three goals in mind:

1. Get newcomers started with a good overview of the system.

2. Help them save money in connect-time dollars by knowing where they are going before they start.

3. Provide them with enough background so they can continue the exploration on their own, able to deal with the everchanging landscape of CompuServe.

While this book is primarily an introduction to CompuServe, it is not intended for new subscribers only. We expect some who come along on this expedition have tried CompuServe on their own, but have perhaps become entangled in the process. All are welcome, so long as we can make certain assumptions about you and your computer. For instance, we must assume that you know a few things about your computer. Ours is not an especially "technical" book; you won't need to write programs or draw flow charts, but we do expect that you can load a program and run it. We also assume you have a modem and that your computer is set up with the necessary cables and materials to communicate. (There are still people out there who think they can talk to CompuServe simply by setting a telephone on the same desk with their computer.) If you are in doubt about the fundamentals of communicating through your system, please check with your computer store and make sure you have all the necessary equipment to go on-line.

CompuServe Information Manager and Other Software

When we started writing about CompuServe a decade ago, we had to keep in mind that there were scores of different ways in which the system might appear on the screens of our readers. It all depended on the kind of computers they were using and the type of communications software they were running. Well, it turns out that even in the fast-paced computer world, some things never change. True, the past 10 years have seen much standardization in personal computing; most new users nowadays have either an IBM-compatible system or an Apple Macintosh. But at the same time, there has been an explosion in communications software development. So, while the variables in hardware have decreased, the options in software selection have multiplied; this means there are still scores of ways to see CompuServe. So, our challenge is the same today as it was with the very first edition of this book: to provide an introduction to CompuServe that is meaningful to you, regardless of the software and hardware you may be using. Some of the most frequent questions we are asked about CompuServe actually deal with communications software rather than the system itself. Many new subscribers wonder if they can get printouts of what they see on the screen. Others ask if they can write letters off-line, then connect to CompuServe and deliver them at a burst. The answer to both questions is yes, if you have smart communications software. We will try to steer you toward the smart programs.

CompuServe itself has taken a giant leap toward standardizing how we all see the system by providing its own communications software, a relatively new package called the CompuServe Information Manager (CIM). Three years in development at CompuServe's Columbus, Ohio headquarters, the new software is a stand-alone package that runs on IBM PC compatibles and Apple Macintosh computers, and offers:

- Pull-down menus.
- Light-bar cursors and dialog boxes.
- The familiar "desktop" metaphors now a part of so much modern application software.
- High-resolution graphics and mouse support.
- Guaranteed error-free displays, no matter how much static is on the phone line.

CIM operates as an effective *front-end* to CompuServe's hundreds of features, because it can:

1. Free you from having to memorize numerous on-line commands. Instead of entering precise letters and words at a prompt, you merely move a bar cursor to quickly choose options from a pull-down menu. This is just the sort of aim-and-shoot computing many of us have come to expect today.

2. Maximize your computing budget by doing much of its work off-line. No longer do you have to log on and spend your connect-time dollars just to write and read a few letters and messages. CIM can do these and other tasks while the money meter is turned off.

3. Allow you to group specific chores for more efficiency. When visiting on-line databases, for example, you can build a list of files to be retrieved and can tell the program to disconnect when the process is complete.

4. Let you make very smart use of your own disk space. While you are off-line, you may use a built-in text program to write electronic letters and replies, then place them in an "Out-Basket" on your disk for delivery in a batch on the next on-line session. While on-line, you may retrieve messages — individual letters as well as strings of messages and replies from the forums — and save them either in an "In-Basket" or in specifically named electronic *folders* on your disk for later reading when you are off-line again.

CIM also improves the *quality* of on-line communications by interacting with CompuServe in a new way: through a recently developed convention that CompuServe calls the "Host-Micro Interface." The HMI standard makes it possible for all on-line data (not just downloaded and uploaded files, but also menus, text articles, stock quotes, news reports, letters, and all the rest) to be transferred to your screen by way of the "B+ protocol," CompuServe's own error-free transfer method. This means that CIM always resists phone line static so that stray characters and garbled text can't interfere with the communications. When errors occur in transmission because of phone line noise, the program automatically detects them and simply directs Compu-Serve to retransmit the material. As a result, you see only the corrected data on your screen.

So, should you be a CIM user? Certainly, at least while you are starting out. Since the powerful CIM software was designed to work specifically with Compu-Serve to afford a hassle-free view of the system, it is especially welcome for newcomers. CompuServe provides first-rate on-line support for the software 24 hours a day through features that are free of connect time. CompuServe is virtually giving away the CIM software, because it is included in most startup kits these days. The latest versions have been offered for downloading at a $10 charge with a $10 usage credit; this means, in effect, a full refund.

To turn the question around, why would anyone not use the CompuServe Information Manager software? There are several reasons:

- The program simply may not be available for your kind of computer; at this writing, CompuServe has developed CIM only for IBM and compat-ibles, and for the Apple Macintosh systems. As noted earlier, most of us now use one of these two platforms, but there *are* still computers outside the two "standards." If you are stubbornly holding on to your computer against the waves of Mac and PC people, you are no doubt accustomed to hearing, "Uh, that software isn't available for you..." You're hearing it again with CIM.

- If you are an experienced modem traveller who visits many on-line systems, you may want a general terminal program that can be used with all of them. (This is an argument against all the currently popular "front-end" dedicated communications programs like CIM. One of the authors of this book has even been heard to grumble about such communications programs, grous-ing that he wants a car that can be driven on the back roads as well as the interstate.)

- You may simply prefer the features of a strong third-party program. Some first-rate "automated" terminal programs, such as TapCIS, OzCIS, and AutoSig, stand ready to help you save money by allowing you to do much of your CompuServing *off-line*. Chapter 14 introduces the major players in this exciting new field of automated terminal software and tells you how to get a program that meets your needs.

Nevertheless, we urge you to give CIM a chance, especially if you are new to this system. Take CompuServe up on its free software offer and give the program a good look. CIM is a great way to meet the system and to get a fix on its organization. You may find CIM is everything you want in Compu-Serve communicating. On the other hand, if you later decide to try some-thing else, CIM will have provided a good basis for making the transition to another program. Or you may join thousands who have decided to meet

CIM halfway, using it for some functions, then switching to a favorite third-party program for other activities. To help you make your decisions, we have filed a backgrounder on CIM in the back of the book (see Appendix B.) This, along with the user manual that comes with the software, should provide all the instructions you need for the program. (If you are *not* a CIM user, there are appendix articles for you as well, including sections about terminal settings, writing on-line, file transfer, etc.)

What Is CompuServe?

CompuServe began in 1969 when a small Columbus, Ohio insurance holding company toyed with the idea of using computers to help manage its business. Not sure of what computers could do, the company hired some experts to determine the cost of setting up a data-processing operation. The report, prepared by a 25-year-old engineering graduate, showed that the data-processing subsidiary would lose money the first year. "Do it," said the insurance company's president.

Engineer Jeffrey M. Wilkins, after convincing some of his associates to join him in building the fledgling company, began leasing time on local computers. For the first 10 years, CompuServe primarily served corporations and governments, providing convenient computer storage for their data. Then in 1979, when the personal computer was still more rumination than reality, CompuServe saw the new PC technology's potential and opened its consumer information service, which has been operating ever since.

Today CompuServe, Inc., still headquartered in Columbus, has broadened its scope from the days when it was recognized as a "time-sharing" company. The firm now offers services in videotex, network communication, and education. It outgrew its parent company in 1975 and "spun off" to become a public company with stock traded over-the-counter. In May 1980, CompuServe merged with H&R Block to become a subsidiary. Today, CompuServe can be accessed with a local telephone call in hundreds of cities. In fact, more than 85 percent of the U.S. population can log on directly. Hundreds more can reach the service through carrier networks like Tymnet, Telenet, DataPac, and others.

Be an Explorer!

CompuServe is more than buildings, big computers, and telephone connections. From time to time in this book, we will refer to it as a kind of *community*. This attitude is common among those who regularly visit this on-line world. As you become familiar with the landscape, you will have the sensation of traveling from one place to another through your keyboard. On-line features have their own personalities, much like neighborhoods in a metropolis. (Some early subscribers even dubbed this electronic environment "Micropolis.")

Unlike real brick-and-mortar communities, however, Micropolis is in a constant state of change. People who work at CompuServe regularly add new features and improve old ones. While this is something we found most appealing in our exploration of the system, this ever-changing landscape does cause a problem for those of us writing books. No matter how quickly we get into print, there is always a chance that some material might be outdated because someone at CompuServe has added a feature or found a better way to do something which involves a changed command or simply a new look for an old service. This edition contains updated material throughout. As with earlier editions, we have worked closely with the people at CompuServe to make sure the chapters are as up-to-date as possible. Nonetheless, the system may have changed slightly since we last passed a particular electronic landmark. Still, if you take to heart what we show you here, occasional changes shouldn't upset you. We have focused this book on the system's *structure*, which won't change significantly, even if a few commands do. If you get the idea of how to move from one area to another, a small change in commands shouldn't throw you. Also, we have noticed that whenever CompuServe makes changes in command structure, it usually allows subscribers to enter either the old commands or the new ones.

So, we hope that instead of being upset by system changes, you are challenged by them. After all, you are a pioneer, one of the first one-third of microcomputer owners in the country to travel on the CompuServe highway. Analysts predict that throngs of newcomers are right behind you. For that reason, it is our goal not only to show specific commands for reaching popular features, like the CB Simulator, on-line games, and forums, but also to give you enough information to allow you to continue the expedition on your own.

What Does It Cost?

Now we have come to the spoiler question: How much does CompuServe cost? To answer that, let's return to our motorist metaphor. CompuServe is both a quiet suburban street and an electronic superhighway where the fast lane connects us to the latest developments in on-line communications. What you pay for this service depends on where you go. This digital frontier is not without its toll roads.

CompuServe offers a flat monthly fee subscription rate of $8.95 to give users unlimited access to scores of products and services. You may visit this home port of services as often as you like without worrying about running up additional costs through hourly access charges.

Of course, this is not exactly a new concept to our modern minds. There is probably a restaurant or two in your neighborhood that offers an evening of all-you-can-eat for $8.95.

But this is more than an occasional special or a way for CompuServe to clear out surplus, unwanted merchandise. Features in this limitless access area include some of the system's most popular services, such as shops and stores of the Electronic Mall and Shopper's Advantage, and facilities of CompuServe Mail, where you may send up to 60 messages a month without additional charges. Also included are the airline services of Travelshopper and Eaasy Sabre, Grolier's Academic American Encyclopedia, weather reports from the National Weather Service, the latest news from the Associated Press, a collection of user support and help features, and more. (A complete list of these features is provided in Appendix E.)

This autonomous suburb of CompuServe becomes a great place to learn how to use the system for several reasons:

1. It's cheap. Besides letting you use all the designed features without hourly connect-time expenses, CompuServe also waives the $8.95 monthly flat fee for the first two months of your subscription. Therefore, you can do a lot of exploring and learning before the meter is ever turned on.

2. It's a microcosm of the entire system. This area includes a couple of features from each of the main branches of CompuServe's enormous system. To explore, you simply follow the menus on the screen and visit each branch at your leisure, from communications, news, and travel services to shopping, games and entertainment, and reference and financial features.

3. It puts a priority on learning. Among the options in this unmetered area are membership support services for getting help in a hurry and finding answers to your questions. Not only that, this section includes several special forums that can be used without hourly charges. The Practice Forum will teach you how to use the commands and options supported in all CompuServe forums, while special support forums stand ready to serve users of the CompuServe Information Manager communications software.

Perhaps best of all, your on-line home port prepares you for future exploration beyond its borders. The system provides additional information so you can plot your course at your own pace. As you visit various branches of the system, you will occasionally see menu options to describe related *extended services*. These signposts mark the entrance ramps to that tolled superhighway.

Extended Services give CompuServe its personality and its power; they are as varied as the districts in a metropolis. Some — like the multiple forums that serve the system's IBM and Apple computer users — operate like cities within a city. They routinely help thousands of visitors every day, around the clock, fielding questions and serving up software from their massive reserves. Others, like the forums that support the special interests of specific hobbies and careers, are like neighborhood watering holes. Here, the conversation is often friendly, funny, sometimes intimate. Still other Extended Services are like the research tools in a top-notch library, with databases and catalogs of information ranging from product reviews to today's world news, census reports, and business demographics.

Extended Services are billed at hourly rates depending on your modem access speed ($6 an hour for 300 baud, $8.00 for 1200 and 2400 baud, and $16.00 for 9600 baud). The same hourly rates apply regardless of the time of day or whether it is a weekday or weekend. CompuServe was the first national service to discontinue a higher "prime-time" rate for business hours.

But wait a minute: There are *so many* extended services — literally hundreds of them—how can you avoid becoming overwhelmed by the possibilities? How can you ever find the ones that you need? Here are some tips that will help you on your way:

- For starters, use the unmetered features in the system to get the lay of the land. Because it is a microcosm of the system as a whole, this electronic suburb can outline a map for you.

- Accept the system's offer to describe related Extended Services as you reach the outer branches in your initial exploration. This is a quick way to see what else is available in the interest area you have already been looking at.

- Look in on the Member Support features. Among them are services that will "index" all the various features on CompuServe.

- Once you've charted your course for further exploration, locate forums along the way and drop in for a visit. We will show you how in Chapter 4. CompuServe is at its best as a person-to-person medium, and questions and answers are its life's blood.

- When you find forums that serve some of your interests, leave messages introducing yourself and strike up a conversation. Remember, fellow visitors can tell you about other features you might be interested in. After all, no one knows all the features of CompuServe (just as no one has visited all the high points of New York or Chicago or Los Angeles), but people of like interests do share some valuable pointers with each other.

Finally, don't feel so alone because you've just arrived. This medium is still so young that everyone you meet on-line is more or less a newcomer. We're all first-generation citizens here.

Our Plan

Now that we are ready to begin the exploration, here is our itinerary.

The next chapter focuses on CompuServe's organization and appearance on the screens of users of the CompuServe Information Manager software, as well as users of third-party, non-CIM programs. The chapter illustrates CompuServe's tree structure, the use of menus, and the method of jumping from branch to branch of the tree using the GO command to bypass many layers of menus. It also introduces some of CompuServe's many support features, such as on-line help and the access phone number database, and covers costs and other issues.

CompuServe is an interactive communications medium; therefore, we will waste no time introducing you to the features that get you talking to your electronic neighbors. Chapters 3, 4, and 5 cover the system's main personal communications tools: mail, forums, and conferencing.

Chapter 3 covers the ever more powerful CompuServe Mail feature which is everyone's on-line post office. The service allows you to write to anyone on the system and even enables you to have letters forwarded to *other* computer mail systems, such as MCI Mail and Internet. It also can maintain an automatic "address book" for the user IDs of your regular correspondents, and filing cabinet features for drafts of letters.

Chapter 4 takes us into the forums, perhaps CompuServe's most famous feature. The potential of these electronic clubhouses is enormous. If CompuServe consisted only of its forums, it still would be the primary computer information service in America. The chapter shows how to use the forums with and without the CIM software.

Real-time conferencing is the topic of Chapter 5. It introduces us to the lively CB Simulator — again, with and without the CIM interface — as well as conferencing the forums and elsewhere, including the system's electronic Convention Center, where "guest speakers" regularly appear to meet the public.

After that, we change directions. CompuServe is different for each of us, but what we all have in common is the computer. So it is no surprise that some of the most popular features on CompuServe continue to be the computer-related services and forums, which are the topics of Chapter 6.

As an international system that thrives on data, CompuServe has always given special attention to news features. Chapter 7 illustrates how to bring the resources of the world's news wires and newspapers to your computer screen. Highlighted are the Executive News Service with its wonderful electronic clipping folders and the searchable Newsgrid database, as well as specialty news shops, from the computer industry reports of Online Today to the entertainment news of Hollywood Hotline.

Then, Chapter 8 brings us to news of another type — the technical data that fuels the business and investment communities. CompuServe has some remarkable tools for investors, such as daily stock market quotes, databases of historical quotes, consultant reports, and demographics for researching plans and ideas.

Research also is the subject in Chapter 9, which covers the growing reservoir of reference materials on-line. Gateways — electronic portals through which we can electronically travel to many other computer systems around the world — are a hot new topic in the on-line community. CompuServe has been a leader in the field. Working with Telebase Systems Inc. on projects such as IQuest and assorted specialized research libraries, CompuServe enables users to search the files of some of the major database vendors in the world, including BRS,

Dialog, NewsNet, and others. This chapter shows how to use the gateways to search back issues of newspapers, magazines, trade journals, government reports, and more.

Travel in the more conventional sense is covered next. Chapter 10 looks at CompuServe's considerable travel services. It shows how to make airline and hotel reservations through the keyboard. You can actually shop for the best deal, since unlike many on-line systems, CompuServe provides more than one reservation service. We also seek out related travel features, such as a database of travel stories and tips.

In Chapter 11 we take a breather and look in on the system's entertainment center. Computers and games have been linked since the beginning, but no one plays games like the modem crowd. On CompuServe, you can play some state-of-the-art games, competing against the computer and/or against human opponents around the world. The chapter is a survey of all the various game worlds waiting to be conquered.

If shopping is your passion, stay tuned for Chapter 12, which covers Compu-Serve's own Electronic Mall (100 stores under one digital roof), as well as the extensive Shoppers Advantage Club (formerly called Comp-U-Store.) The chapter also introduces the system's recently revamped Classified Ads section.

Chapter 13 discusses a variety of hobby/personal-interest topics, including a number of general-interest forums that cover topics as diverse as aquariums, gardening, cooking, wine, sports, music, arts, and automobile racing. These hobby features are some of CompuServe's fastest growing services.

Chapter 14 offers a look at some of the communications program alternatives to the CompuServe Information Manager, with special emphasis on the new breed of automated terminal programs such as TapCIS, AutoSig, OzCIS, and others. The chapter gives you an idea of what these programs offer and how you can check them out.

The book concludes with a look at what the future holds for CompuServe and some thoughts on how you can continue to be part of it.

Finally, our back pages feature The On-Line Survival Kit, which contains appendix material, additional information on subjects such as uploading and downloading, writing on-line, the structure of CIM, getting access numbers, forum lists, terminal settings for non-CIM users, and more.

Signing Up and Logging On

If you have never logged on to CompuServe before, the most important section of the appendix — at least initially — will be the article called "Getting Started," Appendix A.

Two keys to your CompuServe account come with your startup package: a user ID number and a password. The ID number is your public self; it is the address to which other subscribers write to you by CompuServe Mail and in the forums, and it is the information listed in the Members Directory under your name. On the other hand, your password is private; it is the combination that opens the door to your account. You are wise to change your password regularly, a procedure that is also described in the Survival Kit.

The "Getting Started" section in the back of the book shows you how to use your user ID and password. It provides information about signing up and logging on to the system. It will be a good idea for you to read the manual for your communications software, then look over the Getting Started section before proceeding to Chapter 2. As the appendix article says, the signup/logon procedures are different, depending on whether you are using the CompuServe Information Manager software.

2

How the System Is Organized

In this chapter...

Menus and the Evolution of CIM
The GO Command
Keeping up with a Constantly Changing Service
Menu Symbols
Getting Help
Finding Other Information
Your Password

Here is a riddle for you: How is CompuServe like a restaurant? If your answer is that restaurants serve bites of food and CompuServe serves bytes of information, then you are too clever for us. We were thinking more along the lines of how restaurants and CompuServe are both "menu driven." This chapter is about CompuServe's organization; it shows that we begin with the menu.

Most of us have a passing acquaintance with computer menus. Nearly all modern software uses them to give you an overview of a program or service's structure, enumerating the options that are open to you. CompuServe uses the menus in the same way.

In addition, as with menus at a restaurant, CompuServe menus do more than simply tell you what is available; they can also guide you through the ordering process. Suppose you are on your first trip to a French restaurant and the menu lists some dishes that are pretty exotic to your eye, such as "Escargot à la Française avec pomme de terre à la Normandie." You want to try it, so as the waiter waits, you reflect on your three options:

1. Try to say the name as the French do (and hope your pronunciation is better than ours).

2. Translate it into English —"I'll take the Normandy-style snails and potatoes"—then muse upon how much more tempting it sounded in the original language.

3. Look at the little number to the left of the description and discreetly whisper, "I'll take the Number Three."

The last option appeals because it allows you to take advantage of a system already in use. Maybe the chef doesn't understand English, but he knows the number 3, and heads for the pot of snails. When the cashier sees 3 on the check, he knows to ring up a tidy $39.95. So, the numbers are integrated into the restaurant's delivery system.

CompuServe has always used menus in the same way. Visiting the system for the first time is a little like your maiden voyage into that French restaurant, since you may be unsure of what or even how to order. Fortunately, the options are set out in a logical arrangement that CompuServe's computers are programmed to understand. For years now, whenever we log on to CompuServe, among the first things we see is a *top menu*, something like this:

```
CompuServe              TOP

   1    Subscriber Assistance
   2    Find a Topic
   3    Communications/Bulletin Bds.
   4    News/Weather/Sports
   5    Travel
   6    The Electronic MALL/Shopping
   7    Money Matters/Markets
   8    Entertainment/Games
   9    Home/Health/Family
  10    Reference/Education
  11    Computers/Technology
  12    Business/Other Interests

Enter choice !
```

All along the path on CompuServe, your options are outlined on the screen in numbered menu form. You don't have to be able to speak the computer's language to tell the system what to do or where to go. You only need to enter a number, then press the ENTER or RETURN key. (In this book, we use the words ENTER and RETURN interchangeably to mean the *carriage return* or end-of-line key on your keyboard.)

When you see the menu on the screen, think of a waiter standing at your table with pad in hand, patiently waiting for instruction. The emphasis is on *patiently.* The system is waiting for your instructions and will wait, usually up to fifteen minutes, between the commands you enter. (After 15 minutes of silence from your end, the system is liable to get edgy and disconnect you. But, even if you are disconnected, you only need to call back and all is forgiven.)

Once you enter the number corresponding to your choice, the system starts on the path to your selection, which often leads to another menu. Menu-driven CompuServe allows you to "fine-tune" your request, zeroing in on what you want by stepping through a series of menus. You can get to any of the services on the system by going from the main menu to a submenu to a sub-submenu, and so forth, typing one number after another and pressing the RETURN key after each selection. When you run out of menus, you have arrived. You see only one menu at a time; the most recent one is always related to the previous one, like branches on a tree. The arrangement has been called exactly that: *a tree structure*, with each menu branching out into menus of related features. Once you know the structure, you can speed the travel with a function called the "GO command" to jump to specific branches of the tree, bypassing large sections of menus.

To see how the important GO command fits into the big picture, let's first explore some history.

Menus Evolving to the CompuServe Information Manager

Long-time CompuServe subscribers recall that in the late 1970s, the consumer service we now think of as CompuServe was known as "Micronet." Being a CompuServe subscriber in those days meant you were given your own on-line "programming area" (later called an account area) to which you could log on and, from a terse "OK" prompt, reach various features. By entering the command "R CB," you could tell Micronet to "run" (or "request") the CB Simulator feature. Once there, you could chat with friends around the country by just typing messages on the keyboard, then waiting a few seconds for replies to appear on your screen. By entering "R MAIL," you ran/requested the electronic mail program where you could post letters, making them available to recipients worldwide in a matter of minutes. "R BULLET" took you to a general purpose bulletin board while "R SIG" (for "special interest group") could send you toward a discussion forum, and so on. So, in its earliest incarnation, CompuServe was like a collection of programs that could be "run" from your unique little corner of the system.

Today, greatly improved versions of these and other original features (the CB Simulator, forums, electronic mail, and many others, all covered in this book) are still available and just as important to the system. However, later subscribers have gotten to know the lay of the CompuServe landscape in an entirely different way. They picture the system, not as isolated programming islands from which users electronically launch themselves, but rather as an organization of interlocking menus and accommodating navigation commands. When they want to visit the CB Simulator, they select a numbered option from a menu or they travel directly to the feature by entering "GO CB." Other menu items and/or GO commands reach the mail program, the forums, and hundreds of other features. Only old-timers recognize this menu system for what it really is: an extensive, friendly *interface* that CompuServe automatically runs at logon for each user. By producing an elaborate tree of ASCII menus, this famous interface has benefitted the user community for many years. It is descriptive enough to help newcomers, but also offers old hands the flexibility they need to abbreviate or even bypass it all together as they become better acquainted with how CompuServe works.

Because CompuServe was created as an ASCII, text-based system, it remains accessible to virtually any kind of personal computer. No special communications software is required to use CompuServe. Today, as in the earliest days of the service, *any* kind of terminal program — from the plainest to the super system — can log on and use the hundreds of on-line features. This approach— making the system open to all kinds of computers and showing the same menu structure to all comers — has made good sense, especially in the first decade of microcomputing when scores of different kinds of computers were in use, many with different operating systems and different terminal programs. By keeping its on-line system requirements to a minimum, CompuServe opened its arms to all of these computer users. The decision certainly paid off. By the end of its first 10 years in 1989, CompuServe had some 650,000 subscribers, making it the largest information service in North America. Versions of CompuServe now also operate throughout Western Europe as well as in Japan, Taiwan, and the Pacific Rim. In the United States, the system can be accessed with a local telephone call in more than five hundred cities; thus, more than 85 percent of the population can log on directly. Hundreds more reach the service through carrier networks like Tymnet, Telenet (SprintNet), DataPac, and others. So, providing a powerful, basic ASCII system has been a good idea for a long time.

On the other hand, CompuServe didn't become the industry leader by standing still. Right now, big changes are afoot in personal computing. More standardization is evident in hardware and software (virtually all new computers are either IBM compatible or Apple Macintosh systems). Machines are bigger, faster, and more graphically sophisticated than they were a decade ago. For many people in this new wave of computing, the plain ASCII CompuServe is beginning to look a little *too* plain.

"The expectations of our users are increasing daily," says CompuServe Executive Vice President Barry Berkov, in charge of the company's information service division. "As they become used to computer programs that are simple to use, yet take advantage of the power of a personal computer, they expect an interface for their information service that works the same way." This is the thinking that gave rise to the CompuServe Information Manager software, introduced in the previous chapter.

Today we find the CompuServe community divided into two major groups:

- In one group are people who are happy to continue with the text-based system they have used for years. Some are experienced telecomputer operators who use the same general-purpose communication program to access many different on-line services (CompuServe, certainly, but also private bulletin-board systems, other commercial information services, and more). They are quite at home with the features of their present communications software and aren't interested in learning a new program. Also in this group are those who may be using older personal computers that predate the accelerating standardization; for them, the new CIM software may not be available yet.

- On the other side is the growing group of subscribers who are logging on with newer machines and want to be able to take advantage of that extra computing power on-line. They may be looking for good, powerful communications software that is dedicated to CompuServe only. They will probably give a long look at the CIM software CompuServe produces, as well as some of the powerful automated terminal programs produced by third-party publishers.

For both groups, an understanding of the system's structure is a key to making a sound decision.

CompuServe Information Manager's Browse Menu

This book is concerned with how to travel CompuServe with and without CIM. We have talked about the role of menus in the plain ASCII-based version of the system. Now let's get a taste of how CIM operates in terms of menus.

Corresponding with that "top" menu illustrated earlier, the CompuServe Information Manager provides a Services pull-down menu with a BROWSE option that enables you to explore CompuServe's many features as you follow the trail of service menus, as shown in Figure 2.1. Selecting the **Browse** option from the Services pull-down menu causes the software to display the general categories of CompuServe features either in words and phrases (as in the IBM version of the software) or in icons (as in the Apple Macintosh and Microsoft Windows versions). Either way, selecting a service group is the same: CIM makes the communications connection and takes you to the next menu level, which lists choices contained in the group that you selected. So, if you chose the option for "Forums," CIM logs on to the system and shows you a list of forum categories, from which you might choose "Hardware Forums." This causes the system to display another list containing the computer hardware-related forums.

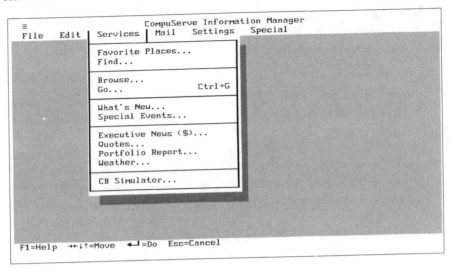

Figure 2.1 CIM's Services Menu

Find: The Quick Path to Locate Topics of Interest

Browsing is easy (and can even be educational); however, when you are look-ing for a specific kind of service, you usually want it in a hurry. A faster, more efficient means to CompuServe travel is the **Find** command, which also illus-trates one of the ways the system itself can help you navigate.

- In the CIM software, Find is on the Services menu, as seen in Figure 2.1. When you choose Find, a dialog box opens; it is a kind of index in which you enter a topic and CompuServe presents a list of places in the system where you might find related information. Once in the Topic dialog box, the software asks you for a topic.

- Those using software other than the CIM package may also use the Find command. At any ! prompt in the ASCII display of the system, enter FIND followed by a keyword, such as FIND APPLE.

Once a Find command has been entered (either through CIM or at the ! prompt in the ASCII version of the system), CompuServe locates all the related services from the system's master index and customizes a menu from which you can choose. For example, if you enter a keyword such as COMPUTERS, the system searches for relative features, then creates a list. Then you can GO directly to any of them. If you are using the CIM software, you simply high-light a service on that customized menu and select the **Go** action button to go directly to it; if you are using third-party ASCII software, you can select the menu number of the feature you want.

CIM'S Favorite Places

CIM also has a **Favorite Places** option that can be selected for use and maintenance from the Services menu. Choosing it lets you create and maintain your *own* menu of services. Then you may use the option to visit your favorite features by highlighting and selecting from the same menu. The display includes these action options:

1. **Go** takes you directly to the service currently highlighted by the bar cursor.

2. **Add** lets you put other features on your Favorite Places menu. You are prompted to supply two kinds of information:

   a) A description, as you want it to appear on the menu.

   b) The service name — the word or code that appears on the introductory screen of the feature you are adding.

3. **Delete** (or **Remove**, in the IBM PC version) allows you to remove the currently highlighted service from the menu.

4. **Open** lets you edit the description and/or service name for the highlighted choice. (**Note**: This option is currently available only in the Macintosh version of the software. IBM PC users, may make the same kind of change by using Remove to delete the current feature, then using Add to put in the corrected version.)

The GO Command

So, the service names of the various features are all-important in navigating CompuServe, whether you are using the CompuServe Information Manager or a third-party communications program. Every feature on CompuServe has a unique service name which the system recognizes as its location or its address. The service name is a series of letters, sometimes an acronym, that identifies the feature. In this book, service names are usually capitalized within parentheses preceded by "GO", as in (GO OLTFORUM).

In CompuServe literature and in on-line help files, these service names are sometimes referred to as "quick reference words" or "page numbers."

GOing with CIM

If you are using the CompuServe Information Manager software, you can **Go...** directly to a service by choosing the **Go...** command from the Services menu to open a dialog box. To use it, simply enter the service name of the feature you want and the service takes you there. All service names can be abbreviated to six letters, which the system will recognize as the service name.

For both IBM and Macintosh versions of the software there is an accelerator key for the Go… function. Those using the IBM/compatible program may press CONTROL-G, while Macintosh users may use COMMAND-G. Using the accelerator key allows you to bypass the Services menu and jump right to the dialog box.

GOing without CIM

Those not using the CIM software — anyone using a general terminal program to see the system in its "natural" ASCII state — can also use the GO command by simply entering GO at a ! prompt followed by the quick reference word, such as GO ENCYCLOPEDIA.

Keeping up with a Constantly Changing Service

Add to death and taxes the certainty that today's CompuServe will not be the same CompuServe next month or probably not even next week. CompuServe is a living, breathing community, and features are added regularly, as the system is fine-tuned. Special events happen frequently. The smart CompuServe user needs to keep abreast of changes and special events to take advantage of what the system offers. That is why **What's New This Week** is an important link to the changing nature of the system.

Twice a week, the What's New feature is displayed. It is updated every Thursday and the new menu appears automatically the first two times you connect to the system after an update. What's New lists important happenings on the system in headline form. If you want to read a complete article related to the headline, select that headline to see more information.

Any time spent reading the articles in What's New is not charged. If you want to see it again after the first two automatic displays:

- And you are using the CIM software, select the **What's New** option from the Service menu (Figure 2.1).
- If you are a non-CIM user, you can view What's New by entering GO NEW at any prompt on the system.

Is the Executive Option for You?

As you Browse the menus of CompuServe, you will sometimes see a code — (E) — beside some options. This means that the feature is available only to subscribers who have what is called the "Executive Option." When you become a CompuServe subscriber, the system usually asks if you want to also sign up for this special service. If you turn down the offer at signup but later decide to give it a second look, you can GO EXECUTIVE for a detailed menu on-line.

The Executive Option, which requires a minimum monthly usage charge, offers access to exclusive financial and news databases, special merchandise offers and discounts, and other special services both on-line and off.

Here is what you receive if you subscribe to the Executive Option:

1. Access to exclusive databases and services, including Executive News Service, Ticker Retrieval, Disclosure II, SuperSite, Institutional Broker's Estimate System, Securities Screening, Return Analysis, and Company Screening.

2. A 50-percent increase in the amount of on-line storage available in your Personal File Area, along with an opportunity to purchase additional storage space at a reduced weekly rate.

3. A six-month storage period for personal files without charge. Thirty days is standard for users who do not subscribe to the Executive Option.

4. A 10-percent discount on the purchase of most CompuServe products.

5. Special direct marketing offers for goods and services from CompuServe's affiliated merchants and manufacturers.

6. Volume discounts on information retrieval from selected transaction price financial databases.

The Costs

Those who choose the Executive Option are subject to a monthly $10 minimum-usage charge. CompuServe's Membership Support Fee is applied toward the Executive Service Option as well as connect-time, on-line CompuServe purchases, and communication surcharges. Also with the Executive Option, the Electronic Funds Transfer monthly minimum is waived.

Menu Symbols

As you explore the system through its branches of menus, you need to be aware of several important symbols related to costs. Chapter 1 gives the details of CompuServe's costs, and Appendix E lays out the specifics of the system's Standard and Alternative Pricing Plans. As you view menus in the system, you will often see service titles marked with a "+" or "$" next to the menu choice. The services marked with a:

- "+" are charged at the CompuServe charge depending on the modem speed. That is to say, they are *outside* the Basic Pricing Plan area.
- "$" are charged at an additional rate, a surcharge.
- "(E)" are part of the Executive Option described in the previous section.
- "(W)" require an 80-character display to view properly.

For additional information on premium surcharges type GO TRANSACTION.

Getting Help

CompuServe is large and complex; no one book or manual can answer every question. Fortunately, the system itself offers much on-line help that is organized to answer nearly all frequently asked questions. In addition, most of the on-line help time is free.

Taking a Tour of the System (GO TOUR)

CompuServe offers a free guided tour through the service to give you the "big picture" of what is available. After each section you have the option of continuing on the tour or learning more about that section. Some of the features you can learn more about on the tour include CompuServe Mail, the CB Simulator, the Electronic Mall, airline reservations and travel services, Grolier's Academic American Encyclopedia and other reference databases, and games and entertainment features.

Information Manager Forums

If you are a CompuServe Information Manager user, some of your first questions might involve the CIM software itself. CompuServe provides two forums. They are free of connect charges, but are subject to communication surcharges, and they allow you to ask questions and receive answers about the program. To access the forums, do one of the following:

IBM DOS users, select the Go... option and specify the address CIMSUPPORT.

Windows users, choose the Go... option and specify WCIMSUPPORT.

Macintosh users, select the Go... option and specify the address MACCIM.

If you are not a CIM user, but are thinking about making the switch, the forums are there to help. Enter GO at a ! prompt on the system followed by the address of the forum you want to visit. CompuServe customer-service employees familiar with the operation of Information Manager as well as some programmers who are involved in the ongoing development of the software monitor the message section and answer user questions quickly.

Since usage of the forum is free, it is an excellent place to practice reading messages and become familiar with the way the program operates within a typical forum.

Note If you have not visited a forum before, you might want to read Chapter 4 before logging on.

General Help in the FEEDBACK Area (GO FEEDBACK)

The Feedback area is free of connect charges, except for communication surcharges, and is your connection to CompuServe's customer service department. The main Feedback menu gives you an option to write a letter with your question to the customer-service people. However, it also includes a "Questions and Answers" section that covers frequently asked questions. Check out the Q&A for the answer, before you take the time to ask your question. Topics include billing, logon and system access, CompuServe Mail, forums, the personal file area, service options and terminal settings, the Executive Option, CompuServe's on-line ordering, the CB Simulator, market quotes, CompuServe software, uploading and downloading files to and from CompuServe, graphics, and games.

If you can't find an answer to your question in the Questions and Answers section, you may write to Customer Service directly. You enter your question in the Feedback area and a customer service representative will answer via CompuServe Mail, usually within 24 hours.

Other ways to contact Customer Service include:

By Phone: Monday through Friday, 8 a.m. to midnight (Eastern time); Saturday and Sunday, noon to 10 p.m. (Eastern time). Customer Service's telephone numbers are (614) 457-8650 from outside the contiguous US, or (800) 848-8990 from within the US, including Alaska, Hawaii, Puerto Rico, St. Thomas, St. John, and St. Croix.

By Mail: Direct all written inquiries regarding your account to:
CompuServe, Inc.
Attn: Customer Service
PO Box 20212
5000 Arlington Centre Blvd.
Columbus, Ohio 43220
Include your user ID number on all written correspondence.

By FAX: CompuServe's fax number is (614) 457-0348.

To ensure prompt delivery of a faxed letter, include a cover page clearly stating your name and User ID number, and the name of the department and/or person to whom the letter is being sent.

Finding Other Information

The GO command (and CIM's Go... option) can also take you to other on-line resources for a variety of information.

Subscriber Directory (GO DIRECTORY)

The on-line directory of subscribers is the place where you can find the user IDs of thousands of members. With hundreds of thousands of users currently on-line, the directory has helped to unite and re-unite many friends and relatives over the years. (In fact, the next chapter begins with an amazing story of how the directory played a part in bringing together family members who had been looking for each other for 30 years.)

The subscriber directory is searchable by name. The state and city may be used as search criteria to narrow a name search. You may omit the first name, state, or city responses by entering a blank line (that is, pressing RETURN). However, if you omit any of these particulars, there is a good chance the resulting list will be too large to be displayed; if that happens, you will be prompted again for the omitted information. You may use /START to terminate any current search and begin a new one.

A subscriber's inclusion in the directory is voluntary. When signing up for CompuServe, a user is automatically asked if he or she wants to be included. Also, the feature itself provides an option that lets you include or exclude your own user ID number in the directory. Any change you request will take a week to be effective.

Finding Access Phone Numbers (GO PHONES)

If you are planning a trip and need to know how to access CompuServe from another city, you can find access numbers for hundreds of locations on-line through the free phone number database. This feature lets you list all the numbers accessible from anywhere in the US and Canada by a specific baud rate, or locate a number in a specific city or area code.

When searching for access numbers by city and state, the state name doesn't need to be abbreviated if you don't know its abbreviation. The entire state name, or as much of the name as you know, may be used.

On the end of each network-access telephone number there is a code identifying the network service for that network-access telephone number. All networks have a surcharge associated with their use. You may GO RATES to check the current rates for communication surcharges.

For more details on the phone database and for tips on using CompuServe's relatively new toll-free 800-number system for finding access numbers, see Appendix C in the On-Line Survival Kit.

Information About Billing and Charges (GO BILLING)

The free BILLING area of CompuServe lets you examine the current CompuServe rates, review all the charges made against your account in recent weeks, and learn about the various billing options CompuServe offers. You may change your billing address, or review and change your billing method from this menu. Other options give you an overview of CompuServe billing methods, request detailed information, inquire about your account, or tell you what to do if you suspect unauthorized use of your account. You can also use the BILLING area to access the Executive Service Option signup discussed earlier. For more information on using this feature, see Appendix E in the On-Line Survival Kit.

Checking Out the Rules (GO RULES)

When you sign up for a CompuServe Account, you agree to abide by certain rules. These rules can be reviewed along with CompuServe's copyright policy, service agreement terms, and business account service terms by choosing RULES as a service name. The RULES area is free of connect charges. The rules and a discussion on copyright are also printed in Appendix G.

Changing Your Password On-line (GO PASSWORD)

One of the best ways to avoid unauthorized use of your CompuServe account is to keep your password secret and change it occasionally. There is always a chance that someone could learn your password. If anyone gets access to the password, that person can log on to CompuServe with your account number. That is why you should never tell anyone your password, on-line or off-line.

If you are not using the CIM software, you can change your password on-line by entering GO PASSWORD and following the prompts. The system will ask for your current password, then direct you to enter the new one you have chosen. The password *will not* display on the screen as you type it (a security precaution). Then, you will be directed to confirm the change by typing the new password again.

If you are using CIM, you need to make the change on-line *before* changing the password in the software itself. To change your password on the system, enter PASSWORD as the service name with the GO option. You are taken to an area where you are asked to enter your current password, then your new password. To make sure you know what you entered as a new password, the system asks you to retype your new password. If you type it correctly a second time, you are told that the password change was successful. Remember that as soon as you change your password on-line, you should change your password in your Information Manager program before attempting to communicate with CompuServe again.

3

CompuServe Mail

In this chapter...

Electronic Mail Today
CompuServeMail Through CIM
Mail without CIM
Mailing to Different Systems
Congressgrams, SantaGrams, Valentines, and More

What better symbolizes the merging of computers and communications than the idea of an electronic letter zipping across the country or around the world in a matter of minutes? Electronic mail is such a widely known medium that it recently qualified as an answer on television's "Jeopardy" game show ("What is 'e-mail?'"). Electronic mail can be the beginning of a friendship, or the means for renewing old acquaintances. Every day, Compu-Serve Mail makes possible on-line reunions of former neighbors, childhood sweethearts, college roommates, and old Army buddies. Sometimes it can even bring together members of a family after they have been lost to one another for decades.

A few years ago, Robert Switzer was heading into the 1990s with a 30-year-old heartache. He had spent more than half of his life unable to find his sons. The two boys were not yet of school age in the early 1960s when Robert and their mother divorced. Although the courts granted Robert custody of his sons, his ex-wife spirited them away to another state where she remarried and changed the boys' last name.

Switzer didn't know where his former wife had gone or that the boys' surname had been changed, but he never stopped looking for them. As a salesman, Switzer traveled in his job; in every new city he visited, he checked telephone books and city directories. He even engaged the help of lawyers, police, and Social Security workers, but by the late 1980s still had no idea where Robert Jr. and John had gone.

It was during the Christmas season of 1989 that Switzer took his search to a new technology; he decided to use the CompuServe Member Directory (GO DIRECTORY) to see if he could locate his sons. It was a long shot, to be sure, but as an experienced CompuServe subscriber, Switzer had recently been able to locate an old friend through e-mail. This time he was encouraged when he discovered an on-line listing for a "John L. Switzer." To the user ID number listed with that name, Switzer quickly posted a simple message:

> I am trying to locate a John Lee Switzer who was born in Chamblee, Georgia, on Nov. 16, 1955. Would you happen to be that person?

On another day when he logged on to CompuServe, Switzer was greeted by a system notice that he had CompuServe Mail waiting in his electronic mailbox. In moments his screen displayed a reply that was almost too good to believe:

> Bob: I hope you are who I think you are. If so, my brother and I have been searching for you for a long time.

It turned out that both of Robert's sons had changed their names back to "Switzer" when they reached the age of 18, and they had been searching for their father ever since. Relatively new CompuServe subscribers themselves, the young men had been using the system to stay in touch with each other, since they were living in different parts of the country. The reunited Switzers have now gotten together in person, and Robert Switzer, Sr. has even discovered that he is a grandfather.

Electronic Mail Today

Of course, few reunions are as dramatic as the Switzers', but most of us can relate to their story. As members of the most mobile society in history, we are aware of the likelihood of losing track of each other. That is why electronic mail is evolving into a powerful tool for keeping tabs on our wandering friends and loved ones. Indeed, "evolving" is the operative word. In its first decade, CompuServe Mail has not only had several different names (from the simple "Email" to the vague "EasyPlex"), but also has grown from a mere note-passer to a full-fledged messaging center that offers international connections.

In its earliest form, electronic mail on CompuServe was small. It limited the length of each piece of correspondence to only a few thousand characters and it required that messages always be written directly on-line . By contrast, messages nowadays can be up to 2,000,000 characters long, and may be written on-line *or* off-line and transmitted to the mail feature. CompuServe Mail can interact with an electronic address book and a filing feature. Also, non-ASCII files (such as binary program files) of up to 2MB in length may now be sent through the electronic post.

CompuServe provides each subscriber with a private mailbox to receive mail on-line around the clock. Other people communicate with you by writing to your user ID number. Incoming letters are automatically placed in your private mailbox and you can collect them the next time you are on-line.

When you want to write to other people, you may compose and edit messages in two ways:

1. While you are on-line (ideal for quick, short messages or brief replies).

2. And/or when you are off-line, saving money on connect-time. Whether you are using the CompuServe Information Manager software, a third-party CompuServe program like TapCis or AutoSig, or a general terminal program, you may compose your messages off-line, save them on disk, and upload them to the system in a burst.

This chapter illustrates how CompuServe Mail also enables you to:

- Forward messages to other subscribers.

- Send messages with "receipts" so you are automatically informed when the addressees have retrieved them.

- Send binary files, such as programs, spreadsheets, and database documents.

- Save names and user IDs of your frequent correspondents in an Address Book for easy future mailing.

- Send messages from CompuServe to other electronic mail systems, including Internet, MCI Mail, InfoPlex, Telex, AT&T Mail, and FAX machines. You may even direct that an electronic letter be printed and delivered on paper by the US Postal Service to any mailing address.

Automatic Notification

Mail is so important that CompuServe is designed to inform you of waiting messages in your private mailbox immediately after you log on. Exactly how this notice comes before your eyes varies, depending on the communications software you are using. A CIM user will see a "Mail!" menu on the screen at logon if letters are waiting; the user clicks on the menu to quickly check the mailbox. Users of other software see a "You have CompuServe Mail waiting" message immediately after the introductory display; then, or at any time during the on-line session, the user can enter GO MAIL to reach the mailbox.

About the Next Sections

The following sections examine how CompuServe Mail appears to CIM users, then cover how the mail feature in its generic form is seen by third-party communications programs. Read the material which applies to your specific software, or read both the CIM and non-CIM sections if you are still undecided about which software you want to use.

Mail Through CIM

Interacting with the mail features is perhaps the CompuServe Information Manager's strongest function. Mail is one of the major groups of options listed on CIM's top menu bar. Either on-line or off-line, the users may select it to see a pull-down menu like the one in Figure 3.1.

The mail options represent the following:

- *Get New Mail* retrieves messages from your on-line mailbox to be either read immediately or placed in CIM's In-Basket for later when you are off-line.

- *Create Mail* composes a message with the built-in editing feature to either send immediately or place in the Out-Basket for later posting.

- *Send Mail in Out-Basket* delivers one or more messages that you have placed in the Out-Basket.

- *Send/Receive All Mail* combines two functions. First, it sends all messages currently in your Out-Basket, then retrieves all new messages and places them in the In-Basket for later reading.

- *Send File* lets you post a disk file, such as a program in binary form.

- *In-Basket* accesses messages currently in the In-Basket.

- *Filing Cabinet* lets you access the messages in CIM's electronic Filing Cabinet.

- *Create Forum Message* is used for composing messages for delivery to discussion forums.

- *Address Book* lets you see and modify the items listed in your Address Book.

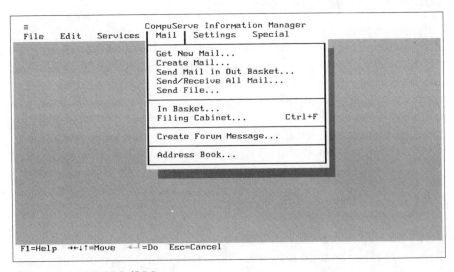

Figure 3.1 CIM Mail Menu

Get New Mail

CIM provides two ways to retrieve and read letters that arrive in your on-line mailbox:

1. Read them on-line, while you are connected to the system.
2. Put them unread into your In-Basket for viewing later after you have disconnected from the system.

Selecting the Get New Mail option from the Mail pull-down menu produces a dialog box that lists the messages currently in your mailbox. (If necessary, CIM will first connect to CompuServe to retrieve this list.) The list provides the subject, author, and size (in number of characters) for each message in the mailbox. A bar cursor may be moved up and down to highlight specific messages. Also displayed are these options:

- *Get* displays the highlighted message immediately (while you are on-line), then gives you a number of additional options.
- *Get All* moves all the messages from the mailbox to your In-Basket for later reading. This time, you are not shown the messages while on-line; instead, you view them later with the In-Basket option on the Mail menu.
- *Delete* marks highlighted messages for removal from the mailbox when you leave the Mail feature.

If you want to view a letter while on-line, highlight it with the bar cursor and select the Get option, which displays the message. It starts with the header containing the subject, author, date, and time of the message, followed by the text. Also on the screen are more options:

- Put this message in the *In-Basket.*
- *Edit* it (in case you want to file or forward it).
- *File* it in the on-disk Filing Cabinet.
- *Reply* to it, composing an answer to a letter-writer while on-line. Both the receiver's electronic mailing address and the message subject will automatically be filled in for you.
- *Forward* it to someone else on-line, adding comments if you like. The system automatically fills in the subject line for you (keeping the same subject as the original). When you forward a message, you actually are creating a copy; the original message is not affected and remains in the mailbox.
- *Delete* this message and return to the list.

You may copy the sender's name and address in your Address Book by highlighting the "From:" area of the message and pressing RETURN (or clicking the mouse).

Similar options are available when viewing letters off-line by reading the contents of the In-Basket.

Creating Mail

Either on-line or off-line, you may compose original letters and replies with CIM's built-in text feature. Selecting the Create Mail option from the Mail pull-down menu results in a dialog box like the one in Figure 3.2.

In this display, you may fill in:

- *TO: Name*, that is, the intended recipient's name. This field is optional.
- *TO: Address*, the recipient's user ID number. This is required. CompuServe considers ID numbers to be the mailing addresses of its subscribers. Or this field may contain an address on *another* electronic mail system, as discussed at the end of this chapter.
- *CC:* ("carbon copy"), the user ID numbers of those who should receive copies of the message. This is optional.
- *Subject:* a brief description of the contents of the note; this is required.

You may also check the Receipt box, which asks the system to automatically notify you by return electronic mail when the message has been retrieved by the addressee. (To use the option, you must select the Receipt function *before* sending the message or *before* placing it in the Out-Basket. Also, if you change your mind before posting, you may erase the X in the brackets by pressing the SPACE bar or clicking the mouse on the box again.)

Below the header is a text box for the message itself. To enter and edit the message, TAB into the text box. When you are through writing and editing the message, IBM PC/compatible users should press F3 or the ESCape key, while mouse-equipped IBM systems and Apple Macintosh users may simply move the cursor to the desired action button.

The options include:

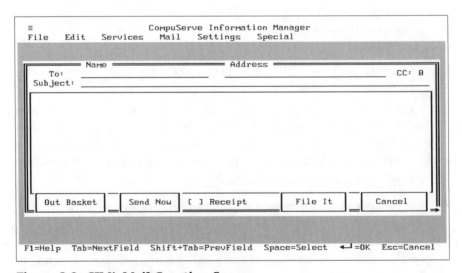

Figure 3.2 CIM's Mail Creation Screen

- Place the message in the *Out-Basket* for later delivery.
- *Send Now*, which works whether you are connected to the system or not. (CIM connects you to the system if you are not already on-line.)
- *File* in the electronic Filing Cabinet. This option is handy to save partially completed messages that can be recalled to work on later.
- *Cancel* or *Delete* in the IBM PC/compatible version to erase messages without sending them.

Distribution Lists

Besides the Receipt function listed in the previous section, later versions of the CIM software offer additional options for handling Distribution Lists, enabling you to specify whether recipients are to receive a Primary, Courtesy, or Blind copy (To, CC, or BC). Define them this way:

1. Carbon copy (CC:) — send a copy of the message to the recipient.
2. Blind copy (BC:) — the same as CC:, but the person's name will not appear on the recipient list of the other receivers.
3. Primary recipient (To:) — send to an additional primary recipient.

The list of To and CC recipients is automatically made available to readers of the message, while the BC list recipients are never disclosed. Users also have the option of keeping the entire recipient list private, so that no readers are shown other recipients of the message.

With the newer CIM versions, each recipient is entered as a To, CC, or BC. Since the recipient list is available to readers of the message, CIM displays it in a dialog box. CIM also helps readers address a Reply To All just by clicking on a single button. The Windows-CIM and the Macintosh-CIM users can keep the recipient list private by unchecking the Show Recipients box on the Recipient List screen; users of the DOS CIM do so by unchecking the Show List box on the CC:List screen.

Also, use the "Get List" option in the CC: field of a message reply (or "Copy Original" in Win CIM or "Reply to All" in Mac CIM) to fetch the recipient list of the parent message before sending your reply. (**Note:** You must be replying to a message to use the "Get List" option.)

Sending Mail from Out-Basket

You may send messages as soon as you finish composing them, whether or not you are currently on-line. On the other hand, if you have several messages and replies to compose, it saves you connect-time money to do your writing and editing off-line, placing the messages in the Out-Basket with the option described in the previous section. When you are finished writing your letters, the Send mail from Out-Basket option on the main Mail pull-down menu will log on and deliver the mail.

The Out-Basket is actually an area of space reserved on your disk by CIM specifically for out-going messages. It is also a handy place to temporarily store partially finished messages until you have time to complete them. You may leave a letter in progress there while you work on other messages or review other messages in your In-Basket.

Selecting Send mail from Out-Basket causes CIM to list the contents of the Out-Basket in menu style, as shown in Figure 3.3.

The bar cursor may move up and down to highlight specific messages. Elsewhere on the screen are the new options:

- *Open* lets you review and edit the message currently highlighted by the bar cursor. You have access to both the message text and the envelope information. Additional options let you specify what is to be done with the message, or you may cancel the Open operation and return the original message to the Out-Basket.

- *Send* posts only the highlighted message. CIM logs on to the system (if you are not already connected), goes to the Mail area, and sends the message.

- *Send All* posts *all* the messages and replies currently in the Out-Basket. Again, CIM logs on to the system if necessary.

- *Delete* erases the highlighted message from your Out-Basket.

By the way, later versions of CIM enhance the Send All function by adding a Disconnect option onto it. You can check this box to optionally have the software automatically disconnect from the system after sending all the mail in the Out-Basket. Also, if you have unsent mail in your Out-Basket when you attempt to leave CIM, the software displays a reminder dialog box to ask you to confirm.

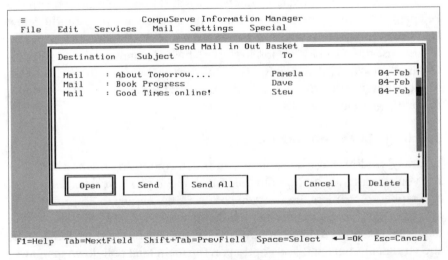

Figure 3.3 Typical Out-Basket Display in CIM

Send/Receive All Mail

Send/Receive All Mail combines the Get New Mail and the Send Mail in Out-Basket options. Choosing it causes the program to:

1. Send all messages currently in your Out-Basket, then
2. Retrieve any new messages and automatically place them in your In-Basket for later reading.

Saving Copies

Starting with version 2.0 of the software, CIM can also automatically save copies of all Mail messages you send. Just select the CIM Desktop option from the Settings option menu on the main menu bar, then mark the Auto-Save Sent Mail selection. When prompted, specify the directory you want CIM to use at the subsequent "Folder:" prompt.

Sending Files

You are not limited to text files when sending material through CompuServe Mail. The Send File option on the main Mail pull-down menu lets you send either binary or text files from elsewhere on your disk, provided the file is not larger than 2MB. This means files you have created with a different text editor or word processor, or with another program, such as a spreadsheet or database manager, may be sent through CompuServe Mail.

When you select Send File from the main menu, the program prompts you to provide the same kind of envelope data you need when writing all mail, including the recipient's name, user ID (address), the message subject, and possible receipt. Then, instead of text, you supply the identification for the file to be sent. You may write up to 73 characters of additional information that will appear along with the subject when the receiver gets the message. If you don't know the name of the file you want to send, you may find it by highlighting and selecting the word "File" on the screen (pressing RETURN or clicking on with the mouse). This instructs the program to search through your disk files on the current directory.

Also on the screen are additional options:

- Place the file in the *Out-Basket* for later delivery.
- *Send Now*, which works whether you are connected to the system or not.
- *Delete* (or *Cancel*) to erase the message without sending it.

You may also send ASCII text files that have been created by *other* word processors by simply copying and pasting the files into a text box.

In-Basket

The In-Basket option on the main Mail menu lets you read, edit, and file messages currently in the In-Basket, as well as write replies. Like the Out-Basket, the In-Basket actually is an area of space that CIM reserves on your disk.

Selecting the In-Basket option displays a list of the messages filed currently in the disk area in menu form. You may move the cursor up and down to highlight and select specific messages. Messages displayed start with a header (including the subject, author, date, and time of the message) followed by the text. Elsewhere on the screen are the following options for selection:

- *Next* to display the next message in the basket.
- *Edit* to change it (in case you want to file or forward it).
- *File* to put it in the electronic Filing Cabinet.
- *Reply;* that is, compose an answer to this letter-writer while on-line. Both the receiver's electronic mailing address and the message subject will automatically be filled in for you.
- *Forward* to send it to someone else on-line, adding comments if you like. The system automatically fills in the subject line for you (keeping the same subject as the original).
- *Delete* to remove this message and return to the list.

You may also copy the sender's name and address in your Address Book by highlighting the "From:" area of the message and pressing RETURN. (More on the Address Book in a moment.)

If you have a printer attached, you may print a message by going to the File pull-down menu and choosing the Print option.

Finally, if you want to save a copy of a message to disk under a specific filename, go to the File pull-down menu and choose the Save As option.

Note Later versions of the software (versions 2.0 and after) provide an option for sorting messages in the In- and Out-Baskets with a Sort button on the menu. You can sort by date, subject, sending, and type (Mail, ENS, forum name, etc.), and you may sort in ascending or descending order.

Filing Cabinet

CIM operates its electronic Filing Cabinet in space reserved on your disk. You may use the Filing Cabinet to store copies of:

- Letters you receive and send through CompuServe Mail.
- Messages from the discussion forums.
- Drafts of letters and messages on which you are currently working.

Filing Cabinet material is kept in electronic *folders* that CIM automatically maintains. Each folder may have a variety of letters and forum messages. You may create as many folders as you want, depending on the size of your disk. Being able to add and delete folders helps you organize messages and letters by topic, source, people's names, or any other way you like. Letters and messages in folders may be read, edited, moved to different folders, or deleted. A message in a folder from another person can be replied to and/or forwarded, regardless of the note's age.

You can access your Filing Cabinet from the Mail pull-down menu (or from the messages area of the forums, as discussed in the next chapter). That brings you to a list of existing folders with a bar cursor highlighting the first one, as shown in Figure 3.4.

The cursor can be moved up and down to highlight different folder names. Elsewhere on the screen are listed the Filing Cabinet options, including:

- *Open* gives you access to the contents of the currently highlighted folder.

- *New* creates a new folder. You are prompted for a name; use any combination of letters, digits, and spaces but begin with a letter. (In the IBM PC/compatible version of the program, filenames may be up to 11 characters; in the Macintosh version, the filenames may be up to 31 characters.)

- *Delete* erases the highlighted folder. Before you may delete a folder, you must erase all messages in it. The idea is to protect you from accidentally removing large groups of messages.

When a folder is Opened, the contents are listed in a display with a bar cursor highlighting the first message. You may move the cursor up and down to highlight and select the one you want. A filed message is displayed, much as it is when using the In-Basket. The options available include:

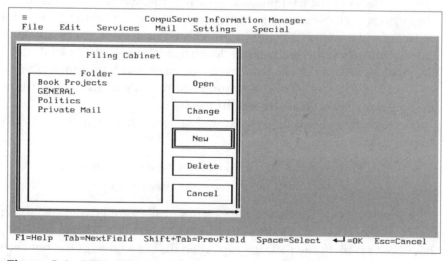

Figure 3.4 CIM's Filing Cabinet

- *Next,* to display the next message in the folder.
- *Edit,* in case you want to forward it by mail.
- *File,* to move this message to another folder.
- *Reply* to it. Both the receiver's electronic mailing address and the message subject will automatically be filled in for you.
- *Forward* it to someone else, adding comments if you'd like. The system automatically fills in the subject line for you (keeping the same subject as the original).
- *Delete* this message from the folder.

Also, you may copy the sender's name and address in your Address Book by highlighting and selecting the "From:" area of the message. You may access your electronic Filing Cabinet at any Mail dialog box with a "File" or "File It" option.

Selecting the File option produces a display from which you may specify the folder to file a message. It lists the names of existing folders with a bar cursor highlighting the top one. The cursor can be moved up and down to highlight different folder names. Options elsewhere on the display list the Filing Cabinet functions, including:

- Save places the letter in the folder whose name is currently highlighted.
- New creates a new folder, prompting you for a name. You may use any combination of letters, digits, and spaces. Names must begin with a letter.
- Cancel ends the Filing Cabinet action and returns you to the message.

Sending with Expiration Dates and Special Designations

Newer versions of the CIM program — such as the new Windows version of the software — enable users to send messages with an *expiration date,* a *notation of priority,* and a *notation of sensitivity,* which affect how messages are displayed to recipients. These messages may be denoted as "*Important*" or "*Private*," designations that reflect the sender's assessment of the importance or sensitivity of the message. (The designations do not, incidentally, affect how CompuServe Mail actually delivers the message.)

Messages may also display an expiration date, which will appear to the recipient if:

- The message was sent from CIM with an expiration date, and
- The message was SAVEd by the recipient after reading.

Text messages are stored in the recipient's mailbox for up to 90 days after they have been read; binary messages are stored for up to 30 days after they have been saved. In the past, the expiration date of a message has not been visible to the reader. You can now make the expiration date appear, as explained above, by choosing to SAVE the message after reading it. The next time you access mail, the message will appear with an expiration date, as in:

```
1 Charlie Bowen/Party invitation
* Expire:(+90) *
```

If you want to save the message for another 90 days, you must choose to go in and SAVE the message again.

Creating Forum Messages

The Mail options also enable you to create messages off-line for delivery to the system's many discussion forums. This and other ways for writing forum messages are discussed in the next chapter.

Address Book

You will come to think of user ID numbers (yours and everyone else's) as "addresses," like the street addresses in a town. Unfortunately, user ID numbers are not easy to remember. "71635,1025" doesn't lend itself to a mnemonic. The good news is that CIM can help manage user ID numbers.

The electronic Address Book is another area of reserved disk space that CIM maintains for you as a place for keeping names and user ID numbers of other people. The Address Book may be as large as you like, depending on available disk space. You may directly access the Address Book for maintenance from the Mail pull-down menu; it can also be updated quickly from inside a letter. When you are reading a letter, you may copy the other person's name and address into your electronic Address Book; later, you can quickly copy that information back to an envelope when you want to send messages. To use this auto-adding feature whenever you are reading a letter, highlight and select the "From:" portion of the message. This causes the program to display a dialog box with three possible options:

- The cursor is already on the Enter (or Save) option, so pressing RETURN or clicking on with the mouse automatically saves the name and address (user ID) as an entry in the Address Book and returns you to the letter you were reading.

- Selecting a Cancel option returns you to the message *without* saving the entry in the Address Book.

- If you want to include a comment with the entry before Saving the address, position the cursor in the Comments box. You may enter up to four lines of text.

An *auto-retrieve* feature also lets you quickly fetch a name and address from the Address Book when you are composing a message. To use it, highlight and select the "To:" portion of the message (the word "To" itself, not the blank space after it), which causes the program to display a list of names in the Address Book in menu form. Highlight and select the name you want. This copies the name and address to the "To:" portion of the letter and returns you to composing.

You may also maintain the Address Book itself by selecting the Address Book option from the main Mail pull-down menu (or from the Message portion of the discussion forums section covered in the next chapter). In the subsequent display (Figure 3.5), a bar cursor may be moved up and down.

The options are:

- *Open* which displays the complete entry for the highlighted name, so that it can be reviewed or edited.

- *Add* which lets you insert another new address. When this option is selected, the software displays its entry form.

- *Delete* (or *Remove)* to delete the highlighted entry.

Incidentally, later versions of the CIM software enhance the Address Book with several new functions, including:

- You can now place multiple addresses into a single entry called a *Group* entry. This makes a recipient list much easier to put together. For example, you could put the addresses of Bob, Sue, Jim, Fred, and Mike into a single entry called SHIPPING DEPT, and easily copy them when sending a message by selecting just the SHIPPING DEPT entry in your Address Book.

- When selected from the CC: dialog, the Address Book supports the marked set capability described in the "CompuServe Mail" section of this

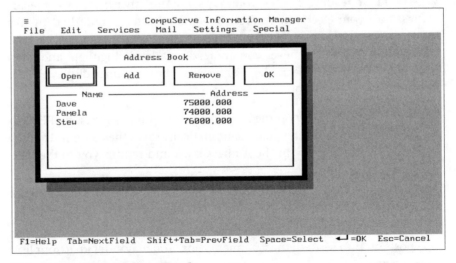

Figure 3.5   CIM Address Book

document. Multiple addresses may be selected for the CC: list by selecting the "Use" button.

- While creating a message, you can now add the message address directly to your Address Book by highlighting the To: field and pressing Enter. Select New and press Enter at the ensuing dialog box.

Enhanced Marking Capability

Incidentally, starting with Version 2.0, CIM enhances its marking capability, enabling you to mark a *set* of messages. In other words, you may mark multiple messages, then perform a common action (such as Delete, Read, Retrieve, etc.) on that marked set. This works with Mail, In-Basket, Address Book, and Filing Cabinet messages, and makes for faster message-processing.

CompuServe Mail without *CIM*

While some think the CompuServe Information Manager is the *only way* to use the electronic post, CompuServe Mail is fully accessible to users of third-party general terminal programs as well. Entering GO MAIL at any prompt on the system brings the user to a numbered main Mail menu that provides the key options, like this:

```
CompuServe Mail Main Menu

 1   READ mail, 1 message pending
 2   COMPOSE a new message
 3   UPLOAD a message
 4   USE a file from PER area
 5   ADDRESS Book
 6   SET options
```

Reading Mail

As noted earlier, when you have mail waiting, you are notified at logon. After you access CompuServe Mail with GO MAIL, a menu displays information about all pending messages, including the name of the sender and the subject of each message. You may read all your messages at one session or select a range of message numbers to be read (1-5), a list of message numbers (5,7,9), or a combination of both (1-5,7,9).

Any message sent to you with "Receipt Requested" (an option discussed later in this section) is denoted on the initial menu with a note reading "* RECEIPT notice pending *." When you read the message, the system automatically sends a "receipt" to inform the sender that the message was successfully delivered.

After reading a message, a menu or prompt asks you to choose your next action. From this menu, you may:

- Reread the message.
- Reply to it. (You are prompted to write a message that the system will automatically send to the original sender.)
- Forward the message to another member, topped by a message of your own.
- Save it in your mailbox.
- Delete it, removing it from your mailbox.
- File it in your Personal File Area on-line. (This generally corresponds with the "Filing Cabinet" option available in the CompuServe Information Manager program).
- Download it to the disk on your PC for later use.

Receiving Binary Files

Binary messages (programs, spreadsheet files, etc.) may also be sent via CompuServe Mail. Such files received in your mailbox are identified on the menu with a "*Binary*" note. These files cannot be "read," but can be downloaded to your disk for off-line use. The system prompts you to download such files. See the appendix article (Appendix I) for more information on file transfer.

Sending Replies

The easiest way to send a message through CompuServe Mail is to select the Reply option after reading a message you have received in your mailbox. The system prompts you to enter your message. You may:

- Type it into a directory, entering the words and pressing RETURN at the end of each screen line. To conclude the letter, enter /EXIT on a new line. (If you are new to on-line composition, see Appendix H, "Writing On-Line," in the On-Line Survival Kit. It provides details on CompuServe's two text-writing/editing programs.)
- Or upload it from a file on your computer's disk. (There will be more about uploading in a moment.)

When you have completed your answer and entered the command /EXIT on a new line, the system closes the message and presents a menu that lists new options, like this:

For current message

1	SEND
2	EDIT
3	TYPE
4	TYPE/POSTAL
5	FILE DRAFT copy
6	SEND with /RECEIPT ($)

These options will do the following:

- SEND tells the system you are ready for the message to be posted. On replies, the system sends the message to the author of the message to which you are replying. With original messages, as noted in the next section, the system prompts you for the user ID of the intended recipient.

- EDIT allows you to edit a message that you previously composed. As noted, CompuServe Mail provides a choice of two edit methods:

  1. A line-numbered editor numbers each line of text as it is entered into your workspace. Then, in edit mode you will be prompted for the line you wish to act upon. You can change words or characters contained within a line.

  2. A nonline-numbered editor (EDIT, sometimes called "Filge") can also be used to compose and/or edit messages. You should be familiar with this editor prior to using it.

- TYPE displays the message being composed or edited, while TYPE/POSTAL shows you the message in the form for a printed postal letter. (More on that later in the chapter.)

- FILE files the messages (whether read or unread) into a file that will reside in your Personal Files Area (GO PER). You may specify a range of messages to be filed (1-5), a list of messages (5,7,9), or a combination of both (1-5,7,9). The word ALL will file all messages. Once messages are filed, they are deleted from your mailbox. (You cannot file Binary messages; they must be downloaded.)

- FILE DRAFT will file the text of a message you just composed. You are prompted for a filename, and the draft is placed in that file in your PER area. "FILE DRAFT filename" also can be entered to eliminate prompting for the filename. FILE DRAFT can be entered before or after choosing the SEND option.

Sending Original Mail

Sending original letters is much like sending replies, except that you need to know the intended recipient's user ID (called an "address" in the CompuServe

Mail documentation). CompuServe Mail's menu offers three ways to create a new message for sending:

- COMPOSE lets you write your message on the spot. (Again, see Appendix H, "Writing On-Line," in the On-Line Survival Kit. It provides details on CompuServe's two text-writing/editing programs.)

- UPLOAD lets you transmit an ASCII text file from your computer's disk to the mail feature.

- USE prompts you for the name of a file previously saved in your Personal File Area (GO PER).

After the letter has been created, enter /EXIT on a new line of the file to close it. Then you are shown the same Send Menu as seen above. It provides opportunities to edit the message.

Finally, when you choose the SEND option, you are prompted for three pieces of information, one at a time:

1. "Send to:" The system seeks the recipient's user ID (or remote mail location address or command if you are sending the message outside of CompuServe; see below.) You may also send the message to *more than one recipient* at the same time by entering each address at the "Send to:" prompt, separating each with a semicolon. Multiple mailing of the same message is currently a surcharged feature, 10 cents for each copy.

2. "From:" Enter your name. You needn't enter your user ID number; the system will supply that automatically.

3. "Subject:" A brief description of the contents of the message.

Tips   The Address Book, discussed later in this section, offers a shortcut on filling in the Send and From fields.

Also, you can have the system bypass the "Send to:", "From:", and "Subject:" prompts simply by embedding that information in the first 10 lines of the message as it is being composed or uploaded. To correctly embed the data in your message, start at the top with "To:" followed by the user ID of the received message. On the next line, enter "From:" followed by your user ID number. On the third line, enter "Subject:" followed by a brief description. Then on the fourth line, begin the message.

Uploading Prewritten Messages and Binary Files

Initially, just about everyone on CompuServe wrote their messages on-line in "real time." Now, however, with improved communications and word-processing software widely in use, many subscribers find it smarter and easier to save on connect-time dollars by writing their messages and replies off-line.

They use their regular word processors to create the files, save them to disk, then log on to CompuServe and transmit them to the system using the Mail feature's UPLOAD. You can do this, too, as long as you keep these few points in mind when composing letters off-line:

1. Have your word processor save the text *in ASCII* format with a carriage return at the end of each screen line. While most word-processing programs routinely save text in their own compressed binary formats, they can usually be directed to save in ASCII instead. Check your user's manual for details of this ASCII option and always use it for text you intend to upload. (In the IBM world, this sometimes is referred to as a "DOS Save," and that may be the term used in your manual.)

2. A single CompuServe Mail letter can be no longer than 2MB (about 2,000,000 characters).

3. Message lines should be no longer than 80 characters. You must not only press RETURN at the end of each line you type on-line, but also have carriage returns in place as your file is transmitted. Make sure there is a *line feed* entered after each carriage return in the file. This is most conveniently done while typing the letter in the word processor, but sometimes it can be done by using your editor to insert the carriage return/line feeds with a search-replace function before the uploading begins.

The UPLOAD option on the main Mail menu can also be used to transfer binary files (programs, spreadsheet data, etc.).

Of course, you will need to be familiar with the transmit/upload facilities of your specific communications program. Check your manual and see Appendix I, "File Transfer", in the On-Line Survival Kit for guidelines.

Sending with Receipt

An option on the Send menu which is displayed when you complete the composition of a message allows you to send your message with a receipt. This means that the system will automatically notify you when the recipient has retrieved your message. At this time, the receipt function is a surcharged feature costing 15 cents per receipt.

The USE Command

Some subscribers have regular introductory messages they send to new friends they meet on the system. Since they don't want to type in the letter each time, they use a kind of electronic form letter. As noted earlier, users of the CompuServe Information Manager load in the prewritten messages from their on-disk filing cabinet. For users of third-party communications programs, such prewritten letters can be loaded into CompuServe Mail from the subscriber's

Personal File Area (GO PER) with the Mail menu's USE command. When selected from the main Mail menu, the USE command causes the system to prompt you for the filename of the text saved in the Personal File Area.

Address Book

The Address Book keeps track of the names and addresses of regular correspondents. The addresses filed there can include CompuServe user IDs, MCI addresses, Internet addresses, Fax numbers, Telex numbers, AT&T Mail addresses, and Postal addresses. You may retain up to 100 addresses in the book.

Once you have started storing addresses in the Address Book, you only need to specify the name of the recipient at the "Send to:" in messages, because the system already has the actual user ID number. So, if you have saved Charles Bowen's user ID number in the Address Book under the name CHARLIE and you want to send him a message, instead of having to spell out his on-line address at the Send to: prompt — 71635,1025 — you can simply enter CHARLIE and the system will check your book.

Remote mail locations (Fax, Telex, Internet, MCI, Postal, etc.) may also be saved in the address book. To do that, enter the name of the recipient at the Name prompt. At the subsequent prompt, enter the full, correct addressing format for the remote mail location. For Fax, Telex, MCI Mail, and Internet, the correct format is >FAX: machine no., >TLX: machine no., >MCIMAIL: MCI address, >INTERNET: Internet address, or >POSTAL, respectively. For postal recipients, you will then be prompted for the address. There will be more on remote mail addresses later in this chapter.

Finally, through another menu option, your own name may also be saved in the Address Book so you will not be prompted for the "From:" information when you send a message. Your return postal address can also be entered in the Address Book.

Mail SET Options

The Mail menu's SET options let you set the mode for viewing and using the Mail feature. You may decide whether the options you choose should be set permanently or for the current session only. The options are:

- Three different MODES for using CompuServe Mail, including:
    a. MENU (providing full menu screens) for the novice user.
    b. PROMPT (providing a one-line list of commands) for the intermediate user.
    c. COMMAND (with a one-word prompt) for the expert user.
- Two switchable editing methods for composing and editing messages. The standard is a line-numbered editor; alternatively, you may also

choose to use a non-line numbered editor. (Again, see Appendix H, "Writing On-line" for a discussion of the two editors.)

- A paging or scrolling option when reading messages. Messages may be paged, according to the type of equipment you are using. Paged is the standard mode. If you do not want your messages to page, set the paging to OFF. Your messages will then scroll continuously, without pausing when the screen is full.

- A "Show Recipients" option allows you to control whether the recipients of your message see the list of other people who got a copy of the same message from you. CompuServe routinely shows this distribution list to all users, but you can keep that list private by toggling the "Show Recipients" to [NO].

Mailing to Different Systems

Whether you are using the CompuServe Information Manager or a third-party communications program, CompuServe Mail also lets you write messages for delivery to people on *other* electronic services including InfoPlex, and to Telex and facsimile (FAX) machines around the world. These are surcharged (extra-cost) features. In addition, as a non-surcharged feature, you may send mail to users of MCI Mail, SprintMail, A&T Mail, and Western Union. Finally, CompuServe Mail can be sent without a surcharge to users on the Internet—an electronic mail system that connects governmental institutions, military branches, educational institutions and commercial companies.

Structuring the Special Addresses

To send to any of these other systems, write or upload the message as usual and then in the To: field in the CIM display (or at the Send To: prompt in the third-party ASCII system display), enter the address of the recipient on the other system, as described in the following sections.

Some of the mail features are extra-cost services. See the "CompuServe Mail" section of Appendix C for the rates as of this writing. For the latest rates, enter GO TRANSACTIONS while on-line.

MCI Mail

To send your message to an MCI Mail address, enter "MCIMAIL:" followed by the MCI address of the intended recipient, such as:

```
MCIMAIL:123-4567
```

You also may use an MCI Mail registered name (such as "MCI MAIL:Charles Bowen"), but the MCI user ID number is preferred. It is unique to the recipient, while there could be several MCI Mail users with the same name. If your message is not uniquely identified, it cannot be delivered.

Telex

You may post a letter to a Telex I or II machine by entering the letters TLX and colon (:) and the machine number, such as:

```
TLX: 1234567
```

You also may follow that with an answer-back code, like this:

```
TLX: 1234567 ABCDEF
```

The answer-back code is optional, but if used, it must be complete for the delivery, so if you are not sure, don't use it. Telexes sent to MCI Mail subscribers require a special prefix—650—before the Telex number. Also, those sent to destinations within the continental United States are considered domestic, while those to destinations outside of the US (regardless of point of origin) are international and require a three-digit country code before the Telex machine number.

The costs vary, depending on the type of machine and the destination. For domestic mail, the cost is sixty cents per three hundred characters sent to a Telex I machine and sixty-five cents per three hundred characters sent to a Telex II machine. For international Telexes, the costs vary depending on the country. The exact charges are displayed for your verification before the message is sent.

Facsimile (FAX) machines

CompuServe Mail also may be routed to Group 3 FAX machines. To send to domestic recipients, enter the letters FAX and a colon (:) and the domestic machine number — that is, a 1 and the area code, followed by the phone number, as in:

```
FAX: 1-614-5551234
```

To send to an international facsimile machine, enter FAX: followed by the country and city codes before the phone number, as in:

```
FAX: 44-1-12345
```

This example would reach Great Britain (44), city of London (1). Compu-Serve makes several attempts to deliver your message within a 24-hour period and returns the message to you if it is undeliverable.

Pricing is divided into three groups. The first, North American faxes (that is, those sent within the United States, Canada, Mexico, and all the Atlantic and Caribbean islands), cost 75 cents for the first 1,000 characters and 25 cents for each additional 1,000 characters. The second group, European faxes (all countries with country codes beginning with 3 or 4), cost 90 cents for the first 1,000 characters, and 90 cents for each additional 1,000 characters. The third group includes FAXes sent to all other countries in the world; these are priced on a country-to-country basis.

InfoPlex

CompuServe Mail also may be sent to users of another CompuServe electronic mail system called InfoPlex, which is used by some corporations and institutions. To send mail to InfoPlex, enter the letters ORG and a colon, followed by the organization's on-line address, as in:

```
Send To: ORG:address
```

"ORG" represents the organization's unique InfoPlex identifier and "address" is the user's mailbox name.

Internet

To send a message to an Internet address, enter INTERNET: followed by the recipient and the "address@domain" in Internet style, such as:

```
INTERNET:Jdoe@abc.michigan-state.edu
```

In this example, the INTERNET: is required by CompuServe to route the message to the Internet system; "Jdoe" is the valid address used by this recipient on the Internet system; the "@" tells Internet that the domain address is following, and the "abc.michigan-state.edu" is the domain address.

> **Note** The domain address elements must be separated by periods and the domain must be separated from the recipient's address by the "@" character with no spaces. Also, you may have a space after the "INTERNET:"

The amount of time it takes to deliver an Internet message varies from half an hour to two days.

Messages which will be forwarded to other networks via the Internet require special addressing formats, such as:

- Bitnet addresses—.BITNET must be appended to the Internet address for it to be delivered via Internet. For example:

```
INTERNET:Charlieb@EDUNAB.BITNET
```

- UUNET addresses usually can be in regular Internet address format. However, occasionally a more complex form is needed, as in:

```
INTERNET:user%organization.domain@UUNET.UU.NET
```

This results in an address such as:

```
INTERNET:harry%edunab.msu@UUNET.UU.NET
```

If your message is undeliverable, you will receive a notification in your CompuServe mailbox. Sometimes the notification also includes the text of your original message, though this depends on the remote mail system (some don't return the text.) Also, you can request a receipt with mail sent via Internet. (**Note**: the receipt is generated *only* when the message is delivered by CompuServe to the Internet. Receipts to indicate whether the user actually receives the messages are not available through Internet.)

Receiving from Internet

You also may *receive* a message from Internet in your CompuServe Mail mailbox. The Internet user needs your correct Internet address. Your address is composed of: (1) Your User ID with the comma changed to a period; (2) the CompuServe domain, which is "compuserve.com;" and (3) the correct addressing format to send the message. (This format varies from one system to another.) Typically, the address is shown as "User ID@compuserve.com", so the address appears as:

```
12345.412@compuserve.com
```

Sending to AT&T Mail Using an X.400 Mail Address

An AT&T user can be addressed by using a surname and given name, in addition to the country and administrative domain values required for all X.400 messages. To ensure uniqueness on the AT&T Mail system, a person's unique ID should also be included, in a style like this:

```
x400:(c=us;a=attmail;s=SURNAME;g=GIVEN;d=id:UNIQUE ID)
```

The capitalized portions of the address above are the user specific variables that you need to supply. For example, if an AT&T user told you his address was "Surname of JONES, Given name of BOB, and AT&T ID of BJONES" in CompuServe Mail you would enter:

```
x400:(c=us;a=attmail;s=jones;g=bob;d=id:bjones)
```

Sending to SprintMail

A SprintMail user can be addressed by using an Organization Name, Surname, and a Given Name, in addition to the Country and Administrative Domain values required for all X.400 messages, such as:

```
x400:(c=us;a=telemail;o=ORGANIZATION;s=SURNAME;g=GIVEN)
```

Note that the information in capitals in the above are the *user specific variables* that you need to supply. So, if a SprintMail user has told you his address is "Organization of BEEZERK, Surname of SMITH, Given name of JOHN," you would enter the following address in CompuServe Mail:

```
x400:(c=us;a=telemail;o=beezerk;s=smith;g=john)
```

The "x400:" must always precede the address, the address must be enclosed in parenthesis, and the elements must be separated by semicolons.

Sending to Western Union 400

A Western Union 400 user can be addressed by using his/her Western Union Number (ELN) along with the Country and Administrative Domain values required for all X.400 messages. The unique ELN should be included as a Domain Defined Attribute. The Western Union 400 address, including the receiver's name, could be entered as:

```
x400:(C=US;A=WESTERN UNION;S=surname;G=given;D=ELN:unique id)
```

So, if an Western Union 400 user's address was "Surname of SMITH, Given name of SAM, and Western Union number of 62044400" in CompuServe Mail you would enter the following address:

```
x400:(C=US;A=WESTERN UNION; S=SMITH;G=SAM;D=ELN:62044400)
```

Receiving Mail from SprintMail, AT&T Mail, or Western Union

The address that you should give to a user of any mail system that can route messages to CompuServe via an X.400 connection is:

- Country = US
- ADMD = CompuServe
- PRMD = csmail
- DDA Type = id
- DDA Value = Your User ID with a period instead of a comma (such as 71635.1025)

> **Note**   AT&T Mail has defined a gateway name of mhs!csmail that can be used in place of the c=, a=, and pd= parameters for a user on the AT&T Mail System.

SprintMail and AT&T Mail users can also send messages to Novell NetWare MHS mailboxes via the CompuServe Mail Hub. The address that you should give in order to be reached at a NetWare MHS mailbox through the CompuServe Mail Hub via X.400 is:

- Country = US
- ADMD = CompuServe
- PRMD = csmail

- DDA Type = id
- DDA Value = mhs:username(a)workgroup

The "@" symbol normally used in a NetWare MHS address must be replaced by "(a)" when used in a X.400 address.

US Postage Service

And here is an option that mixes a little old with the new: Your words can be sent electronically from CompuServe Mail to a regional printing station, where the letter turned into hard copy on high-quality printers and mailed through the US Postal Service. This enables you to send mail via CompuServe to people who are not on-line, and who perhaps don't even have a computer.

The lines must not exceed 80 characters in width and the length of your message must not exceed 279 lines. At the Send To: prompt (or in CIM's To: box), enter POSTAL. After that, the system prompts you for an address, asking for the name, title/company (optional), street address, city, state or province, and zip code. You can enter the state's full name or its two letter postal code. After entering the address, you will be given the opportunity to edit it. Finally, you will be prompted for your return address.

Congressgrams, SantaGrams, Valentines, and More

CompuServe Mail also has extra features, some seasonal in nature. As Christmas nears, the CompuServe Mail menu is expanded to include a "SantaGram" option for sending specialized Christmas greetings to friends and fellow users. In February, a similar Valentine option is added for electronic greetings of the season.

Other extra e-mail services are on-going. Congressgrams are personalized, hardcopy letters you can send electronically from CompuServe to members of the US Senate, the US House of Representatives, the president, or the vice president. Congressgrams are delivered by the US Postal Service and carry a $1 surcharge for each letter.

To use the feature, select the "Send a CONGRESSgram" option from the Mail menu or enter CONGRESS at the prompt. You then are prompted to enter the recipient's name and title (senator, representative, president, or vice president), the text of your message, the subject, your name, and your postal address. CompuServe Mail will automatically enter the recipient's address, the salutation and closing.

A Members of Congress database is provided to help users obtain the names of their congressional representatives, the president, or vice president. To use the database, enter GO FCC-1 at a prompt. It provides a state by state listing of all members in the House of Representatives and the Senate. Each listing includes the name, party affiliation, Washington telephone number, hometown, and committee memberships.

Electronic Mail can even Link to a Battlefield

Finally, electronic mail sometimes can be a hand across the sea to men and women in the military service. During the Gulf War campaign, CompuServe launched "Operation Friendship" to aid in getting letters to the American soldiers in the Middle East.

Started in the months before Christmas 1990, Operation Friendship was a joint program of CompuServe Inc. and Graphnet Inc. The letters were sent electronically like any other CompuServe Mail letters, except that, unlike other e-mail, these messages were sent from the CompuServe network to Graphnet which then forwarded them to its London, England, printing site. The messages were printed on stationery, sealed in envelopes and mailed to Saudi Arabia. The letters could be sent to a specific person, or for those who did not personally know anyone in the Middle East, addressed to "Any Service Member."

This was the first time the resources of the electronic community could be used to boost the morale of people on the other side of the world. It won't be the last.

4

The Forums

In this chapter...

The Big Picture
Message Board, with and without CIM
The Libraries, with and without CIM
User Options
Forum Help

If you had met Don Watkins in early 1989, you would have thought he knew all there was to know about the potential of CompuServe. By then, he had not only been a subscriber for six years, but also managed CompuServe's massive IBM Users Network, a group of on-line discussion forums with active message boards and data libraries. Every day, he had a front-row seat to observe the power of this medium for solving problems. Forums, electronic "clubhouses" that never close, bring together people of common interests from all over the world. Some forums, like those operated by Watkins and his associates, are computer-specific, inviting questions, answers, and comments on technical hardware and software issues. But, besides computer talk, CompuServe's hundreds of forums also include many that deal with broad general topics (politics, religion, sex, education, investing), hobbies (cooking, music, skiing, travel), and professions (law, public relations, medicine, journalism). Having spent a half dozen years at the helm of some of the system's more active forums, Watkins thought he had a pretty good idea of the capabilities of on-line communications.

Then on Tuesday afternoon, October 17, 1989, the ground moved in San Francisco. It was the worst earthquake there since the beginning of the century. Watkins, who lived in nearby Santa Rosa, California, will always remember that day.

> "I was frustrated being so close to the earthquake, being unaffected and really unable to do anything to help without getting in the way of the professionals."

But within hours, Watkins and others around CompuServe discovered there *was* something they could do to help — a job that was uniquely suited for the on-line community.

It turned out that much of San Francisco's telephone equipment survived the quake, but phone service was stymied by a very human problem: the over-working of the long-distance facilities. Everyone was either trying to call in or to call out. At one point, as many as a million long-distance calls a minute were coming into the area, making it nearly impossible to get a call through. As a result, many people in the quake area could make local calls, but not long-distance calls. Since CompuServe's local nodes survived the quake in bet-ter shape than the general Bay Area phone system, people on-line suddenly found themselves in an ideal position to serve the quake victims as a commu-nications link to the outside world.

Soon after the quake, CompuServe subscribers in other parts of the country started posting public messages in various forums, offering to help quake vic-tims in contacting relatives. California CompuServe subscribers who might not be able to dial out directly on the overburdened long-distance lines could make a local call to the system. They were urged to leave notes for the volun-teers who then would relay any "Don't worry, I'm OK" messages to friends and families outside the quake area.

Then Watkins saw the need for something more. Following some harried dis-cussions with his contacts at CompuServe headquarters in Columbus, Ohio, the morning after the quake, Don helped to open a special Earthquake Assistance Forum, which was operational by noon that day. The entire system was used to spread the word that this unique forum had opened as a central point for news reports, information on relief efforts, help in locating people, and a source for details of transportation availability. For weeks to come, forum administrators stayed in contact with San Francisco area agencies and offered up-to-the-minute information, including road closings, and tips on getting emergency assistance. Eyewitness accounts of the damage and injuries were also filed in the forum.

Linked to the forum through on-screen menus were quake-related news features, such as a special Executive News Service clipping folder, a special reports section on the *Online Today* electronic daily associated with *Compu-Serve Magazine,* and information about the Bay area WATS line that served members who did not have local access.

The Earthquake Forum was also a place for action. One forum visitor left a message saying he desperately needed to get to a particularly hard-hit area, but had found that roads were impassable. Seeing the plea, another forum visitor volunteered his own private plane and flew his fellow subscriber in, along with needed medical supplies and food.

The special forum worked so well that its success surprised even the people at CompuServe. (In fact, a month after the disaster, when people in meetings there were still talking about it, one in-house wag reportedly printed up lapel buttons that read: "The Earthquake Forum was *my* idea.")

"The Earthquake Forum worked as well as it did because the quake was in an area where there are lots of folks with computers," said Shel Hall, a Crosstalk Forum administrator who helped Watkins run the Earthquake Forum. "Many of them were savvy enough to log on. When they did, they saw the Earthquake Forum announcement."

Because the quake struck so near the heart of the computer world's famed Silicon Valley, it was a personal tragedy for many people on-line. The disaster's victims included some old acquaintances. Two employees of Ziff-Davis Publishing, a CompuServe business partner, died in the early moments of the quake. John Anderson and Derek Van Alstyne, associates of MacUser magazine, were killed when a wall of a building collapsed on their car. Anderson, who had also been a CompuServe forum administrator, was survived by a wife and two children. CompuServe donated profits earned from the Earthquake Forum to a fund established by Ziff-Davis to aid Anderson's children, to aid the Red Cross, and to a memorial fund established at Van Alstyne's high school.

Sharon Baker Magee was a product manager at CompuServe at the time of the quake. "We learned a lot," she said later, "about providing service to members during a disaster. It was amazing how everyone pulled together."

That lesson is the Earthquake Forum's legacy. While the special forum stayed on-line only a few weeks (it was taken down after things started getting back to normal in the Bay Area), the idea lives on. Now CompuServe routinely establishes special forums and news features in times of emergency. The Persian Gulf War in 1990-91, the breakup of the Soviet Union in 1991, and the Los Angeles riots in the spring of 1992 all prompted the temporary establishment of special forums to help share information.

Forums: The Big Picture

The reason the Earthquake Forum and other special news-related forums work so smoothly is that they offer powerful communications tools with no new learning required for the on-line visitors. CompuServe has some 500 standing public forums that operate around the clock, devoted to everything from computer-specific topics to the professions, to the home and office, to recreation and education. Despite this world of difference in topics, *all* forums have identical commands and features; therefore, learning to use one of them opens the door to them all.

CompuServe forums are administered by *sysops* (systems operators); a large forum usually has more than one, a chief sysop and several assistants. Sysops (sometimes also called "forum administrators") are usually not CompuServe employees; they are independent contractors who keep the forums going. Each chief is paid a percentage of the connect-time dollars that users spend while in his or her forum. Because each sysop is different, each forum is a little different in content, style, and approach. One forum might operate casually like a friendly neighborhood bar tucked away off the highway, while another might be like a busy, self-sufficient shopping mall, buzzing with activity, controversy, and discovery every day.

Most forums are public, but not all. The forum software — with its sophisticated message boards, libraries, and real-time conferences — can be a valuable tool for business, so some companies have private forums on CompuServe for their own use.

All forums have three main components:

1. **Message boards**, for the posting of public messages to which all members may also reply.

2. **Libraries**, or databases, filled with various information related to the interests of the group. This includes public domain and shareware programs that you may retrieve, as well as text files such as news reports and important threads of conversation from the message board on hot topics of the past.

3. **Conference rooms** for immediate real-time on-line discussions. The conference area has multiple "rooms" where members may type their messages to others in attendance and wait a few seconds for replies.

Forums also have an area for bulletins from the sysops and a member directory in which forum members may list their interests. This chapter covers all forum features except the real-conferencing options, which are discussed in the next chapter along with the very similar CB Simulator.

What Software Should You Use?

Forums are the system's most interesting and rewarding features, but they are also the most complex. For example, scores of commands are used to move about the message boards and to review and retrieve files in the data libraries.

The CompuServe Information Manager software greatly simplifies the forums by using its graphic interface to bypass all those commands. CIM helps you read and write messages, makes it easier to retrieve and transmit files in the libraries, and even facilitates real-time conferencing by providing multiple windows for incoming and outgoing messages.

However, when it comes to forums, CIM is not the only game in town. In the mid-1980s, long before CIM was written by the CompuServe staff, independent programmers around the system began to experiment with a new idea in communications software. Instead of writing a general terminal program intended to communicate with all of the modem world (from the local bulletin board system to distant databases), they created software that worked only with CompuServe in an intimate way. These dedicated terminal programs enabled users to *automate* many on-line tasks, especially in the forums. Typically, a user of one of these automated programs starts off-line, making selections from a menu to tell the program what tasks to perform, such as checking new messages in specific forums, posting several original messages on selected boards, and looking at descriptions of new files in data libraries. After the user lays out the jobs, the program automatically logs on and carries out the assignments, saving new messages to disk files as it goes. The user later reads the saved files at leisure, composing replies off-line and instructing the program to log on again and post them. Of course, a big drawing card for such software — and there are now many of them, from free public domain programs to commercial shareware that costs $50 or more — is saving money. That is because the program does so much of its work off-line when the meter isn't running.

If it is going to save money, shouldn't everyone be using automated terminal software? We shall hedge on this answer. Yes, if forums become important to you (and for tens of thousands of users, the forums *are* CompuServe), then you certainly should consider switching to a good automated program for forum hopping. It just makes good economic sense; let your powerful PC help organize all that data. Chapter 14 provides an overview of the latest automated software available for various computer types.

However, it is also wise not to make the move to automation too soon. Those who get the most out of the system are usually those who first learn to navigate for themselves, taking the time to see how the system as a whole is organized and to get a feel for the structure of complex features like forums. Obviously, automated software will work for you if you agree to see the system the way the software's programmers do. However, keep in mind that there are thousands of features on CompuServe, many of which are not on the main road, so to speak. An automated program might routinely zip right past a service you would like. For example, not long ago, we noticed that a computer-savvy friend of ours never seemed to know about any of the new services on CompuServe. Upon investigation, we found that he was never seeing the regular "What's New" announcements of new services mentioned in Chapter 1. That was because the designer of the automated terminal program he used routinely took users by shortcuts around the weekly news feature. Of course, the software could be reset to stop at "What's New," but, because our friend was new to the system, he didn't even know "What's New" existed; so, he certainly didn't know he was missing it and should reset the software.

Moving too early to automated software can lead to a kind of electronic tunnel vision, keeping you in the dark about features that could be valuable to you. A better approach is to start out using CIM or a general terminal program to explore the system and new features, then consider automation for frequently repeated tasks. Some happy CompuServe subscribers let the task determine which program to use. They may use fully-automated terminal software for all forums, then switch to CIM for mail and conferencing, for instance.

Finding and Visiting Forums

Forums are all over the system; each has its own service name (or address), which is a quick reference word that you may use with the GO command (or the Go... option in the CompuServe Information Manager). There are several broad categories of forums, such as:

- Computer-related, including groups interested in specific computers and some more general forums devoted to programming.
- General interest, about topics ranging from games to space to music.
- Professional forums (for lawyers, doctors, aviators, and so on).

You can locate forums by using the FIND command (or the Find... option on CIM's pull-down Services menu). (GO and FIND were discussed in Chapter 2.)

When you visit a forum for the first time, you are greeted with an introductory message. Then the system asks if you would like to JOIN or VISIT. Forums usually restrict most features for members only, but note: by joining, you aren't charged extra. In fact, you are not committing yourself to anything, other than to be guided by the forum's rules for good conduct. JOINing simply enables you to use all the forum's functions. You may JOIN upon arrival or you may decide to visit for a while to see how you like it (remembering that visitors usually don't have all the options of a member).

When you enter a forum as a member, you are greeted with a welcome notice that reminds you:

1. Of the date of your last visit to this forum.
2. Whether there are any new messages addressed to you.
3. If there are any real-time conferences now in progress.

Change in CIM Desktop

CIM users will note that upon arrival, their software makes several changes to the screen, altering the top menu bar. CIM supports different desktops of options for the forums and for the CB Simulator. Inside forums, the menu bar gives you quick access to the three main parts of the forum, the Message Board, the Library, and the Conference area as well as to a group of "special" forum functions. Also, a New Notices icon is displayed if any new announcements have been posted by the sysop since your last visit, similar to the "Mail" notices illustrated in Chapter 3. Finally, the software reserves a portion of the screen to automatically report continuing "events," such as arrivals and departures of other forum members and visitors while you are in the forum.

Message Board Basics

The message board is a forum's communications center, the place where members and visitors share ideas, news, gossip, and suggestions. It often reflects debate, controversy, and compromise, but also support and friendship. Here are some basics about all forum message boards (that are relevant regardless of whether you are using CIM, a third-party general terminal package, or one of the automated programs):

1. The messages are public, from members, visitors, and the sysops. Anyone who has joined the forum may (a) read messages and (b) write and post original messages as well as replies to existing messages. Messages can be up to 10,000 characters (10K) in length.

2. Messages can be gathered in several ways and sorted to help you find discussions of interest. You may collect the messages by:

   a. **Topics**. These are the chains of related messages — the originals and their replies (and replies to the replies and so on) — that are sometimes thought of as *threads*, since all messages in the group are connected by the thread of a single idea. Forums call these message chains "topics" because all the messages in a thread have the same words in the subject line. A reply made to any message in the group keeps the same subject heading. You usually view the messages by topic, reading one group before moving on to the next, because it makes it easier to follow the discussions.

   b. **Sections**. Message boards usually have specialties, and are divided into multiple sections (sometimes called "sub-topics") devoted to specific ideas. Typically, a computer-related forum might have a section for messages relating to hardware, another to software, another to new products, another to user help, and so on. Used along with *topics*, this section structure can help you to quickly target new messages of interest. Also, when writing and posting messages, members are asked to put them in the relevant sections. Sysops may decide to make some sections of the message board private, accessible by invitation only.

3. At any time, you may contribute to discussions by writing replies to existing messages. Also, you may start your own discussion by simply composing a message with a new topic and posting it on the board. The system automatically asks you to identify the subject and the intended recipient. This receiver can be another forum member, or you may indicate the message is for ALL or for SYSOP. Remember that even messages addressed to a specific member may be read and replied to by others in the forum: *All* forum messages between members are public. (Private messages may be sent to the sysops, however, as discussed later.)

4. Besides topics and sections, there are two other ways to find messages on the board. You may search for them:

   a. By a specific writer, recipient, or subject. You may search the entire message board or just a specific section.

   b. With specific message numbers. (Each message on the board is automatically assigned a unique number by the system when it is posted.) This method of retrieval is useful primarily when someone has recommended that you read a particular message and provides you with its specific number.

5. Message boards hold only a limited number of messages. Adding new messages causes the older ones to be automatically deleted by the system. Busier forums have a faster "scroll rate," which means a message may stay on the board only a few days.

6. As you begin visiting a specific forum and reading messages, the system makes note of the most recent message posted. When you exit the message board, the system automatically records the latest posting date as the starting message for your next visit. Then, the next time you read messages, you won't have to see any messages posted before that date. (Another feature in the forum lets you reset that date, as is discussed later in this chapter.)

First let's discuss forum operation through the CIM software, then examine forum usage through third-party software.

Message Boards Via CIM

Users of the CompuServe Information Manager software may look at a forum's message board area by selecting the Message option from the revised top menu bar. A subsequent pull-down menu provides the options illustrated in Figure 4.1.

Browse   selects messages from subsequent section and topic menus.

Search   lets you look for messages by subject, author, or recipient.

Get Waiting   retrieves and displays any new messages addressed to you personally.

Get Single Msg   lets you fetch a specific message by its number. (In other words, you must know the message's unique number in order to use the option.)

Retrieve Marked   puts the marked messages in your electronic Filing Cabinet on your disk for later reading.

Set Date   may be used to set a specific start date for subsequent browsing and searches.

Create message   is used to compose and edit a message with CIM's built-in writing/editing feature.

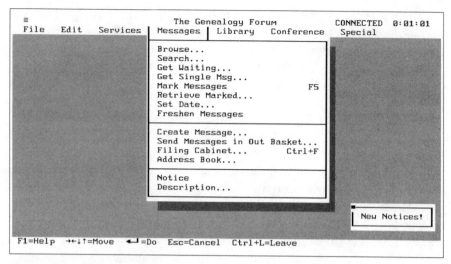

Figure 4.1 CIM Message Menu

Send messages lets you view, then send, the message you have written.

Filing Cabinet gives you access to the electronic Filing Cabinet on your disk.

Address Book gives you access to the electronic Address Book on your disk.

Notice shows you message board-related announcements from the forum's sysops.

Description causes the forum to display a brief report on the message board functions.

Note The IBM PC/compatible version of the program also has a Mark Topic options on this menu. Both the IBM and Apple Macintosh version support the same function for marking a topic to save it on the disk. Each version handles the option a little differently. Both approaches are described later in this chapter.

Getting Messages (BROWSE, SEARCH, GET WAITING, GET SINGLE MSG)

There are several ways to find messages on the boards: by section or topic, by searching subject, author, or recipient, and/or by searching a specific message number. The Browse function on the message pull-down menu uses the first two methods, while the Search function supports the latter two. In addition, the Get Waiting function retrieves messages written specifically to you, while the Get Single Msg lets you retrieve a note by its unique message number.

The **BROWSE** option causes CIM to display a pull-down menu of this particular forum's message board *sections*. As shown in Figure 4.2, the display provides the name of each section, followed by the number of topics (subjects, threads of conversations), then the total number of messages in that section. The naming of sections is a decision by the sysop and the assistants, so section names vary greatly from forum to forum. They are part of the individuality of the forum. The display also shows information about the age of the messages ("Messages since..."). Messages that were posted before that date are not shown (though, as discussed later in the chapter, that date may be reset). Choosing a section from this display causes the software to display a pull-down menu of the *topics* currently in that section, which lists the subject of each discussion followed by the number of messages in that topic. Often the display also has a scroll bar on the menu; therefore, additional choices are available besides the ones in the box.

To select a topic and display the first (that is, the oldest) message available in that thread of conversation, Macintosh and Windows users should highlight the topic, then click on to the Read icon, while IBM PC/compatible DOS users only need to highlight the topic and press RETURN.

Note Besides reading topics on-line, you may also (1) retrieve entire topics and save them in your Filing Cabinet for off-line reading and (2) "map" a topic to get a specific graphic overview of it. These subjects are discussed in later sections in this chapter.

The **SEARCH** option on the Message pull-down menu lets you look through the entire message board or a specific section to find messages either

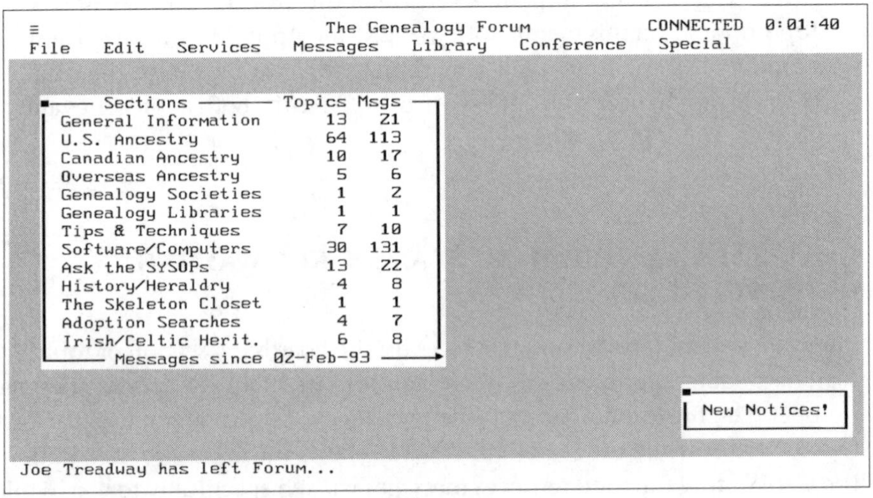

```
  ≡                        The Genealogy Forum          CONNECTED  0:01:40
  File    Edit    Services    Messages    Library    Conference    Special


      ──── Sections ────  Topics Msgs ──
      General Information     13    21
      U.S. Ancestry           64   113
      Canadian Ancestry       10    17
      Overseas Ancestry        5     6
      Genealogy Societies      1     2
      Genealogy Libraries      1     1
      Tips & Techniques        7    10
      Software/Computers      30   131
      Ask the SYSOPs          13    22
      History/Heraldry         4     8
      The Skeleton Closet      1     1
      Adoption Searches        4     7
      Irish/Celtic Herit.      6     8
      ──── Messages since 02-Feb-93 ────▶

                                                          ┌──────────────┐
                                                          │ New Notices! │
                                                          └──────────────┘

  Joe Treadway has left Forum...
```

Figure 4.2 Message Board Sections Display

by subject, author, and recipient, or by message number. To do its work, it displays the dialog box (Figure 4.3) in which you define the particulars of your search. Options let you indicate whether you are searching by message subject, originator, or receiver.

You may specify in a "Search For:" field the name, term, or short phrase for which you are looking. You don't have to enter a complete word or name. In fact, sometimes you probably won't want to use a complete name. For example, if you were searching the board for messages from or to your friend David, you might not know if he joined the forum as "David" or "Dave." In that case, you might want to answer the prompt by entering only as much of the name as you are sure of: DAV. The system then searches the field for all names that contain the letters DAV side by side and in that order. In the same way, if you were searching the subject field of messages for computer-related topics, you might want to enter only COMPUT, which would find "computer," "computers," "computing," "computation," and so on.

Also in the box is a list of active sections. Unless you specify otherwise, the search includes *all* your default sections in the forum, as noted in the display. You may also unmark or mark a section for searching. Two action buttons at the bottom can speed things along. To narrow the search to a specific section of the board, first select the **None** button, then mark the one section to be searched using the procedure discussed in the previous paragraph. On the other hand, to widen the search to cover all sections (including those not currently marked), select the **All** button. In addition, you may change the starting date of the group of messages to be searched.

When a search is completed, the system displays a menu of relevant messages and/or topics. With the cursor bar, you may select a topic to read and see the first (oldest) message in the group.

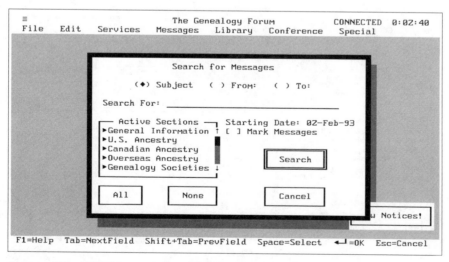

Figure 4.3 CIM Message Search Display

GET WAITING is the option on the Messages pull-down menu that lets you retrieve any new messages written specifically for you. When messages are composed for a forum, the author may fill the "To:" field with the word "ALL," "SYSOP," or the name and address (user ID number) of another member of the forum. In the latter case, although these personally addressed messages are still public, the recipient:

1. Is notified upon arrival in the forum that the messages are waiting, and

2. May retrieve them quickly by using the Get Waiting function, which collects all personally addressed mail posted since the last visit to the forum.

> **Note**   A feature added to later CIM versions (version 2.x) enables you to mark a waiting message for retrieval to disk in a batch.

Finally, the **GET SINGLE MSG** option lets you see a specific message. You are prompted to enter the note's unique message number. This option is useful if someone else in the forum suggests to you, "Be sure to see message #23456." Selecting this option causes the program to prompt you for the message number.

Reading Messages

When reading a forum message board with any of the above four procedures, the messages are displayed one at a time, as shown in Figure 4.4.

A header, displayed above the actual text, contains seven elements:

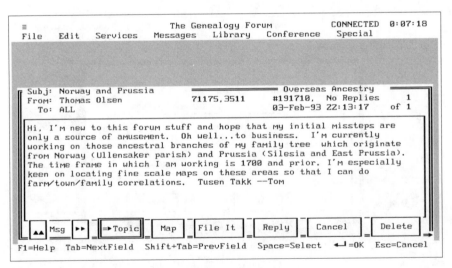

Figure 4.4   Typical Message Display in CIM

- The first line contains (1) the message's subject (or "topic") and (2) the name of the board section where the message was filed. As noted, the subject is the same for all messages in this particular topic (or thread); the system itself makes sure of that by automatically assigning the same subject to all replies to this message or any other message on the topic.

- The second line, preceded by "From:," contains (3) the name and address (user ID number) of the sender, (4) the message's unique sequence number (automatically assigned by the system when the message was posted), and (5) the number of replies that have been posted to the message.

- The last line, preceded by "To:," contains (6) the name and address (user ID number) of the person for whom the message is intended. (Sometimes a message isn't written to a specific person, but rather ALL or SYSOP is written in the "To:" field. Sometimes a symbol (a diamond in the Macintosh version, a "happy face" in the IBM PC/compatible version) appears in front of the "To:" field; this means that the intended recipient of the messages has retrieved it. Also in the last line, the "To:" information is followed by (7) the date and time the message was posted; the time is always displayed as your local time.

Following the header, the message itself is displayed in 10-line pages in a text box. If the message has more than 10 lines, you may move to the other pages with a mouse or the keyboard cursor navigation keys (described in Appendix B, "CompuServe Information Manager Basics").

Elsewhere on the screen are the following options:

Message displays the next message in the topic or group you have chosen. If the one currently on the screen is the last message in the group, the "Message" option is dimmed on the display, to indicate that the option is not currently open. (In the Macintosh version, the appropriate arrow in the icon is dimmed if the message is the first or last message in the topic.)

Topic displays the first message in the *next* topic. Use it to discontinue reading messages in the current subject group and move on to the next one.

Map displays what might be called a "genealogical" map of a forum conversation. (More on this unique feature will follow.)

File copies the message into the electronic Filing Cabinet on your disk, where you may retrieve it later. (This is the same Filing Cabinet used with CompuServe Mail.) Once a message is in the Filing Cabinet, you may retrieve it at any time — on-line or off-line — by selecting the Filing Cabinet option from either the Message or Mail pull-down menu.

Reply enables you to write and post a reply to this message. This is described below in the section about composing original messages and replies.

Delete erases the message from the message board so others can no longer
see it. You may delete only messages that either

   a. You wrote and posted yourself under the current user ID number or

   b. Were addressed to you at the current user ID number.

   (The forum's sysops may delete all messages, including those addressed
to other people.)

Note Starting with version 2.0 of CIM, the software always enables
you to read messages within a forum topic in *reverse* order; just select
the up arrow option while viewing a forum message.

Mapping

The **Map** feature offers a graphic display of messages in a current topic; it is
a quick way to see who is replying to whom in current discussion, as shown
in Figure 4.5.

Consider the following points in a map display:

- The relationship of messages is indicated by the indenting and connecting lines.

- If a map includes a reply message but not a message to which it responded,
  the connecting line will be missing.

- A bullet symbol at the far left of the screen indicates the message you
  have already displayed.

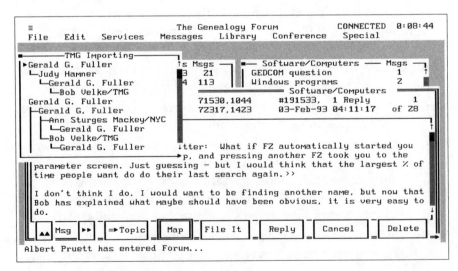

Figure 4.5 CIM's Map Feature at Work

- The cursor bar may be moved up and down to highlight different messages on the map. Selecting one (pressing RETURN in the IBM version, clicking on to the Read icon in the Macintosh version) is a quick way to retrieve a different message on the map (whether or not you have already displayed it).

Saving Topics on Disk (MARK TOPIC/RETRIEVE MARKED)

Individual messages may be copied into the disk Filing Cabinet for later reading. But that's not all: *Entire* topics (or threads of discussion) may be transferred to the Filing Cabinet for off-line use.

From any menu of topics, you may retrieve all the topics you want, copying them to the electronic disk space in your Filing Cabinet. To retrieve a topic this way, first highlight it with the bar cursor, then *mark* it:

- In the Macintosh version, this means simply clicking on the **Mark** icon.
- In the IBM version, there is no such icon, but the same function may be performed by either (1) pressing **CONTROL-T** or (2) going to the Message pull-down menu and selecting the **Mark Topic** option. (Versions of CIM after 2.0 allow you to mark a message for retrieval by pressing the F5 key while reading the message. You can also mark an entire forum message section or topic for retrieval by highlighting it from the list menu and pressing F5.)

Once a topic is marked, a bullet symbol appears in front of the topic name on the display. After marking all of the topic you want to copy to your Filing Cabinet, return to the Message pull-down menu and choose the **Retrieve Marked** option. The system then displays a dialog box which allows you to review the topics you have selected, then choose one of the following options:

Get All,   that is retrieve all the topics on the list. CIM copies all the messages in all the topics to a Filing Cabinet folder named after the forum. Messages already retrieved in the folder remain there as well. If the folder doesn't already exist, the software will automatically create one. The retrieval is reported topic by topic and message by message within a topic.

Remove (or **Delete**)   highlighted topics from the list before beginning the retrieval.

You may cancel at any point during the operation. Once topics have been retrieved on disk, you may read the messages off-line by accessing the Filing Cabinet.

Set Date

CompuServe's forums automatically note the most recent message posted and record the number of the latest message you read while visiting the message board. That last message number becomes the starting point for your next message board visit. This means each visit to the board shows you the messages posted since your last visit. However, you may change the start date for a particular reading of the board, using the Set Date option on the Message pull-down menu.

The Macintosh version displays a calendar with which you may enter a new date by clicking on the month, day, and year to set your message cutoff date. The IBM-compatible version uses a simpler display that prompts you to enter the starting date. In either version, all Browsing and Searching of the board will include the message beginning with the date you have set from then until you leave the forum.

Writing Forum Messages (CREATE MESSAGE/SEND MESSAGES)

Writing and posting forum messages is very much like CompuServe Mail in that it uses the same built-in text feature, may be done on-line or off-line, and can make use of the electronic Address Book.

The two ways for you to get your own thoughts and words on to a forum message board are by composing original messages (thus starting your own topic or thread) and replying to other people's messages (making your message part of an existing topic).

1. **ORIGINAL MESSAGES** may be created with the **Create Message** option from the Messages pull-down menu, which displays a dialog box for composition similar to the Mail text box. Your name and user ID number are automatically filled in for you. (Incidentally, the way your name appears in the "From:" field of messages may be changed, as is discussed later in this chapter in the Forum Options section.) Since writing an original message means starting a new discussion, you need to supply a subject (topic) for the message and specify the section of the board on which it is to be posted. (In later versions of the software, starting with version 2.0, CIM automatically records the current forum or section as the default for your message destination; unless you modify the information, your message will go to that section.) In the last line (beginning with "To:") you are to identify a recipient. You may either:

   a. Manually enter the information by positioning the cursor (with the mouse or the TAB key) on the area following the To: and entering a forum member's name. Follow this with his or her user ID number (address) in the second area. Or, if you don't have a specific person in mind as a receiver, you may enter ALL or the word SYSOP in either field.

   b. Use the electronic Address Book on your disk to get the date for the receiver. To do that, select the To: field (by clicking on with the mouse or by pressing RETURN). This causes CIM to list the names in your

Address Book. Select one and the recipient will be automatically identified in the field. (It works just like CompuServe Mail. For more on the use of the Address Book, see Chapter 3.)

2. **REPLIES** may be created by selecting the **Reply** action button while viewing a message. This causes a similar text box to appear, except that the subject, section, and receiver's address are automatically filled in for you. (The subject of a reply message is always the same as the subject of the original.)

Whether you are writing an original message or a reply, the next step is the same. Use the mouse or the TAB key to reach the text box, then you may begin typing your message, using the built-in writing/editing feature, as shown in Figure 4.6. To stop writing, IBM users should press ESCape, while Macintosh users may simply position the mouse cursor on an option.

The next options are:

Send   posts the message on the board.

Out-Basket   puts it in the disk storage for later delivery.

File   lets you keep it in the electronic Filing Cabinet. This option may also be used to save partially completed messages that may be recalled to work on later.

Delete   erases the message without sending it and gives you a fresh text box.

Elsewhere on the screen is a **Via Mail** option that lets you send the message from the forum to the receiver, not on the message board, but via CompuServe Mail to the individual's private mailbox. To use this option, select the option before selecting **Send**. This puts a mark in the brackets.

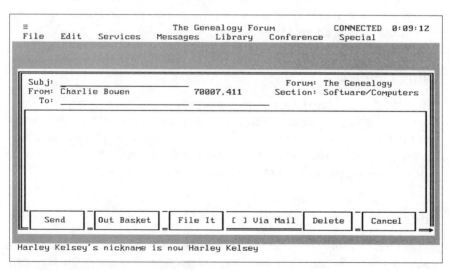

Figure 4.6 Composing Message in CIM

Off-line composing of forum messages is also possible through the Mail pull-down menu, as noted in the previous chapter. This is particularly useful if you have a number of messages to write and want to save connect-time charges. While off-line, pull down the Mail menu and select the **Create Forum Message** option, which produces a new dialog box. You may list the recipient (a forum member, ALL, or SYSOP) after a To: prompt. Then write the message. To deliver the message do the following:

1. Select the **Out-Basket** option. (The program automatically tags it as a message destined for a forum.)

2. Go… to the forum where you want it posted.

3. When you arrive, select **Send Messages** from the Message pull-down menu to take you to the Out-Basket.

4. Select **Send**, which takes you to a dialog box where you select the appropriate section. You may also change the subject, the recipient, and the message text. Then select **Send Now**, which actually posts the message.

Note   Later versions of the software add an option that allows you to automatically save a copy of all forum messages you send in a Filing Cabinet folder of your choice.

Private Messages

Some forums allow visitors to send and receive private messages through the message boards. Later versions of the CompuServe Information Manager software support that feature where available. To use it, choose the Create Messages from the Message menu, then mark the Private checkbox and the message will be sent only to the address specified in the To: field.

Filing Cabinet

When the disk storage space has been stocked with forum messages (with the File option) and with topics (with the Mark Topic/Retrieve Marked options), you may use the Filing Cabinet at any time (on-line or off-line) from either the Message pull-down menu or the Mail pull-down menu. It works the same way here as for CompuServe Mail, as discussed in Chapter 3.

Address Book

Forum messages, like CompuServe Mail, can interact with the electronic Address Book on your disk, since it is the *same* Address Book you use in the Mail program. A helpful feature of CIM is the keeping of names, user ID numbers, and other information on forum regulars. While reading the boards in the forums, you may save a message author's or recipient's name and user ID by highlighting the From: or To: field, and either clicking on it with a mouse or pressing RETURN. This displays an Address Entry dialog box with the name and address filled in. Also, you may access your list from the Message pull-down menu by selecting **Address Book**. This produces a dialog box where you may Add or Remove an entry or Open the book to view and modify the material. In addition, material in a forum's Member Directory may also be copied directly into the Address Book, as will be discussed later.

Message Board with Non-CIM Software

If you're using a third-party communications program rather than the CompuServe Information Manager software, you can look at a forum's message board by simply following numbered menus. (An alternative to *both* CIM and general third-party software is an automatic terminal program, such as TAPCIS or Whap, that performs much of the forum maintenance off-line. An overview of such programs is provided in Chapter 14. For now we are assuming you are using a program that will allow you to operate a forum manually so you can learn its organization.)

With non-CIM software, the introductory menu of the forum looks like this:

```
        1    INSTRUCTIONS

        2    MESSAGES
        3    LIBRARIES (Files)
        4    CONFERENCING (0 participating)

        5    ANNOUNCEMENTS from sysop
        6    MEMBER directory
        7    OPTIONS for this forum

        Enter choice !
```

To reach the message board portion of the forum, select the MESSAGES option.

Note On this and other menus in the forum, you will notice that some words are capitalized, as MESSAGES, CONFERENCING, LIBRARIES, and so on. This capitalization signals that you can enter these words or their abbreviations instead of the numeric menu items.

To start to read a message, choose option 2 or enter MESSAGES or MES at the prompt. This takes you to a Messages Menu, which provides these primary options:

SELECT to read by section and subject.

READ or search messages.

CHANGE the age selection.

COMPOSE an original message for posting.

Select

The SELECT option on the menu allows you to group messages in two ways:

1. By the *section* (or subtopic) of the message board.
2. Then by *subjects* or *threads* of the messages.

A forum's message board is divided into subtopics or *sections* which are departments or categories; the sysop can assign up to 18 different subtopics. Section 1 might be "General Interest," while section 2 is devoted to "News," section 3 is "Help Wanted," and so on. (Some forums start with section 0, while others make section 1 their first subtopic. Also, not all subtopics are public; some forums reserve a few areas of the board for sysop-invitation only.) Choosing SELECT (by entering SEL, 1, or the entire word SELECT) causes the system to list its section names, each followed by two numbers that indicate section activity, like this:

```
Section names (#subjs/# msgs)
 0   General (35/79)
 1   Download Help (1/2)
 2   Library Tools (1/2)
 5   Fun Graphics (1/1)
 6   Gen Fun & Games (9/11)
 7   Ask the Sysops (32/92)
 8   Village Inn (2/5)

Enter choice(s) or ALL !
```

The first number indicates how many different *subjects* or *threads* (the terms are used interchangeably in the forums) are being discussed in the messages posted there; the second number is the total number of messages filed. At the prompt, you may indicate the section or sections you want to SELECT for reading; you do that by entering a single number, several numbers separated by commas, or the word ALL.

The system then becomes more specific by listing the subjects in the selected section or sections. A menu provides a list of the individual subjects followed by a number in parentheses that tells how many messages are in each subject, like this:

```
Subject (# msgs)

Section 0 - General
   1    286 to 386 or 486 (1)
   2    DX2 VS DX at 50 mhz (1)
   3    something like NEW (3)
   4    Giving my PC more brains (1)
   5    ThinkPad 700 Notebooks (1)
   6    Hi! and HELP!! (3)
   7    DOS 5.0 (1)
   8    zip-unzip execs (3)
   9    CompuServe made easy (1)
  10    modem help for notebook (2)
  11    Windows Quicken (3)
  12    AS/400 (1)
  13    Sorry (4)
  14    procomm in host mode (2)
  15    Six pack card (2)
  16    [F]orward (2)

Enter choice(s) or <CR> for more !
```

At this point, you may enter the numbers of any subjects that sound interesting and the system will begin displaying what it has on file. After each message is a prompt that says, "Press <CR> for next or type CHOICES !" Here you may:

- Go directly to the next message in the discussion by pressing the RETURN key. (If there were no more messages, pressing RETURN takes you back to the subject menu.)

- Or you may see other possible actions on this message by entering CHOICES (or simply CHO). A "Read Action menu" is produced with a number of options, including those to:

    a. REPLY with the same subject.

    b. COMPOSE with a new subject.

    c. REREAD this message.

    d. Go to the NEXT reply.

    e. Go to the NEXT SUBJECT (that is, skip unread messages in the current thread and display the first message in the *next* message thread) and READ reply.

Another option ("DELETE this message") is also displayed on the menu if that option is open to you. You may delete a message only if you wrote it or it was written specifically to you (that is, your user ID number was specified by the sender in the TO: field when the message was written or the message was written as a reply to one you wrote.)

Besides the commands on the menu, there are some additional reading commands that can be used at the "CHOICES" prompt (the one that looks like "Press <CR> for next or type CHOICES !"). Choices can also be entered at the Read Action menu, which we have called the "CHOICES" menu. The following options are offered:

- MARK designates the message you have just read for later retrieval with the command READ MARKED. In other words, as you read the board, you can enter MARK at the prompt following selected messages. Then, you can return to the Messages menu and enter the command READ MARKED to see again all the messages you have marked. (We have more to say about command sequences, like READ MARKED, in a moment.)

- ROOT displays the first message available in the current thread of messages.

- PARENT displays the "parent" or "owner" message of a reply.

- SCROLL causes the system to display the current batch of messages consecutively, without your having to press the RETURN key between them. In other words, SCROLL causes the suppression of the "Press <CR> for next or type CHOICES !" prompt for the batch of messages you are currently reading.

Read

The READ option is actually a Read or Search feature. Choosing it from the Message Menu gives you the following options:

```
Read
   1   [NEW] messages
   2   Message NUMBER
   3   WAITING messages for you (0)

Search [new] messages
   4   FROM (Sender)
   5   SUBJECT
   6   TO (Recipient)

Enter choice !
```

In other words, you may either:

Read:

1. All new or marked messages. Messages are grouped automatically in order of threads. This is particularly handy if you have been following conversations over several days, because the READ messages function allows you to automatically catch up on each of them.

2. Specific messages by number. The NUMBER option displays a message whose number you specify. When you select it, the system displays the range of message numbers currently on the board and asks you to specify some boundaries. As a practical matter, you won't use this option as often as the others. Instead of reading individual messages by number, it is wiser to read messages grouped by threads, age, or some other way so you can follow the thread of conversation.

3. And/or messages waiting specifically for you. This WAITING option offers to display messages that have been posted for you, either as original messages or as replies to your earlier notes on the board. They are flagged for your attention; the system tells you about them when you enter the forum. Also, because messages written to you can be deleted, a seventh option—"DELETE this message"—will be added to the Read Action menu reachable through the CHOICES options on any such message.

Search new or marked messages that are FROM a specific person, TO a specific person, and/or about a particular SUBJECT. These commands do not search the text of the messages, but rather the messages' *headers;* that is, the words and numbers contained in the "Sb:," "Fm:," and "To:" fields.

Here are some points about searching these fields:

1. Use quotation marks to enclose strings containing two or more words or names; for example, "Dave Peyton" or "Red Apples" or "Charlie Bowen."

2. You don't have to enter a complete word or name. In fact, sometimes you probably won't want to use a complete name. If you were searching the board for messages from or to your friend David, you might not know if he joined the forum as "David" or "Dave." In that case, you might want to answer the prompt by entering only as much of the name as you are sure of: DAV. The system then searches the field for all names that contain the letters DAV side by side and in that order. In the same way, if you were searching the subject field of messages for computer-related topics, you might want to enter only COMPUT, which would find "computer," "computers," "computing," "computation" and so on.

3. The forum searches the *entire* field, not just the beginning. So, if you were looking for a message from Dave Peyton, you could enter PEYTON or PEY as well as DAVID or DAV.

4. The TO and FROM prompts also accept the user ID, as well as the name, of the person for whom you are searching. However, there is a difference: While the system accepts partial names and words, user IDs entered at the prompts must be complete. (If you are looking for messages from the user of ID number 71635,1025, you *won't* find it if you enter only 71635 at the prompt.)

Change

Forums have another powerful tool for grouping messages by *age* through the Message Menu's CHANGE option.

Generally, forums are set up to display "new" messages each time you visit the forum (any messages that have been posted since the last message number you have read). However, the CHANGE option lets you specify that on the current visit you want to see either: NEW messages, ALL messages, those STARTING message number, or those posted in the past specified number of DAYS. The CHANGE menu interacts with the Read function. There are two points about the CHANGE functions:

- CHANGEs are in effect only for your current forum session. When you leave the forum or log off the system, the age option returns to NEW.

- Except for the ALL setting, CHANGE *limits* the messages you can find, as if you have laid a grid over the material you want to see. That is why the setting is described in square brackets on a number of menus, to remind you of the grid currently in effect.

Other Useful Reading Commands

Not all forum commands are listed on the menus. Certain command words and letter combinations can be entered for some additional functions.

For instance, you can plan imaginary *grids* over the message board to limit your reading and searching to a designated section or sections. The command SS, which means "Set Section," entered at a prompt, causes the system to respond with a list of its section numbers and a prompt. Now you can enter the numbers of one or more sections (separated by commas). From then on, until you enter another SS command, all the messages you read or search will be from the designated sections only. When you log off, the system resets your sections to the original number.

Another useful command is NAME. Entered at a prompt, NAME causes the system to display a menu. Forums can have different sections in the message board, data libraries, and conference areas, so the system is asking which names you need to see.

Other commands offer various kinds of summary data about the messages on the board:

- BROWSE displays a summary of each message thread, one at a time, then prompts you to read the thread or continue to the next one. A prompt indicates you may enter Y to read the messages in the thread or N to continue to the next thread BROWSE has found for you. Also, you can enter X to end the BROWSE session and return to the menu.

- SCAN can also be entered at this menu to see the list of headers for each message filed on the post.

- SCAN QUICK displays a different kind of summary of message threads, listing their subjects, number of replies, etc.

Composing Messages on the Board

Two ways are available for you to get your own words on the message board:

- By composing original messages (thus starting your own thread or subject).
- By replying to other people's messages (thereby making your note part of an existing thread).

The COMPOSE option on the forum's Messages menu enables you to write an original message to post on the board. When you select that option, the system opens a writing area. Two editors are available on-line (EDIT and LINEEDIT), both of which are discussed in Appendix H, "Writing On-Line," in the On-Line Survival Kit. In addition, you may upload a prewritten ASCII file, which is discussed later in this chapter.

When you finish the message and close it with the /EXIT command, the system shows you a Post Action menu like this:

```
        1    POST message on board
        2    EDIT message
        3    TYPE message
        4    MAIL via CompuServe Mail
        5    CANCEL message compose

    Enter choice !
```

The options include:

1. POST message on board.
2. EDIT message using a menu-driven editor (with options to CHANGE characters in a line, REPLACE a line, DELETE a line, INSERT new lines, TYPE (display) all lines, and POST the message on the board). Since the editing works with numbers, it is wise to use the TYPE command to see your message with the existing line numbers.

3. TYPE message.

4. MAIL via CompuServe Mail.

5. CANCEL message compose.

Another command available, but not shown here, on the message is PREview, which allows you to see how the message you are composing will appear once you have posted it. The command is also often used to see how a message will appear in a specific screen width. For instance, if you want to see how the message will appear to those with computers having a 32-character screen, you would enter PREVIEW WIDTH:32.

> **Note** Obviously, this business of references to line numbers applies only when you are using the line-numbered editor described in Appendix H. If, after reading the material in the appendix, you decide to switch to the unnumbered EDIT program, you no longer receive the forum Edit menu when you enter the EDIT command. Instead, the system simply reopens the message for editing and expects you to use those slash (/) commands, such as /P to print the current line, /L/*string* to locate a word or phrase, and so forth. Since you are new to forums, we suggest that you continue to use the line-numbered editor for now, since it provides many menus along the way.

Posting Messages

Once you have your message edited the way you want it, you can put it on the message board by entering the word POST or choosing the corresponding numeral on the menu. The system then prompts with:

> Post for (Name and/or User ID):

New subscribers sometimes misunderstand this prompt, possibly because of the "and/or" business. It means that, at a minimum, you should enter the user ID number of the intended recipient. As an option, you may also enter the recipient's name on the same line. In other words, you could enter "Charlie Bowen 71635,1025" or simply, "71635,1025." Either way, the forum now knows to mark the message for the recipient's next visit to the forum, because you have supplied the user ID number. When the intended recipient logs in, the system will announce that your message is waiting. However, if you enter only the name *without* the user ID number, the system won't know how to notify the recipient. Several ways exist to find user IDs and names, as is discussed in the previous chapter. You can find ID numbers and names on the message board itself by using the searching facilities to search the TO and FROM fields, as illustrated earlier in this chapter.

There are two other ways you can reply to this "Post for (Name and/or User ID):" prompt. You may enter:

- ALL if you are addressing the note to the entire membership.
- SYSOP if you want the message marked for the forum's administrators. If you enter the word SYSOP, you don't have to supply a user ID number.

After you have filled in this blank, the system prompts for the subject of your message. This can be a word or string of words, up to 24 characters; it will appear in the "Sb:" line of the message header. Subject lines are important because they are used by members who are sorting and reading the message by threads. Since you are using the COMPOSE to create an *original* message (rather than a reply), you are automatically creating a new thread on the board.

After that, the system needs to know on what section or subtopic of the board to post your message, and displays a menu of the section names. Once you enter the number of the section which best describes your message's topic, the system posts your message and reports the number assigned to it.

The remaining option on the Post menu allows you to MAIL your message from the forum to the recipient via CompuServe Mail. With this option, your message does not appear on the board as a public pronouncement, but instead is sent privately to the recipient's electronic mailbox. In addition, you are prompted for the recipient's user ID number.

Replying to Messages

Replying to messages is even easier than composing originals. As noted earlier, options to reply to messages occur as part of several Read functions. Selecting one allows you to *answer* the message you have just read. The REPLY option sees to it that your message has the same subject line as the message you are answering; that means it is also in the same thread as the original. Since it is a reply, the system does not prompt you for a subject or a recipient after you are finished writing the message.

Uploading to Message Boards

You can not only compose CompuServe Mail off-line, then log on and send it, but also upload prewritten messages to the message boards of forums. Write the message with your word processor, following the same procedures discussed in the previous chapter. Remember that the file needs to be saved *in ASCII* by your word processor. Then log on, visit the forum where you want the message posted—either as a reply or an original note—and select the Compose option from the menu. When the system prompts you to enter your menu, you need to enter this command on the first line:

```
/UPLOAD <RETURN>
```

Note that the slash (/) must be the first character on the line (this tells Compu-Serve the following is a *command* rather than text) and there is no space between the slash and the command UPLOAD. After you press RETURN, CompuServe will display its upload protocol menu from which you can select the protocol you want to use for the file transfer. (See Appendix I on "File Transfer" in the On-Line Survival Kit for specifics.) After the file has been transmitted, enter /EXIT on a new line to tell CompuServe to close the file. You can then edit and post the message just as you would if you had entered it directly from the keyboard.

A Few Words About Message Board Content

Whether you see message boards through the CompuServe Information Manager, a third-party general program, or an automatic navigating program, it all comes down to the messages. So, before we move on to the forum libraries and how they work, let's take a moment to discuss the *content* of forum messages—those you read and those you send.

Forum Shorthand

When reading message boards, you will find that they often encourage a kind of shorthand with abbreviations of frequently used words and phrases and odd acronyms that can be intimidating to the uninitiated. Here is a list of common abbreviations used in some forums:

- BBS: Computer "bulletin board system," usually a private dialup service.
- BCNU: "Be seein' you."
- BTW: "By the way."
- CIS: CompuServe Information Service.
- CO: Conference, used to refer to real-time conferencing, either as a noun ("At the CO...") or a verb ("When we CO...").
- config: configuration.
- CU: "See you," as in "CU tomorrow."
- DBMS: database management system.
- FYI: "For your information."
- IMHO: "In my humble opinion."
- NBD: "No big deal."
- OIC: "Oh, I see."

- OTOH: "On the other hand."
- params: parameters; that is, communications settings.
- p.d.: public domain.
- PPN: literally "Programmer Project Number," an old term for a CompuServe user ID number.
- prog.: program.
- WizOp: the primary (that is, *wizard*) sysop of a forum.
- w.p.: word processor.
- WYSIWYG: "What you see is what you get."
- xfer: transfer, as in file transfer.

Becoming a Good Guy

The message board is a powerful utility for asking questions of the world but, of course, its success depends on your receiving answers. You are more likely to get replies to your messages if you think before you type. Here are some tips from the Sadder-But-Wiser Department of Interpersonal Electronic Relationships:

1. *Leave public messages only when you really have something to say.* Boards are often inundated with one- and two-line replies that say only, "I agree" or "Haha — that's a good one" or perhaps a personal message of interest to only one other forum member. Since each forum message board holds a limited number of messages, each time a new one is posted, the oldest one is removed. It is always a shame when an old message that might be the beginning of a fascinating topic is scrolled into limbo by a new note that says nothing. So post messages publicly when they contribute to the discussion and have a general interest. For private communication, use CompuServe Mail.

2. *Don't let this inhibit you from asking questions publicly.* Most questions *are* of general interest. For every one questioner who speaks out, there are four or five wishing someone would ask the same question. Just remember to pick a good place to post the question — the appropriate section of an appropriate forum. (Sysops can move a message from one section to another, but they appreciate members who are already savvy enough to post it correctly in the first place.)

3. *Don't be a mass-mailer*, posting the same message in a number of different forums. Because your fellow subscribers often visit a variety of forums, it is inconsiderate if you make them come across an identical message on every board they visit. Pick the one forum that best meets your needs for a specific question or comment.

4. *Research.* Sysops are used to answering the same questions over and over again, particularly when a new piece of major software or hardware is

released, or a forum project is under way. Repetition is part of the job. On the other hand, you do everyone a favor if you read a little before you write. If it is conceivable that your question already has been raised and answered recently, search or browse the board. Also check the library (covered in the next section); perhaps the forum has preserved a thread file that specifically addresses your question. If you don't find an answer on your own, raise the issue in a message. Be sure to ask if there is a library file you might have overlooked.

5. *Watch for your answers*. If you raise a question, be sure to check in again within at least 48 hours to see the replies. It is frustrating to those who take the time to answer a question if the questioner doesn't check back in time to read it before it scrolls off into oblivion. It is bad form to ask the members to answer your question again just because you didn't check back sooner.

6. Remember, *don't leave a message that says, "What's this forum all about?"* Find out for yourself. The sysops have put together special files outlining their goals in the Notices area, as illustrated at the end of this chapter. Check them to see the forum's direction.

7. Finally, *enjoy yourself!* All this talk of conventions and local customs might make the forums sound like stuffy, straightlaced outfits. They aren't. Most forums love good humor and camaraderie. Inject a little of your own personality into your messages. Introduce yourself. People are always interested in other people. You may find others on the forum who have similar backgrounds. After all, talk is what it is all about.

The Forum Libraries—An Overview

The libraries hold the resources and treasures of a forum. Generally, they contain three kinds of data:

1. Public domain and shareware *software* that you may retrieve on your disk. Once retrieved, the programs may be used over and over again off-line.

2. Text files, such as past topics discussed in the forum that may be read on-line or retrieved for off-line reading later. The text may also include reprints of published articles, reviews and commentaries written by other forum members, how-to articles by sysops and forum regulars, transcripts of important real-conferences, and message board conversations of note.

3. Graphics files that may be viewed on-line or retrieved for off-line viewing. These sometimes are referred to as ".GIF" files because they usually have that filename extension (such as "BOARD.GIF"). GIF stands for "Graphic Interchange Format," a widely accepted format for picture files that may be exchanged between different types of computers.

Libraries, like the message boards, are divided into sections, each devoted to a particular aspect of the forum's subjects. Each section has its own name assigned by the sysop and staff. Sections might be named "New Uploads," "General News," or "Library Tools." One section might contain general utility programs, another might have files relating to word processing, while still others might have game software and reviews or programs and articles about computer graphics. (Libraries can also have numbers associated with them. Users with general third-party software use these numbers with commands— the command LIB 1 takes a user to the library number 1—while CIM users are accustomed to ignoring the numbers and simply select a desired library from a menu by name. However, a new function—covered later in the chapter — allows CIM users to have the numbers on library sections displayed as well as their names.)

Any of the files in the library — programs or text — may be *retrieved* ("downloaded"); this means a copy is made on your disk so that you may use it later off-line. In addition, you may *contribute* ("upload") copies of your own files, including original programs and text, for others to use.

As with the message boards, there is more than one way to prowl the forum libraries. You may either:

- Browse sections, reading descriptions of recently contributed files, or
- Search for specific files by name, contributor's user ID number, or keywords.

Either way, when you find a file of interest, you may retrieve it immediately or mark it for later retrieval, perhaps in a batch with other files in that forum.

This section will first examine data libraries as seen through the CompuServe Information Manager, then view them as used through non-CIM software.

Data Libraries Through CIM

When you select Library from the menu bar, the CompuServe Information Manager displays a pull-down menu of library options, as shown in Figure 4.7.

The options on the menu represent the following:

Browse lets you see descriptions of files in a section of the library. As you go, you may elect to retrieve the file described, saving a copy on your disk.

Search enables you to look for files by name, contributor's user ID number, or keywords.

Retrieve File causes CIM to fetch a specified file, automatically saving it on your disk. You are prompted for the name of the file you want.

Retrieve Marked lets you get a file or files previously marked.

Contribute lets you send a copy of a file on your disk to the forum's library.

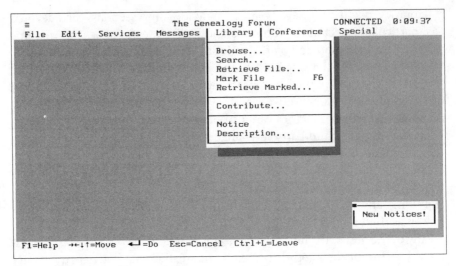

Figure 4.7   CIM Library Menu

Browse

Selecting the Browse option displays a list of the names of the library's sections used in that particular forum. (Often these names are the same as those used on corresponding sections of the message board.)

After you highlight and select a section to view, the system lists the names of that section's files, putting the newest files first. Each file listed includes:

- Name, with its optional extension, which may be either an extension of the name or, more commonly, an abbreviation for its file type.

- Date — when it was contributed to the library.

- Number of accesses — the number of times it has been retrieved or viewed. (**Note**: If this is a large number, it is a pretty good indication that the file has been popular. However, a small number doesn't necessarily mean it is a less popular file. The number is reset to zero when a sysop edits or moves the file from one library to another, so the number can be misleading. A better way to judge a file is to read a description of it, as illustrated in a moment.)

- Title, that briefly describes the contents.

As usual, the bar cursor may be moved up and down to highlight files.

At this point, there is a slight difference between the IBM and Macintosh versions of the software:

- In the Macintosh version, icons representing a half dozen options are displayed at the top. The first icon — **Info** — lets you see additional information about the currently highlighted file. Presented in a summary box are these items: The user ID number of the person who contributed the file to the library, the size in bytes or characters, and the "title," a one-line description of the file's contents or what the file does. Also, on new displays are two additional icons. One shows up and down arrows; you may click on to the appropriate arrow to see the same summary information about the next or previous file in the list. The other icon is **List**, which reports you to the file list.

- In the IBM version, you need to select a file from the list (highlight it and press RETURN). This produces the summary box of information (User ID number of the file's contributor, the file size, and one-line "title") and action buttons that correspond with the Macintosh icons. (The action buttons include a **Next** that lets you see the summary information on the next file in the list.)

Once the file list is displayed, several major options are added:

Abstract produces even more information on the current file, including a longer description and a list of keywords that the contributor has assigned to the file.

Retrieve lets you make a copy of the current file on your disk. (More on file retrieval in a moment.)

Mark causes the program to mark the current file for later retrieval.

Delete lets you delete the highlighted file from the library, *if* you are the person who submitted it in the first place.

Note Later versions of CIM (2.0 and beyond) add an option allowing you to browse library files by titles instead of filenames.

Viewing Files While On-line

While it generally saves time and money to retrieve files to the disk for off-line use, it is possible to *view* plain text and graphics files while you are on-line. In the IBM version of the software, a **View** option is provided, when relevant, as part of a dialog box that comes whenever you select the **Abstract** feature. Similarly, in the Macintosh version of the program, a **View** icon is provided when you select **Info** or **Abstract** on a text or graphics file. Files that are "viewed" as displays are not automatically saved on the disk.

Search

Browsing is best for casual use of the libraries and for keeping up with the latest contributions for favorite sections. On the other hand, sometimes you are looking for specific programs and other files about particular subjects. For those times, the Search option might be more useful.

Selecting Search from the Library pull-down menu causes the program to display a dialog box, as shown in Figure 4.8, in which you may specify the search particulars. You may type the letters in upper or lower case; Compu-Serve treats both cases the same. By filling in or leaving blank the elements in this form, you instruct the system what to look for.

The elements are:

1. The **File Name:** field, where you may specify a name, an extension, or both. The asterisks, called *wildcards*, also may be used to mean "any name" and/or "any extension." You could enter MEMORY.* to look for all files with the name MEMORY, regardless of the extension. Similarly, you could enter *.BAS to look for files that have the extension of ".BAS," regardless of the name. More on extensions and wildcards later.

2. The **User ID:** field, where you may enter the user ID number of the person who contributed the file. If you found several interesting files by a member with the ID number of 71635,1025, you could fill in that number in this field to look for other contributions by that member.

3. The **Keyword:** field lets you zero in on topics of interest. It is the most useful field in the form. Those who contribute files to the library are asked to assign several keywords to help others find them. You may use this field to locate files of interest. Keywords actually aren't restricted to *words*; they may include any combination of letters, numbers and special characters. You may use the asterisk "wildcard" to search for any letter or group of letters. Suppose you are looking for articles and programs related to telecommunications programs and you wanted to find files

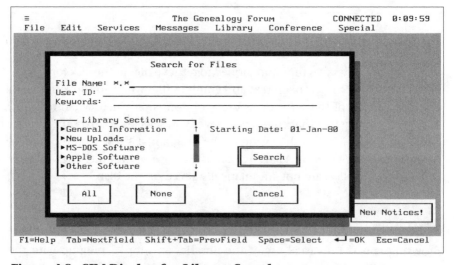

Figure 4.8   CIM Display for Library Search

with keywords of "telecommunications," "telecommunicate," or "tele-computing," for example; that is, any keyword beginning with "TELE-COM-." You simply enter TELECOM*. Also, you may narrow your search by specifying more than one keyword, separated by a space.

4. **Sections** — what portions of the library to search.

5. The **Starting date:** field. The specified search covers only those files contributed on or after the date shown in this area. You may change this date to broaden or narrow the search.

Once you have the criteria outlined in this form, you may begin the search by selecting the **Search** button. (Or you may cancel the search with the adjacent button.)

When files meeting your specifications are found, the system provides the same options as illustrated in previous sections. You may ask to see abstracts, retrieve the files immediately, mark them for later retrieval, or view them now (if they are text or graphics files).

Note that in later versions of the software (starting with version 2.0), CIM allows for the search of several library sections in a forum at the same time to find a file. (Previous versions enabled users to search only one library at a time.) To use the option, follow the same basic search technique just outlined: Choose the Search option from the Library menu, then choose the multiple sections to search, or select the ALL or NONE button to tailor the search.

Retrieving Files (Downloading)

You may retrieve a file with one of the options in the dialog box that appears with both the Browse and Search options. In addition, **Retrieve File** is also an option on the main Library pull-down menu. It is useful if you *already know* the name and extension of the file you want to retrieve. Selecting Retrieve File from the menu causes the program to prompt you for the name of the file to receive. (Another alternative on the Retrieve File option is to Mark a file for later retrieval; this is discussed in the next section.)

Whether you activate the retrieve function from a dialog box or from the main pull-down menu, the next dialog box prompts you for the *name* and the *destination* of the retrieved file: Where on your disk you want the file to be saved, and under what filename it should be saved. CIM is designed to assume two answers to these questions:

- You want the file to have the same name and extension as it has in the library on-line.

- It should be saved in the same directory on your disk where you were when you started CIM.

You can change these defaults if you like, as discussed below. When you have it set the way you want it, select the Save button on the box to begin the file retrieval. CompuServe then begins transferring a copy of the library file to your computer, displaying a graph that tells you the total size of the file being retrieved and approximately how much longer the entire copying procedure will take. As blocks of data are received, verified, and copied on your machine, the number in the "Bytes Transferred" field is increased and the bar graph indicates how much of the file has been retrieved so far. The dialog box remains on the screen throughout the file transfer. Note that you may Cancel a retrieval at any point.

Changing the Destination

If you want the retrieved file to be saved on the disk somewhere other than where CIM assumes, you may change the information. Macintosh users may click and drag on the folder title and select the destination specification from a resulting menu. IBM users should press the DELETE key and enter new specifications. You may also TAB into a list box and select a directory or a disk as the destination.

Retrieving Marked Files

Just as the message board enables you to retrieve groups of topics (or threads of messages) on the disk in one operation, the libraries also let you mark and retrieve groups of files. There are two ways to mark library files for later retrieval:

- **Mark** is one of the action button alternatives offered in the dialog box that appears with the Browse and the Search functions.
- You may also choose between **Mark** and **Retrieve** if you select the Retrieve File option from the main Library pull-down menu.

(Files selected this way stay marked until you retrieve them or until you leave the forum.)

Once you have finished marking files for retrieval, you may return to the main Library pull-down menu and select the **Retrieve Marked** option, which provides a dialog box, shown in Figure 4.9, to determine your next action. All the marked files are listed and a bar cursor may be moved up and down to highlight each.

The options are:

Abstract (or **Show** in the IBM version), which displays information about the highlighted file. A subsequent dialog box gives you the option to delete it from the list.

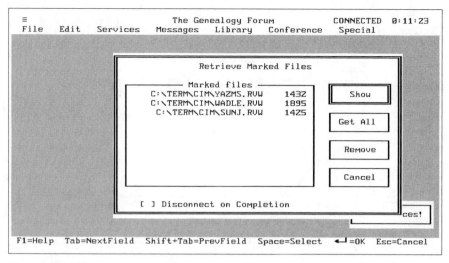

Figure 4.9 Dialog Box for Retrieving Marked Files

Get All, which retrieves all the files on the list to your disk. A progress report
is displayed as each file is retrieved.

Delete removes the highlighted file from the retrieval list.

Also on the display is a "Disconnect" box that you may check if you want
your computer to automatically log off from CompuServe after all the marked
files have been retrieved. This allows you to leave the retrieval unattended
without running up extra connect-time charges.

Contributing Your Own Files to Libraries

Suppose you have written, edited, and polished a text file or a program, and
now you want to share it with the world. The first decision is to which forum
to contribute it and to which of the forum's libraries should it be uploaded.
Make a quick field trip to the prospective forum. Peek into the library sections
and, with the Browse option, get an idea of the kind of files stored there.

When you are ready for the actual upload, select the Contribute option
from the Library pull-down menu. In the Macintosh version, a standard file
dialog box is shown from which you may select the file you want to upload.
Click on the Open option to choose the highlighted file and the program
produces a dialog box for additional information, as shown in Figure 4.10. (In
the IBM version, the program goes directly to the dialog box. However, as
described below, the system does provide some assistance in selecting the file
to be contributed.)

The fields represent the following:

- **File** refers to the name of the file on your disk that you want to contribute.
    IBM users note: If the file is in any directory other than the current

```
≡                    The Genealogy Forum            CONNECTED  0:11:41
 File   Edit   Services   Messages   Library   Conference   Special

   ┌──────────────────────────────────────────────────────────────┐
   │ File:  _____       │
   │ Title: _____       │
   │ Keys:  _____       │
   │ ──────────────────── Description ────────────────────         │
   │                                                                │
   │                                                                │
   │                                                                │
   │                                                                │
   │                                                                │
   │ ┌ Type ─┐ ┌ Section ──────────┐                                │
   │ │ Binary│ │  General Information│    ┌────────┐    ┌────────┐   │
   │ └───────┘ └────────────────────┘    │   OK   │    │ Cancel │   │
   │                                     └────────┘    └────────┘   │
   │ Under the Operating Rules, you must own or have sufficient    │
   │ rights to anything you contribute.                            │
   └──────────────────────────────────────────────────────────────┘
 F1=Help  Tab=NextField  Shift+Tab=PrevField  Space=Select  ⏎=OK  Esc=Cancel
```

Figure 4.10 Contributing Files

one, you must include the complete directory specification, or you may select it from a directory menu. To do that, press RETURN at the File: field to see a menu of files in the current directory as well as options to list files in other directories.

- The **Title** is a brief (50 characters or less) indicator of what the file contains or does. (This is the information you see when you are Browsing or Searching sections of a library.)

- The **Keys** refers to the *keywords* you want assigned to this particular file. You may enter up to 80 characters worth of keywords. Choose the keywords carefully, since they are the link that makes it possible for others to Search for files like this one. Choose brief keywords that describe your file uniquely, and consider several words that describe the same thing. If it is an accounting program, you might use ACCOUNTING, BUSINESS, STATISTICS, for example.

- The text box below the Keys: line lets you put in a longer **Description** of the file. You may enter up to 465 characters. Tell the users what, if any, additional files are needed, with a line such as, "You will find the instructions in the file called HOTONE.DOC." Also, include a summary of system requirements, such as color graphics card or hard disk. The usual built-in text feature is in effect, so you may use the writing/editing commands.

Elsewhere on the screen, the **Type** of file you are contributing should be specified.

1. Binary
2. Text
3. RLE

4. NAPLPS

5. GIF

6. Image

Here the system is simply asking in what format the file should be *saved* in the library. The biggest mistake new users make is uploading a binary file (such as a program or specially formatted data file from a database or word processor), but having it saved on-line in Text format. You won't make mistakes like that, if you keep this in mind. Your file should be saved:

- In Text if it is already saved in ASCII format on *your* disk.

- In binary, if it is a program, such as machine language or a "tokenized" BASIC file and specialized data file (or it is a compressed file as discussed later in this chapter).

The other options refer to graphics files. RLE are "run-length" encoded graphics; NAPLPS are graphics formatted in the North American Presentation Level Protocol Syntax; and GIF are graphics files formatted in Graphics Interchange Forum.

When the form has been completed, select the appropriate action button (**Contribute** in the Macintosh version, **OK** in the IBM version), then CompuServe and CIM begin the file transfers, reporting the progress as they go along. Forum sysops review all contributed files before making them publicly available. This means there may be a delay of a day or two before the contribution appears on-line for others to retrieve.

Data Libraries Through Non-CIM Software

If you choose to visit forum libraries with software other than the CompuServe Information Manager, you will operate from a general on-screen menu.

When you select LIBRARIES from the main forum menu, the system lists the names of the libraries associated with this particular forum, and asks you to indicate when you wish to visit. When you enter a numbered choice, the system links you to that library and displays a Library Menu, like this one:

```
    1   BROWSE thru files
    2   DIRECTORY of files
    3   UPLOAD a new file
    4   DOWNLOAD a file

    5   LIBRARIES

Enter choice !
```

Most of the options available with CIM are also available in the generic, ASCII version.

Browse

The BROWSE command displays the contents of a Library one file at a time. Selecting the BROWSE option causes the system to ask you which libraries you wish to see. Press RETURN if you want to BROWSE only the current library (the one you are linked to), or you can enter more than one. For instance, if you enter 1,3,5-7, the option would search libraries 1, 3, 5, 6, and 7. You may also enter ALL to search all of the libraries.

After that, the system prompts for keywords and for "Oldest files in days." To each of these two prompts, you enter a specification, or just press RETURN to signify "all." The system then displays the first file it finds meeting your criterion, and shows you something like this:

```
[76702,542]
COMPRS.DOC/Asc Bytes: 12252, Count: 8000, 13-Jun-91
(09-Dec-92)
Title : Generic information about compressed files
Keywords: ARC ZIP ZOO LZH SIT CPT ARCHIVE
COMPRESSION DECOMPRESSION HELP

Text file explaining Compressed Files (i.e. ARC, ZIP, ZOO,
 LZH, SIT,
CPT file extensions). Generic information with pointers to the
appropriate support forum, library, and file names for the
decompression
utilities. Covers Apple 128K IIe, IIc, IIgs, Amiga, Atari,
Commodore 8-bit,
DOS (IBM), OS/2, Windows, NeXT, Macintosh, and Unix
platforms.

Prepared - Ed Girou, PRACTICE/HELPFORUM forum
```

Included in the display are the user ID number of the person who uploaded the file, the filename and the date it was uploaded, followed by the size of the file in bytes, and the number of times the file has been retrieved. Next are the file's brief title, the keywords associated with it and, finally, the actual file description.

> **Note** As discussed later, in the section on Forum Options, you can direct the forum to show you *less* information about each file in this BROWSing. By resetting a switch in the User Options area, you can specify a *short* file description when BROWSing (limiting the data essentially to a filename and brief title).

As on the message board, the display is followed by a prompt that says, "Press <CR> for next or type CHOICES." The choices menu includes:

> (1) READ this file
> (2) DOWNLOAD this file
>
> or press RETURN to library menu.

You actually have four options:

1. If the file you have found is text (ASCII) — identified either by the description and/or a ".TXT" extension, and/or described as an article or such — you might want to REAd it (option 1). Subsequently, you can stop and start the display with CONTROL S and CONTROL Q as you have elsewhere in the system. If you want to stop reading it before the end, CONTROL P interrupts the displays and returns you to a prompt.

2. If the description indicates the file is binary, such as a program written to run on your kind of computer, you might want to DOWnload it onto a disk. After you enter the DOW command, you are shown a familiar menu that prompts you to identify a file transfer protocol, such as CompuServe's B Protocol, Xmodem, or Kermit. If you are unfamiliar with download, you need to consult the manual that came with your software, then look over the material in Appendix I.

3. If you want to see if the system has found another file for you, press RETURN, as the bottom line says. (The list produced by the BRO command is always in reverse chronological order, with the most recent files listed first.)

4. Or you can stop BROwsing and return to the Library menu by entering the letters RET or the entire word RETURN.

Some other points about BROwse are:

- The display is sometimes interrupted with a "paging" prompt that says, "MORE !" at which point you need to press the RETURN key to continue. Some users like to eliminate this prompt and let the BROwsed information scroll uninterrupted. There are two ways to do it: (1) enter the S navigation command (S for "scroll") at the first MORE ! prompt, or (2) at the LIB prompt, enter SET PAGE OFF, which eliminates all paging functions for the current session. With paging turned off, you can still control the display with control keys: CONTROL S and CONTROL Q to freeze and "unfreeze" the display, CONTROL P to interrupt the display and return to the previous prompt. To turn paging back on, enter SET PAGE ON.

- BRO's file descriptions can be misleading. Sometimes a file's description says, "Download with XMODEM." Does that mean it can't be downloaded with another error-checking technique, such as B Protocol or Kermit? Not at all—*any* file transfer protocol can be used, so long as:

   a. It is supported by CompuServe (that is, listed on the menu illustrated in Appendix I).

   b. It is also supported by your *own* communications program (consult your manual).

   c. You make the appropriate menu selection to tell CompuServe which protocol you intend to use.

   d. You follow the correct command sequence in your own terminal program to initiate the download with the specified protocol.

- You can BROWSE more than one forum library at a time, as will be described later in this chapter.

Directory

BROwse isn't the only option available for seeing filenames. The second option, DIRectory (or SCAN), is similar to BROWSE, except that it gives only the filenames (no descriptions). A typical display with a DIR command is:

```
[76702,542]
COMPRS.DOC/Asc Bytes: 12252, Count: 8000,
13-Jun-91(09-Dec-92)
```

It is handy for a quick list of filenames. Then at a prompt, you may enter REA or DOW followed by the filename, such as REA APPROV.TXT and DOW WOOD.COM. In other words, use DIR for a quick look at the files, note the filename or names you want, then return to the Library menu and use the REA or DOW command.

Command Linking with Switches

Forum commands in the library and elsewhere can be *linked* to save time. BROwse is a particularly powerful command when it is linked with other information. Suppose you want to search a library for any files with RECIPES as a keyword. The long way is to enter BRO, then wait for the system to prompt you to enter a keyword. The fast way is to link the command, bypassing the menu, and getting right down to business by entering BRO KEY:RECIPES.

Here is a variation on that theme, one that is popular with devoted forum-hoppers. Suppose it has been five days since you visited the libraries of your favorite forum. You could access the library and enter this linked command: BRO AGE:5, which means, "Show me everything that has been added to this library in the past five days."

Such linking of commands is done with a space followed by a *switch* (AGE: and KEY: are both called "switches"), followed by the additional information. You can even link a specification for a transfer protocol when downloading, using a command such as DOW GAME.BAS PROTO:B. (Of course, if you use a transfer method other than CompuServe's B Protocol, you would specify *it* after the PROTO: switch, as in DOW GAME.BAS PROTO:XMODEM.)

Another such switch — DES (for "description") — is useful with the DIRectory command we just discussed. You can enter DIR DES to receive a description with the filenames. It can be added to other switches, too, as in DIR DES KEY:BASIC. (Of course, DES is *not* needed with BRO, since the BROwse command already produces file descriptions.)

Wildcards and Connectors

You can use "wildcards" with the BRO command, which is especially useful when you are searching large libraries. Some computer hobbyist forums have thousands of articles and programs on-line. Suppose you wanted to BROwse to find all of the BASIC game programs submitted in the past 30 days. Since most forums use .BAS as the extension for BASIC programs, you might enter:

```
BRO *.BAS KEY:GAMES AGE:30.
```

The asterisk (*) is the wildcard. This command tells the system to check all files with the extension of .BAS and display a description if they also have a keyword of "GAMES" and an age of 30 days or less.

You can search filenames in some interesting ways. Suppose you are looking for telecommunications programs and you want to find files with the keywords of "telecommunications," "telecommunicate," or "telecomputing"— any keyword beginning with "TELECOM-." To do that, you enter DIR KEY:TELECOM* or BRO KEY:TELECOM*.

In addition, wildcards don't have to be at the end of a phrase. KEY:*XYZ finds files that include keywords ending in "XYZ"; KEY:*XYZ* finds those with keywords containing the letters "XYZ" somewhere in the middle. Wildcards can also be used in the filenames. If you had heard of a program in a library called "MEMORY," but didn't know the extension, you could use BRO MEMORY.* or DIR MEMORY.* to find "MEMORY.BAS," "MEM-ORY.BIN," and "MEMORY.ASC," for example.

Another wildcard — the question mark — can be used to limit the number of characters in a search phrase. BRO TEST?.TXT would find "TEST1.TXT," "TEST8.TXT," and "TESTB.TXT," but not "TESTER.TXT" or "TEST10.TXT." The ? is a wildcard for one space only. More than one question mark can also be used, as in BRO TEST??.TXT.

You can search for files that contain more than one keyword, too. If you wanted to find BASIC programs dealing with memory checking, you might enter BRO KEY:MEMORY BASIC. (A space means the connector "AND".) Only files containing *both* the keywords BASIC and MEMORY are shown. You can mix and match these options in some interesting ways, such as: BRO MEM*.* AGE:2 or BRO AGE:5 KEY:DBASE HELP.

Because keywords help you search libraries quickly, CompuServe provides an easy way to determine if a particular keyword is in use. It is the KEY command. At a library prompt, you can enter KEY: followed by a word, and the system reports back with the number of files containing that keyword. Then you can follow up with a DIR or a BRO command. You can also get a complete list of *all* keywords used in a particular subtopic by entering KEY <RETURN> (KEY with no specified search word). However, that could produce a long, long list. It is better to use a wildcard, such as KEY:TELECOM* to get a report on how many files contain a keyword that begins with those letters.

Incidentally, command linking and wildcards can be a great shortcut when you want to BROWSE more than one of a forum's libraries at the same time. The BRO command can be used with a LIB switch to specify multiple libraries for browsing. The "current" library (the one you are in when you give the BROwse command) is always assumed. You may specify additional libraries, as in BRO *.BAS LIB:3,4-6,12 or BRO *.* LIB:1,2,5-7. In addition, you may specify that all libraries be browsed with BRO LIB:ALL.

Contributing

Contributing to a library (uploading) is essentially downloading in reverse. Suppose you have written a text file or a program you want to share with the world. The first decision is in which forum to share it and to which of the forum's libraries should it be uploaded. In many forums, specific libraries are reserved for new uploads. Almost always the name of the library — listed with the NAMES command — will tip you off. If the forum doesn't have a library specifically for new uploads, then choose the library subtopic whose subject most closely fits your contribution. After that, look into the library subtopics and, with the BROwse or DIRectory command and the KEY: switch, get an idea of the kind of files stored there.

Note Many busy forums request that all files over a specific length be compressed (packed and squeezed) before uploading, using an archiving utility similar to those discussed in the previous section. Check the ANNOUNCEMENTS section of the forum (see the forum's main menu) for details, including where to find the necessary utilities for the packing. If in doubt, consult the sysop.

When you are ready for the actual upload, two methods are available: selecting options from menus, or entering a command string that bypasses the menus by anticipating a prompt. We will look at the menu-driven approach first, in order to see what's going on. Then we will examine the preferred (faster) command-string method.

To have menus available to guide you in uploading, simply enter the command UPL (for UPLoad) at the Library prompt. The only problem you might encounter at this point is that sometimes a subtopic is already full. If so, you receive a message that there is not enough room for new files. Then you might post a short note about the situation to the sysop. The sysop will probably get back to you when the space situation improves.

Assuming space is available, the system asks you to enter the filename as you want it to appear in the library, having up to six letters plus a three-letter extension. You can use a combination of letters and numbers, as long as the first character is a letter. Also, check the ANNOUNCEMENTS area to see if the forum has preferred extensions to certain kinds of data.

After entering the filename, you need to tell the system which transfer protocol you want to use for the upload, selecting from this menu:

Library Protocol Menu

Transfer protocols available -

```
1   XMODEM
2   CompuServe B+ and original B
3   DC2/DC4 (Capture)
4   YMODEM
5   CompuServe QB (B w/send ahead)
6   Kermit

0   Abort transfer request
```

If file transfer with your communications software is unfamiliar to you, consult the user manual that came with your program, then read Appendix I.

The key to successful uploads and downloads is to make sure that your communications program and CompuServe are using the *same* transfer protocol. For users of the CompuServe Information Manager software, this is no problem, since CIM automatically selects B Protocol for transfers, a protocol CompuServe itself wrote and incorporated in the program. Non-CIM users can select a different protocol but, in exchange for that freedom, are required to sweat the details by making sure their own software supports the chosen protocol and that CompuServe has been alerted to the selection.

> **Note**　For uploading program — binary — files, use any of these options except number 4. As discussed in Appendix I, DC2/DC4 CAPTURE is an ASCII dump, and provides no error-checking.

After determining which protocol you are planning to use, the system sometimes asks, "Filename for your computer:"— in other words, what is the name of the file you want to upload as it exists on your disk? If you are using a two-drive floppy disk system, you should specify the drive on which the file resides, as in "B:TEST.TXT". If you are using a hard disk, you should specify the path to the file, if it is not on the currently addressed subdirectory.

Finally, CompuServe needs to know the format of the file. The system is simply asking in what format the file should be *saved* in the library. Note that error-checking can be used to transmit files to be saved in any format. At this point, the biggest mistake new users make is uploading a binary file but having it saved on-line in ASCII format. You won't make mistakes like that if you keep this in mind. Your file should be saved:

- In ASCII, if it is something that should be readable by the users while they are on-line with the REA command and it is already saved in ASCII format on *your* disk.

- In binary, if it is a program (machine language or a "tokenized" BASIC file), or it is a compressed file (.ARC, .LBR, .PIT, .SIT) as discussed later.

Once familiar with the uploading procedure through menus, you might prefer using the faster *command linking* approach, which allows you to bypass menus by using additional information with a PROTO: switch. Suppose you are uploading a text file called HOTONE.DOC using B Protocol, and you want it saved on CompuServe in ASCII. You could enter at the library prompt: UPL HOTONE.DOC PROTO:B TYPE:ASCII. This supplies all the anticipated information: PROTOcol B and file TYPE ASCII. If it is a program to be saved as a binary file and you are using XMODEM to transmit, the commands could be strung together as UPL HOTONE.COM PROTO:XMODEM TYPE:BIN. Options available after the PROTO: switch are B, KERMIT, XMODEM, and CAPTURE. (CAPTURE is offered for the ASCII dump.) Following the TYPE: switch, you can enter BIN (for binary), ASCII, GIF, or RLE. (Actually, the command string can be abbreviated even further, to just the first three letters of each element, as in UPL HOTONE.COM PRO:XMO TYP:BIN.)

When you have answered all the system's questions, either through menus or command linking with switches, the upload begins. The operation is virtually the same as a download, except, of course, that your machine now is the sender and CompuServe is doing the listening.

Keywords and Descriptions

When the upload is complete, the system notifies you with a message about how long the transfer took, then prompts you for the keywords you wish placed on your file when it is made public. Select keywords carefully. Because you now know how valuable they are when you are searching libraries, choose brief keywords that describe your file specifically, and consider several words that describe the same thing. If it is an accounting program, you might use ACCOUNTING, BUSINESS, STATISTICS, for example. You may enter up to 132 characters' worth of keywords.

Next, the system requests a description (in up to 500 characters) and a title (80 characters or less). Tell the users what, if any, additional files are needed, with a line such as, "You will find the instructions in the file called HOTONE.DOC." Also, include a summary of system requirements, such as color graphics card and hard disk. A good convention recently instituted in some forums is to include specific information about the file in the last lines, like, "Shareware. DL via protocol. Unpack with ARC-E (8-bit). Uploader/Author: (your name)." Of course, if you are not the author, the last line should state "Uploaded by:" followed by your name, and the description should say who is the author, if known. Of course, even if you leave off this line, interested fellow members can find you through the user ID that will appear with the file, but it is nice to have a real name associated with it.

When you have finished, the system will display what you have written as keywords and a description, and ask you to confirm it. (Answering No allows you to re-enter data.) When everything is okay, the file is "copied" into the library, but it won't be made public immediately. All new files are flagged for the sysops' review. If the file came through properly, the sysops will then "merge" it into the library; if they discover a problem, you will receive word either on the board or via CompuServe Mail.

Frequently Used File Extensions

Whether you use the CompuServe Information Manager or third-party communications software, you will see the *contents* of forum libraries (filenames, descriptions, keywords, titles, etc.) in essentially the same way. You will notice that filenames in libraries usually have three-letter extensions that commonly denote the file type. .BAS is commonly used to indicate the file is a BASIC program, while the extension .TXT means a text file. Names of library files are assigned by the people who contribute them (though a sysop may modify a filename before including the material in a subtopic). In addition to .BAS and .TXT, some other extensions have particular meanings in most forum libraries, for example:

- .ASC means ASCII format. Sometimes this is used instead of .TXT to indicate text files. It is sometimes used to indicate a BASIC program saved in ASCII rather than tokenized BASIC, also.

- .DOC often stands for documentation; that is, the instructions for a particular program. Also used sometimes are .MAN for users manual and .INS for instructions. Nearly always .DOC, .MAN, and .INS have been saved in ASCII. Often the extensions are used in connection with another file of a similar name. MEMORY.BAS might be the program, while MEMORY.DOC contains the instructions.

- .HLP is "Help." These are primarily ASCII files written by the sysops, containing answers to commonly asked questions.

- .INF stands for "information." Usually this is an ASCII file containing background information on a topic.

- .THD or .THR stands for thread. Important discussions from a forum's message board are often stored in the library with these extensions.

- .CNF or .CO or .CON represents a conference transcript — discussions that occurred in the real-time conferencing section of the system — saved in ASCII.

- .FIX represents a file that corrects an error. It might refer to a specific program (MEMORY.FIX might apply to MEMORY.BAS), or it might be a general article with programming tips.

- .PAT is "patch," a bit of programming that can be incorporated in another file to change the program.

- .ASM is a source code listing for an editor/assembler.

Compressed Files

However, the most common file extensions in many forums these days are *not* on the above list. Instead, they are .ZIP and .ARC, .LBR and .PIT or .SIT— all extensions that represent *file compression*. To understand them, we need to give some background.

Software development today is more sophisticated than it was five years ago. Today's public domain and shareware programs are often much longer, taking advantage of the larger memories in our computers. Sometimes, instead of a single program, good software is actually an integrated *system* that requires several linked programs and data files to interact on the same task. This used to cause big headaches for sysops and forum members, because one word processing program or complex spreadsheet or communications program might be represented by not one, but four or five lengthy files in a library. This made retrieval — particularly for those new to on-line communications — complicated.

Fortunately, in the mid-1980s the on-line programming wizards came to our rescue. Now, many forums use one or more file compression methods for these large software systems. The new utility programs developed by the wizards solve the problem of long, multiple files by performing two vital operations:

- Pack together several programs into *one* large file.
- Then "squeeze" (compress) the file as tightly as possible — sometimes by up to 50 percent — to prepare it for uploading to the library.

This idea of packed/squeezed files saves other forum members retrieval time and, of course, also saves space in the library, because one tightly compacted file, rather than four or five files, can be contributed to the library. A file that has been uploaded in a compressed format appears in the library with a special extension. In the world of IBM and compatibles, the extension is often either ".ZIP" or ".ARC" (meaning "archived") and, less frequently these days, ".LBR" (meaning "libraried"). In the Apple Macintosh community, the extension is often ".SIT" or ".PIT," referring to files compressed with the Stuffit and Packit programs.

When you browse libraries and find a file with such a special extension, be prepared to unpack it and unsqueeze it off-line. This isn't as complex as it sounds. It simply means you need unarchiving software tools. Those utilities are usually available for retrieval in the same forum in which you found the compressed file. Check with the sysops for specifics.

The IBM New Users Forum (GO IBMNEW) has a "Data Library Tools" section for utilities. Members of the Macintosh Personal Productivity Forum (GO MACPRO) have a number of similar programs available for that system.

Good Citizenship and File Transfer

Just as there are rules of common courtesy on the message boards, using libraries also requires some thoughtfulness. Here are some tips — ideas contributed by assorted sysops over the years — for the courteous contributor.

Before You Contribute

Is your text edited? Is the program debugged? Perhaps you should look it over again or run the program through its paces for a few days to get the kinks out. Some people think that because they are *giving away* the text or their original program, they have no obligation to edit it. There is no legal obligation, to be sure. On the other hand, if you appreciate it when software you retrieve works as described, you should be inspired to reach the same standard. Naturally, when a number of people start using your program, they may find obscure bugs, but they will be happy that you already have swatted the big ones.

Is the program annotated? Whether it is a BASIC program or an assembly language source code, users are pleased when you take time to include remarks and comments in the listing to explain what is happening.

Is the program documented? Beyond the embedded comment lines, have you written users' instructions? Most good library programs are accompanied by documentation, uploaded with the .DOC extension. The instructions don't have to be long; some of the most sophisticated programs have only a page or two of instructions. Here are some tips for preparing instructions:

1. Write the file off-line and, at the top, insert a sentence or two that describes what the program does.

2. At the beginning, include details of any special requirements for the program, such as a printer, additional memory, color graphics, and so forth. Briefly summarize how to use the program, in step-by-step examples, if possible, as if you were telling a friend who was sitting beside you at the keyboard.

3. At the end, remind the reader of your user ID number, so you can be reached through CompuServe Mail or on the message board with comments or questions.

A final question concerns just *how free* your program should be. Not all programs in the libraries are public domain. Some are shareware; the author gives us the original software, putting us on our honor to make a suggested "donation" if we like it and intend to use it regularly. Should you plan to make the same appeal for funding from those who use your creation? It's your call. All good programming should be rewarded, with praise, certainly, and sometimes with cold hard cash. The shareware phenomenon is a laudable, positive movement in software creation. At the same time, though, it is not in the spirit of these libraries to make *everything* carry a price tag. The libraries are intended mainly for the distribution of the public domain works. However, if your program is unique and you sincerely think you ought to be compensated, by all means, make it shareware.

After the Contribution

When the file has been contributed, you should enjoy checking in to the library from time to time to see how many people have retrieved it. Make yourself available to field questions or comments. Some users may even want to make some revisions of their own. That could be the beginning of a new on-line friendship, since you obviously have found someone with similar interests.

Additional Help in Finding Files

Besides the options discussed earlier, there is a feature outside the forums that helps you find library files. It is File Finders, a keyword-searchable database for quick reference to files in assorted data libraries of the multiple IBM and Apple Macintosh forums, as well as forums supporting other platforms. Instead of having to search databases in each forum, subscribers may make one stop at the File Finder and search them all. Mac File Finder is a database of files from Macintosh-related forums, including the forums of the Micronetworked Apple Users Groups, Aldus, Adobe, and Microsoft. IBM File Finder offers file information from the IBM Users Network, Microsoft, Borland, and others.

Among the file databases are:

- Amiga File Finder (GO AMGFF).
- Atari File Finder (GO ATARIFF).
- Graphics File Finder (GO GRAPHFF).
- IBM File Finder (GO IBMFF).
- Macintosh File Finder (GO MACFF).

Real-time Conferencing — An Overview

In addition to the message board and the libraries, real-time talk is the third major area of all forums. Each forum has a number of electronic "conference rooms" that may be used for live chats among forum members. These electro-talks can range from informal gabfests to formal lectures, panel discussions, and interviews. Forum conferencing is similar to several other CompuServe features—including the CB Simulator and the Convention Center—so we shall defer that discussion to the next chapter.

User Options

Forums have several additional features for seeing announcements from the sysops, altering aspects of the forum display, and using a database of information about fellow forum members.

CIM'S Special Forum Options

Selecting the Special option from the main forum pull-down menu produces a menu with these options:

Notices, which displays different kinds of announcements from the sysops.

Forum Option, which lets you change some of the ways this particular forum interacts with you.

Forum Status, which displays the forum's welcome page. (This option is not included in the IBM version of the software.)

Join Forum, which lets you become a member of the forum. You are invited to join when you first visit the forum; if you decline, you may use this option later to sign up.

Search Membership, which gives you access to the Membership Directory to search for information about other forum members. (Incidentally, this option is further empowered in later CIM versions, enabling you to automatically add forum members to your Address Book. Select the name you want from the member list and press RETURN, then select the Add option and press RETURN to copy the data to your Address Book.)

Change Member Entry, which lets you add, change, or delete information about yourself in the Membership database.

Note   Later versions of CIM (2.x) add a **Remove Forum Info** option on the Special menu that lets you remove information from your forum database. Background: Each time you visit a forum, CIM quietly stores some forum-specific data, such as the message section names, library names and numbers, information the software uses in database form to get you into the forum faster and to show you choices for forum messages section names that are off-line. If you change your forum-hopping habits, you might opt to remove the forum data to allow the software to rebuild its forum database on subsequent visits.

Notices

Eight different kinds of announcements from the forum sysop are on file and may be viewed with the Notice option on the Special pull-down menu. It is unnecessary—and sometimes considered rather rude—to leave a note on the message board asking a sysop or the membership to explain the forum. Such information is already on file in the Notice area. The notices, which differ in terms of content from forum to forum, include:

News Flash. This usually reports recent developments, announces upcoming events, and so on. It is often shown automatically as you enter a forum.

New Member. This welcomes first-time visitors to the forum, explains the usage rules, and tells how to get additional information and assistance. The notice is automatically shown after you use the Join Forum option.

General Announcement. This includes information of more lasting interest to the group than that contained in the News Flash notice. It usually summarizes functions and operating instructions and gives tips on usage and etiquette.

Messages. This may tell you about the latest hot message topics. It also might outline the various message sections and the subject matter in each. It may be used from the pull-down menu for the Messages options.

Conference. This notice tells of regular real-time conferences held in the forum, or reports upcoming special conferences and provides tips. It may be used from the pull-down menu for the Conference options, as illustrated in the next chapter.

Library. This one usually summarizes what each library section contains and may list recently contributed files along with other library news. It may also be retrieved from the pull-down menu for the Library options.

Membership. This notice usually contains additional information about membership and provides general conduct guidelines.

Sysop Roster. It details the sysops' backgrounds, with information on how they came to be here in the first place.

Forum Options

CIM works intimately with CompuServe to regulate how your screen appears throughout the system, coordinating the on-line features with the software's pull-down menus, cursor controls, action buttons, and so on. However, you may modify three aspects of the individual forums. Selecting Forum Options with the Special pull-down menu produces the dialog box with a number of alterable items, as shown in Figure 4.11.

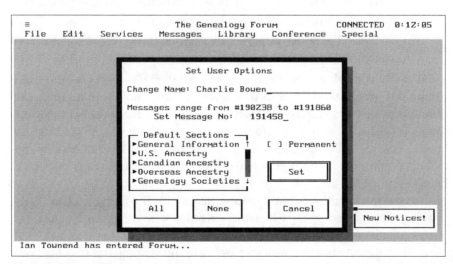

Figure 4.11 CIM Forum Options

The options include:

1. **Name**. The field lets you change the way your name appears in the forums, such as in the header of any message you post. Note some forums request members to sign up with their full names. If you sign up with first name only or a nickname, the sysops may ask you to use this option to provide a full name. (Incidentally, this is the name under which you appear when you log into the forum's conference area, as discussed in the next chapter.)

2. **Set Message Number**. This field contains what the forum "thinks" is the number of the last message you read in the forum. As noted earlier, each forum routinely records the number of the last message you read in order to use that as the starting number next time. Ordinarily, the updating is automatically handled by CompuServe, but sometimes you might want to have access to messages posted *before* your last visit to the message board, or you might want to skip over a number of messages. You may use this option to look at the current range of messages and to set a new message starting point. (This procedure is considered more precise than changing the message starting date with the Set Date option provided on the Messages pull-down menu.)

3. **Default sections**. This lets you specify the message board sections that you routinely access when you Search for messages. You may exclude any message board sections that don't interest you. Earlier, the chapter illustrated how to select sections when Searching for messages; this option allows you to make such a setting more permanent. To use the option, move the cursor down the list, then highlight and select the sections. Also, the two action buttons at the bottom can be used:

   a. To narrow the search to a specific section or two. First select the **None** button, then mark the sections to be searched.

   b. To widen the search to cover all sections (including those not currently marked), select the **All** button.

Setting the default this way means that from then on when you enter this forum, the system "knows" your interests in advance and displays messages only on the sections you have marked. Note, though, that even with the defaults established, you may override them in the Search option on the message board by simply indicating that you want to search all sections. The command will affect only that current search and will not alter the defaults on record here.

Changes made in the Forum Options area are for the current session only unless you also mark the [ ] **Permanent** check box. Permanent settings remain in effect for this forum until you change them again. Also note that changes apply only to the forum you are currently visiting, not to others you access now or in a later on-line session.

Search Membership/Change Member Entry

Since you are drawn to forums because of particular interests, the last two options on the Special pull-down menu help you find like-minded people and let them find out about you. The Membership Directory allows you to use a database where forum users voluntarily place information about themselves. The feature also lets you add information about your own interests. Selecting Select Membership from the menu displays a form that may be filled in to help in finding and reviewing entries. You may search by any or all of the following fields:

User Name: You don't have to enter a full name. If you are not sure about the spelling, enter part of the name and the system finds all entries that contain the same series of letters that you have entered.

User ID number: If you select this option you must enter the *complete* number. The system will search for "71635,1025" but will not look for "71635."

Interests: You may enter the first part of a word, such as SAIL, to find all those who list "sailing" and "sailboats" among their interests.

Once the form is filled in as you want it, select the Search button. The subsequent display includes these action buttons:

Next lets you see the next entry, if there is a group found by your search.

Add copies the names and user IDs to your electronic Address Book for use in writing CompuServe Mail and messages on forum message boards.

Finally, from the Special pull-down menu you may also select Change Member Entry to add, modify, or remove your own entry from the forum's membership directory. To create your entry the first time, the system displays a text box in which you may enter up to 149 characters to list your interests. It is a good idea to list each interest on a separate line. Then you may save the material on-line for others to find. If you use the option to modify an existing entry, the file is displayed in the box and you may edit it with the built-in text feature.

Forum Desktop Setup

Starting with version 2.x of CIM, the main menu bar's Settings menu includes a selection of forum-related preferences that can also be set. Selecting Settings from the main menu, you can store preferences for:

- Forum nickname (that is, the name you want to use in forums). For instance, perhaps you would rather go by the informal "Charlie" in all the forums you join, rather than "Charles."
- Whether to show the library section *numbers* in addition to the section names.

- Whether to display a specific menu each time you enter a forum. (For instance, if you always want to start in the database libraries rather than the menu board when you enter a forum, you can make that designation in the Settings and, in effect, change the front door of every forum you enter.)

User Options in Non-CIM Software

If you are using non-CIM software, you need to know about the forum's USER OPTIONS feature for customizing the displays. OPTIONS is a selection on the forum's main menu. Selecting it causes the system to take you to a new, powerful area with an introductory menu that looks like this:

```
FORUM OPTIONS

    1    INITIAL menu/prompt [Forum]
    2    Forum MODE [MENU*]

MESSAGES OPTIONS
    3    PAUSE after messages [Always]
    4    NAME [Charlie Bowen]
    5    Prompt CHARACTER []
    6    EDITOR [LINEDIT*]
    7    SECTIONS [...]
    8    HIGH msg read [32007]
    9    REPLIES info [Count]
   10    TYPE waiting msgs [NO]
   11    SKIP msgs you left [NO]

Enter choice !
```

Notice the OPTIONS menu uses square brackets to indicate the *current settings* (defaults) for each of its 11 options, such as "[Forum]" in the first item. Asterisks beside some of these settings—such as Forum MODE [MENU*]—indicate the forum is using a setting defined in your Profile area, discussed elsewhere in this book.

Forum Options

As the menu subheadings tell you, the first two options here determine aspects of the forum structure itself—where it should put its front door, and how it should look inside.

Option 1, INITIAL menu/prompt, tells the system at what point you want to enter this forum. Right now, the front door of this forum — the default, as specified in the brackets — is the main forum menu. However, you can have it your own way. Suppose that from now on when you enter this forum, you want the next menu you see to be, not the main menu, but the Message menu, or the Libraries menu, or the Conferencing menu. If you enter INITIAL, INI, or 1 at the prompt, the system gives you this list which includes Forum, Messages, Libraries, or Conferencing. At the prompt, you indicate with a number where you want the *starting point* to be in this particular forum.

Option 2, Forum MODE, is more powerful; it determines whether you are shown full menus or abbreviated prompts in this forum. Some experienced forum users turn off most menus and run in a kind of expert mode, made possible by Option 2. If you enter 2 (or MODE) at the prompt, the system displays options including: Use PROFILE setting, MENU, and COMMAND. Three settings are possible — MENU (the current setting, which allows detailed menus), COMMAND (or abbreviated expert mode), and a setting retrieved from the Profile area of the system, discussed elsewhere. If you change this variable to COMMAND mode by entering COM or 3 at the prompt, the entire look of the forum changes. No longer are you presented with full numbered menus at every turn in the forum; instead you receive abbreviated prompts. You are expected to remember the letters of the commands you want to use (REA NEW to Read New messages, SELECT to choose sections and threads, etc.).

Message Options

The remaining options on the menu deal with how messages in this forum are displayed on your screen.

Option 3, PAUSE after messages, tells the forum whether to (1) stop and display a prompt after every message you read, (2) stop only after messages addressed to you, or (3) never stop between messages (that is, keep displaying the messages until it reaches the end and returns to the main menu or prompt).

Note If you were to disable the PAUSE with Option 3, you could use a slightly different method to reply to messages: At a ! prompt, you would simply enter the word REPLY (or the letters REP) followed by the message's number.

Option 4, NAME, allows you to change the way your name appears in the header of any message you post. This is important because some forums request that members sign up with full names. If you sign up with your first name only or a nickname, the sysops may ask you to use the NAME variable option to provide a full name.

Option 5, Prompt CHARACTER, lets you change the forum prompt. As a rule, this function isn't used by most members. However, some specially-designed communications programs use it. Some, for instance, direct you to change the CHARACTER variable to a Control-G (the ASCII code for the sounding of a "bell" on your computer). Once changed, a tone sounds each time you reach a major menu or prompt in that forum.

Option 6, EDITOR, deals with writing messages, letting you specify which of CompuServe's two editing programs — the line-numbered LINEDIT or the unnumbered EDIT — you wish to use for writing your messages. (This option, like Option 2, also allows you to defer to a setting in the Profile area.) The editors are discussed in Appendix H, "Writing On-Line."

Option 7, SECTIONS, lets you specify your defaults for subtopics. Enter SEC and the system displays all the subtopic names with an asterisk beside your current defaults, followed by an "Enter choice" prompt with three alternatives. You can enter the numbers to "toggle" the settings for subtopics. If a section currently is "on" (that is, marked with an asterisk, as is subtopic 2 in the example), you can turn it "off" by entering its number (2) at the prompt. Or you can enter the letter C to *clear all* (remove) the currently marked defaults, or the letter A to *add all* available subtopics. Setting your permanent defaults this way means that from then on when you enter the particular forum, the system "knows" your interests in advance and displays messages only on the sections you have marked. However, even with the defaults established, you can override them with the SS command, such as SS ALL if you decide on one particular visit that you want to view the entire board.

Option 8, HIGH message read, is the variable that contains the number of the last message you read in the forum. This allows the system to "know" where to start reading if you enter a command to read or scan *new* messages. Note you can change the HIGH variable, raising or lowering it. If you leave it alone, it automatically updates itself as you read messages. You can also set it to L, meaning the *last* message you read on the current session.

Option 9, REPLIES info, lets you specify how you want to be told about replies to messages you are reading. At the end of the messages you can have a *count* of the replies, a *list* of the *numbers* of all replies, or *no* reply information at all.

Option 10, TYPE waiting messages, determines how the system will behave when you enter a forum. If TYPE is set to Yes, the forum displays messages addressed to you; if set to No, then it simply informs you of the numbers of the waiting messages.

Option 11, SKIP messages you left, lets you indicate whether, during a routine reading of the board, you want to see or skip the messages you wrote and posted.

Library Options

Another option — *Option 12* — affects Library Display: that is, how filenames and descriptions of library entries are displayed when you enter a BROWSE command. The DISPLAY option can be set to either:

- LONG (the default), meaning that for each file, you are shown the user ID of uploader, filename, submission date, size of file in characters, number of accesses, title, keywords, and description when using BROWSE.
- SHORT, meaning that for each file, the BROWSE command produces only the file's name, file type, size of file in kilobytes (1024 characters), date of last modification, and title.

Permanent or Temporary

Each time you change one of these defaults, the system displays the revised menu. Finally, when you have changed everything you wish to change, you enter T to return to the top of the forum. You see a message that says, "Would you like current settings to apply to this Session only, or to be Permanent? Enter S or P, or H for help." CompuServe realizes that sometimes a customer wants to test-drive possible changes before accepting them. So, any time you make changes in defaults, the system gives you an option to make them either "temporary" (for this session only) or "permanent" (permanent until we change them again).

More Forum Help

You are now ready to begin exploring the forums. Here is a reminder about some of the *free* forums with which you might want to start.

CompuServe Help Forum (GO HELPFORUM)

The Help Forum is open to all CompuServe members for assistance with or discussion of the CompuServe Information Service. Here is where you can post a message with questions or comments concerning CompuServe and its use. The subject content of messages and responses is limited to information relating to using the CompuServe Information Service. Forum Manager and Primary Sysop Mike Schoenbach (76703,4363).

Practice Forum (GO PRACTICE)

This forum is designed to assist new CompuServe subscribers in learning how to use the CompuServe forum and the text-based (ASCII) forum command interface. Primary Sysop is Mike Schoenbach (76703,4363). Help and information concerning CompuServe HMI (Host-Micro) interface products is provided in the following free forums:

- DOS CIM Support Forum (GO CIMSUPPORT)
- Mac CIM Support Forum (GO MCIMSUPPORT)
- Navigator Support Forum (GO NAVSUPPORT)
- Win CIM Support Forum (GO WCIMSUPPORT)

More to Come

More forums will be introduced throughout the rest of the book. Most of the remaining chapters contain sections describing forums that are relevant to the subject at hand. Besides that, Appendix J in the On-Line Survival Kit is intended as a road map for the forum traveller. It lists the names and on-line addresses for hundreds of forums. Enjoy.

5

CB Simulator and Real-Time Conferencing

In this chapter...

Getting Started with the CB Simulator
About CB's Structure
CB-ing with CIM
CB-ing with Non-CIM Software
Conferencing in the Forums
Electronic Convention Center

Many of Terry A. Biener's friends don't know she has an accent. They don't know, for instance, that when she speaks of "chatter data," the New Yorker makes those words rhyme. Thousands of her friends around CompuServe don't know that because, even though they may chat with her every day, most have never heard the sound of Terry's voice.

In fact, many don't even know her real name. But that's okay; they prefer the name she has given herself. Around these parts, Terry Biener is Cupcake, chronicler and chief booster of CompuServe's CB Simulator. For more than 10 years now, she has written a much-loved on-line newsletter called CB Society—*Cupcake's Column* in which she covers the news and activities (the chatter data) of CompuServe's most popular feature, its 72-channel, international real-time conferencing service. Who is better to be CB's eyes and ears? Cupcake has been conferencing on CompuServe almost from the beginning.

The CB Simulator was the 1980 brainchild of Alexander "Sandy" Trevor, then CompuServe's vice president of technology. At first, Trevor was virtually alone in believing computer users would enjoy "talking" to one another on-line in real-time, typing messages on the keyboard and, after a few seconds, reading replies on the screen. Nay-sayers said there was no way people would pay good money to chat by keyboard when they could just pick up the phone and call somebody. Undaunted, Trevor programmed the first CB software over a weekend and brought it on-line the following Monday. Terry Biener recalls those early days of computer CBing.

"My son had just turned two," she wrote in *CompuServe Magazine* on the 10th anniversary of Sandy Trevor's vision. "As a former teacher turned full-time mother (and a computer widow, to boot), I felt shut out from the outside adult world and craved mental stimulation. When my husband, Alan, prodded me to look at his 'new service,' I reluctantly eyed a response from a question he typed on his monitor. Someone, somewhere, had answered him. 'Let me try this,' I said, and began typing to someone 3,000 miles away. The rest, as they say, is history."

CompuServe innovated this kind of real-time conferencing, allowing any number of computer users to type messages to each other as if on some enormous telephone party line. The talkers gave themselves "handles" similar to the imaginative aliases used in the citizens band radio craze of the day. (Biener's original handle was "Blondie," until she ran into someone on-line who had already claimed that name, so she switched to Cupcake. "I happened to be baking that day," she recalls. Since then, CB has evolved to add features enabling its regulars to reserve and register their handles for exclusive use.)

In the early days, programmers in CompuServe's fledgling consumer wing didn't really know what they had in Trevor's idea. As one long-time employee commented several years ago, "We called it 'CB' (the whimsical name stuck) and we thought it would be an interesting diversion." Most subscribers in those days were computer professionals or "serious hobbyists" interested in on-line programming tools. It was not unusual, he said, to be logged in to the new conference area for an hour or more, waiting for someone else to come along to talk. Finally a message like this might appear:

```
(FRED:) WHAT KIND EQUIP U USE?
```

Those clipped messages, mostly technical in nature, were the CompuServe equivalent of "What hath God wrought?"

Then, a busy night would mean seeing 30 people CBing. Nowadays it is not uncommon to find hundreds of people chatting on the channels around the clock. Chatting about what? Oh, nothing. And everything. Early on, the CB conversation was often limited to technical talk of hardware, software, and little else. In time, though, the "non-techies" discovered CB and turned it into a kind of electronic town square. Now as then, people meet, talk, fuss, become friends. Sometimes they even marry. The first on-line wedding happened on CompuServe on Valentine's Day 1983. The bride and groom typed their vows from one computer, while the minister typed from another. Seventy-seven invited CB guests were present in a private area of the on-line service, some acting as members of the wedding party. The reception lasted for hours, with people typing their good wishes and throwing their electronic rice.

Cupcake launched *CB Society* in November 1982 and has been covering the people and events of this new kind of community ever since. The newsletter (GO CUPCAKE) is now updated twice a month, available electronically, of course, on the menu that also offers the CB bands themselves. During the first decade on-line, Cupcake collected her share of war stories. "I remember a man from Argentina who was living in the United States," she said. "He was so excited one night when he bumped into a girl from Argentina — until he discovered she was his ex-wife. I know two guys who met at a CB party — one had logged on from Kansas City and the other from Memphis — and discovered they had the same great-grandfather. Then there were the two men who came on-line, got acquainted and found out they both were in Italy but were talking by way of Columbus, Ohio ..."

Entering its second decade, CB has evolved from a novelty into a sophisticated, imaginative medium that, for many users, is the heart of this kind of communication. It is a place not only for good times, but also for finding a shoulder to cry on, or a willing ear to hear a new idea.

"I, like many users, see CB as a window to the world," Terry Biener says, "a unique way to have 'mind to mind' communication. Affinity runs deep among CBers... They can travel to any city and find friends to chat with, dine with, and even ones who offer a place to stay. The CB Society has come to mean unconditional acceptance. Day or night, a friend is just a keystroke away."

Getting Started with the CB Simulator

If you use the CompuServe Information Manager software, getting to the real-time conferencing area is a matter of selecting CB Simulator from the pull-down Services menu. If you use a non-CIM third-party program, enter GO CB at any CompuServe prompt. This brings you to an introductory menu, like this:

```
CB SIMULATOR CB-10

    1    ** Welcome New CB Users **
         Read This First (FREE)
    2    Guidelines for Behavior (FREE)
```

```
3    Access CB General Band
4    Access CB Adult Band

5    Entertainment Center
6    Special Pricing - The CB Club
7    Cupcake's CB Society Column
8    CB Forum
9    CB Profiles
```

Options include those for CB guidelines, access to the channels themselves, the latest copy of Cupcake's newsletter, background of the "CB Club" and the CB Forum, and more.

As illustrated by the menu, the CB Simulator is reconfigured into two new bands:

- The friendly neighborhood atmosphere of the General Band, where you can meet both old and new friends from all around the world on a variety of channels devoted to various interests. To reach the General Band directly, enter GO CB-1.

- The Adult Band is for members age 18 and older, for conversation away from the younger CB membership. To access the Adult Band, GO CB-2.

If you are a newcomer, you are invited to visit the General Band, Channel 2, any evening from 6:00 p.m. to 2:00 a.m. Eastern Time where a team of CB Helpers is always ready to welcome and assist you. (Think of it as the free swimming lessons at the on-line world's version of the Y.)

CB Club (GO CBCLUB)

You don't have to join the CB Club in order to use the CB Simulator but, if you become a regular on this feature, you would do well to check out The Club. CB's main menu has an option that tells you about special discount offers and pricing plans that can save you money. (The club also enables you to reserve your favorite "handle," to be used by you alone.) At this writing, there are two versions of the CB Club, each with different optional pricing plans, available to anyone who wants to use CB frequently and save money:

Monthly Signup Fee	Hourly Charge	Availability
$ 25	$ 4.30	24 Hours/Day
$ 85	$ 0.30	24 Hours/Day

No matter which plan you select, the following apply:

- You may use modem speeds of up to 2400 bps.
- Your Club membership becomes effective immediately after you join the current month, or on the first day of the next month if you sign up early.
- Communication Surcharges do apply if you use a supplemental access number.

Club months are based on *calendar* months (12:00 am local time on the first day of the month until 11:59 pm on the last day of the month). To determine local time for your location, type DAYTIME at any prompt. If you join the Club at any time during a month, Club rates will apply only to your time on CB (or in the Entertainment Center) after you join until the last day of the month. That is, the Club is not retroactive.

Also note that you may switch from the $25 CB Club plan to the $85 plan during a month. You will pay the full signup fee for the $85 Club, though, with no refund for the previous Club signup fee, and your lower hourly rate will only be in effect for the time you spend on CB or in the Entertainment Center after signing up for the $85 plan; previous hours will be billed at the $25 plan rate.

Participation in the Club grants you a reserved handle on CB. It also provides discount access in the Entertainment Center, a games area discussed elsewhere in the book.

How the Signup Works

Select the Signup option on the CB/Entertainment Center Club menu. Sign up at any time during the month and immediately begin getting your special pricing in the Entertainment Center or on CB. You may sign up for the next month up to six days ahead of time. You must reapply for each month you wish to participate in the Club.

At the time you sign up, you are asked to submit your choice for a reserved handle (this is optional). To see CompuServe's guidelines for handles, select the Reserved Handle Description from the Club menu or type GO HANDLE.

Restrictions

CB/Entertainment Center Club membership is for your individual use; you cannot share your account with anyone other than your immediate family members when they are with you. Any account sharing its Club membership will result in cancellation of the membership and billing of all CB or Entertainment Center time at full rates.

Club membership is based on your prepayment of the monthly signup fee. You will not receive any refund for cancellation during a month. Your account will be charged the signup fee on the day you sign up for the Club. Payment rejection or delay will result in immediate suspension of your Club participation and no credit will be issued for days lost. If your account is suspended or canceled by CompuServe for violation of service terms or guidelines, you will not receive any refund.

CB Forum

The main menu also introduces the CB Forum where the growing number of fans of this real-time medium gather to exchange forum messages. It works like other forums, following the structure outlined in Chapter 4 on forums. The sysop is Pat Phelps (known in these parts as *LooLoo*), a CompuServe employee. Her user ID is 70006,522. You may also reach the forum by entering GO CBFORUM.

CB Profile

Another main menu option is to create and file a CB "Profiles." This is your own personal profile that others may read while in the CB Simulator. You are asked for information, such as where you live, your age, the type of computer you use, interests, and so on.

About CB's Structure

CB's two bands (General and Adult) each have 36 individual *channels*, so there is lots of room for conversation. In addition, as we will see in a moment, you can create private and semi-private groups for conversation away from public eyes.

Your Handle

As you enter either of the CB bands, you are prompted for a *handle*, a name that identifies you on the CB handle. Almost everyone chooses a "handle" over their real name while using CB. Your handle may contain up to 19 characters, but can't include asterisks (*), pound signs (#), or braces [].

CBing with CIM

If you use the CompuServe Information Manager software and select the CB option from the Service menu, a new "desktop" is automatically implemented, adding three new command groups:

1. **Channels,** with options of tune to various channels, monitor other channels, and so on.

2. **People,** allowing you to locate other users on-line and invite them to a private discussion, and so forth.

3. **Special,** which has options for changing your handle, tracking other users, recording talk sessions, and the like.

Channels

When you first arrive in CB, you may:

1. Tune to a public channel and begin receiving and sending real-time messages with those already tuned in.

2. Join an existing group for private conversation with other members of that group.

3. Start your own group conversation and invite others to join you.

CIM automatically displays its Channel Selector screen, a grid-like display like the one shown in Figure 5.1:

The display illustrates the 36 channels of the current band with a cursor positioned on one of them. You may move this cursor to select any of the channels, then use one of the options elsewhere on the screen to implement one of these actions:

- *Tune* takes you to the selected channel, where you may exchange messages with others already tuned there.

- *Monitor* allows you to "listen in" on the selected channel, reading the messages being exchanged, by not sending any of your own.

- *Who* provides a list from the system of the handles of the people currently tuned to the current channel (and other channels).

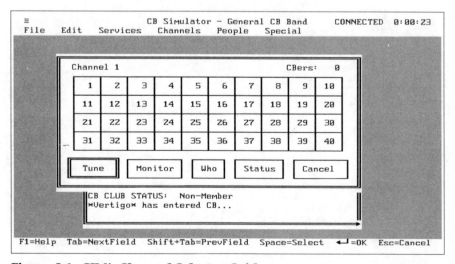

Figure 5.1 CIM's Channel Selector Grid

- *Status* displays information about how many people are on all the channels, provided as a graphic representation.

Tune

When you have *Tuned* to a channel, the conferencing window appears on your screen showing the current conversation, as shown in Figure 5.2. Handles of those already tuned in and talking to each other appear to the left of the screen; their messages follow. *SYSTEM* precedes informational messages, such as what channel you are tuned to.

To listen: Simply read the messages. If the channel is busy, there may be several conversations going on at once, so keep in mind that you are entering in the middle of things. It is a good idea to read for a few moments to get an idea of the direction of the conversation. Also, CB conversations often use abbreviations and acronyms, much like the messages in the forums. After you have been tuned to the channel for a time, the message display scrolls if there are others on the channel typing messages to each other. After the conference box is full, a line scrolls off the top every time a new line appears at the bottom of the box.

To track: At the bottom is a Tracking Window that keeps you informed of the people who come and go on CB, with messages such as, "*BLUE-GRASS* has tuned to channel 14." The window displays information about other CB users, including who has tuned in, tuned out, switched channels, changed handles, and so on. (To personalize the types of information that appear in the notice line, see the Track option on the Special menu, discussed later in this chapter.)

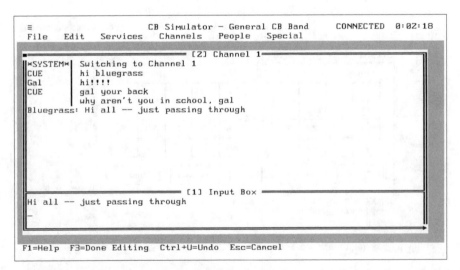

Figure 5.2 CIM Conference Window

To talk: When you are ready to talk to the others on this channel, you use the input box at the bottom of the screen. Just begin typing and you see it in the Input Box as you type. Compose your message away from the hubbub of incoming text; nothing actually is sent to the others tuned to the channel until you press RETURN. This means you may back up to change a message before transmitting it. Once you have pressed RETURN to send it, the other people tuned to or monitoring the current channel may read it. When it is displayed on their screens, it is automatically preceded by your handle.

Monitor

While tuned to one channel, you may *Monitor* another, meaning you may listen in. To do that, highlight the channel with the Channel Selector (the grid-box), then choose the Monitor option. The display automatically splits into multiple windows. One window shows you what's happening on the channel you are monitoring; you may listen in but may not send messages to this channel (unless you decide to return to the Channels menu and Tune to it). The other window continues to display the conversation on the channel to which you are tuned; you may send messages to this channel by typing in the input box and pressing RETURN.

To stop monitoring a channel, Macintosh users click on the close box of the screen; IBM users go to the pull-down Channels menu and select the Monitor option, specifying the channel again (in effect "toggling" the monitor option off).

Who

The *Who* option listed in the Channels pull-down menu gives you a list of user ID numbers and names for the people using the CB channels. The software provides a dialog box so you may search for a specific group of users. (This is the same option as the *Who's Who* feature discussed later in the People section of this chapter.)

Status

CIM can also provide a graph of activity on the various channels of the band you have selected. Choosing the *Status* option from the Channel Selector pull-down menu gives you a quick overview of the channel traffic. A display features bar graphs representing the channel's activity relative to the currently most active channel. The number above the bars is the actual number of talkers currently tuned to the channel. (It does not reflect how many people are monitoring each channel.)

People

The *People* pull-down menu provides options for dealing with specific individuals on-line. Selecting it produces a display with new options, including:

- *Who's Who,* a list of people on the channels.
- *Invite* lets you ask other talkers to join you in a private group discussion.
- *Squelch* blocks messages from other talkers whom you specify.
- *Friends,* a kind of specialized electronic address book for conferencing acquaintances.

Who's Who

CB maintains a list of handles of those who are currently talking on its channels. As talkers log on and log off, CB adds and removes handles from the list. This option, available on the People menu (as well as on the Channels menu discussed earlier) lets you search and list all or portions of this potentially massive record of the comings and goings on the channels. Selecting the *Who* option causes the system to display a dialog box with check boxes that let you control the search to:

- *Show* (1) all, (2) only those on a specified channel, or (3) only those in semi-private "group" discussions.
- *View by* (1) handles or (2) user ID numbers.
- *Friends* to look for subscribers you have previously identified on your "Friends" list, as described later in this section.

The resulting list, like the one shown in Figure 5.3, includes a bar cursor that may be moved up and down to highlight a user. When a name is highlighted, the system displays that talker's user ID number and location.

Either of two action buttons may be used in conjunction with highlight names:

Profile allows you to find personal information about someone currently using CB (assuming that person has created a profile). These profiles say where people live, their ages, types of computers they use, and their interests. Just highlight and select the handle of the person about whom you want to know more.

Talk lets you invite another talker into a private one-to-one message area. To use it, highlight a name and select the action button. After that, a conversation window opens automatically with your cursor in the input box. Type the message you want to send. If someone sends you a talk message, the window opens automatically on the screen with your cursor in the input box, ready for you to type a reply. Pressing ESC removes this Talk box from the screen at any time.

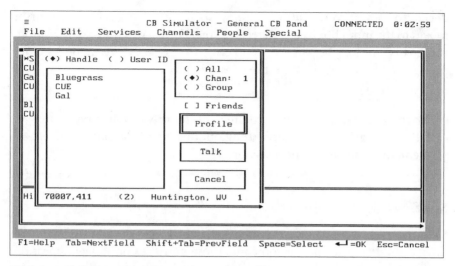

Figure 5.3 Typical Who's Who List in CIM

Invite

The public channels on CB can become extremely busy places. It is common for 20 or 30 people to conduct a half dozen or more conversations at the same time on a single CB channel. This is fine if you want the party atmosphere that CB is famous for, but there are times when you might want to talk with only a few people. The *Talk* option is fine as a kind of electronic whisper; it lets two people talk privately with one another. On the other hand, when you want to talk privately with *more* than one person, you should think in terms of a private *group*. This is an out-of-the-way room where a party may go on within a larger party. When you are participating in private conversations, only those in the group may read messages sent by other group members. You may, however, be tuned to one channel and monitoring another while in a private conversation.

To initiate a private group discussion, use the *Invite* option on the People pull-down menu. This lets you invite one or more current talkers to a private group conversation, away from the noise of the busy channels. To use the option, select Invite and the system opens a dialog box similar to the one used with the Who's Who option, except that the names have checkboxes beside them. Use the *Show* and *View By* controls to narrow your list, then select and X the boxes of the names you are inviting to your private group. Another checkbox, labelled "Friends," enables you to automatically invite subscribers on your Friends list to a group chat. (The Friends option is discussed later in this chapter.)

After you have checked all the names, select the Invite option and the system automatically sends a privately displayed invitation to each person. Recipients then choose to either join the conversation or decline the invitation. If you decide to join, a conversation window opens on your screen. Your cursor moves to the input box, ready to receive your words. Anything you type from this box is sent to others in the group only. To close a Conversation window, press Esc or click the mouse on the Close box.

> **Note**　You may also control requirements for private talks and/or invitations for group discussions, using options on the *Special* pull-down menu discussed in the next section.

Squelch

Squelch allows you to block the messages of anyone you find disruptive or offensive. After you squelch someone, those messages no longer appear on your screen. When you select Squelch from the People pull-down menu, you see a list of handles of everyone using CB. You may use two options — *Show* and *View By* — to narrow your list, then highlight and mark the check box beside the name or names of those whose messages you want to squelch. Once the handles are marked, select the *Squelch* action button. To "unsquelch" someone you have previously squelched, highlight his or her handle, and remove the check mark. Also provided is a **Not Friends** check box, so you may easily squelch all except the subscribers you have identified on your Friends list (described in the next section).

Friends

Friends operates as a kind of CBing electronic address book. When you select Friends from the menu, CIM opens a dialog box with which you can add and remove names and user IDs from a list of people you have previously identified as your on-line buddies. Then, from different places in the software, you may search to see if any of your friends are currently on-line. The feature also lets you quickly invite your acquaintances to such happenings as private groups.

CB Special

The final pull-down menu on the CB desktop is Special, which displays the following collection of options:

- **Change Handle** allows you to change the name you are using on CB.
- **Tracking** lets you control what types of information appear in your tracking window.
- **Recording** lets you save a copy of discussions on your disk.

- **Accept Invitations** tells the system whether you are currently accepting invitations to group discussion.

- **Accept Talks**, similarly, tells the system whether you are currently accepting requests from others for private one-to-one talks.

- **Bulletin** displays summary information and news of the CB world.

Note Later versions of the software organize these options a little differently, including a **Settings** option on the Special menu. Under Settings are options for controlling Tracking, Recording, and automatic acceptance or rejection of invitations and talk requests. Even though these are located in different areas of the program, the functions work the same as described in this section. Later CIM versions also include a **Set Function Keys** option here for defining keys.

Change Handle

The Change Handle option allows you to change the name you are using on CB; that is, the name seen by others reading your messages. You may change your handle any time while in the CB area. You are shown your current handle and provided with an input box for the new name. It may contain up to 19 characters, but can't include asterisks (*), pound signs (#), or braces [ ]. Also, you aren't allowed to use a handle reserved by someone else through the CB Club.

Tracking

The Tracking option lets you control what types of information appear in the tracking window at the bottom of the screen. When you select this option, the program provides a dialog box; by selecting and checking the appropriate boxes, you may direct the system to track:

- People entering the CB band you are using.
- People leaving the band.
- Those changing locations.
- And/or those changing handles.

You may select one or more of these to track and, unless you specify otherwise, all activities will be noted.

Recording

You may *Record* — that is, save — a copy of the messages sent on an open channel or in a private or group discussion to the disk files on your computer.

- If you select Record while tuned to a channel, the conversation that occurs from that point on is stored in a file (CHANNEL.LOG in the IBM PC/ compatible version; Room Log File in the Macintosh version).

- If you select the option while in a group, the conversation that appears on your screen is stored in a different file (GROUP.LOG in the IBM version; Group Log File in the Macintosh version).

The recordings are cumulative files, so each time you use Recording, that session log is appended to logs of past sessions. You may create new names for the log files. The saving of text continues until you select the Recording option again or you leave the CB feature.

Accept Invitation and Accept Talks

The previous section illustrated how to send requests for private one-to-one discussions (*Talks*) and multi-user private group discussions (*Invitations*). When you are on the receiving end of these requests, you are shown an invitation. However, whenever you are not in the mood for private talks, you may have the system automatically turn them down for you using these options on the Special pull-down menu. You may mark and unmark these options. When either has a check mark beside it, it means you are accepting requests. If you turn off the check mark, the system will inform anyone who asks that you are not accepting private conferencing requests. If you change your mind later, you may return to the option and restore a check mark.

CBing with Non-CIM Software

While many CB regulars think CompuServe Information Manager is the tops when it comes to conferencing, it still is possible to use the service with a non-CIM program. All of the CB features outlined in the previous section are also available to users of third-party programs.

The main rules to remember when communicating without CIM are:

- To talk on the CB channels, just enter a message and press RETURN.

- To enter *commands*, precede them with a slash (/) in the first position of a new line.

All conferencing commands may be abbreviated to the slash and the first three letters. In the following discussion of commands, the required first three letters are in upper case. For instance, /HANdle means that the slash and the letters "HAN" are required; the rest of the letters are optional.

Once you have entered an accepted handle, the system reports how many people are on the 36 channels of that band with a message like this:

```
(channel) users tuned in
(1)21 (3)4 (5)2 (6)2
(7)8 (10)1 (11)2 (12)1 (13)2
(14)1 (16)8 (17)5 (18)3 (21)2
(22)1 (23)1 (24)1 (27)2 (29)1
(30)1 (33)12 (34)9 (36)3 (Grp)18
```

In this example, 21 participants are on channel 1, four are on channel 3, two are on 5, two are on 6, and so on. The late entry means that 18 users are in private **Group** discussions ("Grp").

The system now asks what channel you wish to visit. When you enter the number of the desired channel, you begin seeing incoming messages from others already talking there.

No matter what band or channel you are using, the messages appear in the same format. Here is a typical display. When someone types a message and presses RETURN, it appears to the other users logged on to or monitoring that channel as something like this:

```
(9-205,Bluegrass) Hi folks. Good to see all of you!
```

The first section includes the channel number (1-36), then the *job number* assigned by the system (more on that later), the speaker's handle, and the message.

Your Handle

You don't have to keep the handle you came with. At any time on-line, you may change your handle by entering:

/HANdle, which causes the system to prompt with, "What's your handle?" Now type in your new name (up to 19 characters with no asterisks or pound signs); the system verifies the change.

As noted earlier, a favorite handle may be reserved so that you are the only CB Simulator visitor who can ever use it. The option is a feature of Compu-Serve's "CB Club," which also provides regulars with an optional pricing plan. To join the club, you pay a monthly fee. To check out details, enter GO CBCLUB at any ! prompt on CompuServe or /GO CBCLUB from a talk channel.

Listing Commands

The CB Simulator offers two major commands for listing other talkers on-line.

/STAtus

/STAtus provides a status report on the number of users on each channel and the number in private group talks. It is similar to the report you see when you first come to the CB area, but includes a couple of extra symbols, something like this:

```
(1)5 (3)5# (6)3* (30)10* (Grp)18
```

In this display:

- The # sign indicates the channel to which you are tuned (in this case, channel 5).
- The asterisk denotes channels which you are *monitoring*.

/USErs

/USErs provides a "user status" report of all the users on your current channel or in your private group, and looks something like this:

Job	User ID	Nod	Chn	Handle
32	70000,010	QAK	6	Old Fella
203	77777,375	QAK	6	Bluegrass
214	70000,1331	ALT	6	Hermit

In this display:

- The numbers on the left are *job* numbers. A job is a one-, two-, or three-digit temporary number which the host computer automatically assigns to each user at login to the CB area. You also need job numbers with some special features, which will be discussed later in this chapter. At any one time, no two job numbers are the same.
- The user ID numbers of all the talkers.
- The *node* ("NYN," "CWV," "QAK," etc.), a code for the cities from which the users are calling.
- The channel to which the users are tuned.
- The handle of each user.

/USER Variations

You may also enter:

/USER followed by a channel number (such as /USER 10) to see only the talkers logged to that particular channel.

/USERS ALL to see the names and numbers of everyone on *all* 36 channels of the band to which you are tuned.

/USERS OPEN for a list of all users currently on all open channels.

/USERS GRP for the same data on all users currently talking in private groups.

Node Codes

You can receive more information about the nodes or city codes by entering:

/NODE followed by the code in question. If you wanted to know where the node HWV is located, you could enter /NODE HWV, and the system should report, "NODE = Huntington WV." This means a person identified with the HWV node is located in Huntington, West Virginia. Sometimes, however, the location of a node isn't given.

Navigation and Monitoring Commands

Other commands let you change channels and listen in on channels to which you are not currently tuned.

/CHAnnel

/CHAnnel, the primary command in this group, allows you to move to another channel. If you want to move to channel 1, enter /CHA 1. Now a /STAtus command shows you something like this:

```
(1)6#,(3)4,(6)3,(30)10,(Grp)8
```

Note the pound sign confirms that you are now tuned to channel 1.

/MONitor and /UNMonitor

/MONitor allows you to eavesdrop on other channels, hearing what is being said in other places besides the channel to which you are tuned. You may monitor up to two other channels on your current band without actually tuning to them. Remember, whatever you type is transmitted *only* to the channel to which you are tuned, *not* to the ones you are monitoring.

/UNMonitor causes you to stop monitoring a channel, such as /UNM 3.

Other Navigators

Other navigation commands include:

/TOP or **/MAIN** takes you out of the CB Simulator and back to the main general menu of CompuServe.

/GO, followed by a CompuServe page address, takes you out of CB and to the specified page elsewhere on CompuServe.

/FIND, followed by a topic, leaves CB and finds the requested topic.

Finding Other Talkers

With such a busy, popular feature as conferencing, there have to be faster ways, besides the /USErs command, to locate your friends and identify newcomers in all those crowded electronic rooms.

WHOs

An important locating command is:

/WHO, which helps you to put names, handles, and user IDs together. Suppose your friend with user ID 71635,1025 is somewhere on CB, but you don't know the handle or channel. Enter /WHO 71635,1025; the system will scan the CB channels on that band and, if it finds the user ID you have specified, it reports that user's current job number, node, channel, and handle. /WHO also works if you know your friend's current job number, as in /WHO 23.

Paging — The System Beeper

Another command allows you to *page* or signal an acquaintance from across a crowded CB:

/PAGE   followed by the other person's current job number, as in /PAGE 23, causes the system to send your friend what amounts to the conferencing version of a beeper—a message something like, "*** Job 214 [70000,000] BitWise has just /PAGE'd you." You then might send your friend a request for a private talk, or just look him up on the public channels with the /WHO command to see where he is.

/NOPAGE is for those times when you don't want to be interrupted by /PAGEs, turning off your own beeper. That tells the system you are not accepting /PAGE requests at the moment. Anyone who tries to page you is told you aren't available. When you are ready to turn the beeper back on, enter /PAGE.

Your Own JOB Number

Finding other people's job numbers is easy: They appear on the /USERS list, can be located with the /WHO and /WHERE commands, and are automatically displayed with every received message. Meanwhile, you can find your *own* number without having to resort to a possible lengthy /USErs list. The command is

```
/JOB
```

which causes the system to report a one-, two-, or three-digit number it assigned to you.

Profiles of CB Users

Profile is a way to learn a little something about those who are using CB. A CB Profile is a voluntarily submitted public file that contains a user's handle, user ID, birthdate and age (computed from the birthdate), city and state, the computer in use, occupation, and interests.

To install your own CB Profile, enter GO CBPROFILE (or /GO CBPROFILE while on a CB channel), which takes you to the CB Profile menu from which you may add, change, or delete your current profile. Once your profile is on file, other CBers have instant access to it, by entering:

/PROfile followed by either the user ID (/PR 71635,1025), a handle (/PRO Bluegrass), or a job number (/PRO 52). You may double-check your own profile by typing /PRO followed by your own handle, user ID, or job number while on a CB channel.

Squelching Other Talkers

CompuServe has commands to block out messages from other users, a process the system calls *squelching*. The command is:

/SQUelch, followed by the handle, the user ID, or the job number of a subscriber, causes the system to discontinue sending you messages from a particular user of the conference. If you entered /SQU HARPO, /SQU 23, or /SQU 70000,010, the system would report that a particular user ID number has been squelched, "% Squelching [70000,010]."

To "unsquelch," enter /SQU with no handle, and the system says, "% No longer squelching."

You may squelch as many as 10 users, one at a time, for any conferencing session. The system keeps track of those you aren't interested in listening to. A single /SQU command (that is, /SQU without any data following it) lifts the ban against *all* you have squelched.

Other characteristics of the squelch are:

- A user remains squelched during your current CB session, even if he changes his handle.
- You don't have to be on the same channel with a particular user to squelch.
- Targets of your squelches are not notified. There is no public system message that you are squelching someone.

Talking Privately

A popular conferencing feature is the CB Simulator's Group talk feature, which allows you to communicate *privately* with one or more other members. Once inside a group, your messages are displayed, not to those on public channels, but only to those inside your group. The privacy continues until you exit to a public channel again. Ask another talker to join you in a private area by entering:

/INVite followed by the other user's job number, such as /INV 23. A message will appear on your screen, such as "% Entering group — /BREAK exits group—/USERS lists group members. Inviting job 23 to join group." When this prompt appears, you no longer see the conversation on the public channels, but reside in a kind of limbo. No messages appear as you await the reply to your invitation. As the message indicates, you may enter:

/BREAK to exit the group and return to the public channel from which you came.

/USERS to see who else is in the group. As noted, the /USERS command always displays the talkers on the *default* channel which, in this case, means the private group.

Actually, you may enter *any* of the usual CB commands in private groups, including /STAtus, /PAGE, /MONitor, /UNMonitor, USErs, and so on. You can also invite others into your group, one at a time, by entering /INVite and another job number.

Meanwhile, on the other end of the /INVitations, each of your recipients sees something like, "% Job 4 [71635,1025] Bluegrass invites you to /JOIN 4." The message provides the recipient with your current job number, your user ID number, and your current handle. The recipient can turn down your /INVitation by simply ignoring this message, or accept the offer by entering:

/JOIn followed by your job number (in this case, /JOI 4). This takes a user out of the public channels and into a private talk area, where the user is greeted by, "% Entering group—/BREAK exits group—/USERS lists group members." When someone /JOIns, the others already belonging to the private group are informed, with a systems message like, "Lady Editor has joined the group." Once two or more people have joined a private group, their messages are displayed only to each other. In private groups, the system slightly changes the format of messages, to something like this:

> (#23,Lady Editor) Hi folks. Thanks for inviting me!

Since talkers in groups are no longer on public channels, the messages omit the usual band and channel number before the handle, instead displaying only a pound sign and the talker's job number (#23 in the example above). Compare this with the example of the "typical display" at the beginning of this section.

Anyone inside the group may /INVite others to /JOIn by entering the /INVite command followed by a job number. The person who started the group has no special authority over future members; everyone on The Inside has the power to bring in more talkers.

When someone is ready to leave a private group and return to the public channels, the person enters /BREAK and receives a message like "Entering channel 6." Meanwhile, others remaining in the group see a message like, "Lady Editor leaves the group." Once you leave a group, you may not return with a /JOIn command unless someone in the group /INVites you again.

Saying "No" in Advance

If you are on a public channel and don't want to be disturbed with /INVitations to private talks, you may enter:

/NOInvite. This causes the system to automatically (and politely) decline any /INVite requests directed your way, with a message like, "Job 6 is busy." The /NOInvite is in effect for the current session only. To turn off /NOInvite, enter /INVite with no trailing job number.

You may also see a list of your current INVitations by entering:

/JOIn *without* a job number. The system will display something like, "%
Pending invitations from 4 — /JOIN # to accept an invitation." If the
sender of the invitation enters /BREAK before you accept, the message
is, "% No invitations pending — /INVITE another user to join you."

Other Group Commands and Functions

Here are a few more notes on Private Groups:

- Inside and outside of Private Groups, you may see selective lists of other
talkers.
- You don't have to be on the *same* public channel with an intended recipient to /INVite that user to a group.
- If you enter the /JOIn command without being /INVited by someone else,
the system informs you with a message like, "No invitation to JOIN 6 —
/INVITE 6 to join you."
- You may send an /INVitation to someone already in a private group from
a public channel or from a Group. The recipient receives the usual systems
notification of the /INVitation and, if the invitation is accepted, the recipient
automatically leaves the current Group for the new one with you.

Leaving CB

Several commands are available for leaving the conferencing area:

/OFF   causes you to leave the conference and log off CompuServe.

/EXIt   lets you leave the conference area and return to a menu.

/TOP and **/MAIN**   cause you to leave the conference area and go to
the TOP of the system.

Getting Help

To get help with any conferencing command, enter /HELp. This is a brief list,
intended to jog your memory, not to provide complete documentation. For
more extensive help, see the CB menu, by entering GO CB from a ! prompt,
or /GO CB from a channel.

ECHOing and Repeating

CompuServe offers commands for controlling the display in conferencing:

/ECHO,   in which mode CompuServe (1) bounces back the characters it
receives but (2) does not repeat the transmission to you as others see it.

/NOECHO, in which CompuServe does not bounce back the characters you receive, but *does* repeat the transmission with your handle affixed.

CompuServe's default setting is the former one, (echoing characters and not repeating).

Getting the Time of Day

/DAY displays the current time and the date.

/WTIme shows the local time in major world cities.

Conferencing in the Forums

As noted in the previous chapter, nearly every forum on CompuServe has its own conferencing area and, with a few exceptions, using them is like using the CB Simulator. In content, some of the conferences in the forums are somewhat different from the "chatter" you usually see on CB. Forum conferences are often held to discuss a single topic or issue related to the interests of forum members. Sometimes, depending on the forum that is hosting the event, the topics are serious and complex; other conferences are conducted in a relaxed and friendly atmosphere. If you enter one of these conferences as a newcomer, it is a good idea to watch the conversation for a time to get a sense of the conference tone.

For CIM Users

To reach the conference area of a forum, select the pull-down Conference menu from the Forum menu, which produces a menu of conferencing options, such as:

Enter Room displays a list of available conference rooms, which are similar to the channels in the CB Simulator. In some forums, only one room is available; in other forums, a dozen or more rooms are open. You may find out how many people are currently using a room, if any, by highlighting the name of the conference room. After you select a room, the forum conferencing window appears on your screen just as in CB. Also, the CB simulator, handles, or names appear along the left side of the screen and are followed by conversation display. The Input Box allows you to enter your own messages. The notice line reports ongoing activity in the conference rooms and the forum. The status line indicates the number of people in conference.

Who's Who lists the people currently using the forum. Unlike the CB Simulator, there is no Profile information available in forum conference areas.

Set Nickname is the same as Change Handle. Unless you use this selection to change your name, the name shown in the conference is the name you have chosen to use in the forum. As with a CB Handle, you may pre-record your forum nickname in the Personal Preferences area of the Information.

Listen works the same way as Monitor in the CB Simulator, and **Ignore** works the same as CB's Squelch option.

Notice displays the conference announcement, which usually tells about all regularly scheduled conferences and any special conferences planned for the forum conference area.

Description displays any announcements about the particular use of specific rooms, if any, in the conference area.

Other options, including **Track, Record, Invite, Ignore Invitations, Accept Invitations, Ignore Talks,** and **Accept Talks,** work the same way as they do in the CB Simulator.

For Non-CIM Users

To reach the conferencing area of a forum, select the Conferencing option from the Forum main menu (or enter CO at any prompt in the forum).

The subsequent display is similar to the open options in the CB Simulator, though the terminology is different. Instead of "channels," for instance, the forum conferencing area is divided into "rooms," though the function is the same. In the conferencing area, enter /HELP to get the latest list of commands.

Electronic Convention Center (GO CONVENTION)

When a special kind of conference is called for or when a celebrity is in conference on CompuServe and hundreds are expected to attend, the Electronic Convention Center is available for the special need. The conference center allows as many as 300 people to attend a conference in this special area. The conference may take one of three formats:

1. *Roundtable discussions* that allow all present to comment and ask questions. This is the same kind of "free-for-all" conferencing that is available on the CB Simulator and in the forum conferencing areas.

2. *Moderated conferences* that allow questions in turn from those who are recognized to ask questions. Unsolicited comments are not allowed. This is the most popular kind of conference in the Convention Center.

3. *Lectures* that do not allow comments or questions from those attending.

You see "Enter a Conference in Session" on the menu 30 minutes before the start of a conference and while a conference is in progress.

Special conferences are often announced in What's New, in forum notices, and by choosing 2 in the main Convention Center menu. That also is the choice for making reservations for conferences when reservations are necessary.

Some conferences require reservations or a fee. If that is the case, you see an (R) on the menu beside the conference name if a reservation is required or a (R$) if a reservation fee is required.

Enter the word RESERVE followed by a space and the menu choice from the reservations menu to reserve a place at the conference. Cancellations must be made at least 24 hours before the conference begins in order for you to be credited with a refund.

Chapter

6

Computer and
Software Support

In this chapter...

Using FIND to Get What You Want
Getting to Know the Sysop
Is it Hardware or Software?
The Survey of Support Forums

Betty Knight sometimes calls herself the grandmother of CompuServe forums. She certainly meets the specs. At 70, she has the wit and insight for the job, not to mention all the love of fun, poetry, and story-telling that you could ask for in a grandmother.

But she is also something of a cliché-buster, a star witness against the notion that computing is an interest reserved for male Baby Boomers and their sons. The fact is Betty Knight was a computing professional before some of her on-line acquaintances were even born. It was 1960 when her company trained her to be a mainframe computer programmer, one of the first women in the field.

"I loved it," she told a *CompuServe Magazine* reporter a few years ago. "I felt like a pioneer. We never knew what was going to work and we had to program everything because there wasn't much software."

For more than 20 years, Knight learned to expect to teach herself her new profession, to read the technical manuals, and to experiment. It was with the same pioneering spirit she bought her first *personal* computer, a Commodore-64, in the early 1980s and discovered CompuServe.

"I fell in love with telecommunications," she said. A widow who was still working in those days, she welcomed the companionship she found on-line. "I could be alone in my living room, dial up CompuServe and be in another world. I could talk with people, make friends and do all sorts of things."

When Betty Knight was eventually recruited as a sysop, she helped expand the original Commodore Forum into an entire network of related forums and services. It is there that she now presides/resides in a position found somewhere between wizard and welcome-wagon-of-one.

Newcomers always are surprised to find "a social life" in those forums that are primarily technical in nature. True, the computer support forums surveyed in this chapter are, first of all, problem solvers. ("The 24-hour manual of everything" was the definition one long-time forum hopper coined at the 10th anniversary of CompuServe's Micronetworked Apple User Groups, or MAUG, forums in 1991.)

The computer-related forums are at their best in providing specific technical assistance on all manner of hardware and software. In the case of machines that are a little out of the mainstream of current computing, CompuServe can become the sole resource for important data. Consider, for instance, the highly successful Atari forums.

"Atari computer users have been the underdogs of the computing world from Day One," says Ron Luks, the New Yorker who founded and still manages the Atari forums. "The forum was the only place people could go to get support for Atari machines."

Luks was working as a stock/options trader in a Wall Street brokerage firm in 1981 when he discovered his Atari. He was thinking about buying an IBM PC when he saw an Atari 800 running a video game called *Star Raiders*. "I was so mesmerized by the game that I bought the Atari, figuring I would play with it until I got a 'serious machine,' but that old 8-bit machine did everything I needed, so I never bought the IBM."

Computerists tend to develop an intense loyalty to their machines, Luks observes, "*and* to each other."

That's something Dave Groves learned in the late 1980s. A car accident in Miami near the bank where he worked put Groves in a body cast for three months, followed by nine months of therapy. During that extended recovery, he was buoyed by the on-line camaraderie of the Atari forums.

It is pointless to try to determine where the *technical* aspects end and the *social* functions begin, but Betty Knight has figured it out. Visitors may first be drawn to a forum by the subject, but what brings them back is the setting and the atmosphere of these remarkable waystations.

"We bend over backward," Knight told her interviewer. "I love it when new people visit the forum and ask questions because I know they're going to get the same thrill I got when I first came on-line."

The Overview

Computers are what we all have in common, so it is no surprise that computer-related forums — dealing with hardware and software, programming and applications, communications and graphics, and the like — are some of the most popular on the system.

Forums discussing computers and their operation were the first to be organized. When new computer systems have come along over the past decade, new forums have been added to support them. As various software becomes popular, forums devoted solely to software have increased in popularity.

In time, software companies themselves have found forums to be an efficient, economical way to keep in contact with customers. Today most of the major software companies and scores of small companies are represented with one or more forums. A presence on CompuServe is just good business.

This chapter covers the forums and on-line text material that provide the instant, international hardware and software support, through both the user-helping-user phenomenon that has characterized personal computing from the beginning and the direct contact with technical support for most of the major hardware and software companies.

Using FIND to Get What You Want

Most of the chapter is an overview of CompuServe's services in the complex arena of computer and software support. Keep in mind what we said at the outset of this book: This landscape is constantly changing, especially in the areas devoted to computer-related topics. New forums are added almost weekly. Sometimes more than one forum debuts every week. A few of them even disappear, though more often two or more forums merge into one or, less often, the name changes. For these reasons, it's important for you to remember the FIND command when you're looking for on-line support for your hardware or software.

The FIND command should be your constant companion when looking for CompuServe services:

- If you are using the CompuServe Information Manager, select Find... from the Services menu and fill in the subsequent dialog box with a keyword describing what you are looking for.

- If you are using general terminal software, enter FIND at any ! prompt followed by a keyword, such as FIND IBM.

Either way, the system responds by building a specialized menu of the services meeting your keyword specification.

A Tip About Names

You can quickly FIND out if your hardware or software is supported by typing a brand name for the hardware or software. CompuServe is diligent about adding the names of all the products supported in the forums. For instance, at this writing, there was not a forum specifically dedicated to Northgate computers, but Northgate products *were* supported in the PC Vendor A Forum (GO PCVENA), a forum where a group of hardware and software vendors are grouped together in a single location to provide customer service and a place for discussing their products. Although you couldn't find a Northgate Forum or support for Northgate by going through the list of forums, you could quickly find where that support was located by typing NORTHGATE at the FIND command prompt.

FIND also enables you to sidestep problems with unusual names. You won't see a forum for Procomm, one of the most famous of all terminal programs for PC and compatibles. That's because support for the program is found in the Datastorm Forum (GO DATASTORM), a forum operated by Datastorm Corp., the company that publishes Procomm and Procomm Plus.

This brings us to an important hint. When using FIND to look for support of a specific product, be certain to enter the exact name of the product for which you're seeking support. In lieu of that, enter the name of the company that produces the product. Remember, the more specific you are with your request to the FIND function, the faster you're likely to hone in on what you want.

Getting to Know the Sysop

With the increased complexity of the forums have come larger staffs of sysops who operate the forums. In addition, forums differ in how they are administered. Most forums have chief administrators, or sysops (system operators), as well as one or more assistants. But that's not always the case. In some forums, a group shares sysop duties equally. With company-run forums, the entire technical support staff may share duties. In others, a sysop may be assigned to monitor and administer only one message and/or library section.

You should get to know the sysops. Many of them have been forum administrators for 10 years or longer. They are often your first line of help in solving the problems you are having with the system. Don't be afraid to ask them for help with navigating the system. Most of them are extremely knowledgeable in the mysteries of CompuServe. If they don't know the answer to your question, most of them can point you in the direction where help is available.

How to Write to a Sysop

In some busy forums, the chain of command can become confusing for someone trying to make contact with a sysop. That's why knowing how to address a message to SYSOP or *SYSOP is important. Even if you don't know the sysop's name or user ID number, a message addressed to SYSOP will always get the attention of a forum administrator. A message addressed to *SYSOP (note the asterisk in front of the word) will make the message private and visible only to a forum administrator.

We've tried to include the names and user IDs of forum administrators where possible, but a complete list would probably fill half the book with names and user IDs. Besides, the sysop rosters change frequently, so listing them would be futile.

As a user, all you really have to remember is SYSOP or *SYSOP for addresses; These get the attention of forum administrators as quickly as their names and user IDs.

Is It Hardware or Software?

In the early days of CompuServe, and the early editions of this book, it was a simple matter to list the hardware support forums and the software support forums as separate entries. Now, it's not that easy, partly because the distinctions between "hardware" and "software" are not always so clear. Is desktop publishing a hardware issue or a software issue? Scanners for digitizing images are hardware, but it takes software to optimize the images and create the document in which it is placed. Is MIDI music a function of hardware or software? Well, uh, both. The days are over when someone can point to a lot of forums and say "That's hardware," or "That's software." Therefore, we're listing forums that deal with hardware and/or software in one group.

Also, note that a large number of forums are grouped together in a "display area." This means they can be accessed directly by GO words or from a submenu. From here you can access everything from company news releases and company newsletters to repair sites (for hardware) and special feedback areas where you can write letters directly to the company that maintains the forums and related display area. In the case of Aldus, for example, you can access the display area by typing GO ALDUS. if you want to access the Aldus Customer Services Forum, you can choose the menu item from this display area or type GO ALDSVC at any prompt.

Support: An Overview

Here is an overview of the hardware and software forums and display areas you can find on CompuServe, listed in alphabetical order.

ACIUS Forum (GO ACIUS)

The ACIUS Forum is designed to support all of ACIUS Incorporated products. John Beaulieu (76702,1021) is the primary sysop.

Adobe Forum (GO ADOBE)

The Adobe Forum provides an area where users, dealers, service bureaus, third-party developers, and others can communicate directly with Adobe. Forum sysop is Michael Shahamatdoust (76704,21).

AI Forum (GO AIFORUM)

AI Forum, devoted to topics about artificial intelligence, is an electronic edition of *AI Expert* magazine offering program listings from each monthly issue and supporting code, executable programs for many machines, and more. Primary sysop is Susan Shepherd (76703,4326).

Aldus Online (GO ALDUS)

This area offers a menu of services provided by Aldus. They include:

- Customer First Online, a subscription-only interactive electronic support service for Aldus customers with registered products.
- Silicon Beach/Aldus Forum (GO SBSALD), providing technical help for Aldus subsidiary Silicon Beach Software.
- Customer Services Forum (GO ALDSVC), to answer public questions about pricing, upgrade, address change, and pre-sale questions. It's also home to a Developer's Corner and more.
- Product Information, a display area listing of text articles on each Aldus and Silicon Beach Software product.
- Services Information, a listing of text articles on each Aldus service program. Each article outlines the features, price, requirements, and other information about each program.

Apple Forums (GO APPLE)

These forums, part of the Micronetworked Apple Users Groups (MAUG), support the older Apple II computers. (Macintosh-oriented forums follow this section.)

- Apple II Programmers Forum (GO APPROG) offers help in the many ways to program your Apple II. There are sections on BASIC, Pascal, and other programming environments. Neil Shapiro (76703,401) is the primary sysop of all Apple forums.
- Apple II Users Forum (GO APPUSER) is for discussion of all of the application software available for the Apple II as well as the add-on hardware.
- Apple II Vendor Forum (GO APPIIVEN) is where companies offer on-line support.

Apple Macintosh Computers (GO MAC)

A major player in today's computer market, the Mac is supported on CompuServe by:

- Applications Forum (GO MACAP) offers support for application programs. Neil Shapiro (76703,401) is the primary sysop for all Mac forums.

- Communications Forum (GO MACCOM) is the place to learn all the many ways that the Mac can be used to communicate with other Macs, other computers, and FAX machines.

- Community Clubhouse Forum (GO MACCLUB) is where you can interact on a more personal level than is typical on the other forums.

- Developers Forum (GO MACDEV) focuses on all of the ways and techniques to program Macintosh computers, with special sections on languages such as Pascal and C.

- Entertainment Forum (GO MACFUN) covers all the entertainment uses of the Mac.

- Hardware Forum (GO MACHW) is for discussions of the various models of Macs, from the Classic through the Performa, the Quadras, the Mac II, and LC.

- Hypertext Forum (GO MACHYPER) supports the Apple's HyperCard program. Libraries contain thousands of HyperCard files.

- New Users and Help Forum (GO MACNEW) is designed for new members and all those who need help in using the Mac forums.

- Systems Forum (GO MACSYS) has discussions of the system software for the Macintosh (System, Finder, DAs, FKEYs, INITs, cdevs) as well as the hardware you can attach to your Mac (printers, monitors, disks).

- Mac Vendor Forums (GO MACAVEN, GO MACBVEN, and GO MACCVEN) is for vendors of Mac software and add-on hardware.

- File Finder (GO MACFF) MAC File Finder is an on-line comprehensive keyword-searchable database of file descriptions from MAC-related forums. It is designed to provide quick and easy reference to some of the best programs and files available in the following forums: Adobe Forum, Mac Hardware Forum, Mac Applications Forum, Microsoft Applications Forum, Microsoft Excel Forum, Borland Applications Forum, MIDI A Vendor Forum, Borland Pascal Forum, MIDI B Vendor Forum, Mac Communications Forum, MIDI/Music Forum, Community Clubhouse Forum, Music and Performing Arts Forum, Mac Developers Forum, MS Word Forum, Entertainment Forum, Mac New Users and Help Forum, Fox Software

Forum, Silicon Beach/Aldus Forum, Fifth Generation Forum, Symantec Apps Forum, Mac Hypertext Forum, Mac Systems Forum, Lotus Spreadsheets Forum, and the Mac Vendor Forums.

APPC Information Exchange Forum (GO APPCFORUM)

IBM offers this open forum for the discussion of all topics related to the design and implementation of applications that use Advanced Program-to-Program Communications (APPC). The sysop is Lance Bader (76711,151).

Artisoft ArtiFacts Forum (GO ARTISOFT)

The forum is operated by Artisoft's Technical Support Department as a service to all users of Artisoft's hardware and software. The sysop is Rick Roth (75600,1377).

3COM'S On-line Information Service (GO THREECOM)

3Com Corporation's on-line information service is sponsored by 3Com's Customer Support. The display offers a menu from which you can access:

- About 3Com Corporation — The choice contains the latest corporate backgrounder, a list of telephone numbers and addresses for contacting 3Com, and a description of the various service options that you can buy.
- What's New — This menu choice will list new additions to the Ask3Com service.
- Technical Articles — 3Com's Technical Database, the option has over 700 articles, many taken from questions and answers on 3Com's internal network.
- Product/Service Notes — This is the text portion of most of 3Com's more technical pre-sales information.
- Education Services Catalog — The menu choice gives the latest education services course catalog, as well as class schedules for upcoming months and registration/payment information.
- Find a Service Center — This is a database of 3Com Authorized Service Centers and Certified Network Centers. You can search by name, area code, state, or city.
- Ask3com Forum (GO ASKFORUM) — For user-to-user discussion, join the Ask3Com Forum.

Atari Users Network (GO ATARINET)

You'll find the following forums and services on AtariNet, headed by Ron Luks (76703,254).

- Atari ST Arts Forum (GO ATARIARTS) specializes in graphics/entertainment-related software and information relating to the Atari 16-Bit (ST) series of computers.

- Atari ST Productivity Forum (GO ATARIPRO) specializes in productivity-related software and information relating to the Atari 16-Bit (ST) series of computers. It includes a private area for communication among registered Atari Developers who are approved by Atari Corp. for access.

- Atari ST Vendors Forum (GO ATARIVEN) supports commercial hardware and software by participating vendors.

- Atari 8-Bit Forum (GO ATARI8) supports the Atari 8-Bit line of personal computers.

- Atari Portfolio Forum (GO APORTFOLIO) provides information and technical support for the Atari Portfolio palmtop computer system, and includes a private area for communication among registered Atari Portfolio Developers who are approved by Atari Corp. for access.

- Atari ST File Finder (GO ATARIFF) is an on-line comprehensive keyword-searchable-database of file descriptions from the Atari ST related forums.

- What's New In The Atari Forums (GO ATA-1) is an area containing help and information relating to the Atari support services on CompuServe.

Autodesk Forums (GO ADESK)

Autodesk AutoCAD Forum (GO ACAD) is reserved for questions about Auto-CAD and its related products: AutoLISP, ADS, AME, AutoShade, AutoFlix, and Autodesk RenderMan.

Autodesk Retail Products Forum (GO ARETAIL) is for the support of its Mass Market CADD and CADD-related products: Generic CADD (PC and Mac), AutoSketch, Generic 3D, GenCADD, and the HOME series.

Autodesk Software Forum (GO ASOFT) is for questions about Autodesk's Multimedia products, Autodesk 3D Studio, Autodesk Animator and Animator Pro, and Autodesk Multimedia Explorer, and about Autodesk's Science Series products, CA Lab and Chaos: The Software.

Banyan Forum (GO BANFORUM)

The forum provides computing support for Banyan Software products. The sysop is Deb Penny (76702,1151).

BASIS International Forum (GO BASIS)

The forum supports BASIS products. BASIS President and CEO Thom Olson (76702,1426) frequents the forum.

Blyth Forum (GO BLYTH)

The forum offers technical support for Blyth Products. The sysop is Rick Moen (76711,243).

Borland (GO BORLAND)

From this display area, you can read the latest news releases, learn of Borland's product line, leave suggestions for Borland's Research and Development Division, obtain product support, ask questions about product registration, and read of Borland's latest employment opportunities. In addition, you can access the following forums:

- Borland Development Tools Forum (GO BDEVTOOLS) for help with Object-Vision, Paradox Engine, Interbase, Brief, and Borland Version Control.
- Borland Pascal Forum (GO BPASCAL).
- Borland C++/DOS Forum (GO BCPPDOS) for help with Borland C++, TC++, TC, TD, and Tools.
- Borland C++/Windows Forum (GO BCPPWIN).
- Borland Quattro Pro Forum (GO QUATTROPRO) for both DOS and Windows.
- Borland Applications Forum (GO BORAPP) for help with Sidekick and utilities.
- Borland Paradox/DOS Forum (GO PDOXDOS) for help with Paradox and Reflex.
- Borland dBASE Forum (GO DBASE).

Cabletron Systems (GO CTRON)

This display area offers text files that include the corporate background of Cabletron, a list of sales offices, information about training and presentations, and the Cabletron Systems Forum (GO CTN-48), a manufacturer of computer networking hardware and network management software.

CADD/CAM/CAE Vendor Forum (GO CADDVEN)

Third-party vendors of CAD and related applications are in this forum.

Canon Support Area (GO CANON)

This display area offers information about Canon, a list of regional offices and service facilities, and entry to the Canon Support Forum (GO CAN-10) designed for users to be able to exchange information on Canon's various products.

Canopus Research Forum (GO CANOPUS)

Sponsored by Canopus Research, it's a place to discuss information industry technologies and products, and serves as an on-line newsletter with analysis, commentary, and reviews written by Canopus Research President William F. Zachmann (76004,3657).

CD ROM Forum (GO CDROM)

The forum is sponsored by Metatec/Discovery Systems. Rich Bowers (71333,1114), executive director of the Optical Publishing Association, is a sysop.

Central Point Forums (GO CENTRAL)

Central Point DOS Forum (GO CPSDOS) is for Central Point Software DOS applications.

Central Point Win/Mac Forum (GO CPSWINMAC) is for Central Point Software Windows and Macintosh applications.

Clarion Software Forum (GO CLARION)

The forum gives support for Clarion Software. Sysops are Greg Whitaker (76711,1035) and Paul Schomaker (76711,1034).

Computer Club Forum (GO CLUB)

This forum provides hardware/software support for computers whose manufacturers have gone out of business or no longer support their machines, and for computer users without a forum specifically dedicated to their hardware. Computers currently supported in CLUB are: ACTRIX, ADAM, AMSTRAD, APRICOT, EAGLE, KAYPRO, OHIO SCIENTIFIC, PANASONIC, SANYO, all TIMEX/SINCLAIR equipment, and the VICTOR 9000. Primary sysop is Dave Yaros (76703,4332).

Commodore and Amiga Support (GO CBMNET)

CBMNET includes services for both the Commodore line of computers as well as Amigas. For the Amiga there are:

- Amiga Arts Forum (GO AMIGAARTS) devoted to the creative Amiga user and the entertainment-oriented user.
- Amiga Tech Forum (GO AMIGATECH) devoted to programming your Amiga or finding out more about how things work internally.
- Amiga User's Forum (GO AMIGAUSER) is for all topics of interest to Amiga users.

- Amiga Vendor Forum (GO AMIGAVENDOR) allows multiple vendors of Amiga products to share one forum to provide support for their products.
- Amiga File Finder (GO AMIGAFF) is a comprehensive keyword-searchable database of file descriptions from Amiga-related forums.

For the Commodore there are:

- Commodore Arts and Games (GO CBMART) supports music, graphics/ GEOS, games and their related utilities for the Commodore 8-bit computers. While much of the material on this forum is related to the Commodore C64 and Commodore C128, there are also a few programs for the Commodore VIC-20 computer as well. Primary sysop is Betty Knight (76703,4037).
- Commodore Applications Forum (GO CBMAPP) is a forum for all who enjoy Commodore 8-bit computers and their applications. Primary sysop is Gary Farmaner (76703,3050).
- Commodore Service Forum (GO CBMSERVICE) is maintained by Commodore Business Machines, Inc. employees and is a place to exchange ideas, suggestions, and experience.
- Commodore Newsletter (GO CBMNEWS) is an on-line area sponsored by Commodore Business Machines that contains such features as Commodore announcements, resources for education, user group information, a service center directory, and Commodore software updates.

Compaq Connection (GO COMPAQ)

The Compaq Connection is designed to provide our customers with accessibility to the highest quality support and information on available COMPAQ products. It provides information on Compaq product support services, authorized training for both users and resellers, and Compaq worldwide addresses and phone numbers. In addition there are two forums:

- Compaq Forum (GO CPQFORUM) provides users with access to Compaq technical support and downloadable files, drivers, utilities, and software solutions.
- ISHV Forum (GO CPQISHV) is a private forum for use by authorized Compaq Independent Hardware and Software Vendors (ISHVs).

CompuAdd Forum (GO COMPUADD)

This is the place for CompuAdd customers to communicate with CompuAdd's technical support and engineering staff as well as share tips and techniques with other users.

Computer Associates Resource Center (GO CAI)

The Computer Associates Resource Center is a display area that provides information concerning Computer Associates Micro, VAX, and UNIX products as well as current news about Computer Associates. It includes:

- What's New — Current information about Computer Associates.
- Technical Support — Information on the different types of support offered clients using any of the CA micro products.
- Product Information — A brief product description on each of the CA micro, VAX, and UNIX products.
- Productivity Solutions Forum (GO CAIPRO) — Information on CA Productivity Products.
- Application Development Forum (GO CAIDEV) — Used to exchange information on the CA micro application development tools.
- VAX and UNIX Forum (GO CAMINI) — Used for the exchange of technical information on CA VAX and UNIX products.

Computer Consultant's Forum (GO CONSULT)

This is a forum especially for computer consultants and others interested in any aspect of computer consulting, sponsored by the Independent Computer Consultants Association (ICCA). Primary sysop is David Moskowitz (76701,100).

Computer Language Magazine Forum (GO CLMFORUM)

Here's where you'll find how to program code and extended listings mentioned in *Computer Language Magazine*, public domain programs mentioned in the "Public Domain Software Review" column in the magazine, and a database of public domain software for all major operating systems. The forum also offers a place for feedback to magazine editors, writers, and support people.

Corel Forum (GO COREL)

This is a forum for support of and information about Corel products. The sysop is Steve Cockwell (76711,563).

CP/M Forum (GO CPMFORUM)

The forum is a source for the exchange of information about CP/M and the related hardware and software. It is managed by Ross & Associates–Communications Management. The primary sysop is John Ross (76703,551).

Crosstalk Forum (GO TALK)

The forum is devoted to the software products developed and marketed by DCA/Crosstalk Communications. Sysops are Maria Forrest (76701,104) and Steve Johnson and Jacek ("Jack") Sadkowski, both using account number 76702,1216.

Data Access Corp. (GO DAC)

This display area offers a menu that provides Data Access Corp. product news releases, sales and marketing information, technical support services, and Data Access Forum (GO DACCESS), which provides interactive support for DAC products.

Data Based Advisor Forum (GO DBADVISOR)

This is the electronic version of three magazines — *Data Based Advisor, FoxPro Advisor,* and *Access Advisor*. Primary sysop is David Frier (76702,1417).

DataEase International Forum (GO DATAEASE)

The forum supports all aspects of DataEase International US products and services. Primary sysop is Chris Griffith (76702,2017).

Datastorm Forum (GO DATASTORM)

This is the place on CompuServe where Datastorm supports its Procomm communications products and more.

DBMS Forum (GO DBMS)

This is the CompuServe home of *DBMS*, a monthly magazine devoted to database management systems programming, client-server systems, front-ends to databases, and other technical DBMS hardware and software issues. Primary sysop is Tom Genereaux (76703,4265).

DEC Users Network (GO DECUNET)

All forums on the DEC user's network lend support to various Digital Equipment Corp.'s products. The forums are:

- DEC PC Forum (GO DECPC) is dedicated to Digital's line of Personal Computers. Primary sysops are Bill Leeman (76703,3055) and Bill Mayhew (76702,502).

- DECPCI Forum (GO DECPCI) is dedicated to the discussion of Digital's PC Integration products.

- PDP-11 Forum (GO PDP11) provides communication between users of the LSI-11 series of DEC microcomputers, and encourages the exchange of software designed to run on the LSI-11/PDP-11 computer systems.

- VAX Forum (GO VAXFORUM) discusses Digital Equipment's line of VAX 32-bit computer systems, the VAX/VMS operating system and its utilities, VAX applications, and Digital's versions of the Unix operating system known as Ultrix-32 and Ultrix-32m.

Dell Forum (GO DELL)

The Dell Forum offers technical support for Dell computers. Primary sysop is Ron Clark (76702,1601).

Desktop Publishing Forum (GO DTPFORUM)

Run by people who are all actual users of desktop publishing systems, this forum calls itself a worldwide independent users' group.

Digitalk Forum (GO DIGITALK)

This is a place for Digitalk Smalltalk/V users to talk to Digitalk and other users, exchange technical and other information, receive technical support, and keep up with the latest information on Digitalk products and activities. Primary sysop is Brenda Friederich (76711,366).

DTP Vendor Forum (GO DTPVENDOR)

This is a forum where vendors of desktop publishing software and hardware hang out. The forum is supported by the same people who run the Desktop Publishing Forum.

Dr. Dobb's Journal Forum (GO DDJFORUM)

This provides the electronic connection to *Dr. Dobb's Journal*, one of the oldest magazines devoted to programming languages, techniques, tools, utilities, and algorithms. Primary sysop is Tom Genereaux (76703,4265).

Eicon Forum (GO EICON)

The forum provides information and technical support on Eicon products by Eicon personnel, including Eicon technical support.

Epson Forum (GO EPSON)

The Epson Forum is a source for the exchange of information about Epson computers and printers, and the related hardware and software. The primary sysop is John Ross (76703,551).

FED Forum (GO FEDERATION)

This is the forum of the Federation of International Distributors and The International Managers' Club. The Federation is an association of international Macintosh, OS/2, Windows, NeXT, UNIX, and MS-DOS distributors and republishers. The International Managers' Club (IMC) brings together people within the computer industry involved in international operations, and provides them with information resources and various forums in which to network more effectively. Sysop is Lynne Patkin (75300,3070).

Fifth Generation Forum (GO FIFTHGEN)

The forum offers support for all Fifth Generation Systems products. It's managed by Joseph Katz, Inc.

CSI Forth Net Forum (GO FORTH)

This forum, devoted to Forth and its applications, is sponsored by Creative Solutions, Inc. (CSI). Sysop is Don Colburn (76703,4160), founder of CSI.

Fox Software Forum (GO FOXFORUM)

This forum is designed to support Microsoft's Fox database management and graphics software. It's managed by the Technical Support Department of Microsoft, Inc. Primary sysop is Gloria Pfeif (75300,3606).

Graphics (GO GRAPHICS)

No area of CompuServe has grown faster in recent years than graphics. Since most of the newer computers come equipped with graphics adapters, CompuServe has met the demand with a veritable explosion of graphic services. The GRAPHICS menu is a one-stop area where you can learn the fundamentals of creating, uploading and downloading graphics, find the graphics you want to download, and get help from experts and well-informed hobbyists. Some of the offerings from the GRAPHICS menu are:

- Introduction to Graphics: A tutorial which covers all of the information you may need to successfully find, download, and view your first graphic art files.

- The Graphics File Finder: A fast, convenient way to locate particular files in the various 'Go Graphics' Forums. In addition, CIM users can download files directly from the File Finder listings without having to actually move to the forums. File Finder permits searches by a variety of criteria, including keyword, forum, uploader's ID, file size and type, and others.

- Graphics Support Forum (GO GRAPHSUP): The place to go to learn about graphics and your computer from those who are professionals and learned hobbyists.

- Graphics Gallery Forum (GO GALLERY): Image libraries from private and public collections around the world. It's the home of Smithsonian Online, with five entire libraries devoted to images from this famous Washington institution, and includes images direct from NASA.

- Graphics Corner Forum (GO CORNER): Photographic images from around the world, from people and animals to star clusters and galaxies.

- Fine Art Forum (GO FINEART): An on-line art gallery, where the work of artists from the Old Masters to present-day artists is displayed.

- Computer Art Forum (GO COMART): A large collection of images generated by hand, by using painting and drawing programs.

- Graphics Developers Forum (GO GRAPHDEV): Four work groups, each devoted to the concept of software development based on the voluntary contribution of each person's expertise, resulting in software that anyone can run.

- Quick Pictures Forum (GO QPICS): A repository for Clipart, Missing Children, and Smaller Images.

- Graphics Plus Forum (GO GRAPHPLUS): A place filled with images that push the limits of consumer graphics technology. The images in the Graphics Plus Forum are larger than the commonly found 640x480 resolution, with close to 256 colors per image. In fact, no image that is less than 800x600 in size will be found in this Forum.

- Graphics Vendors Forums (GO GRAPHAVEN or GO GRAPHBVEN): Direct support from manufacturers of hardware and software products.

Hayes Forum (GO HAYFORUM)

This is the forum which provides Hayes modem customers technical support. Primary sysop is Joey Browning (76702,1365).

Hewlett-Packard Forums (GO HP)

HP Systems Forum (GO HPSYSTEMS) deals with questions about Hewlett-Packard systems and discusses programming techniques and other technical aspects of HP systems. Primary sysop for all HP forums is Ted Dickens (76701,272).

- HP Peripherals Forum (GO HPPERIPHER) for discussions and support of all HP peripheral products.
- HP Handhelds Forum (GO HPHANDHELDS) for support of your HP handheld computer, HP palmtop computer, or HP calculator.

IBM Desktop Forum (GO IBMDESK)

This forum is operated by IBM Programming Systems. Primary sysop is Gary Vieregger, Administrator (76711,35).

IBM LMU/2 Forum (GO LMU2FORUM)

This is a forum for discussion of topics related to IBM LAN Management Utilities/2 (LMU/2). Forum administrator is Steve Pace (76711,724).

IBMOS2 Support (GO IBMOS2)

In addition to IBMOS/2 User Forum (GO OS2USER), IBM OS2 Support Forum (GO OS2SUPPORT), and two IBMOS/2 Developer Forums (GO OS2DF1 and GO OS2DF2), this display area offers an IBM OS/2 ServicePak download area which contains OS/2 product fixes for reported customer problems and problems identified by IBM as well as product enhancements.

IBM Users Network (GO IBMNET)

The IBM Users Network is independent; although not affiliated with IBM, it is recognized as an authorized user group. The primary sysop for IBMNET, Don Watkins (76703,750) and other sysops are independent as well. Here are the highlights of IBMNET:

- IBM New User's/Fun Forum (GO IBMNEW): The place to start if you're just becoming acquainted with the PC or with the CompuServe Forum software. IBMNEW also has an excellent selection of games, graphics, and music in its libraries.
- IBM PC Hardware Forum (GO IBMHW): The forum for discussing hardware-related issues. In addition to reviews and other comments on hardware, there are hardware diagnostic programs, hardware-specific utilities (printer utilities, disk managers, special video programs [especially for the EGA and VGA]), and other hardware-specific software in the libraries.
- Software Applications Forum (GO IBMAPP): The place to find the "core" applications for the PC; word processing, database management, business

and personal accounting, business graphics, desktop publishing, and educational software.

- Systems/Utilities Forum (GO IBMSYS): The latest in general utilities and information on the various operating systems and environments available for the PC, including multitasking and OS/2. In the libraries here you'll find various utility programs, including DOS additions, improved DOS utilities as well as resident desktop utilities and all those programs that make living with the PC easier.

- Programming Forum (GO IBMPRO): Offerings assemblers, source code in a variety of languages, and help from fellow members can be found here. IBMPRO contains not only valuable information for experienced programmers but also hints, tips, and tutorials for those just starting to program.

- Communications Forum (GO IBMCOM): Discussions on how to use various communications programs and hardware. In the data libraries, you'll see the best public domain and shareware communications software available.

- Bulletin Board Forum (GO IBMBBS): Contains bulletin board programs, utilities, door programs, and the discussion of issues concerning bulletin board operators and users. You'll find a wide variety of bulletin board programs, bulletin board utilities, and helpful advice from other bulletin board operators if you currently run a board or plenty of startup advice if you're interested in starting one.

- Shareware/ASP Forum (GO ASPFORUM): The Association of Shareware Professionals (ASP) is a non-profit group dedicated to educating computer users about the "try before you buy" software marketing concept and to setting standards for the author and user community. If you'd like some info on shareware or joining the ASP, or you just want to discuss shareware issues drop by.

- IBM European Users Forum (GO IBMEUROPE): This Forum is devoted to the topic of the European user of the PC and compatibles with an interest in sharing information and programs.

- PC Vendor Forums: A total of six forums at this writing — GO PCVENA, GO PCVENB, GO PCVENC, GO PCVEND, GO PCVENE, and GO PCVENF. Check section names in each forum to find the vendors represented.

- IBM File Finder (GO IBMFF): A special database containing information on all IBMNET and most IBM-related forum files. The IBM File Finder will allow you to search on filename or keyword, or use a variety of search methods to help you quickly locate files of interest.

Intel Corporation Forums (GO INTEL)

The Intel Forum (GO INTELFORUM) supports the Intel Personal Computer Enhancement (PCED) or Development Tools Operation (DT) products. Primary sysop is Paul Crandall (76702,366).

Software Developers (Intel Access/iRUG) Forum (GO INTELACCESS) is a communication channel between Intel and software developers. The Real-Time side of the Forum is intended to help you achieve the most value from your Intel iRMX Operating System software and hardware products. The Intel ACCESS/Real-Time Forum allows you to send feedback to Intel via the SYSOP, as well as trade tips and techniques with other software developers and iRMX users, or to simply ask questions. Primary sysop is Roe Fowler (76711,374).

IRIFORUM Javelin/EXPRESS Forum (GO IROFORUM)

Sponsored by Information Resources, the forum supports the company's products. Primary sysop is Tom Genereaux (76703,4265).

League for Engineering Automation Productivity Forum (GO LEAP)

Also known as the CADD/CAM forum, the forum is for discussion of anything related to engineering or design automation.

Logitech Forum (GO LOGITECH)

The Logitech Forum provides technical support to owners of Logitech products, such as mice, ScanMan family of scanners, and software packages (PaintShow Plus, Finesse, and Logitech Windows).

Logo Forum (GO LOGOFORUM)

This is the place to explore Logo and similar computer languages, from the simplest turtle graphics and drawing exercises to complex list processing, CASE simulations, and behavioral studies for professionals.

World of Lotus (GO LOTUS)

This display area offers a launching point for Lotus forums and a database, including:

- LDC Spreadsheet Forum (GO LOTUSA) for support for 1-2-3 and Symphony.
- LDC Words & Pixels Forum (GO LOTUSB) for support of Agenda, Magellan, cc:Mail, Notes, Freelance, LotusWorks, and Express.

- LDC Word Processing Forum (GO LOTUSWP for support of Ami Pro, SmarText, Word4, and Manuscript.

- Lotus Technical Library (GO LTL-1), a comprehensive collection of Lotus product information. It contains answers to common questions, tips and techniques for using Lotus products more effectively, and troubleshooting guidelines for identifying and resolving technical difficulties.

Macromedia Forum (GO MACROMEDIA)

This is a forum where users of Macromedia products can communicate directly with other users and the Macromedia Technical Support Staff. Primary sysop is Doug Wyrick (75300,2303).

McAfee Virus Help Forum (GO VIRUSFORUM)

This forum is not restricted to McAfee Associates customers, nor is it limited to discussions of McAfee Associates products. Questions about all aspects of viruses and other anti-virus packages are encouraged. Primary sysops are Aryeh Goretsky (76702,1714) and Spencer Clark (76702,1713).

MECA Forum (GO MECA)

The forum is sponsored by MECA Software for users of their software to obtain support for products and to enable users to communicate with each other.

Microsoft Connection (GO MICROSOFT)

The Microsoft name, a giant in personal computing, only naturally has one of the largest areas of CompuServe devoted to it. The area provides customers with technical support and information about all Microsoft products not only for US customers but also for international customers. Microsoft promises additional areas in the future. Here are some highlights of the Microsoft Connection:

- Client Server Computing Forum (GO MSNETWORKS).
- Developer Relations Forum (GO MSDR).
- Developer Technical Library (GO MSDNLIB).
- Microsoft Applications Forum (GO MSAPP).
- Microsoft Benelux Forum (GO MSBF) for the Benelux customers in Europe.
- Microsoft DOS 5.0 Forum (GO MSDOS).
- Microsoft SQL Server Forum (GO MSSQL).

- Microsoft Software Library (GO MSL), a keyword-searchable library containing downloadable text, graphics, sample code, and utilities files.
- Microsoft Windows Advanced Forum (GO WINADV).
- Microsoft Windows Extensions Forum (GO WINEXT).
- Microsoft Windows SDK Forum (GO WINSDK).
- Microsoft Access Forum (GO MSACCESS).
- Microsoft BASIC Forum (GO MSBASIC).
- Microsoft CE Systems Forum (GO MSCESYSTEM).
- Microsoft Central Europe Forum (GO MSCE).
- Microsoft Excel Forum (GO MSEXCEL).
- Microsoft Knowledge Base (GO MSKB), an up-to-date database containing thousands of developer-specific technical articles.
- Microsoft Languages Forum (GO MSLANG).
- Microsoft WIN32 Forum (GO MSWIN32).
- Microsoft Word Forum (GO MSWORD).
- Windows Third-Party Forums (GO WINAPA, GO WINAPB and GO WINAPC).

MIDI Forums (GO MIDI)

For those fascinated by marrying computers and music, the MIDI area is for you. It features:

- The MIDI/MUSIC Forum (GO MIDIFORUM) which provides highlights of interviews, columns, and synthesizer sound banks and patches. Primary sysop is Jim Maki (76701,33).
- Two MIDI Vendor Forums (GO MIDIAFORUM and GO MIDIBFORUM), offering vendors of MIDI hardware and software.

Modem Vendor Forum (GO MODEMVENDOR)

This forum is shared by the following modem vendors: Supra Corporation, Boca Research, Global Village Communications, US Robotics, Telebit, PSI Integration, Inc., Zoom, Megahertz, and The Complete PC.

Multimedia Forums

Under the general heading of multimedia, you'll find the following forums:

- IBM Ultimedia Tool Series A Forum (GO ULTIATOOLS and GO ULTIB-TOOLS), two forums for support of the Ultimedia tools that offer a full range of authoring, content creation, capture, and editing facilities for video, audio, animation, graphics, image, and music.

- Macromedia Forum (GO MACROMEDIA) provides support and user communication for Macromedia products. Primary sysop is Doug Wyrick (75300,2303).

- Multimedia Forum (GO MULTIMEDIA), concerned with computer-based interactive multimedia technologies, products, and markets, sponsored by Multimedia Computing Corporation. Nick Arnett (75300,1324), president of Multimedia Computing Corp., is the chief sysop.

- Multimedia Conference Forum (GO MULTICON) is the electronic side of major multimedia-related conferences.

- Multimedia Vendor Forum (GO MULTIVEN), a place for vendors of multimedia products to provide support for their products. Primary sysop is Jim Ogilvie (75300,2253).

NeXT Users Forum (GO NEXTFORUM)

This is an on-line users group for fans of the NeXT computer. Primary sysop is David Bowdish (76711,143).

Novell NetWire (GO NOVELL)

This link between Novell and its customers offers the following:

- Novel NOVLIB Forum (GO NOVLIB), a forum that primarily contains libraries of Novell information.

- Novell NOVA Forum (GO NOVA), a forum that covers topics relating to some NetWare Operating Systems and Novell's Communication Products.

- Novell NOVB Forum (GO NOVB), a forum for discussion of network topologies, file servers, workstation issues, backups, printing, cabling, and media.

- Novell NOVC Forum (GO NOVC), a forum about NetWare Requester for OS/2 or the NetWare environment.

- Novell NETW2X Forum (GO NETW2X), a place for questions relating to NetWare v2.x.

- Novell NETW3X Forum (GO NETW3X), a place for questions relating specifically to NetWare v3.x.

- Technical Bulletin Database provides technical information about Novell software and hardware.

- Novell Vendor Forum (GO NOVVEN)

Oracle Forum (GO ORACLE)

This is the forum for questions about Oracle software. Primary sysop is Chris Wooldridge (76711,1014).

Packard Bell Forum (GO PACKARDBELL)

This forum offers technical support for Packard Bell computers and a place for users to exchange ideas. Primary sysop is Tom Gilmore (75300,2261).

Palmtop Forum (GO PALMTOP)

The forum is designed to support all aspects of the evolving technology of super-small computers. It supports the broad range of palmtops as well as specific models and brands. Primary sysop is Ron Luks (76703,254).

PC Plus Online (GO PCPLUS)

Britain's two best selling PC magazines, *PC PLUS* and *PC ANSWERS,* join forces by creating this combined service. In addition to lots of information about the magazines in this display area, you can access the PC PLUS/PC ANSWERS Forum (GO PCPFORUM) where you can talk to editors, other readers, and computer users. Primary sysop is Robin Nixon (70007,5547).

Pen Technology Forum (GO PENFORUM)

This forum supports PEN computers, which utilize writing, marking, and gesturing on a display screen with what looks like a pen. Primary sysop is Ron Luks (76703,254).

Practical Peripherals Forum (GO PPIFORUM)

Sponsored by Practical Peripherals, Inc., the primary purpose of this forum is technical support for users of telecommunications PPI products. Primary sysop is Paul E. Hansen (76702,475).

Quarterdeck Forum (GO QUARTERDECK)

This forum provides technical support, a review of product descriptions, and files related to Quarterdeck products. Primary sysop is Michael Chapman (76004,2310).

Revelation Technologies Forum (GO REVELATION)

This forum provides support and discussion of Revelation Technologies products. Primary sysop for support is Thom Dieterich (75300,2270).

Santa Cruz Operations Inc. Forum (GO SCOFORUM)

The forum supports SCO end-users, resellers, developers, and partners.

Software Publishers Association Forum (GO SPAFORUM)

The forum is operated by the Software Publishers Association (SPA), the principal trade association of the microcomputer software industry. Primary sysop is David Frier (76702,1417).

Software Publishing Forum (GO SPCFORUM)

The forum provides on-line support and user interaction for Software Publishing Corp. products. Primary sysop is Kelly Gang (76702,541).

Spinnaker Forum (GO SPINNAKER)

Spinnaker software is the focus of this forum.

Stac Electronics Forum (GO STACKER)

Stac Electronics, the Data Compression Company, offers this forum for users of its hardware and software. Primary sysop is Keith Dunlea (75300,2755).

Standard Microsystem Forum (GO SMC)

This forum is devoted to the topics of Ethernet, Arcnet, Token-Ring, and Network Management, both hardware and software issues.

Symantec Forums (GO SYMANTEC)

Symantec Applications Forum (GO SYMFORUM) is devoted to the discussion of Symantec's software products. Primary sysop is Bill Hall (76707,14).

Symantec/Norton Forum (GO NORUTL) is for discussion of all Symantec utility products including all Peter Norton products as well as the Symantec utilities for the Macintosh and Symantec Anti-Virus. Hall is primary sysop for this forum as well.

Tandy Users Network (GO TANDYNET)

The Tandy Users Network is composed of five forums and a newsletter from the Tandy Corp.

- Color Computer Forum (GO COCO) specializes in the TRS-80 Color Computer. Primary sysop is Wayne Day (76703,376).
- LDOS/TRSDOS 6 Forum (GO LDOS), sponsored by MISOSYS, INC., is for users of MISOSYS and Logical Systems products. These include LDOS 5 for the Model 1, 3, and LOBO MAX80, TRSDOS 6 for the TRS-80 Model 4/4P/4D, and many related products. Primary sysop is Joe Kyle-DiPietropaolo (76703,437).
- Model 100/Portables Forum (GO M100SIG), is a forum intended for the users of the TRS-80 Model 100, Tandy 200, NEC portables, Olivetti M-10, Tandy 600, and compatible portables. Primary sysop is Wayne Day (76703,376).
- OS-9 Forum (GO OS9) is the place for exchange of information and software amongst users of the multiuser, multitasking OS-9 Operating System available for most 6809 and 68000 computers. Primary sysop is Wayne Day (76703,376).
- Tandy Professional Forum (GO TRS80PRO) is dedicated to the Tandy Z-80, 8088, and 68000 microcomputers in their various forms and shapes. Primary sysop is Wayne Day (76703,376).
- Tandy Corporation Newsletter (GO TRS-1) is a newsletter display area from the Tandy Corporation. It includes news from Tandy, customer service and feedback, and the Tandy User Group Newsletter.

TapCIS Forum (GO TAPCIS)

This is the forum for helping users make the most out of the capabilities of TapCIS, the automated program for utilizing CompuServe forums, libraries, and mail.

Telecommunications Forum (GO TELECO)

The Telecommunications Forum is devoted to topics ranging from which long distance service you may want to consider to advanced topics in telecommunications, such as local area networking and mainframe communications. The primary sysop is Marilyn DePaoli (76702,1626).

Thomas-Conrad Forum (GO TCCFORUM)

Thomas-Conrad technical support, the latest adapter drivers, network diagnostics software, product availability and information, and more are available here. Primary sysop is Mark Voisinet-Anderson (75300,3477).

Toshiba Computer Forum (GO TOSHIBA)

Toshiba computers and their uses are the themes of this forum. Product support specialists from Toshiba America are in the forum to answer your questions. Primary sysop is Jim Rohrer (76702,1300).

UK Computer Shopper Forum (GO UKSHOPPER)

The Computer Shopper UK forum is designed to complement the magazine of the same name.

UK Computing Forum (GO UKCOMPUTING)

This is another CompuServe Europe forum offering discussion of computing in Great Britain. Primary sysops are Steve Manners (70007,4737) and Andy Johnson (75300,1504).

UK Shareware Publishing Forum (GO UKSHARE)

The forum is shareware for the PC and compatibles from Shareware Publishing of Devon, England. Primary sysop is Steve Townsley (70007,4725).

Unix Forum (GO UNIXFORUM)

This is the place for users to discuss UNIX-related issues and exchange UNIX-related code, and find a list of some of the relevant issues.

UserLand Software Forum (GO USERLAND)

The developer and publisher of the Frontier scripting system for the Macintosh is in charge of this forum. Dave Winer (76244,120) co-author of Frontier and president/founder of UserLand Software is primary sysop.

Ventura Software Forum (GO VENTURA)

Managed by Ventura Software Inc., the forum focuses on the products of Ventura Software Inc. Primary sysop is Karl Anthony (76702,1206).

Wolfram Research Forum (GO WOLFRAM)

Use this forum to exchange information, make contacts, share resources, and solutions to problems. Primary sysop is Bruce Pea (76702,1400).

WordPerfect Services (GO WORDPERFECT)

This display area, concentrating on the most popular word processing program in the world, offers the following two WordPerfect related forums:

- WordPerfect Customer Support Forum (WPCS) managed by WordPerfect's Customer Support Department provides an alternative means of support to users who prefer to or need to communicate electronically with WordPerfect Corporation.

- WordPerfect Users Forum (WPUSERS), a private company independent of WordPerfect Corporation.

WordStar Forum (GO WORDSTAR)

Operated by WordStar International Corporation, the forum provides help, information, and supplemental material to you, the users of WordStar.

Zenith Data Systems Forum (GO ZENITH)

This forum is the on-line center for users of Zenith Data Systems computer products and the hardware and software used with them. Joseph Katz (76703,662) is primary sysop.

ZiffNet (GO ZIFFNET)

This surcharged area (you can read about the surcharges before you enter), sponsored by Ziff-Davis Publishing, offers the following:

- Ziff Buyers' Market — a buyers' service with current specs, prices, and ordering information on more than 10,000 products.
- ZiffNet Product Reviews Index and Product Awards Listings.
- Weekly computer industry news from *PC Week* and *MacWEEK*.
- ZiffNet Support forum.
- ZiffNet/Mac Buyer's Guide — information on over 3,000 Macintosh products.
- ZiffNet/Mac's Technical Support Database.
- MacUser/MacWEEK Index.
- All member support databases — Help, ZiffNet Highlights, and others.
- Plus, you get a subscription to *ZiffNet Threads*, a newsletter full of hints, tips, and other valuable information for using ZiffNet, ZEUS, and ZiffNet/Mac.

7

News, Weather, and Related Services

In this chapter...

When Cathy Conroy needed a new business telephone line, she had it installed in the kitchen of her Gaithersburg, Maryland, home.

"Hey, lady, you sure *this* is where you want the line?" the installer asked.

Oh, yes, she was sure. As a full-time freelance writer, she had an office elsewhere in the house, complete with a desk and desktop computer. But, she found that from the kitchen table she had a view of half the neighborhood. From there she knew what children were visiting in her home at any moment and she was within earshot of the first call of "Mom!" from her own kids. At the same time, with her laptop attached to that new phone line, she could also be *at work* in a matter of seconds. Sometimes speed is critical to her job, because Cathy Conroy is among a new wave of electronic journalists who cover the news for the electronic community.

Conroy is a regular contributor to *Online Today*, CompuServe's own electronic daily publication that has been providing the news to on-line readers for nearly 10 years now. Every day, Cathy joins others on a staff of freelance writers and editors around the country who monitor and present the computer-related news from around the world. These are reporters without a newsroom who have worked together for almost a decade, though most have never met face to face; their communications with each other and with their editors is by electronic mail.

Online Today is dependable. Seven days a week, just like clockwork, the publication provides new reports on its menus. The editors' and writers' devotion to this routine has made their publication one of CompuServe's more popular features. Thousands of users have come to rely on *Online Today* for the first reports of developments in the on-line world and the computer industry. However, it is the breaks in routine reporting that provide the biggest challenges; it is in the emergencies that *Online Today* shines brightest.

Chapter 4 told the story of how response to the 1989 California earthquake inspired the creation of a special Earthquake Forum. *Online Today* played an important part in supporting that forum by reporting on activities on-line so subscribers would know about the special forum, and by keeping people updated on relief efforts.

Cathy Conroy played a primary role in this coverage. "I worked non-stop from 9:00 a.m. until about midnight," she recalled. "As I finished one article, something else would happen, and I would write another story. Editors and writers were sending me information from around the world. We were constantly messaging one another so no one duplicated anyone else's efforts. The messages also contained information that would offer help to different writers."

Online Today (OLT) is produced by many of the same editors and writers who produce the monthly *CompuServe Magazine*. The on-line publication, which can be reached by entering GO ONLINE at a command prompt, provides daily stories from the computer world as well as reviews of hardware, software, and books, reports from the activities around the system, and more. Like many publications, *Online Today* is composed of a number of separate sections, including the latest news about the happenings in the system's forums and conferences as well as daily news from the computer industry as a whole.

OLT's loyal readers have come to think of it as CompuServe's "hometown" paper, locally owned and operated. But, like any metropolis, CompuServe has more than one paper on its newsstands. This chapter focuses on the system's formidable resources for news, as provided by the world's top news wires and newspapers. It introduces you to "electronic clipping folders" which enable you to capture future stories of interest as well as news databases to search for news of the recent past.

Executive News Service (GO ENS)

The Executive News Service provides access to current news from various resources, as many as 4,000 fresh stories each day, including reports from:

- The Associated Press (national, Washington, sports, and business).
- United Press International (national, regional, sports, business).
- Today's *Washington Post* (selected articles).
- OTC NewsAlert (press releases from companies).
- Reuters (world, sports, European, and financial news).

ENS, which is a surcharged feature ($15 an hour), can automatically save any stories containing keywords about subjects that you want to follow in personalized electronic *clip folders*. In that way, ENS works around the clock, even when you are not on-line, instantly clipping stories and offering them to you the next time you visit the feature. You may browse ENS's wires yourself in "real-time" as well as search for recent stories about specific companies and corporations.

To use ENS, you must first sign up for the Executive Option, which, as you learned in Chapter 2, provides a number of additional services. (For more details, enter GO EXECUTIVE.) Once signed up, you may use the news feature by entering GO ENS, which displays an introductory menu, like this:

```
Executive News Svc. ($)

1   Introduction to ENS
2   Review Current News
3   Search by Ticker

4   Create/Change/Delete a Personal Folder (E)
```

There are three ways to use ENS:

1. Search for news from specific companies.
2. Browse current news from the various resources.
3. Collect future stories in clipping folders.

Search by Ticker

Search by Ticker gives you access to the hot business news from the previous 24 hours, located by stock market ticker symbols. Selecting it causes the system to prompt for "Ticker:" Enter the appropriate letters, such as AAPL for Apple

Computer Inc. or MSFT for Microsoft Corp., and the system compiles a menu of article titles from Reuters' Financial Report and OTC NewsAlert. Select each article by number from the menu to read the full text of the story. If your corporation of interest has not made the news in the last 24 hours, the system tells you that no stories were found. Ticker symbols may be searched on CompuServe by company name by selecting GO LOOKUP.

Browsing

When Browsing, the system prompts you to identify the wires you wish to scan, using a menu listing the available wires. The Associated Press offers its national and world news wires, as well as its sports and financial wires. United Press International provides national, business, sports, and regional wires. Reuters is a British wire service with financial reports of a decidedly international bent. OTC NewsAlert is a business wire concentrating on news of companies traded over-the-counter in the stock market. *The Washington Post*, the larger newspaper in the nation's capital, brings on-line selected stories from that morning's editions. (And, of course, look for this menu to change as ENS adds new resources.)

After you have entered your selection or selections (you may choose more than one, separating the numbers with commas), ENS finds the stories you have requested and asks how you want to see them, prompting with a menu of options to:

- Scan by story titles, a word or two, or perhaps a screen line about each one; you then select the stories you wish to read.

- Scan by story leads, which shows you more information, the opening three lines of each story ("leads"), and prompts for the numbers of the ones you want to read.

- Read all stories. This option skips the intermediate step by displaying ("Read") the text of each story already found.

Browsing or searching by ticker symbol is fine for some applications, but that is not where ENS shines. What this feature does best is its third method of news gathering: Electronic Clipping Folders.

Folders

Suppose election fever has hit your household and you want ENS to follow news of your favorite candidates. You may set up a folder to capture election news as it is transmitted over the various wires. The stories then stay in the folders until your next visit to the ENS.

Creating a Folder

To create a folder, start by selecting the Create/Change/Delete a Folder option from the main ENS menu. The system displays a folder maintenance menu that includes options to:

1. Create a Clipping Folder.
2. Change a Folder.
3. Delete a Folder.
4. (And/Or) List a Folder.

After you choose the "Create a Clipping Folder" option, the system asks you to name the folder, using up to 10 characters, such as ELECTIONS. Next, the system asks for a "Folder Expiration Date (MM/DD/YY):" How long do you want the folder to exist? Enter the date in the common numbers/slashes format, as in 11/30/94. A folder may exist up to one year, (but that date can be extended with a revision option illustrated at the end of this section). After that, you are prompted for "Number of days to retain clipped stories." If you plan to check in every other day, enter 2.

News Wires

Now ENS focuses on the most important part of the work — choosing the news resources and subjects to clip — by starting with a menu which lists the available wires (such as "AP US and World," "AP Sports," "UPI Financial," "The Washington Post"). You may select a single wire or more than one; enter the numbers separated by commas, such as 1,4,5,7.

Keywords

Next ENS prompts for up to seven keywords or phrases, such as the candidates' names. Phrases may be up to 80 characters long and may be enclosed in parentheses (LEAGUE OF WOMEN VOTERS). Also, some powerful commands are available for linking them.

- An asterisk (*) is a wildcard, so VOT* clips stories containing "vote," "votes," "voters," and so on.
- You may also qualify your phrase with a plus sign (+) to require that two or more words or phrases be clipped. This means "AND" as in SMITH+VOTERS and SMITH+ELECTION.
- To indicate that a story should be clipped if it contains one keyword but *not* another, use a minus sign (–), such as ELECTION–NATIONAL.
- To clip a story that matches any of two or more phrases, use the I sign to mean OR, as in ELECTION I VOTE I RUN-OFF.

Actually, sophisticated commands for narrowing and broadening keywords and phrases in ENS clipping folders can be mixed and matched in some interesting ways, using parentheses to enclose complex concepts. Some examples that CompuServe has offered on-line are:

- OHIO ST* + FOOTBALL finds stories containing both the phrase Ohio St *and* the word football.

- MERRILL LYNCH – (DAILY TREASURY INDEX | TELERATE) lets you follow Merrill Lynch announcements, such as initial public offerings it is underwriting and corporate news on itself, but *not* daily reports on its bond index.

- MERRILL LYNCH – (CAPITAL MARKETS) finds stories on Merrill Lynch but *not* those regarding the initial public offerings it is underwriting.

- APPLE + COMPUT* finds any story containing both the word Apple *and* any variation of compute. Since both combinations are required, it avoids stories dealing with apple growers and those about computers other than Apple's computers.

- COMPUT* + (SECUR* | CRIME | PRIVACY) finds stories containing variations of the word compute, *and* one *or* more of the words secur*, crime, and privacy.

- COMPUT* + (VIRUS – DISEASE) finds stories containing variations of the word compute *and* the word virus, but *not* the word disease.

Using the Folders

After you have answered all the questions, the system stores the ELECTIONS folder and is ready to go to work. From now until the folder's expiration date, ENS monitors the wires and news categories you have specified, setting aside any stories that contain at least one of your keywords or phrases. You may read the clipped news any time you are on-line by entering GO ENS, because the system automatically revises its main ENS menu to add new options such as, "Review folder ELECTIONS." Selecting a folder option causes the system to give you a menu from which you may scan and/or read your clipped stories.

Revising and Deleting

You may revise or delete a folder by choosing the "Create/Change/Delete" option on the main ENS menu. The option provides an opportunity to add and delete key phrases, news wires, and categories. Note the revision option also lets you change the expiration date and the retention days.

ENS With CIM

The CompuServe Information Manager software provides a little extra flexibility in using ENS. With CIM, the feature is directly accessible from the Services pull-down menu. Selecting **Executive News** from the Services menu causes

CIM to connect to CompuServe (if you are not already connected) and to display a revised menu bar with two new options:

- **Folders**, which lets you create, maintain, and delete your clipping folders.
- **Stories**, which lets you look at reports from the news wires, including those collected in your electronic folders, as well as stories from the current wires retrieved by company stock symbols.

Stories

The Stories menu provides options to access:

- **Clipping folders**: The ones you create for specific types of reports. Selecting it displays a list of your folders by name and the number of stories currently in each. A bar cursor may be moved up and down to highlight a folder. Action buttons elsewhere on the screen allow you to **Browse**, or **Search** by keyword, the stories in the highlighted folder.
- **Public folders**, including current and late breaking news from the various wires. Again, action buttons let you **Browse** or **Search** the folder. Another option gets you search for news from a specific company by its ticker symbol.

When **Brows**ing either group of folders you are shown a display with various action buttons for each highlighted story on the list. You may:

Get it, that is, read it immediately.

Preview it — see the first few lines.

Mark it for later retrieval from the Filing Cabinet. Stories marked this way then may be fetched with the **Retrieve Stories** option.

Delete it from a personal clipping folder. (Obviously, you cannot delete stories from public folders.)

OK, to discontinue the browse and return to the previous menu.

When **Search**ing for stories in the folders, you are prompted with a dialog box with which you may specify the wire to search in the folder as well as:

- Search on company ticker, headline, lead, or text.
- Keywords.
- Dates.

Stories found in the folder may be reviewed immediately or saved in the Filing Cabinet.

Folders

Selecting the CIM Folders option from the main ENS menu bar produces a pull-down menu with new options — Create, Update, Delete, and Clear —

that allow you to set up and maintain your clipping folders through a dialog box. This form lets you specify a folder name, expiration date, retention time, wires to be scanned, and keywords to search for.

NewsGrid (GO NewsGrid)

NewsGrid is a *non*-surcharged news feature provided by Comtex Scientific Corporation of Stamford, Connecticut. Compiled from major wire services throughout the world, the feature is searchable, and there is a main menu entry that provides detailed tips on how to search it:

```
NewsGrid (sm)

    1   US/World Headline News
    2   US Business Headline News
    3   World Business Headline News

    4   Market Update

    5   Search by Keyword
    6   How to use NewsGrid

A product of Comtex Scientific Corp.
```

Each business day, NewsGrid's editors capture thousands of stories from major wire services around the world, including United Press International, PR Newswire, Deutsche Presse-Agentur (Germany), Pacific Rim News (Japan), Itar/Tass (Russia), Xinhua (China), and more. During business hours, a new story is added to the database about every two minutes.

Ways to Use NewsGrid

Like the Executive News Service, NewsGrid offers more than one way to view its reports:

- By scanning the headlines of stories the editors have selected.
- By searching the current database with a keyword.

Scanning

The top options on the main NewsGrid menu—US/World headline news and US and World business headline news—represent the first of the two viewing approaches. The headline news is updated continuously throughout the day as news breaks. Stories are prioritized by NewsGrid editors. Also, as stories fall off the Headline News lists, they remain available in the keyword-search database for seven days.

Another option on the main menu—Market Update—represents a variation on the headline feature. Each market update story appears on a regular basis, some updated every half hour, others updated daily, weekly, monthly, or quarterly. Only the most current stories are available in the Market Update section, with all Market Update stories from the past seven days available in the Keyword Search database. If you select the option from the main menu, the system prompts you to narrow your request by choosing NYSE, AMEX, OTC, Bonds, Currency, Commodities, etc., from a menu.

Searching

NewsGrid's most powerful feature is its searching capability. It allows you to quickly locate stories on topics of interest to you. As noted, all NewsGrid stories, including headline and market update stories for the previous seven days, are in the keyword-search database. NewsGrid editors assign each story 5 to 10 keywords. If you entered a keyword that matches one assigned by an editor, that story is included in the list of stories found.

NewsGrid automatically searches for keywords that begin with the string of letters you specified. This is indicated by an asterisk (*) succeeding the word when it is re-displayed to you. To instruct NewsGrid to match only on the exact word or string you specified, end your keyword with an exclamation point. If you enter CAT at the search prompt, the system looks for keywords that *begin* with those three letters; if you enter CAT!, it looks only for the keyword "cat."

Keywords most often used by NewsGrid editors are proper names (Clinton, Bush), country names (USA, Israel), regions of the world (Middle East, Caribbean), industry names (financial services, autos), company names (Sony Corp., Eastman Kodak Co.), ticker symbols (IBM, GM), or any of the following category-type words: sports (or the name of a particular sport), feature, election, capitol (for congressional stories), annual report, earnings, market, weather. Ordinary words may be used, but they occur less frequently.

Industry Groups

In terms of industry groups, NewsGrid uses these keywords:

advertising	banking	business services
aerospace	beverages	chemicals
agriculture	biotechnology	computers
autos	broadcasting	construction
aviation	building material	consumer products

defense contracting	machinery	real estate
education	metals	restaurants
electronic publishing	mining	retail
electronics	nuclear energy	rubber
entertainment	office equipment	ship building
environmental service	personal care	telecommunications
financial services	petroleum products	textiles
food	pharmaceuticals	tobacco
forestry products	photography	toys
freight	plastics	travel services
health care	precious metals	trucks
industrial products	publishing	utilities
insurance	railroads	

Countries

For countries, NewsGrid uses these keywords:

Africa: Algeria, Angola, Benin, Botswana, Burundi, Cameroon, Cape Verde, Central African Republic, Chad, Comoros, Congo, Djibouti, Egypt, Equatorial Guinea, Ethiopia, Gabon, Gambia, Ghana, Guinea, Guinea Bissau, Ivory Coast, Kenya, Lesotho, Liberia, Libya, Madagascar, Malawi, Mali, Mauritania, Mauritius, Morocco, Mozambique, Nambia, Niger, Nigeria, Principe, Reunion, Rwanda, Sao Tome, Senegal, Seychelles, Sierra Leone, Somalia, South Africa, Sudan, Swaziland, Tanzania, Togo, Tunisia, Uganda, Upper Volta, Western Sahara, Zaire, Zambia and Zimbabwe.

Asia: Afghanistan, Bangladesh, Bhutan, Burma, Cambodia, China, Hong Kong, India, Japan, Kampuchea, Laos, Macau, Maldives, Mongolia, Nepal, North Korea, Pakistan, Singapore, South Korea, Sri Lanka, Taiwan, Thailand and Vietnam.

Caribbean: Antigua, Aruba, Bahamas, Barbados, Barbuda, Cuba, Dominica, Dominican Republic, Grenada, Guadeloupe, Haiti, Jamaica, Martinique, Netherland Antilles, Puerto Rico, St. Lucia, Trinidad, Tobago and Virgin Islands.

Central America: Belize, Costa Rica, El Salvador, Guatemala, Honduras, Nicaragua and Panama.

Europe: Albania, Austria, Belgium, Bulgaria, Czech Republic, Slovakia, Denmark, Finland, France, Greece, Greenland, Hungary, Iceland, Ireland, Italy, Liechtenstein, Luxembourg, Malta, Netherlands, Norway, Poland, Portugal, Romania, Spain, Sweden, Switzerland, United Kingdom, Germany, Yugoslavia, Serbia, Bosnia, Russia, Ukraine, Latvia, Lithusania, Estonia, Belarus, Armania, George, Uzbekistan, Slovenia, Turkmenistan, Kazakhstan, Azerbaijan, Kyrgyzstan, Crotia, Macedonia.

Middle East: Bahrain, Cyprus, Iran, Iraq, Israel, Jordan, Kuwait, Lebanon, North Yemen, Oman, Qatar, Saudi Arabia, South Yemen, Syria, and Turkey.

North America: Canada, Mexico, and USA.

Pacific region: Australia, Borneo, Brunei, Cook Islands, East Timor, Fiji, French Polynesia, Indonesia, Kiribati, Malaysia, Nauru, New Zealand, Papua New, Philippines, Solomon Islands, Sunda Islands, Tuvalu, Vanuatu, and Samoa.

South America: Argentina, Bolivia, Brazil, Chile, Columbia, Ecuador, Falkland Islands, Guyana, Paraguay, Peru, Suriname, Uraguay, and Venezuela.

AP Online (GO APO)

The Associated Press, the nation's primary news wire service, has been a presence on CompuServe for more than a decade. In the early days of the Executive News Service, AP provided most of the reports; today it is still the primary information provider there. In addition to the surcharged ENS, the news service also provides the non-surcharged AP Online, a specially edited report, usually containing between 250 and 300 stories that make up the top national, international, Washington, financial, and sports news of the day, available from a menu:

```
AP Online

 1   Latest News-Updated Hourly
 2   Weather
 3   Sports
 4   National
 5   Washington
 6   World
 7   Political
 8   Entertainment
 9   Business News
10   Wall Street
11   Dow Jones Average
12   Feature News/Today in History
13   Science & Health
```

One valuable option — "Latest News–Updated Hourly"— offers summaries of the top stories of the hour. The feature is transmitted around the clock every day.

Also, sports fans take note. If you press RETURN at APO's main menu, you will be taken to a second menu for news stories about assorted sports, including baseball, football, basketball, hockey, soccer, tennis, golf, college, and scoreboards.

The Business Wire (GO TBW)

Throughout each business day, the Business Wire brings on-line press releases, news articles, and other information from the world of business. Information on hundreds of different companies is transmitted daily.

Hollywood Hotline (GO HOLLYWOOD)

This is a daily collection of news items from the entertainment world, including TV, film, stage, and recordings. Two other popular news-like features from the entertainment world are:

1. **Soap Opera Summaries** (GO SOAPS), which offers daily summaries, news of primetime soaps, news and gossip from the industry, and related features.
2. **Hollywood Hotline's Movie Reviews** (GO MOVIES) provides reviews of current movies and picks hits.

Other News Services

CompuServe offers the Newspaper Library database that provides surcharged access to the full text of articles searched from more than 40 newspapers across the country. This feature is covered in Chapter 9, along with other *gateway* services.

Forums that Cover News and Current Events

Regardless of the fears of some that electronic communications are a threat to the printed word, some publications have set up on-line extensions, particularly computer- and science-related magazines.

Broadcasters and Engineers (GO BPFORUM)

John Hoffman, 76703,1036, a broadcast engineer at the NBC Television Network in New York, runs the Broadcast Professionals Forum and presents an electronic magazine called *InCue OnLine*. The forum is open to individuals and companies involved in radio, television, cable television, professional audio and video communications, and so on. It also provides on-line services for two professional organizations, the Audio Engineering Society, and the Society of Broadcast Engineers.

Journalists and Writers

Journalists and writers have a number of forums to serve them.

- Journalism Forum (GO JFORUM) was established by Jim Cameron, 76703,3010, who is president of Cameron Communications, Inc., a Connecticut-based consulting firm specializing in radio news and program syndication. The forum is designed to serve professional journalists, those in related fields, and students considering careers in the profession.

- Literary Forum (GO LITFORUM) is an information exchange for writers of fiction, poetry, and non-fiction. It is open to working writers and aspirants alike. The primary sysop is CompuServe veteran, Alex Krislov, 76703,243, of Cleveland, Ohio.

- Public Relations and Marketing Forum (GO PRSIG) began in January 1984 as a medium for electronic dialogue between professional publicists (as well as students) in the communications field. The founder is primary sysop Ron Solberg, 76703,575, who owns and operates his own Chicago area public relations agency. He has more than twenty years experience in the public relations industry.

- Florida Today Newslink (GO FLATODAY) is operated by Florida Today newspaper as a new way for newspapers to relate to readers. The forum has a special interest in the space program and in all Florida-related issues. It is managed by Kristen Zimman, 76711,1111, and Mark Decotis, 71333,1616.

- The Global Crisis Forum (GO CRISIS) is devoted to discussing the world's hot spots. On-line pro Shel Hall, 76701,103, is the primary sysop. He was the founder of Crosstalk Communications, and was a sysop with Don Watkins in the Earthquake Forum (discussed in Chapter 4) as well as in the Persian Gulf Crisis Forum and the Hurricane Andrew Forum. He currently also runs the Automobile Forum (GO CARS).

And Now a Word from Our Weather Bureau

Sometimes weather is news too; and CompuServe has an on-line around-the-clock weather feature to help get forecasts for your own region, as well as for virtually anywhere else in the country, and around the world. And, if you have a computer equipped with a compatible graphics card, the system can draw a variety of weather maps right on your screen.

Weather in an Instant

When you are on CompuServe, weather information is never more than a few keystrokes away.

- If you are a non-CIM user, you can enter the command WEATHER <RETURN> at any prompt on the system. CompuServe responds by providing you with the latest forecast for your region.
- If you are a CIM user, you can select the **Weather** option from the Services menu and the software prompts you to indicate whether you want:

    a. A *local* forecast (for your present location).

    b. A forecast for a different *city*. The same dialog box has data entry lines for state/province and country. Note that you can request forecasts for cities around the world, as well as those inside the US.

    c. A forecast for a *station* (letting you indicate with a three-letter weather reporting station code).

CIM then goes on-line (if you are not already connected) and fetches the requested forecast.

More Weather

Besides these quick, back-pocket forecasts, CompuServe provides other more extensive weather information, including on-screen weather maps. To reach them through the CompuServe Weather feature:

- If you are a CIM user, select the Go . . . option and specify WEATHER in the resulting dialog box).
- If you are a non-CIM user, enter GO WEATHER. The system then will ask about the graphics capability of your computer, prompting you with a menu of types of graphics supported. Since CompuServe supplies color and black-and-white versions of its weather maps, it needs to know what you can see.

A subsequent dialog box or menu lets you specify a location. This can be an international city as well as a US city, since CompuServe provides forecasts for some 85 cities abroad. Now, you may view a variety of reports, including a short-term forecast, a state extended forecast, a severe weather alert, the precipitation probability, a regional summary, the daily climatological report, the sports and recreation forecast, or the marine forecast. (Not all reports are available for all locations.) If you are using the CIM software, select the options you want to see and choose the **View** option to see the reports.

Weather Maps

The GO WEATHER area also has options that allow you to see on-line weather maps. These are automatically shown to you in high-resolution graphics and they may be retrieved for off-line viewing later. Obviously, successful viewing depends on the graphic capabilities of your system. If you are using CIM, the program itself makes screen adjustments for best viewing.

Among the maps available:

- The latest **radar map**, which shows precipitation measured by echo intensities recorded at radar stations. Each time a map is created, information from radar locations across the country is gathered to create a comprehensive graphic. Each echo intensity is shown as either solid white or shaded, or in a different color if viewed on a color monitor. The upper left corner of the map shows the maximum and minimum observation times of the radar reports used to make the map.

- **Depiction maps**, for which the system takes information from surface reports to create a graphic representation of flight conditions throughout the United States. Every 15 minutes a new map is created, and a range of the report times used for that map is shown after the menu selection.

- A **Temperature map**, updated around the clock, showing the current temperature bands across the country.

- **Satellite maps** for the continental US and the Pacific, showing the current cloud formations and the high and low pressure fronts.

- About a dozen **Accu-Weather maps** for the US, including Current Weather for the nation, Tomorrow's Weather, the 48-Hour Weather forecast, the Current Temperatures, Tonight's Lows, Tomorrow's Highs, and the Wake-Up Weather Maps for the Northeast, Southeast, North Central, South Central, Northwest, and Southwest.

Note When you specify a city outside the US, a smaller selection of weather maps is available. Usually they are limited to the current satellite map, the current weather conditions, and the forecast for the next day. Note, too, that on non-US maps, temperatures are often reported in Celsius rather than the Fahrenheit readings listed on US weather maps.

8

Investing and Finance

In this chapter...

A medium, by definition, has no voice and purpose of its own. Television, radio, film, print, and other media take on the objectives and personality of each communicator who uses them. This is especially true with the new media. Each of us sees something different when we come to CompuServe: a chance for fresh experiences, amusements of a kind once reserved for sci-fi and fantasy, a global platform for self-expression, or light-speed tools for support of all kinds of informational quests.

When Chuck Spear looked into this same magic mirror a decade ago, he saw a business opportunity, a chance to do what he had dreamed of for years: to bring computers and instant automation to individual investors. Spear established one of the first discount brokerage houses to reside in a different kind of business district, the downtown electronic community.

Spear, who started his career as an attorney with a major Chicago bank, had observed the inefficiency of traditional stock brokerages. In every half dozen incoming calls, only one would be a trade, with the rest seeking only stock quotes or account information. Not only was the resulting phone tag a major irritant to customers dispatched with the Hold button, but commissions also had to increase to cover the high cost of providing all that inconvenience.

The alternative Spear envisioned — one of those "simple" ideas that always turn out to be so revolutionary — was to put the power of administering and monitoring an account in the hands of the person who owned it, enabling the owner to use a personal computer at home or the office to follow the market. The no-commission Spear Securities Inc. was launched in the mid-1980s, originally on an information service called The Source. When that McLean, Virginia, system ceased operation about five years ago, Spear moved his service uptown to CompuServe, where he could reach five times as many potential customers. Today the feature — now called Spear Rees and Company — is one of several electronic brokerages and is among the scores of financial resources and services this chapter covers.

The original Spear brokerage service has diversified over the years, but Chuck Spear says he hasn't forgotten his on-line roots. Electronic users not only continue to account for a healthy percentage of the business, but they also serve to remind the company of a goal. Not long ago, Spear told a writer with *CompuServe Magazine* about an Australian investor who described himself as being "in the middle of nowhere." On-line brokerage was his way of keeping on top of the market.

"The point was well made," Spear observed. "If you're removed from information sources, this is tremendous."

Another story illustrates that distance is not the only way someone can be isolated in modern society. Spear recalled that one time a group of people came into his Glendale, California offices and handed his receptionist a note requesting to see him. She asked them a question but they didn't respond. The visitors were deaf, but active users of Chuck Spear's on-line service. They had come to thank him.

Overview of the Financial Features

Not so long ago, the professional financial reports and analyses that CompuServe puts at your fingertips were reserved for the wizards of Wall Street. These decision-making tools were the very factors that made today's Wall Street giants of finance. Until recently, only the biggest investment banking houses could afford the kinds of databases that you find in the part of the system covered in this chapter:

- Stock quotes, available on a 20-minute delayed basis for 10,000 securities traded on the New York, American, Philadelphia, Boston, and National exchanges, as well as over-the-counter. Price and volume information are reported as a composite of the exchanges.

- Historical quotes, the pricing history on 46,000 stocks, bonds, warrants, and mutual funds available on a daily basis, dating from 12 years back, up to the present. Dividend and interest payment history for these issues is available from January 1, 1968 to the present. Pricing history for options begins with the day the option starts trading and remains in the database for three to four weeks after it expires. Exchanges covered include NYSE, AMEX, Philadelphia, National, Boston, Toronto, and Montreal, as well as over-the-counter.

- Forecasts from the professionals of corporate earnings and other key financial items for three to five years in the future. Coverage includes some 1,800 companies and 80 industry aggregates. Also available are consensus forecasts for the current and next fiscal years.

- Public company data, including expert evaluations, names of their officers, products and services available, credit ratings, and their affiliations with other companies.

With information like this, the individual investor can compete on the same level with those who prowl the canyons of Wall Street and make their living in high finance.

Some financial features are included in the standard, basic pricing plans; many additional money features are available as extended services in the "pay-as-you-go" metered area of the system.

Quick Quotes

The latest trading information for stocks, equities, options, and market indicators is one of three money options included in CompuServe's basic services package.

Quotes with CIM

If you use the CompuServe Information Manager, you'll find it is as easy to get stock information as selecting the "Quotes…" option on the Services pull-down menu. Choosing it opens the dialog box.

A few ticker symbols are initially supplied with the program, but you may add as many as you like. (Only ticker symbols may be used, not CUSIP numbers or company names.) If you don't know the ticker symbol for an issue, you may Go… LOOKUP (discussed later in this chapter).

To see the latest quotes for all the symbols on the list, select the **Get All** option. The displayed report lists the ticker symbol, volume traded, high and low price, the most recent (or last) price of the day, the change from the previous day, and the time or date the report was updated.

If you check Quotes during a trading day, the Update column will probably list a time; major exchanges require that trading information be delayed at least 15 minutes, so the time will usually be at least 15 minutes behind the current time of day.

If you check a quote on a non-trading day (weekend or holiday) or in the evening after an exchange has closed, you will see a date. The "Change" column reflects the change from the previous day's last trading price. "High" is the highest price of the day for the stock, while "Low" is the lowest.

More About the Dialog Box

The dialog box provides the following options:

- You may see a specific issue by highlighting that ticker symbol in the box and selecting the **Get** option. The Apple Macintosh version lets you highlight multiple tickers by holding down the OPTION key and clicking on to each one before selecting Get; the IBM version also lets you select more than one ticker by providing an additional **Mark** option that may be used before the Get.
- To include a new stock ticker in the field at the left, choose the **Add** option and enter the symbol.
- To remove a ticker symbol, highlight it, and select the **Remove** option.

Portfolio Report Built into CIM

Besides instant stock quotes, CompuServe Information Manager includes a built-in Portfolio Report option accessible from the Services pull-down menu. It allows you to maintain a list of stocks on your disk. From that list, you may retrieve a quick report on the current value of the stocks and their profit or loss since your purchase of them. Selected from the Services menu, Portfolio Report displays a dialog box that displays the symbols for the securities in the portfolio. Action buttons elsewhere on the screen include:

Report causes CompuServe to seek the latest values of the stocks listed.

Add lets you put more symbols in the portfolio.

Edit lets you change the information on-file for the highlighted stock.

Delete removes the highlighted stock from the portfolio.

Cancel discontinues the operation and removes the display from the screen.

Add and Edit

Selecting the Add button causes the program to display a dialog box that lets you add a security. It prompts for a symbol, the number of shares you own, the value per share at the time of purchase, and the date of purchase.

Selecting Edit from the action buttons produces a similar display with which you may change current information on file.

Report

When you select Report, CIM logs in (if you are not already on-line) and collects the current information on each issue in your collection. When it is done, it displays a report which includes the data for each issue as well as the total value of the portfolio and the amount of the change since the earliest purchase date.

Quick Quotes for Non-CIM Users

If you are using a general terminal program rather than CIM, you can visit the Quick Quote feature in two ways:

1. You can type GO QQUOTE to get the latest Dow Jones stock average report. At the prompt which follows, you may enter a ticker symbol or a series of ticker symbols separated by commas. If you don't know the ticker symbol, you may enter an asterisk followed by the beginning of a company name; a menu of possible choices will be displayed.

2. At nearly any ! prompt on the system, you can type QUOTE followed by a ticker symbol or a series of ticker symbols followed by commas to get the latest information about a security or a series of securities.

Company News

Incidentally, if there is an asterisk by one or more of the quotes, it means that there is current news about the company. At the next Issue: prompt, you may enter /CONEWS to go to a surcharged news area (discussed later) where the current news of that company or companies will be displayed.

Issue and Symbol Lookup

Besides Basic Quotes, the Issue and Symbol Lookup area is also included in CompuServe's standard, flat-fee pricing plan. These features enable you to determine what securities and indexes are covered in other securities databases and to access the symbols needed to make efficient use of most databases. The two areas for Basic Service subscribers include:

1. Search for Company Name, Ticker Symbol, and CUSIP (GO LOOKUP), which allows you to search by name, CUSIP number, ticker symbol, CNUM or SIC code, and list all the issues for a company you select. This service finds the ticker symbols or CUSIP numbers that you may use in other investment services.

2. Menu of Available Indexes (GO INDICATORS), which gives the ticker and CUSIP number for all the indexes included in the MicroQuote II database

along with the time period for which the index has data. Indexes are categorized into manageable groups designated by market/industry indexes, bonds/yields, exchange rates, volumes, advances and declines, and any issues that are new or don't fall into one of the other categories. Another option lets you list all the indexes (more than 700) without going through additional menus.

Lookup Options for Extended Financial Services

In addition to the services listed above, CompuServe offers the following among its extra-cost extended services.

- List Bonds for Company (GO BONDS), which displays all active bonds for a company. The report displays the ticker symbols, CUSIP numbers, issue descriptions, yield, and current selling price for each bond. In addition, a quality rating is provided, expressed by both *Standard and Poor's* and *Moody's*.
- Menu of Available Commodities (GO CSYMBOL), which covers the availability of such commodity groups as foods, grains, metals, financial, petroleum, fibers, currencies, and indexes. Access symbols, active contracts, exchange, where traded, and commodity description are shown for each commodity.

Mortgage Calculator

Another entry on the Money menu available as part of Basic Services is the Mortgage Calculator (GO MORTPAY).

You supply the basics in this on-line loan amortization program—the amount of the loan, the annual percentage rate, the number of years, and the number of payments per year.

The program responds by giving you the amount of each payment and offers to give you a display of the payment schedule, including the term, payment, interest, and principal paid in that payment, and the balance of the loan after that payment.

More Extended Financial Services

Quick stock quotes and the other financial features are all listed on a Money Matters/Markets menu. If you are using the CIM software, you can use the Browse option on the Services pull-down menu to see a list of the general CompuServe topics. If you are using a general terminal program, type GO MONEY to see the same main MONEY menu:

```
Money Matters   MONEY

BASIC FINANCIAL SERVICES
  1   Basic Quotes
  2   FundWatch Online By MoneyMagazine
  3   Issue/Symbol Lookup
  4   Mortgage Calculator
EXTENDED FINANCIAL SERVICES
  5   Market Quotes/Highlights
  6   Company Information
  7   Brokerage Services
  8   Earnings/Economic Projections
  9   Micro Software Interfaces
 10   Personal Finance/Insurance
 11   Financial Forums
 12   MicroQuote II ($)
 13   Business News
 14   Instructions/Fees
 15   Read Before Investing
  !
```

Market Quotes and Highlights (GO QUOTES)

Each of the main items on the money menu takes you to submenus. The Quick Quotes services illustrated earlier are part of the Market Quotes/Highlights option which takes you to the QUOTES submenu. Other features in that area are described in the following section.

Current Market Snapshot (GO SNAPSHOT)

The Current Market Snapshot is a surcharged area that gives a quick overview of current stock market trends by displaying key indicators in a one-page statistical report. The page contains highlights of current trading trends by displaying the highest, lowest, and latest values for the Dow Jones 30, Standard and Poor's 500, and NASDAQ Composite and London Gold Fix indexes. The strength of the trend is displayed in a summary of New York Stock Exchange activity, including percent change and number of shares traded in the current session. Advancing and declining issues with a separation into up and down volumes are presented. Snapshot also presents the value of the US dollar in Japanese yen, German Deutsche marks, and British pound sterling.

Historical Stock/Fund Pricing (GO SECURITIES)

For the serious investor, the history of how a security has performed is invaluable. Various surcharged databases, most updated overnight, offer historical looks at securities. A summary of the features follows.

Pricing History/1 Issue (GO PRICES)

This feature displays historical prices for a single issue by day, week, or month for more than 12 years. Data available includes CUSIP, exchange code, volume, high/ask, low/bid, and close/average for the given security. You have the option of choosing the beginning and ending dates or a number of time periods.

Multiple Issues/1 Day (GO QSHEET)

This one gives volume, close/average, high/ask, low/bid, and CUSIP number for several issues for a single trading day.

Price/Volume Graph (GO TREND)

This option provides both the traded price and the trading volume for the requested days, weeks, or months in chart form. Current earnings, price, dividend, and risk information for common stocks are displayed with a graph produced by CIM.

Dividends, Splits, and Bond Interest (GO DIVIDENDS)

This feature gives historical information about these events for an issue over a given period. Mutual fund distributions are also available. You specify the number of dividends you wish to view. The report includes the ex-date, record date, payment date, distribution type, and the rate or amount of each distribution.

Pricing Statistics (GO PRISTATS)

Pricing Statistics gives a quick look at the performance price and volume performance for an issue over a given period, including indications on whether the issue is trading closer to contemporary high or low prices. Also included are the current high/ask, low/bid, and close average as well as the highest high, the highest close, the lowest low, the lowest close, the close and volume, the beta factor, and the beta centile rank.

Detailed Issue Examination (GO EXAMINE)

This feature describes a single issue, including trading status, recent price, dividends, risk measures, and capitalization. For stocks, it shows the shares outstanding, 12-month earnings-per-share, beta factor, indicated annual dividend, and the dividend yield. For bonds, it displays the maturity date, bond rate, yield to maturity, interest payment history, and amount outstanding. Options information includes shares per contract, open interest, expiration date, and exercise price. The 52-week high and low prices are included for all securities.

Options Profile (GO OPRICE)

The Options Profile lists all options currently trading on a given common stock or market index. It includes put and call options trading on major US and Canadian exchanges, listing the name, closing price, pricing date, ticker symbol, and exchange code for the company. The exercise price and closing option price are displayed for each active option.

UK Historical Stock Pricing (GO UKPRICE)

This feature offers pricing information for over 5,000 UK equity issues and approximately 350 market indexes. Most securities in the service have data from as far back as July 1, 1990. The update times will vary. Generally, the service will offer updated UK equity issues by 9:00pm ET (2:00am, GMT). Market Indexes are updated by 12:00am ET (5:00am, GMT). Refer to the last update (which is displayed when you first enter the service) to ensure that prices have been updated prior to using the service.

Highlights for Previous Day (GO MARKET)

This feature analyzes the markets' most recent history. It includes a look at the New York Stock Exchange, American Stock Exchange, and over-the-counter markets, and the preparation of 19 different reports. Included are the most active stocks, the largest gainers and losers, stocks for which the price has risen or dropped over the past three, four, or five trading days, stocks with new six-month highs or lows, stocks with a low above yesterday's high or a high below yesterday's low, and stocks that have traded twice their average volume.

Commodity Markets (GO COMMODITIES)

The Commodities Markets option offers:

- Commodity Pricing (GO CPRICE) is the pricing history for one contract. It presents historical performance by day, week, or month for the requested commodity contract (or optionally the contract nearest delivery). Displayed are open, high, low, and setting prices along with volume and open interest. Also available are aggregate volume and open interest for some contracts for the requested commodity along with the cash market price for the commodity.

- News-A-Tron Market Reports (GO NAT-1), a service of News-a-tron Corp., provides news, analytical features, and cash quotes for selected commodities, market indexes, and financial instruments. The reports are provided daily.

- Agri-Commodities, Inc. (GO ACI-1) shows past issues of a weekly newsletter for the futures trader, featuring the TSF trading system, trading recommendations, a market overview, and tips on how to improve your trading performance. "Futures Focus" is available to subscribers every Friday. It is published by News-a-tron.

Mutual Fund Analysis (GO FUNDWATCH)

The highlight of this menu is Fundwatch Online by *Money Magazine* (GO FUNDWATCH) where you may retrieve details of a particular fund by entering its name or ticker symbol. You may also screen top performing funds by their return over the year-to-date, one-year annualized, three-year annualized, five-year annualized, ten-year annualized, the latest bull market, or the latest bear market. Also from the MONEYMAG menu, you may access current quotes (QQUOTE).

Investment Analysis Tools (GO ANALYSIS)

In addition to providing a menu gateway to Mutual Funds Analysis (see above), this area provides various menu-driven databases from MicroQuote II investment data and the screening capabilities of DISCLOSURE II to search for facts on thousands of companies, letting you comparison shop before buying. Additional options let you track purchased securities and gauge their success. All are surcharged and most are updated overnight. These investment analysis tools are described in the next sections.

Company Screening (GO COSCREEN)

Company Screening lets you search the DISCLOSURE II database by menu and produce a list of companies that meet your criteria based on your own guidelines. Selection categories include various growth rates and financial ratios as well as industry codes, state, total assets, book value, market value, annual sales, net income, cash flow, latest price, and so on.

Securities Screening (GO SCREEN)

With this feature you may select a type of investment, then screen the Micro-Quote II database to find securities that meet your demands. For example, if you were considering common stocks, you might search by price, earnings, dividends, risk, capitalization, recent highs and lows, exchange, and industry. Securities Screening is useful for buying into or selling short, and for picking bonds with specific maturity dates and yield targets.

Return Analysis (GO RETURN)

Return Analysis calculates the holding period and annual returns for as many as 30 requested securities. Because you enter the holding period, this product is useful for analyzing historical performances of specific issues, such as mutual funds in bull and bear markets.

Portfolio Valuation (GO PORT)

This feature finds the value of a portfolio for dates you select and displays unrealized gains and losses.

RateGram (GO RATEGRAM)

RateGram enables you to search for the best current rates for money market accounts, certificates of deposit, and money market mutual funds, and see predictions about future rates, among other things.

Company Information (GO COMPANY)

Of course, the more you know about a company, the better you are prepared to make a decision on an investment. This part of the system provides several areas in which you may get the latest information about all aspects of American and foreign corporations and businesses.

Company Analyzer (GO ANALYZER)

The Company Analyzer, a service available only with a subscription to the Executive Option, described in Chapter 2, offers a menu of the information available for the requested company along with the current market quote for the company's common stock. Options include price, volume, dividend history, a statistical analysis of the market performance, descriptive data from DISCLOSURE, Standard and Poor's projections from the Institutional Brokers Estimate System, financial statements, and ownership information from DISCLOSURE. You may also choose an options profile and a return analysis program.

S&P Online (GO S&P)

This service, from Standard and Poor's Corporation, offers data on about 5,600 companies, including business summaries, earnings outlooks, historical earnings, and dividends and summaries of product lines. All information is dated to indicate when it was last reviewed. The S&P Master List has buy recommendations for various investments. S&P investment "Ideas" present stocks that the analysts expect to out-perform the market over the next 12 months.

DISCLOSURE II (GO DISCLOSURE)

The DISCLOSURE II database, available only with the Executive Option, is a compilation of information from the 10K filings and other reports of publicly-owned companies that are required to be filed by the Securities and Exchange Commission. This includes the 10K management discussions, detailed financial statements, business segment data, five-year financial summaries, company name and address, a list of SEC filings, a business description, officers and directors, a list of subsidiaries and insider owners, institutional owners, and owners of five percent or more of the company's stock. It is updated every Sunday, with market prices updated every night.

CITIBANK's GLOBAL REPORT (GO CITIBANK)

Launched by Citibank in 1986, Global Report is an information resource for a number of large corporations worldwide because it integrates and organizes news and financial data from sources, allowing for quick and easy information retrieval. Global Report is updated around the clock from sources around the world. You'll find real-time foreign exchange and fixed-income rates from major market-makers worldwide, in-depth company profiles on more than 10,000 major US-traded firms (which may include up to six months of historical company news), country profiles, and more. Many screens are dynamically updated so that you can actually watch price and rate changes as they occur.

> **Note** To create these dynamic screens, Global Report uses special commands to display information on your screen (known as ANSI escape sequences). Many communication programs support these commands (such as the CompuServe Information Manager and other commercially available programs). If your software does not support these commands, you will notice that additional characters will be displayed.

D&B Dun's Market Identifiers (GO DUNS)

Dun's Market Identifiers is directory information on more than two million US establishments, public and private. Companies with more than five employees or with one million dollars or more in sales are included. The information on a company includes the name, address, and telephone number, and company characteristics such as sales figures, number of employees, corporate family relationships, and executive names. An individual reference may not include all of this information. You may retrieve records by entering the company name, geographic location, product or service, executive name, number of employees, or sales as your search criteria.

Similar databases exist for Canadian and International companies from the same DUNS menu.

Business Database Plus (GO BUSDB)

This service contains more than 580,000 full-text articles from more than 500 business and trade journals, plus more than 300,000 articles from industry newsletters. Search Business and Trade Journals for access to articles from more than 500 business magazines and journals. Search Industry Newsletters for access to articles from a variety of specialized business newsletters. The databases are updated whenever a significant amount of new material is available, usually weekly. Business Database Plus has been structured to permit menu searching; you can shortcut some of the menus by entering compound search expressions.

Business Dateline (GO BUSDATE)

Full text of articles from more than 115 regional business publications in the US and Canada are featured in this service. Coverage includes local economic conditions, retailing, real estate, people and management, financial institutions, transportation, and electronics. Articles from 1985 to the present are included in the database. The information includes the article's author, title, publication, date of publication, the dateline, as well as the complete text of the article. Articles may be retrieved by subject words, author name, company name, geographic location, or publication date.

Corporate Affiliations (GO AFFILIATIONS)

Most of the large US public and private companies and their affiliates are covered in this database. It includes all companies and affiliates from the New York Stock Exchange and the American Stock Exchange, and any company from the OTC Exchange that has affiliates. The information available for a company or affiliate includes company name, address, phone number, business description, executive names, and its place in the corporate family hierarchy.

You may retrieve company references by entering the company's name or ticker symbol, city, state, ZIP code, or telephone area code; executive name or executive position title, or board of directors member.

TRW Business Credit Profiles (GO TRWREPORT)

Included here are credit and business information on more than 13 million organizations. Use this database to find actual account information for over 70 million business account relationships as reported by participating corporations. Available are credit histories, financial information and ratios, key business facts such as size, ownership, and products, UCC filings, tax liens, judgments, bankruptcies, and an executive summary.

Reports may be retrieved by entering a company name and either the state or ZIP code of the specific company location. If no company name exactly matches the name you entered, the database will try to retrieve and display up to 24 companies with similar names. Likewise, if you enter a ZIP code, it will also retrieve similarly-named companies from adjacent ZIP areas.

InvesText (GO INVTEXT)

These reports—by analysts in more than 50 Wall Street, regional, and international brokerage houses and research firms—cover more than 8,200 US public companies and more than 2,300 publicly-held foreign companies. Company reports include historical information, such as company profiles; revenues, earnings, and other financial operating results, and stock performance. The reports may also include the brokerage's recommendations with analysis and forecasts of the company's future performance.

Industry reports are available for some 50 predefined industry groups, including assorted high-technology fields, consumer goods and services, energy and natural resources, finance, construction, and real estate. Industry reports are comprised of information on trends and conditions in the industry, new technology and product development, competition, and market share. Many reports contain analysis as well as descriptive text and statistics.

InvesText offers four ways of searching. You may access:

- Company reports by entering the company name or ticker symbol to retrieve all of the Company Reports on the entered company.

- Industry reports by entering an industry group name to retrieve all of the Industry Reports for the entered industry.

- By topic to retrieve individual report PAGES containing topics of interest to you. Enter a word or phrase describing the subject. The search retrieves all pages in which the entered word or phrase appears. Searches may include company, industry, and product names.

- By report number, its unique six-digit InvesText code. The report number is usually obtained from previous searches in InvesText. Searching by InvesText Report Number retrieves complete industry or company reports.

International Company Information

Many of the previously mentioned databases in the COMPANY area contain information about international companies. In addition, there are some country-specific databases, described in the following sections.

Canada

Canadian Dun's Market Identifiers (GO CMI-1) is a database of directory information on about 350,000 Canadian companies. The information includes the name, address, and telephone number, as well as company characteristics such as sales figures, number of employees, and executive names. An individual reference may not include all of this information.

Europe

European Company Library (GO EUROLIB) library contains selected financial information on more than two million European companies. Information is available from leading business databases such as:

- D&B-European Dun's Market Identifiers: Current; updated quarterly. Contains summary descriptions of major public and private companies in Europe. Includes industry classifications, chief executive name, and sales in US and local currencies.

- Europe's Largest Companies: Current; updated monthly. Provides directory and financial information on European companies, including banks, insurance companies, construction firms, and industrial concerns.

- Hoppenstedt Austria: Current; updated semi-annually. Provides directory information on leading Austrian businesses. Information provided includes company name and address, management, ownership, affiliations, line of business, financial, and import/export data. Full text records in German.

- Hoppenstedt Benelux: Current; updated quarterly. Provides directory information on companies in the Netherlands, Belgium, and Luxembourg. Records are in Dutch, French, German, English, and Spanish.

- Irish Company Profiles: Current; updated monthly. Provides directory information on companies of all types located in the Republic of Ireland. Records include company name, address, telephone number, key personnel, trade description, and number of employees.

- Kompass Europe: Current; updated annually. Provides directory information on companies and their products in selected European countries. Coverage emphasizes industry, manufacturing, and related services.

Germany

German Company Library (GO GERLIB) contains selected financial information on more than 48,000 German companies. Information is available from leading business databases such as:

- Credit Reform: Profiles companies of all sizes, in western Germany and the former West Berlin, registered in one of the following legal forms: Einzelfirma, OHG, KG, GmbH & Co KG, GmbH, or AG. Records include company name and address, registration details, ownership, management, capital/sales/employees, type of business, and a summary of products and services.

- D&B-German Dun's Market Identifiers: Descriptions of major public and private companies in Germany. Includes industry classifications, chief executive name, and sales in US dollars and German marks. Data taken from the D&B-European Dun's Market Identifiers database.

- Hoppenstedt Directory of German Companies: From 1989 to present; updated quarterly. Provides directory information on German companies with more than 20 employees or over DM 2 million in sales volume. Includes ownership and subsidiary information.

- Kompass Germany: Directory information on companies and their products in Germany. Coverage emphasizes industry, manufacturing, and related services. Data taken from the Kompass Europe database.

United Kingdom

UK Company Library (GO UKLIB) has selected financial information on more than 1.2 million UK companies. Information is available from leading business databases such as:

- D&B-European Dun's Market Identifiers—UK COUNTRIES: Summary descriptions of major public and private companies in the UK. Data taken from the D&B-Dun's European Market Identifiers database.

- ICC British Company Directory: Name and address directory and summary information on every limited liability company in the UK.

- ICC British Company Financial Datasheets: Financial results for leading UK companies. Provides detailed figures for about half the companies and abridged information for the other half.

- Infocheck: Credit and financial information on British Registered Companies. Records include name, address, account information, ratios, trends, and comments added by InfoCheck, including credit limits.

- Key British Enterprises: Profiles of the top companies in the UK, as determined by annual sales.

- Kompass UK: Covers the UK business-to-business sector with emphasis on manufacturing, industrial, and associated service sectors.

UK Marketing Library (GO UKMARKETING) contains market research reports from top marketing analysts. Information is available from:

- ICC Key Note Market Research: Provides the full text of research reports from the Key Note series, reviewing individual consumer, business, and industrial markets in the UK. There is also increasing coverage of the European market as well. Reports cover industry structure, customers, market size, recent developments, future prospects, and more.

- Management & Marketing Abstracts: From 1976 to present. Contains abstracts from journals worldwide on the practical and theoretical areas of management and marketing.

- Marketing Surveys Index: Comprehensive directory of published research on European and world markets.

- Mintel Research Reports: Full text of original market research from four Mintel publications: *Market Intelligence, Retail Intelligence, Leisure Intelligence*, and *Personal Finance Intelligence*. Markets in the UK are reviewed for size, purchasing patterns, distribution, and advertising expenditure.

- Mintel Special Reports: Text of special one-time market research reports analyzing an industry in the UK — its products, markets, and consumers. Report subjects include food, retailing, insurance, cosmetics, and many other industries.

- MSI Market Research Reports: Reports of markets and industries in the UK and other European countries. Contains information on size and segmentation of markets, trends, advertising, and sales.

UK Trademark Library (GO UKTRADEMARK) provides information on technical standards and trademarks in the United Kingdom. Information is currently provided by two sources:

1. BSI Standardline: Provides citations to current British technical standards. Includes Codes of Practice, Drafts of Development, Automobile, Marine, and Aerospace Series, and Drafts for Public Comment.

2. British Trade Marks: A database of all registered UK trademarks and pending applications, as well as lapsed trademarks and applications since 1976 that have been filed with the Patent Office of the United Kingdom's Trade Marks Registry. Records include trademark name and design

description, owner name and address, the types of goods or services trademarked, international class numbers, and the date and status of the application. Graphical displays of marks are not available.

Australia and New Zealand

Australian and New Zealand Company Library (GO Anzcolib) is a selected directory and news information on more than 95,000 businesses, both public and private, in Australia and New Zealand. Information is available from these leading business directory and news databases:

- D&B-Australian Dun's Market Identifiers and D&B-New Zealand Dun's Market Identifiers: Summary descriptions of major public and private companies in Australia and New Zealand. The directory information for a company includes the name, address, and telephone number, as well as company characteristics such as sales figures, number of employees, net worth, date of incorporation, parent company name, and chief executive name.

- Asia-Pacific: Covers the business and economic news of Asia and the Pacific, from the Pacific Rim to the Middle East from 1985 to the present. Records consist of abstracts or bibliographic references to newspapers and other publications, including *The Wall Street Journal* and *The New York Times*.

- Reuter Textline: Offers access to a collection of prominent newspapers and news wires in the English language, originating in Australia, New Zealand, China, Japan, Korea, India, and other Asian countries. Provides comprehensive coverage of world, national, domestic, political, economic, financial, industry, and commercial news for the Asian/Pacific Rim and Australian/Oceania regions. Most records in the database are full-text articles (9 out of 10), the other 10 percent are article abstracts. Coverage is from 1985 to the present.

Thomas Companies and Products Online (GO THOMAS)

Two financial services, both databases, are included here, as described in the following sections.

Thomas Register Online

Thomas Register Online contains information on almost 150,000 US and Canadian manufacturers and service providers, and is updated annually. It includes the company name, address, telephone number, and products or services provided. Also available for some companies are trade names with descriptions, TELEX and cable address, asset rating, number of employees, exporter status, names of parent or subsidiary companies, and executive names and titles. You can retrieve company records by entering the company name, words describing its line of business, SIC code, product, trade name, city, state, zip code, or telephone area code.

Thomas New Industrial Products

Thomas New Industrial Products contains the latest technical information on new industrial products introduced by US (and some non-US) manufacturers and sellers. The database is updated weekly. A wide variety of industrial products is covered, with each database record supplying key technical data including features, attributes, and performance specifications. The information in each record includes the product name, any applicable product synonyms, SIC codes, trade name, model number, product use, attributes and specifications, plus manufacturer name, address, and telephone number. An individual record may not contain all of this information. You can retrieve product records by entering the company name, company location, product name, trade name, model number, SIC code, or publication date.

Brokerage Services (GO BROKERAGE)

Electronic versions of brokerage houses allow you to trade securities on-line and mesh well with the ability to examine securities with your computer.

Each brokerage service on CompuServe offers its own services and brand of on-line buying and selling of securities. If you're looking for an on-line brokerage service, spend some time exploring all of them before you make a decision.

On-line brokerage services are described in the next sections.

*Quick & Reilly Quick*Way (GO QWK)*

With Quick*Way, orders are executed as they are received when the stock market is open. Orders placed during the evening or on weekends are executed when the market opens the next business day. Quick Way offers 24-hour access to your account and provides full account monitoring capabilities. You may place stock and option orders, review, change, or cancel your orders, check your portfolio value, income, unrealized gains and losses, and check year-to-date realized gains and losses. Quick Way also provides quotations on stocks, options, indexes, and mutual funds with optional real-time quotations on these items.

Spear Rees & Company (GO SPEAR)

In Spear Rees, in addition to on-line activity, you may trade via a toll-free phone number and your on-line portfolio records are automatically updated. On-line access is 24 hours a day to place, review, or change your stock and option orders. You may also see your current holdings and what they are worth based on current market prices; review your transaction history for tax or other purposes, and check prices for stocks, options, mutuals, and indexes. A commission-free program designed especially for individuals who actively trade via their computers, the service permits unlimited transactions, with certain restrictions, in selected companies. The stocks — at this writing, Advanced Micro Devices, Blockbuster Entertainment, Compaq Computer, Conner Peripherals, Glaxo Holdings, Reebok International, RJR Nabisco Holdings, Tandem Computers Inc., Telephone de Mexico, and Toys R Us — are widely held volatile issues particularly suited to profit-making from short-term trading opportunities. Spear offers a full spectrum of services including cash, margin, option, retirement, corporate and custodial accounts. In addition to stocks and options, customers can purchase mutual funds, tax-deferred annuities, real estate income trusts, investment oriented insurance, and unit investment trusts.

E*TRADE Securities (GO ETRADE)

Some of E*TRADE's features include deep discount commissions with no connect time surcharge on Compuserve, online ordering of stocks and options, quotes on stocks, options, market indices, mutual funds, commodities, and futures. You can receive news alerts on your stocks at the moment the news hits the wires, automatic confirmation when your orders are executed, and the ability to review your portfolio's value, income, and unrealized gains and losses. In addition E*TRADE Securities conducts two realistic stock market games (GO ETGAME) which you can play using current stock market data. One game is for stocks only, the other is for stocks and/or stock options. The monthly winner of each game is paid $50.00 by E*TRADE. You can start your participation in the games anytime.

Max Ule's (GO TKR-1)

Max Ule offers clients who can't get to their computers a 24-hour real-time NYSE, AMEX, and OTC stock quote service called Maxi-Quote, available in major metropolitan areas. To qualify for the service, clients must maintain an active account with Max Ule that has a cash or equity balance of $5,000.00 or more. Maxi-Quote users call a local phone number, and can obtain individual quotations or follow a portfolio of up to 27 stocks with a single command. If the user wishes to place an order during market hours, a single number transfers him or her to the Max Ule trading room. Maxi-Quote is available in New York, Chicago, Washington DC, Philadelphia, Boston, Long Island, Northern New Jersey, Atlanta, Detroit, Pittsburgh, Cleveland, St. Louis, Dallas, Houston, Beverly Hills, Newport Beach, Encino, San Diego, San Francisco, Seattle, Denver, San Jose, Hartford, McLean, Albany, Providence, Baltimore, Ft. Lauderdale, Minneapolis, Indianapolis, and Louisville. More areas are expected to be added.

Earnings and Economic Projections

We already have seen some of the areas where earnings projections are available, including Standard & Poor's Online and InvesText. This section contains some others.

I/B/E/S Earnings Estimates (GO IBES)

Available only to subscribers of the Executive Option, this is the Institutional Broker's Estimate System. It represents a consensus of annual and long-term forecasts from more than 2,500 analysts at 130 brokerage and institutional research firms, including the top 20 research firms in the country and 100 percent of the all-star analysts as ranked by *Institutional Investor* magazine. The database includes information about 4,500 companies and reports the most optimistic and pessimistic EPS estimates as well as median, mean, and variation. Current share price, earnings per share, and price/earnings ratio are included.

MMS Financial Reports (GO MMS)

This service is available from MMS International, a multi-national corporation specializing in financial and economic research. MMS focuses on monetary theory and forecasting of central banking policies and operations. It produces a series of economic reports released on a daily, weekly, and biweekly basis. Reports offered include FEDWATCH, which focuses on interest rate trends and Federal Reserve Board activity, daily analysis of the debt, currency and equity markets, and special briefings on economic data, including expectations.

Personal Finance and Insurance (GO FINANCE)

Other services in this part of CompuServe are useful for your personal financial and insurance decisions.

Information USA/Finance (GO INFOUSA)

This is a portion of the larger Information USA database that provides a list of government publications on finance and how to order them. You can learn about banking, consumer credit laws, safeguarding your investments, and bill collection. Borrowing money is explained in publications on credit, types of loans, loan applications, and interest rates.

U.S. Government Publications (GO GPO)

This feature comes in two parts. The first is a catalog of government publications, books, and subscription services. In addition to obtaining ordering information, any CompuServe subscriber with a valid MasterCard or VISA may order on-line any publication handled by the Government Printing Office. The orders are compiled and forwarded directly to the Government Printing Office at least once a week, and more frequently as volume dictates. The second part has on-line consumer information articles from government publications, including articles on personal finance. The entire database is updated weekly or as important changes occur.

MICROQUOTE II (GO MQUOTE)

MicroQuote is the basic engine that drives many of the features of databases you may access. It also is a place you may go to work at the command level with the financial databases, where you may create files for downloading to your computer, and where you may perform most of the functions we have discussed from a single command prompt without going through menus.

If you become a frequent visitor to the financial programs, you might want to order the Financial Services Users Guide by going to the CompuServe On-line Order area (GO ORDER), as described in Chapter 14. The guide will give you a complete rundown on how to use the capabilities available in this area. To give you some idea of what you can do at the MicroQuote command prompt, here is a list of the names that may be typed at the prompt and a description of their functions:

ANALYZER	Company Analyzer
BONDS	List all bonds for issuer
CATALOG	Brief list of files
CHARGES	List surcharges for session
COMMANDS	List of available features
COPY	Copies a file
COSCREEN	Disclosure database screener

DATA	Data retrieval program
DELETE	Delete a file
DIRECTORY	Detailed list of files
DISCLOSURE	Disclosure II Reports
DIVIDEND	Dividends, splits, interest
EDIT	FILGE editor
EXAMINE	Description of an issue
FILTRN	Up- and download files
IBESB	Brief IBES earnings forecast
IBESE	Expanded IBES earnings forecast
LOOKUP	Find issues by name, ticker, CUSIP, or SIC
MARKET	Market highlights
OPRICE	List options for issuer
PORT	Portfolio valuation
PRICES	Price, dividend display
PRISTATS	Price summary over date range
PROTECT	Protect file, directory
QQUOTE	Current-day prices
QSHEET	Multiple security quotes
RENAME	Rename a file
RETURN	Return Analysis
S&P	S&P Online
SCREEN	Screening for securities
SNAPSHOT	Current market indicators
TREND	Price/Volume Chart
TYPE	Type file contents

Micro Software Interfaces (GO INTERFACES)

Software interfaces for MicroQuote II can increase the ability of your computer to interact with the command driven area and increase your efficiency.

MQINT Securities Prices — (GO MQINT)

MQINT is designed to meet the need to automate the process of downloading data files. CompuServe guarantees an unchanging dialogue. All prompts end in a colon. MQINT allows access and interfacing with MicroQuote II, Quick

Quote, and Commodity databases. Subscribers may retrieve single-day quotations for one or several issues or a time-series of quotations for a single issue or contract. The program shortens data transmission time and employs a check sum, if requested, to assure correct data.

IQINT—Company Information (GO IQINT)

Like MQINT, IQINT is designed for program-controlled downloading to your microcomputer. IQINT, however, is designed to get descriptive items about a specified issue from MicroQuote II, company financial information from DISCLOSURE II, and earnings information from I/B/E/S.

MQDATA—Prices, Dividends, Securities Descriptions (GO MQDATA)

MQDATA creates files for transfer to your computer and allows access to MicroQuote II data. Subscribers may select one or more issues for a range of days, weeks, or months, and create files formatted for use in spreadsheets, databases, or BASIC programs. Subscribers may also download dividends, earnings, yields, and other descriptive and performance data.

Error Free File Transfer (GO FILTRN)

FILTRN is CompuServe's file transfer program; in the financial area, it facilitates accurate transfer of data files between your computer and CompuServe. B protocol, which is supported by CIM software, and XMODEM protocol are available to ensure accurate transfer. Other popular transfer protocols may also be selected.

Instructions and Fees (GO FINHELP)

In this area, you may read more instructions about the various financial areas as well as related forums. In addition, you may find a rundown of all the surcharges that apply to the financial areas on CompuServe and to review your on-line surcharges during any one session in the financial area.

Financial and Professional Forums

A number of forums support interests in finances and securities, and various professionals:

The Investors Forum (GO INVFORUM), where investors of all kinds meet to discuss their passion. The forum's libraries are filled with computer programs aimed at assisting the investor. The forum is co-administered by Harry Knutowski, 76703,4214, and Mike Pietruk, 76703,4346.

The NAIC Forum (GO NAIC), for value-oriented long-term investors who aren't concerned with day-to-day changes in market prices, but who focus on finding quality companies and buying them at good prices. It is sponsored by the National Association of Investors Corporation which supports both individual investors and those who belong to clubs. The concepts in this forum focus on investing in common stocks for the long term—from three to five years at a time.

And here are some forums devoted to specific professions:

AMIA Medical Forum (GO MEDSIG) serves medical professionals and those interested in health-related work. The sysop is Dr. Alan Rowberg, 76703,4421.

The Court Reporters Forum (GO CRFORUM), with participation by the National Court Reporters Association and the *Journal of Court Reporting*, serves anyone interested in the profession. Richard A. Sherman, 71154,61, is the administrator.

The European Community Teleworkers Forum (GO ECTF) supplies information on teleworking, telematics, and advanced broadband communications. David Brain, 76004,3453, is the chief sysop.

The International Trade Forum (GO TRADE) is intended for those working in or interested by international trade. The sysop is Thom Hartmann, 76702,765.

The Legal Forum (GO LAWSIG) serves those working in or interested by any aspect of the legal profession. Old CompuServe hand, Noel D. Adler, 76703,264, is the sysop.

The Office Automation Support Forum (GO OAFORUM) focuses on issues of interest to those who use office automation products in their business or professional lives. Thom Hartmann, 76702,765, is the manager.

The SafetyNet Forum (GO SAFETYNET) shares information on any aspect of safety, such as occupational health, engineering, fire protection, or law enforcement. It is administered by Dr. Charles M. Baldeck.

Note Another group of business data tools — demographics from the U.S. Census Bureau as well as major private reports such as SuperSite — are covered in Chapter 9.

9

References Library and Education

In this chapter...

Chuck Lynd and Georgia Griffith know something about the soul of this medium. That is not because they have any particularly rare insight into hardware or software or high-tech marketing strategies. Rather, it's because they have a special appreciation for something more fundamental to the system: the actual information that fuels it. Together the two Ohio educators have more than two decades' worth of first-hand evidence that electronically shared information enriches lives.

Since 1984, Lynd has administered CompuServe's Education Forum, where one night he might be counseling a parent on how to deal with a local school board, then the next night he might be talking about the school of the 21st Century or the bright promise of the electronic classroom. His forum has brought together contacts from scores of national organizations, professional associations, universities, and school districts. Visitors range from the president of the American Federation of Teachers to a psychologist with expertise in learning disabilities to the director of a federally funded project that uses telecommunications to deliver instruction.

Even before he started his forum, Lynd began to see how fundamental the sharing of information was to his new electronic environment. While he, himself, was certainly no computer slouch — as a former Columbus, Ohio teacher in regular classrooms and special education, he had been using computer databases and modems as early as the mid-1970s — but he found that launching a forum was a whole new experience. Needing a mentor, he turned to one of CompuServe's earliest on-line stars: Georgia Griffith. She not only helped him through the forum technicalities in his first days on-line, but also showed him a new twist on education along the way.

"She has inspired me to patiently explain to newcomers the myriad facets of uploading and downloading, parameter settings and transfer protocols," Lynd said in a 1990 article in CompuServe's Online Today electronic publication. "I have not forgotten the initial pains and frustrations; and, therefore, I derive personal satisfaction if I can shorten the learning curve for someone else."

Today Griffith continues as an assistant sysop in Lynd's important Education Forum, but that is only one of her many on-line activities. In fact, Georgia Griffith is one of the hardest working information providers on all of CompuServe, with friends and admirers in every corner of the system.

Georgia is a music educator by profession and came onto CompuServe in 1982, where she helped out with a short-term computer experiment by a group of newspapers around the country. From that work arose the Issues Forum which Georgia still manages. The following year Griffith launched another project that was especially important to her — the Handicapped User's Database, an ever-growing collection of articles and reports of interest to subscribers with disabilities. She has operated the HUD database ever since, along with the IBM/Special Needs Forum which she coordinates with IBM.

Many people who communicate with Georgia through the Issues Forum or the Education Forum never realize that she has overcome her own obstacles to become part of this electronic world. Griffith has been blind since birth and lost her hearing as a young woman. She was the first blind student at Capital University in Columbus, Ohio, and was graduated Phi Beta Kappa with a bachelor's degree in music. Since her first days on CompuServe, she has talked with the on-line world through a device that alters modem data into a form of communications she can read like braille.

Georgia's story would be remarkable enough if her on-line work were the extent of her activities, but that's just part of it. In 1971 she became the Library of Congress' only proofreader of braille music through the National Braille Association. She also works with LINC Resources Inc., a Columbus, Ohio nonprofit organization that assists educators in locating instructional materials and training resources. In 1990, Georgia Griffith was nominated as an Outstanding Woman of America, one of only 2,000 in the country, and she received a presidential citation for her work with the Library of Congress.

Her friends are proud and amazed at her accomplishments, but Griffith has always taken it in stride. Not long ago, she told *CompuServe Magazine* the philosophy she has shared with on-line friends over the years: "Whatever your lot in life, build something on it."

Overview

This chapter concerns the on-line stomping grounds of Chuck Lynd and Georgia Griffith, and scores of others devoted to education and learning. CompuServe is rich in such materials, ranging from forums to reference libraries of magazines, newspapers, and journals, encyclopedias and other reference books, statistical reports from the US Census Bureau, and more.

These are the kinds of reference materials we have come to rely on in a busy world; CompuServe makes accessing them easy. The same computer that connects you with forums, electronic mail, real-time conferencing, games, and stock quotes also provides the link to remarkable new electronic reservoirs of data. An innovation in on-line communications has been *gateways*, a technology that links one entire computer system with another. You may go through this electronic portal to use other systems, whether the destination computers are in a building next door or in a city on the other side of the world.

The chapter introduces various on-line reference facilities, including the major gateways. Among the features covered are:

IQuest, a gateway to hundreds of databases from major research services around the world.

Grolier's Academic American Encyclopedia, a massive electronic reference that is updated four times a year.

Computer Database Plus, a timely database from Ziff Communications that provides material from assorted computer-related publications, including hardware and software reviews.

Medical References, including a database of material from medical journals and health reports.

Demographics, from business-related market data to specific current reports from the US Census Bureau.

Other references, from *Books in Print* and *Who's Who* to discussion forums devoted to education, teachers, students, and parents.

Since many of the features are surcharged (extra-cost), this chapter will tell you how to find the latest rates.

Some Tips

If you are using the CompuServe Information Manager software, you can reach the system's libraries by selecting the Reference option on the Service menu. (Note that the software routinely goes into Terminal Emulator mode when accessing the reference/education features.) If you are using a third-party communications program, you can reach the same features by entering GO REFERENCES at any prompt.

Here are some tips for using these features:

1. Since you usually visit these services to search for specific data, it is wise to prepare in advance by familiarizing yourself with your communication software's facilities for a capture buffer feature and how to save and print data from it. (For CIM users, this means reviewing the manual's discussion of Terminal Emulator mode and the capture buffer.)

2. Before visiting a reference feature, you might want to increase the size of the capture buffer to hold more than 100 lines of text.

3. If you frequently search for the same topics in reference features and are using CIM, consider saving your search terms in the Terminal Emulator's function keys. (See your manual.) If you are using a third-party program, it too may have function keys for saving frequently entered keystrokes; see the software's instructions.

IQuest (GO IQUEST)

IQuest, a joint gateway project of CompuServe and Telebase Systems Incorporated of Devon, Pennsylvania, came on-line in 1985, allowing subscribers to link up with nearly a thousand specific databases provided by such major vendors as Dialog, BRS, and NewsNet. With IQuest, you pay your usual CompuServe connect-time and also pay for material retrieved through the gateway.

IQuest has three different approaches:

1. **IQuest-I**, designed for inexperienced subscribers, is menu-driven. IQuest-I actually helps you select an appropriate database by prompting you to:

   - (a) Make selections from a series of categories listed by menus.

   - Then (b) enter your question in the form of a keyword or keywords.

   After that, IQuest-I takes you through the gateway to a relevant database it chooses and automatically translates your query into a command language understood by that particular database.

2. **IQuest-II** is for more experienced searchers and offers a larger selection of databases. It asks you to:

  • (a) To name the database you wish to search.

  • Then (b) enter the keywords that make up your query.

  IQuest-II then takes over, making the call to the remote service and, again, translating your question into the database's own language.

3. **SmartScan** lets you make a preliminary scan of several relevant databases at one time to see which ones contain information on your search topic. It then builds a menu from which you may access specific databases.

Beginners usually choose IQuest-I, letting the system handle more of the work. The system seeks to narrow the search to a broad area of interest. Note that the service keeps a running tab of your charges. Generally, IQuest bills only for the searching and the information actually retrieved from a database. Consider the following costs:

  • $9.00 is charged for searching and retrieving information from a database. However, if a search does not turn up any files that meet your search specifications, the charge will be only $1.00.

  • Some of the databases carry an additional $4.00 to $25.00 in surcharges. These databases are identified on-line to alert users in advance; therefore, you are given an opportunity to back out of a search before incurring such an extra charge.

  • Standard CompuServe communications connect-time charges are also in effect in IQuest.

  • Additional on-line purchases, such as abstracts of references or full-text of articles, are charged on a per-item basis.

IQuest-I uses a series of menus to zero in on a topic of interest. After you select a topic from the first menu, the system displays a series of new menus, each becoming more specific about the information for which you are looking, giving the system the background it needs to decide which database to access for you. Surcharges remain zero until after the actual trip through the gateway to a database. (However, you are incurring the usual CompuServe connect-charges during this time.)

Kinds of Data

Information in IQuest is available in two forms:

Bibliographic, basic information about published material, such as the name of the publication, date, author, and title of the article. Many bibliographic databases also provide abstracts (brief summaries) of the cited articles, for an extra charge.

Full-text, the complete text of the articles you have located.

Most of the databases accessible to IQuest contain either bibliographic references only or full-text articles only; when there is a choice, IQuest asks which you prefer.

After you have made your selections on all the menus, IQuest is ready to determine your question with a prompt that says, "Enter your specific topic." (Type H for important examples or B to back up). At this point, the system is looking for a keyword or keywords to describe what you are looking for. You may enter:

- H for Help (which provides examples of search strategies). Some databases have their own syntax for searches, so examples are useful.
- B to back up (return to the previous menu).

H and B may be used at virtually any IQuest prompt. Two other commands are T (for "TOP") which returns you to the main IQuest menu, and L (for "Leave") to log off IQuest and return to the main CompuServe system.

After verifying your keyword, IQuest reports the name of the database it has selected for the job and makes its way through the gateway. This could take a few minutes as the system automatically:

1. Accesses a communications network and dials into the chosen database vendor.

2. Submits a password for admission (because IQuest is your representative, the password is sent from the gateway to the host computer; it isn't displayed to you).

3. Navigates to the database it has selected.

4. Translates your query into a local language that the database understands.

After the search is finished, IQuest reports a number of "hits," that is, the number of references it has found that meet your keyword specifications.

If your destination is:

A bibliographic database, your $9.00 charge provides a list of up to 10 of the most recent references. Each is displayed with a heading number along with the title of the article, the name of the author and the publication, the publication date, volume number, and usually the page number. For additional charges, you may sometimes see abstracts of selected articles ($3.00 apiece) and/or the next 10 headlines in the haul ($9.00), or you may order reprints of the selected articles to be mailed to you directly ($18.00 by US mail, $42.00 via overnight courier).

A full-text service,   your initial $9.00 provides up to 15 of the latest references. For no extra charge, you may enter a heading number to view the complete text of one article. Usually, for extra charges you may also display the text of other articles, or see the next 15 references from the search.

After a search, the system reports the amount of your charges so far and provides options for additional services, including the next collection of headings, another search, paper reprints of articles, and so on.

IQuest-II

After you become familiar with IQuest-I, you might want to step up to the advanced service, IQuest-II. It is faster, since it provides fewer menus to study, and it offers access to a wider variety of databases. The difference is that you select the database you wish to search, rather than turning the responsibility over to the system. You may also request information on specific IQuest databases at the -> prompt; just enter DIR followed by a subject, such as DIR MUSIC, to find databases devoted to a specific subject.

When you are ready, select IQuest-II and, when prompted to enter the name of the database to search, enter a name, such as D&B — Dun's Million Dollar Directory. IQuest prompts for keywords that describe your subject, then logs on and makes the search. Incidentally, you also may enter DIR LIST at the -> to get a list of IQuest's various search areas.

SmartScan

SmartScan is a convenient way to make a preliminary scan of several relevant databases at one time to determine which ones contain information pertinent to your subject. It then lets you choose from a menu the databases from which you want to retrieve the data. To start, select the SmartScan option from the main menu. Subsequent menus narrow the topics, similar to those used with IQuest-I. The system then prompts for keywords and ultimately produces an *occurrence menu*, showing you how many records relevant to your keywords may be retrieved from each database; therefore, you know up front where the coverage is — and isn't — for your particular topic. Pressing H (for Help) retrieves database descriptions. Once you have reviewed the menu, you may retrieve references from the databases by making your selection from the menu. The system conducts a standard search, after which, if you choose, you may start a new search.

The cross-database scan and resulting occurrence menu are billed as one standard search, $5.00 at current rates. Each subsequent access to a database from the SmartScan menu is billed as a separate standard search, including any applicable database surcharges.

About Keywords

With IQuest-I, IQuest-II, or SmartScan (as with many other resources discussed in this chapter), the key to success is the same: the *keywords* and how they are defined. The best place to start your search strategies — in IQuest and in other extra-cost, keyword-searchable features — is off-line. Before you log on, you can save money by giving some thought to what you want to specify at the keyword prompt. Here are some guidelines for entering IQuest keywords:

- Omit common words, like OF, THE, FOR, and AT. (Instead of "the Department of the Interior," make it DEPARTMENT INTERIOR.)

- Use words and phrases that are unique to your subject. ("Convertible" is a more specific term than "Automobile.")

- Don't worry about capitalization. IQuest views upper- and lowercase letters the same.

- The slash (/) character is a wildcard and may be used at the end of a keyword to retrieve references to text that include words beginning with specified letters (COMPUT/ to retrieve COMPUTER, COMPUTERS, COMPUTING, COMPUTATIONS, and so on). The slash may also be used in the middle of words; for example, PRACTI/E retrieves both "practice" and the British spelling, "practise."

IQuest recognizes three connectors:

- **AND** to narrow your search. (APPLE AND IBM to fetch only those files that contain *both* keywords.)

- **OR** to expand your search. (APPLE OR IBM retrieves files containing *either* the word "Apple" or the letters "IBM.")

- **NOT** to exclude a specified topic. If you are looking for references to the country of Libya that do not deal with the political violence, you might enter LIBYA NOT TERRORIS/. That collects files that mention "Libya" but do *not* also mention words that begin with "terroris," such as "terrorism" and "terrorist."

Finally, you may combine (or *nest*) searches by using parentheses around groups of words you have connected with AND, OR, or NOT. (LIBYA OR SYRIA OR IRAN) AND TERRORISM retrieves files that contain a mention of at least one of the three countries and the word "terrorism."

The Vendors

Major database vendors represented in IQuest include:

- Dialog Information Services Incorporated of Palo Alto, California, provided by Knight-Ridder Company. It offers more than 200 databases and was originally conceived by Lockheed Corporation as a tool for NASA researchers. The data-bases deal with a wide range of topics from law and government to medicine and science, engineering and technology, patents and agriculture.

- BRS (Bibliographic Retrieval Service) of Latham, New York, with some 80 databases. It was designed in the mid-1970s as a dialup service for research librarians. Since then, it has been expanded to cover science and medicine, business and finance, references, education, and humanities.

- SDC/Orbit of Santa Monica, California, a subsidiary of Burroughs Corporation, is considered the oldest modern database vendor. Brought on-line in 1965, it has about 80 databases, including some not found anywhere else, such as SDC, the provider of Accountant of the American Institute of CPAs; MONITOR, an index of *The Christian Science Monitor* newspaper, and SPORT, covering sports literature.

- NewsNet of Bryn Mawr, Pennsylvania, brings together hundreds of newsletters from 34 industry groups, including computing, telecommunications, electronics, medicine, business, education, law, social sciences, and others. Publications are daily, weekly, monthly, and quarterly.

- DataTimes of Oklahoma City, Oklahoma, another newspaper service with full-text of additional papers.

- Questel of Washington, D.C., a subsidiary of the French Telesystems, contains more than 40 databases, including its best-known DARC chemical files.

- DataSolve of London, a product of the British Broadcasting Corporation, offers summaries of world radio broadcasts from 120 countries and foreign news agencies, as well as BBC news.

In addition, IQuest has added Datastar of Switzerland, G. Cam Serveur of Paris, QL Systems of Kingston, Ontario, Canada, and Timeplace of Waltham, Massachusetts.

In recent years, Telebase Systems has brought on-line other reference databases that work essentially like IQuest. These are illustrated later in the chapter.

Grolier's Academic American Encyclopedia (GO ENCYCLOPEDIA)

CompuServe has an encyclopedia on-line that is updated and revised four times a year. It is Grolier's Academic American Encyclopedia with more than 33,000 articles, fact boxes, bibliographies, and tables. If you were to have it in print, it would be a twenty-one-volume work containing some ten million words. What is special about AAE, besides its timeliness, is that it is:

- Easily searchable by keywords. You may enter something quite general, like HORSE, and then zero in on the specific subject by examining the menu of articles it retrieves; or you may start by entering something like ITALY, HISTORY OF, and get right to heart of the matter.

- Quickly readable. Because of the way complex subjects are presented. If you ask AAE for its article on FRANCE, it produces an outline with a menu that lets you jump into the middle, directly to portions dealing with "Land," "People," "Economic Activity," "Government," and so on.

- Thoughtfully organized. Some topics are broken down even further. Under the "Land" section usually is a sub-menu to take you to the discussions of soils, climate, vegetation, animal life, resources, and so on.

The feature also uses three kinds of cross-reference entries to guide you to relevant information: Article heading cross references, "See also" references listed at the end of an article, and internal cross references found within an article (usually in ALL CAPS).

Keywords

With most searches, the encyclopedia finds all entries beginning with the letters you enter. Entering CAT finds some 75 articles, ranging from *cat* and *cat family* to *catacombs*, *catalpa*, and *catalytic converter*. Remember to enter at least three letters; if you enter only one or two letters at the Search prompt (such as ID), the encyclopedia will try to find only only that specific word.

Here are some tips for planning a search:

1. Have alternate terms in mind. If you can't find an entry under FILMS, try MOVIES, CINEMA, or MOTION PICTURES.

2. As with IQuest, include in your plans some broad, categorical terms. For instance, AAE has no entry for BALD EAGLE, but information about the bird can be found under EAGLE.

3. If in doubt about spelling, enter only as much of the word as you are sure of. If you enter BRZ, the service finds BRZEZINSKI.

4. Check the spelling before going on-line. A misspelled keyword is the most common reason for failure to find entries.

5. Search for the singular form of a term (HORSE rather than HORSES).

Statistics

Having access to such an up-to-date encyclopedia is particularly valuable if current statistics are important to your research. Many AAE articles are accompanied by summary "fact boxes." Expect to find them with all articles about countries, continents, states, Canadian provinces, and US presidents. Several hundred entries also display statistics tables, such as sports records, awards and prizes, and industry production data. If an article has an accompanying table, the system calls your attention to it on a menu displayed before the text begins.

Computer Database Plus (GO COMPDB)

Computer Database Plus, sponsored by Information Access Company in conjunction with magazine publisher Ziff-Davis Company, contains full-text and summaries of computer-related articles in more than 120 magazines, newspapers, and journals, covering hardware, software, electronics, engineering, communications, and the application of technology. The publications include *PC Magazine, Personal Computing, Electronic News, MacWeek*, and *Electronic Business*. Articles cover companies, people, products, trends, corporate finances, case histories on the use of computer products, industry projections, programming, and computer design.

Such comprehensive coverage comes at a price. The database carries a surcharge of $15.00 an hour. In addition, you are charged $2.50 for each complete record (abstract and full-text), and $1.00 for abstracts only; if no abstract is available, the charge is reduced to $1.50. You may read about how to use the system (option 3 in the example) *before* accessing the database and turning on those surcharges. This feature has elaborate options for search strategies, so if you plan to use the database, you are advised to examine the articles under option 3 before going on.

Computer Database Plus is fully menu-driven. Most searchers begin with the "Words Occurring Anywhere" option on the main menu. Subsequent menus give you the opportunity to narrow or broaden your search field. When you are ready to see the selected stories, an option allows you to request a menu. The database allows users to call up the entire text of more than 70 percent of indexed articles. Most coverage begins with the January 1987 issues. The database is updated weekly with material from current issues of the publications.

The service also incorporated a feature called Computer Directory (GO COMPDIR for direct access), which provides information on more than 55,000 computer hardware and software products sold in North America. Updated monthly, the directory may be used to pinpoint an exact product or group of products and encompasses information on software packages, computer systems (micro-mainframe), peripherals, data, and telecommunications products. Included is summary information on more than 9,500 manufacturers.

Medical References

CompuServe connects with a number of medical-related databases, including collections of articles from medical journals.

Health Database Plus (GO HLTDB)

This database is provided by Information Access Company, the same firm that produces Computer Database Plus. It covers consumer and professional publications in the areas of health, nutrition, and fitness. The database covers more than 18,000 articles and is updated weekly. It is made up of three kinds of publications, including:

1. **Core journals**, those with health, medical, and nutrition coverage oriented to the lay reader, such as *Food & Nutrition*, *Health*, and *Psychology Today*. In general, articles include full text, with coverage beginning in January 1989.

2. **Technical and professional journals**, such as *Patient Care*, *RN*, and *The New England Journal of Medicine*. These generally do not include full text but do offer synopses for the lay reader and authors' abstracts. Coverage begins with June 1989.

3. **Consumer publications**, selected by topic, beginning in 1983. Articles generally include full text.

The database connect-time is surcharged at $15.00 an hour plus $1.50 for each full-text article retrieved. Abstracts are $1.00.

HealthNet (GO HNT)

This is one of the older on-line home medical reference sources for personal computer users. The database is in three parts: the HealthNet Reference Library, the HealthNet Newsletter, and HouseCalls, in which you may submit questions to the HealthNet staff to be answered publicly and anonymously.

PaperChase (GO PAPERCHASE)

PaperChase puts MEDLINE, the National Library of Medicine's database of references to the biomedical literature, at your fingertips. The service is surcharged at $24.00 an hour during weekday business hours and $18.00 an hour in the evenings and on weekends.

The feature contains more than five million references from 4,000 journals, all references indexed since 1966. Each month some 25,000 more references are indexed and abstracted. The service is provided by Boston's Beth Israel Hospital. There are two major sections:

1. LOOK FOR, in which you create lists of references that meet your specifications. Each list will be labeled with a single alphabetic character, or a number and alphabetic character. To create such lists, you may enter a title word, medical subject heading, subheading, author's name, journal title, year of publication, or language of publication. Often, it is best

to enter less than a full word and let PaperChase find all references containing the prefix or root word.

2. OPTIONS, where you may combine your lists in various ways or display them. A particularly important option in PaperChase is "Find References Common to 2 or More Lists." For example, to find out if LITHIUM can cause HYPERCALCEMIA, you can *Look For* LITHIUM, *Look For* HYPERCALCEMIA, then *Find References Common* to these two lists. When you display the result, you should have what you want. In many cases the best search strategy is to identify a single medical subject heading, identify another medical subject heading, then use the Find References Common option. The system provides on-line help files.

Search commands are quite powerful and you are advised to read the sections available under options on the main menu before accessing the data-base.

Rare Disease Database (GO NORD)

The Rare Disease Database is made up of the on-line reports by the National Organization for Rare Disorders, a non-profit, voluntary health agency dedicated to the identification, control, and cure of rare "Orphan Diseases." Each entry has a "Resources" section containing names and addresses of other agencies, organizations, and clinics that provide further assistant to those with each rare disorder.

The database is funded by the Generic Pharmaceutical Industry Association with additional aid from the Pharmaceutical Manufacturers Association, REVCO Drug Stores Foundation, and the Robert Leet and Clara Guthrie Patterson Trust. In addition to the database, it provides access to newsletters, information on prevalent health conditions and concerns, and an AIDS Update.

Peterson's College Database (GO PETERSON)

This famed database contains descriptions of more than 3,400 accredited or approved US and Canadian colleges that grant associate and/or bachelor's degrees. It is provided by the same company that published the printed *Peterson's Guide to Four-Year Colleges* and *Peterson's Guide to Two-Year Colleges*.

The database lets you search for colleges based on more than 500 characteristics, arranged in 19 primary categories, including: location, coed/ single sex, size, level of study, public/private, campus setting, entrance difficulty, majors, sports, housing, costs, campus life and activities, special programs, freshman data/enrollment patterns, ethnic/geographic mix, admission requirements, admission policies, application deadlines, and entrance difficulty-transfer.

After you have chosen all of the characteristics that are important to you, the system displays your final list of colleges from which you may choose some for in-depth profile.

Some abbreviations used in the profiles include:

- Degree levels — A for associate, B for bachelor's, C for master's and D for doctorate.
- Athletics — S after a sport indicates availability of grants-in-aid. Roman numerals indicate NCAA divisions.
- Majors — A means associate and B means bachelor's.

Consumer Reports (GO CSR)

This database allows you to search for reports prepared by the Consumers Union staff. The reports are similar to what you find in *Consumer Reports* magazine, modified slightly for placement in this electronic database.

Reports are listed in one of four categories — appliances, automobiles, electronics/cameras, and home — and are alphabetized within each category. The reports generally cover products and services that cost $50.00 or more, or lower-priced products and services that are typically bought frequently or in bulk.

Most non-automotive reports are divided into four sections: introduction/overview, what to look for, recommendations, and models tested/ratings. Occasionally, other choices, such as features/specifications or article updates, are available. A guide explains ratings symbols and a full description of each characteristic.

Demographics

Demographic information is a cornerstone for many businesses. Whether you are searching for a location for a new regional office or finding the best areas in which to sell your wares, the characteristics of various parts of the country are all-important. The same information may be invaluable if you are considering a move to a new city and want to compare it with your current home. CompuServe offers assorted resources for demographic information for business or general research.

CENDATA (GO CENDATA)

This service of the US Census Bureau includes reports on population, manufacturing, foreign trade, agriculture, business, and so on. It is menu-driven. The frequently updated service also provides a "what's new" feature, accessible from the main menu, to help you keep up on the latest additions. At this writing, the feature is *not* surcharged; on-line basic connect rates apply here.

Neighborhood Reports (GO NEIGHBOR)

Neighborhood Reports let you find age, income, occupation, and household statistics, searching by ZIP code, county, or state. The reports are available to all CompuServe Information Service subscribers, while the *full* set of demographic reports that comprise SuperSite is available to Executive Service Option subscribers only. The Neighborhood Reports provide the demographics for a ZIP code. The surcharge for each report is $10.00.

SUPERSITE (GO SUPERSITE)

SuperSite provides demographics for the United States as a whole as well as for every individual state, county, Standard Metropolitan Statistical Area (SMSA), Arbitron TV Market (ADI), Nielsen TV Market (DMA), and ZIP code area. Fourteen reports are available for each area, covering general demographics, income, housing, education, employment from the latest census, along with updates and forecasts. In addition, sales potential reports for 16 major types of retail stores and consumer potential for three types of financial institutions are included. ACORN (A Classification of Residential Neighborhoods), available as part of SuperSite, classifies all households in the US into one of 44 market segments based upon the demographic, socioeconomic, and housing characteristics of the neighborhood.

What is best about SuperSite is that it is easy to find the information you are looking for, as easy as answering prompts from a menu. All you have to do is indicate the kind of geography and report you need and turn on your printer for an 80-column printout. (In the event of a printer problem, the reports may be redisplayed immediately at no additional charge.) Most charts give the latest actual census information, a current update based on interim figures gleaned from several sources, a forecast for future dates, the percentage of change expected between now and the projection, and the annual growth or decline predicted in the various categories.

SuperSite reports, surcharged from $20.00 to $100.00 depending on the information, include:

Demographic Reports for housing, Hispanic population, education, energy, employment, income and component area and forecast summaries, housing value by age, combined demographic and income forecast, age by sex, age by income.

Sales potential reports for various businesses, including appliance store, consumer finance, dry cleaner, hair salon, ice cream store, optical center, photo outlet, retail bakery, savings and loan, apparel store, automotive aftermarket, commercial bank, department store, drug store, footwear store, grocery store, home improvement, restaurant, and shopping center.

ACORN Target Marketing Reports for population profile, household profile, financial services, investment services, convenience store, restaurant, shopping center retail and media analysis, and media.

An option on the main SuperSite menu provides the current costs for specific reports.

As noted, SuperSite is accessible to subscribers who have signed up for the Executive Option.

Business Demographics (GO BUSDEM)

The Business Demographics Reports, based upon information from the US Census Bureau and developed by a firm called Market Statistics, are intended to help businesses analyze their markets. Two types of reports are available:

1. **Business to Business Report** includes information on all broad Standard Industrial Classification (SIC) categories, including the total number of employees in each category for a designated geographical area.

2. **Advertisers' Service Report** includes data on businesses which comprise the SICs for Retail Trade.

Each report breaks down the total number of businesses for each specified geographical unit in relation to company size, and may be requested by ZIP code, county, state, Metropolitan area, ADI (Arbitron TV Markets), DMA (Nielsen TV Markets), or the entire US Reports are $10.00 for any geographical unit.

Phone Directories

The newer databases to arrive on CompuServe are the reservoirs of business and home phone numbers around the country. Are you looking for a long-lost friend or lover? Do you need the number of a potentially important business contact on the other side of the country? Do you wish you could search the Yellow Pages of a business elsewhere? Then, these are the databases for you.

AT&T Toll-Free 800 Directory (GO TOLLFREE)

This is a free database sponsored by AT&T and CompuServe that helps you find toll-free 800 numbers for assorted services across the country.

An option on the main menu is "Look up an 800 Number" which allows you to search by product or service in a number of categories, including advertising, marketing, sales, business equipment and supplies, business services, computers and telecommunications, consumer and public services, education, libraries, schools, finance, insurance, legal, government, real estate, and housing.

The system also provides tips on using the directory most effectively and on ordering print 800 directories, and gives news about special offers.

Phonefile (GO PHONEFILE)

This surcharged database contains some 84 million households nationwide. It is a 25-cent-a-minute ($15.00 an hour) feature that allows users to search by last name, phone number, ZIP code, and other means.

The feature is offered by MetroNet, which already has provided businesses with access to the database. MetroNet is part of Metromail, which in turn is a subsidiary of R.R. Donnelley, the directory publishing company that sells mailing list information to direct marketing firms.

Backers of the venture noted that, rather than being dependent solely on telephone books, data in Phonefile comes from white pages directories as well as published birth announcements, real estate transactions, and other data from public sources. Phonefile has about 100 primary sources of information and 300 to 400 other sources; data is updated at least once weekly.

Phonefile offers three types of searches:

- Name and address
- Surname and geographical area
- Phone number

(CompuServe notes that these types of restricted search methods are designed to retrieve individual names and discourage use of their compilation for mailing or telephone solicitation.)

An opening menu informs users of surcharges and gives five choices, each with three search options, plus directions for use and exit command. A search by name and address prompts for the person's name, street address, city/state, and ZIP code. For a surname search, the system gives users a choice of searching by city and state, by state only, or by ZIP code, then asks for a last name.

This means the service could be used to look up every person with a specific last name in any city or state. Phone search option asks users to enter either a three-digit area code or a five-digit ZIP code. In addition to address and telephone information, the database can include the name of the spouse and the length of residence at the address listed.

*Biz*File (GO BIZFILE)*

Similar to Phone*File, Biz*File provides access to names, addresses, and phone numbers for companies throughout the United States and Canada. The surcharged database is compiled from more than 5,000 Yellow Page directories, containing information on more than 10 million establishments.

Dun's Electronic Yellow Pages (GO DUNSEBD)

This database contains directory information on nearly eight million businesses in the United States. It covers both public and private companies of all sizes and types.

The information for a company includes the name, address, telephone number, type of business, SIC code, number of employees, professional's name, Dun's number, industry, city population, and parent company information as compiled by Dun & Bradstreet Incorporated.

The surcharge amounts to $5.00 for the first 10 titles located, $5.00 for each additional 10 titles, and $2.00 for each full reference retrieved.

Other Databases From Telebase Systems

Besides the massive IQuest gateway system discussed at the beginning of this chapter, Telebase Systems Incorporated also provides access to a number of other database services on CompuServe. In some of the databases, on-paper reprints are also available as extra-cost services, usually $16.00 each for normal delivery, and $36.00 to $39.00 each for express delivery.

Books in Print (GO BOOKS)

This database lists most books currently in print at US trade publishers, books currently out-of-print, and those slated for publication.

Data includes bibliographic references describing books distributed in the United States for single- or multiple-copy purchase, currently in print, to be published in the next six months, and those that went out-of-print or out-of-stock during the last two years. Most records include author, title, publisher, date of publication, edition, binding (such as, "paperback"), list price, and subject as published by R.R. Bowker Co.

The cost is $2.00 for the first 10 titles located, $2.00 for each additional 10 titles, and $2.00 for each reference retrieved.

Commerce Business Daily (GO COMBUS)

This database, published by the US Commerce Department, includes the full text of US Commerce Department publications listing contracts, requests for proposals, and other data related to government contracts. The data includes listings from the printed publication of the same name, as well as from the printed "DMS Bluetops," published by the Office of the Assistant Secretary of Defense. It is updated daily and includes only listings from the most recent 90 days.

The information includes a summary that usually describes the contract/procurement, contracting agency, the "Section Heading" or category of needed product/service, and date of issue. You may retrieve listings by entering subject words, sponsoring agency, or the ZIP code of the sponsoring agency as your search criteria.

The cost is $2.00 for the first 10 titles located, $2.00 for each additional 10 titles, and $2.00 for each full listing retrieved.

Computerized Engineering Index (GO COMPENDEX)

This contains abstracts of articles from significant engineering and technological literature, including journals, publications of engineering societies and organizations, papers from the proceedings of conferences, selected government reports, and books from around the world. Related subjects covered include properties and testing of materials, fluid flow, pollution, ocean technology, applied physics, food technology, and measurements.

Surcharges for the database are $5.00 for the first 10 titles located, $5.00 for additional titles in groups of 10, and $5.00 for each full reference retrieved, with abstract where available. In addition, reprints are $18.00 each by normal delivery or $42.00 for express delivery.

Dissertation Abstracts (GO DISSERTATION)

This database contains bibliographic references for nearly all Ph.D. dissertations published since 1861 and for selected masters' theses. Abstracts are available for dissertations published after 1980.

Data on each dissertation includes author, title, date of publication, and college and degree for which the dissertation was submitted. Surcharges for the data-base are $5.00 for the first 10 titles located, $5.00 for additional titles in groups of 10, and $5.00 for each full reference retrieved, with abstract where available.

Educational Resources Information Center (GO ERIC)

ERIC, a well-known educators' database, contains abstracts of articles covering all aspects of education, including vocational education, counseling, teacher education, and testing. The data goes back to 1966 and is updated monthly. Also included are two subfiles:

1. The Resources In Education (RIE) file, which contains research/technical reports, conference papers and proceedings, program descriptions, opinion papers, bibliographies, reviews, dissertations, teaching and curriculum materials, lesson plans, and guides.
2. The Current Index to Journals in Education (CIJE) file, which contains abstracts of articles from 750 education-related professional journals.

The cost is $2.00 for the first 10 titles located, $2.00 for each additional 10 titles, and $2.00 for each reference retrieved.

IQuest Business Management InfoCenter (GO IQBUSINESS)

This gateway reaches databases covering such topics as management research, marketing studies, company ownership, and mergers and acquisitions. It carries bibliographic and full-text business information provided from magazines, books, and other published sources, and may be obtained from single-database or multi-database SmartScan searches.

The surcharge is $9.00 for the first 10 titles located, $9.00 for each additional 10 titles, and $2.00 for each abstract retrieved. A "SmartScan" for the databases costs $5.00.

Among the specialized services available are:

- PTS PROMT, considered to be one of the best sources of international business information anywhere with more than 1,500 international business journals that offer summary abstracts on-line. Every facet of information is covered, including projections, market and industry share data, corporate structure and news, and trade literature.

- The full-text of the Harvard Business Review, one of the most prestigious scholarly business journals in the world. The emphasis in this database is on applicable and theoretical management; it is ideal for the practicing manager as well as the undergraduate or graduate business school student.

- ABI/INFORM, with abstracts dealing primarily with company, corporate, and industry management applications. ABI/INFORM, notes Schoenbrun, is a popular choice of those working in the insurance and personnel management fields.

IQuest Medical InfoCenter (GO IQMEDICINE)

This is a gateway to more than 20 major medical databases covering various aspects of medicine, including medical practice and research, pharmaceutical news, and allied health studies. These databases contain information from journals, books, government publications, special reports, and many other published sources.

The surcharge is $9.00 for the first 10 titles located, $9.00 for each additional 10 titles, and $2.00 for each abstract retrieved. A "SmartScan" for the databases costs $5.00.

Legal Research Center (GO LEGALRC)

This resource includes indexes to articles from more than 750 law journals, publications, studies covering practical and theoretical aspects of criminal justice, law enforcement and related areas, summaries of legislative, regulatory, judicial, and policy documents covering federal tax issues, legal issues in banking and finance, and more. The information is made available by Dialog Information Services Incorporated.

The surcharge is $4.00 for the first 10 titles located, $4.00 for each additional 10 titles, and $4.00 for each full-text article retrieved.

Magill's Survey of Cinema (GO MAGILL)

Magill's Survey of Cinema contains descriptions of most major films from 1902 to the present. Information on file includes:

- Title
- Release date
- Running time
- Country of release
- Cast and credits
- Production studio
- Motion Picture Association of America rating
- References to reviews

In addition, the plot and significant influences on the film are summarized and discussed.

The cost is $2.00 for the first 10 titles located, $2.00 for each additional 10 titles, and $2.00 for each complete text of movie information retrieved.

Marketing/Management Research Center (GO MKTGRC)

This database links up with indexes and full-text of major US and international business, management, and technical magazines, market and industry research reports, market studies and statistical reports, and US and international company news releases. The information is made available by Dialog Information Services Incorporated.

The surcharge is $4.00 for the first 10 titles located, $4.00 for each additional 10 titles, and $4.00 for each full-text article retrieved.

Marquis Who's Who (GO BIOGRAPHY)

The on-line Marquis Who's Who includes biographical information describing key North American professionals. Most information is obtained directly from the profiled individuals. Included are name, occupation, date and location of birth, parents, spouse and children's names, education, positions held during career, civic, military, and political activities, memberships, awards, and other organizational affiliations. You may retrieve biographies by entering the subject's name, birth (year, city, or country), occupation, research specialty, creative works, awards/honors, or military service as your search criteria. The feature provides "Search Guidelines" that are similar to those used with IQuest. The material is made available by Dialog Information Services Incorporated.

Who's Who carries transaction charges in addition to base CompuServe connect rates. A running total of transaction charges is displayed on Marquis Who's Who menu pages. Connect-charges are not included in the displayed total. Search (retrieves up to 10 names) is charged at $5.00, with additional names (in groups of 10) costing an additional $5.00. Each full biography retrieved is charged at $5.00.

National Technical Information Service (GO NTI)

This resource, published by the US Department of Commerce, contains nearly 1.5 million references to articles from government-sponsored research, development, and engineering reports, usually with corresponding abstracts. Coverage goes back to 1970 and the database is updated every two weeks.

Available for most articles are the titles, authors, corporate sources, sponsors, report numbers, publication years, contract numbers, and abstracts. You may retrieve abstracts by entering subject words, author names, or the publication year.

The cost is $2.00 for the first 10 titles located, $2.00 for each additional 10 titles, and $2.00 for each listing retrieved.

Newspaper Library (GO NPL)

Newspaper Library has selected full-text articles from scores of newspapers from across the United States. (Classified ads are not included.) The database is updated daily, but there is a two-day delay in making today's newspapers available.

The information is made available by Dialog Information Services Incorporated.

The cost is $4.00 for the first 10 titles located, $4.00 for each additional 10 titles, and $3.00 for each full-text article retrieved. As with most Telebase databases, only regular connect-time charges are levied if a search does not retrieve any titles.

A list of the newspapers currently searchable is provided on the main menu.

Patent Research Center (GO PATENT)

The patent gateway reaches summaries of US patents granted in chemical, mechanical, electrical, and design categories, and summaries of patents granted internationally since the mid-1970s. The information is made available by Dialog Information Services Incorporated.

The surcharge is $5.00 for the first 10 titles located, $5.00 for each additional 10 titles, and $5.00 for each full-text article retrieved. As with most Telebase databases, only regular connect-time charges are levied if a search does not retrieve any titles.

PTS Newsletter Database/Communications (GO DPNEWS)

This is the computer and telecommunications section of PTS Newsletter Database, which includes the full text of articles from several of the leading newsletters covering the computer, electronics, and telecommunications industries. They are seen as a good source of facts, figures, analyses, and current information in that market.

Surcharges for the database are $4.00 for the first 10 titles located, $4.00 for additional titles in groups of 10, and $4.00 for each full reference retrieved, with abstract where available.

PTS Newsletter Database/Media (GO MEDIANEWS)

This is the broadcast and publishing section of PTS Newsletter Database, including full text of articles from several major newsletters covering the broadcasting and publishing industries.

Surcharges for the database are $4.00 for the first 10 titles located, $4.00 for additional titles in groups of 10, and $4.00 for each full reference retrieved, with abstract where available.

Other References of Interest

In addition to the above-listed databases, there are other reference features.

Magazine Database Plus (GO MDP)

Ziff Communications Company, the same magazine publisher that produces Computer Library Plus and Health Database Plus (discussed above), has also brought on-line this service, which contains full text of articles from more than 90 general-interest magazines, including *Changing Times*, *The Atlantic*, *The Nation*, *New Republic*, *The Economist*, *Popular Science*, and *U.S. News & World Report*.

Topics covered include current events, business, science, sports, news, people, personal finance, family, arts and crafts, cooking, education, the environment, travel, and political and consumer opinion. Also available are book and movie reviews. Coverage for most titles begins as of January 1, 1986, and is updated weekly.

Besides the base connect-charge, the service charges $1.50 for each full-text article retrieved.

Information USA (GO INFOUSA)

This is an on-line product by author Matthew Lesko, whose *Information USA*, published by Viking Penguin Books, is a 1,250-page reference to nearly everything. The on-line service specializes in telling Lesko's techniques for getting questions answered, with tutorials such as "The Art of Obtaining Information from Bureaucrats."

Book Review Digest (GO BRD)

This database, produced by the H. W. Wilson Co., is available directly or through IQuest. The database provides references to more than 26,000 fiction and non-fiction English language books and is updated twice weekly. It goes back to April 1983. Reviews are drawn from some 80 American, Canadian, and British periodicals covering general and social sciences, humanities, and general reference. The service is searchable by subject, title, author, or person named as subject, and the cost of a search is $9.00. The same rules for searching apply here as in IQuest.

Journal Graphics Transcripts (GO TRANSCRIPTS)

CompuServe also can help you get transcripts of important news broadcasts and TV specials through this database operated by Journal Graphics of New

York. It is a keyword-searchable feature that provides names, shows, networks, and air dates for thousands of programs that have been transcribed, some from as early as the mid 1970s.

The database covers transcripts for several dozen current and previous shows, including ABC's *Nightline, Prime Time Live*, and *20/20*; CBS's *60 Minutes, 48 Hours*, and *CBS Reports*; and PBS's *NOVA* and *Adam Smith's Money World*. It also has transcripts from a number of syndicated shows (Oprah Winfrey, Geraldo, Sally Jessy Raphael, The Wall Street Journal Report, etc.), from Bill Moyers (including The Secret Government, God & Politics, Joseph Campbell, and World of Ideas), and many specials.

The database may be searched by show name and category, by show date, and by topic.

The printed transcripts may be ordered on-line for $10.00 each and will be shipped to you within 24 hours by first-class mail. The expense can be billed to your regular CompuServe account.

Knowledge Index (GO KI)

Evening and weekend access is offered to more than a hundred databases, including over 50,000 journals on various topics. It provides two methods of locating information, menu-based and more advanced command-based versions. The resource has three types of databases: bibliographic, full text, and directory. The introductory menus offer instructions on searching and lists of available databases.

The feature is provided by CompuServe and Dialog Information Services Inc. You are charged $24.00 an hour (40 cents a minute).

Educational Meeting Places

CompuServe has a number of on-line meeting places for teachers, administrators, students, and parents.

Education Forum (GO EDFORUM)

Chuck Lynd is the primary sysop of the Education Forum (GO EDFORUM). Lynd, 76703,674, is a former classroom teacher with experience in both regular and special education settings. He also has more than 10 years experience in education and computer-based retrieval systems.

Education Research Forum (GO EDRESEARCH)

Education Research Forum (GO EDRESEARCH) is set up to share, compare, and comment on research findings in the field. Many of its regular members are associated with the American Educational Research Association. The primary sysop is Dr. Jean W. Pierce, 76703,445, an associate professor at Northern Illinois University, and past president of the Mid-Western Educational Research Association.

Foreign Language Forum (GO FLEFO)

Foreign Language Forum (GO FLEFO) is for teachers and students of all languages. The primary sysops are:

- Jerry Ervin, 76703,2063, who holds Ph.Ds in foreign language education from Ohio State University. His languages are French, Spanish, German, and Russian.
- Doug Lacey, 76702,1245, who holds a Ph.D. in Classics from the University of California, Berkeley. His interests in modern language focus on French, German, and Italian.

Science/Math Forum (GO SCIENCE)

Science/Math Forum (GO SCIENCE) is operated by Rick Needham, 76703,627, chairman of the Science Department of the Mercersburg Academy in Mercersburg, Pennsylvania, as a gathering place for teachers, students, and other subscribers with an interest in science and math. Among the items in the data libraries is an extensive collection of practice problems for students studying for college board achievement tests in math, physics, chemistry, and biology.

Students' Forum (GO STUFO)

Students' Forum (GO STUFO) is intended for students of all ages from the early grades to college; teachers are also welcome. The primary sysop is Dave Winslow, 76703,2033, who has devoted more than twenty years to teaching high school and middle school, and currently teaches math and computer science at the Columbus Academy in Gahanna, Ohio.

Issues Forum (GO ISSUESFORUM)

The most current and hottest news issues have their own sections in this forum which is a place for the free exchange of thoughts and feelings. Politics, handicapped issues, human rights, and more are all welcome topics on the Issues Forum. As new social issues arise, they are often given their own topic area in this forum. Georgia Griffith, 76703,266, is the forum's primary sysop.

Handicapped Users' Database
(GO REHABILITATION)

This is a collection of information specifically for those with handicaps. It includes the latest news about handicapped issues, a reference library, rehabilitation research and development, lists of self-help organizations for those with handicaps, sources of special computer software and hardware for the handicapped, and related issues.

Chapter

10

Travel

In this chapter...

Eaasy Sabre
Worldspan Travelshopper
OAG Electronic Edition
Other Travel Features
Forums

Working smart in the new Information Age means schooling yourself in the basics, then being prepared to welcome the unimagined opportunities the technology will offer. That has certainly worked for California freelance writer Lee Foster.

When he graduated from Stanford with a degree in literature in 1975, Foster could not foresee that in 20 years he would be a grand old man of electronic publishing. It happened naturally when he combined writing with a passion for travel, all the while embracing the emerging computer technology to get the job done.

Since 1984, Foster has shared his experiences on the road in two Compu-Serve features, Adventures in Travel (GO AIT) and West Coast Travel (GO WCT). Foster, on the road about one week out of four, has told his readers of a bicycle trip across the Netherlands and a journey along China's Great Wall, as well as state-side visits to places such as San Francisco's Chinatown and Upper Michigan's Royale Isle National Park. While he has followed a traditional freelancer's career (he has written more than 15 books and appeared in more than 50 newspapers and magazines), Foster is especially excited about his electronic publications.

"I like presenting travel on-line," he recently told a reporter with Compu-Serve's *Online Today* electronic publication, "because a consumer knows it is always there whenever he wants it" and because it is interactive. His features include a section for reader feedback. "Folks, for example, often ask me who will be playing Las Vegas when they plan visiting," so he has made the answer a regular part of the "Nevada Travel" area of the West Coast Travel feature.

Believing that electronic media will one day overtake print travel journalism, Foster has produced four on-line tour guides. As part of the West Coast Travel feature, the guides include material on Monterey-Carmel-Big Sur, Silicon Valley, a statewide adventure guide, and San Francisco.

Overview

No on-line market has grown more rapidly in recent years than the travel services. With them, you become your own travel agent, plotting your business and pleasure trips on-line whenever you want. Often you can use these services to reserve airline seats, hotel rooms, even rental cars.

All travel services are listed on the Travel menu, to which you have access either by entering GO TRAVEL or by highlighting and choosing Travel from the CompuServe Information Manager Services menu. Whether you are using CIM or a third-party general communications program, the menu includes the following options:

```
BASIC TRAVEL SERVICES
Air/Hotel/Car Information
Electronic Mall Merchants (FREE)
Dept. Of State Advisories
Visa Advisories
AT&T Toll-Free 800 Directory
Zagat Restaurant Guide
EXTENDED TRAVEL SERVICES
Air Information/Reservations
Hotel Information
U.S. Domestic Information
International Information
Travel Forums
Aviation
```

Many of the services discussed in this chapter are *gateways* — you leave the CompuServe computers to connect automatically with computers elsewhere. This is similar to the gateway used in some of the reference services, as discussed in Chapter 9, and in the shopping services, such as Shoppers Advantage, illustrated in Chapter 12.

Two major travel services are listed in the Basic Services Air/Hotel/Car Information section of this CIM box (or by choosing No. 1 from the ASCII menu with a general communications program). The subsequent screen lists the primary air reservation services:

```
BASIC AIR/HOTEL/CAR INFORMATION
1   WORLDSPAN Travelshopper
2   WORLDSPAN Travelshopper (CIM)
3   EAASY SABRE
4   EAASY SABRE (CIM)
```

Eaasy Sabre (GO SABRE)

Suppose you are going on a plane trip and you decide to use Eaasy Sabre to check out flight schedules or perhaps even make a reservation. Eaasy Sabre is a very special gateway service. Unlike most gateways where you must use CIM in a terminal emulation mode to access them, CompuServe and Eaasy Sabre have joined to provide a CIM link with the service. Therefore, if you are using CompuServe Information Manager DOS version 1.32, the Windows CIM, or Macintosh version 1.6 or a later version, you can interact with Eaasy Sabre via the boxes and pull-down menus that CIM offers in other parts of the system.

If you are using a general third-party communications program, choose EAASY SABRE from the introductory menu. If you are using CIM, choose EAASY SABRE (CIM) (or enter SABRE with the GO prompt in CIM). In either case the system displays similar introductions:

```
EAASY SABRE

    1    Introduction
    2    How to Use
    3    What is EAASY SABRE (CIM)
    4    Bargain Finder
    5    Talk to EAASY SABRE
    6    Talk to Travelers Access

    7    Access EAASY SABRE
    8    Access EAASY SABRE (CIM)
** HELP DESK 800-331-2690
(Outside the US) 817-355-2936 **
```

Eaasy Sabre enables you to look for scheduled flights on 600 airlines as well as for 18,000 hotel properties worldwide and 45 car agencies. You can choose from more than 43 million fares which are updated at the rate of a million changes daily. You can also access current weather information provided by the National Weather Service for over 600 cities in the US, Canada, and the Caribbean.

You may make actual reservations for flights, hotels, and cars if you sign up as a registered user of the service. Even if you don't subscribe to the reservation service, you may browse the databases as much as you like. The database is a service of American Airlines (which explains the unusual spelling of "EAASY"). Actual departure and arrival information, including gate numbers and baggage claim information, is available for American Airline flights.

Whether you are using CIM or a general terminal program, you see introductory bulletins and announcements from the operators.

In the ASCII display shown to a general third-party program, the bulletins are followed by a message to "Press <CR> to continue" or a prompt that is a "greater-than" symbol (>) at which you may enter commands. The prompt may be unfamiliar, but it is used much like the ! prompt you see on CompuServe whenever you are in terminal emulation of CIM or using a third-party communications program. For third-party terminal program users, follow the instructions on the screen to move on until you get to the main menu:

```
                        EAASY SABRE MAIN MENU


    1  System Quick Tips             6  Profile Review and Change
    2  Travel Reservations and       7  Travelers Access
       Information
    3  Weather Information            8  Official Recreation Guide
    4  AAdvantage                     9  Sign Off
    5  Application to use EAASY SABRE


  To select one of the options above, enter the number:

  **Quick Tip: These system navigation commands are always available:
          /Help or ? for assistance
          /Res or /R to go to the Reservations Menu
          /Top or /T to return to the Main Menu
          /Exit or /E to return to your System Operator
```

From this menu you may search the Reservation and Travel Information database (and may apply for membership in order to make on-line reservations). You may also check weather information for all the cities that have

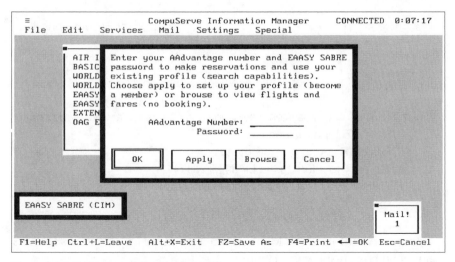

Figure 10.1 Eaasy Sabre's Intro

airports. The System Quick Tips menu choice contains on-line documentation on how to use Eaasy Sabre at a command level. Later, if you decide to use the service for reservations, return here and select the appropriate option to begin the application process.

If you are using CIM, you see an introductory bulletin. Choose Proceed until you see a box like the one in Figure 10.1.

At this point, you may enter your AAdvantage Number and Password if you have become a member, or you may Apply for membership or simply Browse the system.

Navigating the Service

If you are using Eaasy Sabre via a third-party (non-CIM) program, the basic navigation commands are entered at the > prompt. They are preceded by a slash (/):

- /T to return to the main (*top*) menu.
- /E to *exit* to go back through the gateway and return to CompuServe.
- /R to go to the *reservations* menu.

Selecting the reservation options (/R or option 2 in the example) takes you to the main reservation menu:

RESERVATIONS MENU	
1 Flight Reservations and Availablility	5 Airline Fares
2 Flight Arrival/Departure Information	6 Itinerary Review and Change

```
    3   Hotels                         7   Sign On for Reservations
    4   Rental Cars                    8   Flight Schedules
                                       9   Specific Flight Details

   To select one of the options above, enter the number:

   Quick Tip: The following system navigation commands are always available:
            /Help or ? for assistance, or
            /Res or /R to return to this menu or
            /Top or /T to return to the MAIN MENU or
            /Exit or /E to return to the System Operator
```

CompuServe Information Manager offers a similar list of options from its main menu box, as shown in Figure 10.2.

Highlighting any of these choices will allow you to choose that menu item. In this case, highlight and choose Flights to get to the Destination or flight planning box.

Flight Schedules

If you want to review and compare flights in ASCII version (third-party communications programs, that is, non-CIM), you select option 1 and the system asks you for specific information, including:

- From what city will you be departing?
- To what city will you be traveling?
- What date will you be traveling?

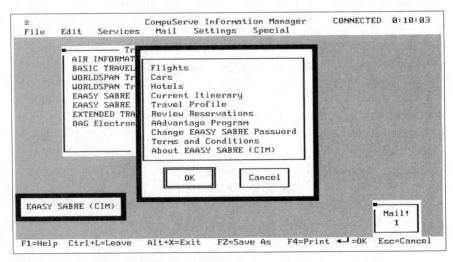

Figure 10.2 Entering Eaasy Sabre

- Which flights do you want to see? (A menu gives you options to specify a certain class of service, a particular airline, a specific connecting city, etc. Or you may press RETURN to leave the option blank and see all available flights.)

- What is your desired departure time? If you enter 7:00 a.m., the list isn't restricted to only those flights, but presents flights closest to that time first. Again, you may leave the option blank by pressing RETURN to indicate no preference.

After the questions are answered, the system displays something like this:

```
FLIGHT AVAILABILITY
From: (HTS) HUNTINGTON, WV
  To: (MSY) NEW ORLEANS, LA                          MONDAY APR-05-93
------------------------------------------------------------------------
                                             On
   Flight    Leave      Arrive    Meal  Stop Aircraft Time  Classes of Service**
1*DL 3057  HTS 640A  CVG  735A           0   SF3           Y B M Q H K L
   DL 1075      908A  MSY 1010A  S        0   M80    8    F Y B M Q H K L
2 US 659   HTS 700A  PIT  745A           0   D9S    5    F Y B H Q V M K
   US 210       945A  MSY 1130A  B        0   M80    8    F Y B H Q V M K
3*NW3439   HTS 645A  DTW  815A           0   SWM          Y B M H Q V K
   NW1473       935A  MSY 1121A  S        0   D9S    7    F Y B M H Q V K
------------------------------------------------------------------------
To SELECT a flight, enter the line number, or

 8  View MORE flights              11  View all FARES
 9  CHANGE flight request          12  Translate CODES
10  View FIRST flight display      13  View LOWest one-way fares

**Quick Tip: Select your flight, then choose Bargain Finder when prompted and
  EAASY SABRE will select the class of service for the lowest available fare.
```

If you are a regular flier, you know that airlines don't run on jet fuel; they run on codes. There are lots of codes here. If it looks vaguely familiar, it might be because you have looked over a shoulder as a travel agent made reservations and have seen this system. It is used by many travel professionals in a slightly modified form.

In the left column, the numbers 1,2, and 3 each represent a different series of flights through various "hubs." You may find out the code for any airport by choosing option 12 (" Translate CODES") on this menu, which produces a menu that allows you to translate codes for cities, airports, airlines, and equipment. Using that menu, you can determine, that "PIT" means Pittsburgh, Pennsylvania, for instance.

With CIM, you choose Flights from the main menu to see a Destination box like the one shown in Figure 10.3.

```
≡                 CompuServe Information Manager    CONNECTED  0:11:10
 File   Edit   Services   Mail   Settings   Special
                    ▀▀▀▀▀▀▀▀ Destination ▀▀▀▀▀▀▀▀
         Departure City or Code: _____
                         Date: 08-Feb-1993_ Time: 8:00am___
         Arrival City or Code: _____
         Number of Passengers: _
         (Optional)
           Airline Name or Code: _____

          ┌──────────┐  ┌────────┐  ┌────────────┐  ┌────────┐
          │ Flights  │  │ Fares  │  │ Preferences │  │ Cancel │
          └──────────┘  └────────┘  └────────────┘  └────────┘


 ┌────────────────────────┐
 │ EAASY SABRE (CIM)      │                          ┌────────┐
 └────────────────────────┘                          │ Mail!  │
                                                      │  1     │
                                                      └────────┘
 F1=Help  Ctrl+L=Leave   Alt+X=Exit   F2=Save As   F4=Print ↵=OK  Esc=Cancel
```

Figure 10.3   Destination Box

You fill in the Departure City or the airport code, the date and approximate time you want to leave and the arrival city or the city's airport code. Next, you enter the number of passengers, including yourself, who will be on the flight with you. You may choose an airline (or enter the airline's code) as an option.

CIM users may also choose the Preferences box which will take you to a Flight and Fare Preferences window where you can choose the class of service and a connecting city, and enter a return date to view applicable fares for your travel dates.

From the Destination window, choose Flights to see a list of all flights Eaasy Sabre has chosen, as shown in Figure 10.4.

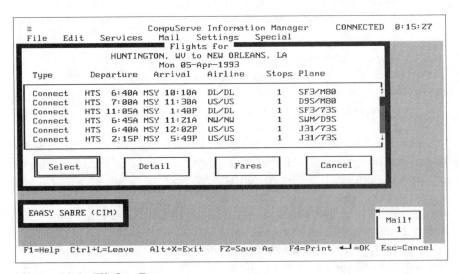

Figure 10.4   Flights Box

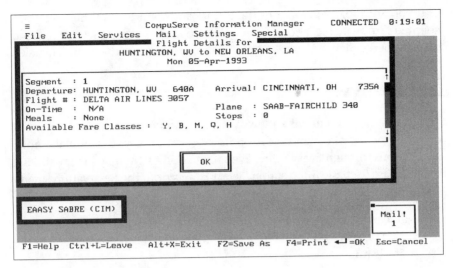

Figure 10.5   Details Box

There may be more flights than the window can hold, so you may use the standard way to scroll up and down the window to see them all.

The Fares button gives you the fare for the highlighted flight. Detail gives you the detail of the highlighted flight, as shown in Figure 10.5.

If there is more than one segment of the flight, scroll down to see the remaining segments.

When non-CIM users choose to inspect a single flight from the display more closely, they are asked to indicate the number of passengers, up to four, or simply press ENTER for one. After that, you see something like:

```
Flight:  COMAIR INC             3057            APR05
From:    HUNTINGTON, WV         (HTS)            640A
To:        CINCINNATI, OH             (CVG) 735A
Meal:    No meal served


Flight:  DELTA AIRLINES         1075            APR05
From:    CINCINNATI, OH             (CVG)        908A
To:        NEW ORLEANS, LA         (MSY)       1010A
Meal:    Snack


1  Use Bargain Finder to locate lowest discounted fare available
2  Select class of service for each segment
3  Return To Availability
>
```

If you are a registered user of the feature and want to find the lowest discounted fare available, choose 1. To select your own class of service for each segment of the flight, choose 2. Option 3 takes you back to the flight schedules.

Hotel Listings

The Reservations menu also allows you to examine hotel listings in various cities. If you elect to sign up for on-line reservations, you may make hotel reservations through Eaasy Sabre. Even if you don't sign up, you may still use the database for basic information. Select Hotels from the Reservations menu and the system prompts for specifics, including:

- Name of the city in which the hotel is desired. (You may enter a full name, such as "NEW ORLEANS," or a code, MSY, which is the same used in the flight listings.)
- Desired check-in and check-out dates.
- Number of adults in a room and number of names in the party.
- The number of rooms needed.
- Other qualifiers, such as a specific hotel or hotel chain, location, transportation, maximum room rate, or corporate rate.

If you're using CIM, the Hotel Selection window looks like the display in Figure 10.6. You fill in the blanks, including the city, check-in and check-out times, single or multiple occupancy, the number in your party, and the number of rooms. Choose the Preferences button to see a screen which will allow you to focus on a hotel according to special rates, bed type, and location (city, suburban, airport, etc.)

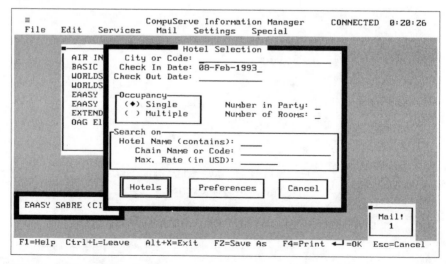

Figure 10.6 Hotels Box

A typical display of a list of hotels looks like this:

```
Hotel availability in NEW ORLEANS, LA
Check in:  05APR MONDAY       Check out: 07APR WEDNESDAY
Preferences:  Chain:                     Name:
              Location:                  Zip:
              Bed type:                  Area:
              Special rate:              Trans:
- - - - - - - - - - - - - - - - - - - - - - - - - - - - - - -
  Chain code    Name               Miles from MSY  Lowest rate

  1  SI   -  SHERATON NEW ORLEANS      13E          $170.00
            NEW ORLEANS,LA
  2  HH   -  NEW ORLEANS HILTON RV     14SE         $130.00
            NEW ORLEANS, LA
  3  VP   -  HOTEL ACADIANA            150W         $ 55.00
            LAFAYETTE, LA
- - - - - - - - - - - - - - - - - - - - - - - - - - - - - - -
For details or reservations enter the line number, or
4  View MORE hotels          7  Translate CODES
5  NEW hotel request         8  Change PREFERENCES
6  Repeat FIRST display      9  Change DATES
```

The hotel name is accompanied by information about mileage and direction in relation to the airport. For example, the Sheraton New Orleans is located 13 miles west of the airport. For details about one of the hotels, choose the corresponding number. If you have signed up to make reservations on-line, you would choose the same number. As elsewhere in the feature, navigation commands are led by slashes, such as /T command to go back to the main menu. No matter where you are in Eaasy Sabre, you may get back to "System Operator" — that is, CompuServe — by entering /E.

CIM's window looks basically the same and allows you to Detail a highlighted motel with one button, get more information about Rates with another, or Select a hotel for a reservation if you are a member.

Other Notes

Frequent visitors to Eaasy Sabre via third-party programs often take a short cut called "FAASTTRACK," which lets them enter codes separated by commas. You learn how to do that by choosing option 1 "System Quick Tips" on the main menu.

If you think you might be interested in signing up for the on-line reservation capability, called "AAdvantage," you may read about it and apply to join using options on the main menu. Once you are a member, you are given an AAdvantage number and password. If you are using non-CIM software, you may also put a "personal profile" on-line with the system to save time in searching for flights and making reservations.

Travel Profile

When you use Eaasy Sabre with CIM, the system offers Travel Profile in which your personal travel profile information is stored with your AAdvantage number. You must be an EAASY SABRE Member to store a travel profile. The Travel Profile will optionally store any or all of the following information for you:

- Address and Phone Information.
- Credit Card number (for hotel/car confirmation or Ticket-by-Mail).
- Seating and Meal Preferences.
- SABRE Travel Agent information.
- Departure City/Airport (The information will be pre-filled for you on your Destination Screen.) Store a frequently traveled Arrival City/Airport as well.
- Preferred Airline.
- Display flight schedules using a 12- or 24-hour clock.
- Default departure and arrival times.
- Currency (US dollars or other) for fares and car rates.
- Class of Service (Store Bargain Finder) to always see the lowest prices for your reservation.
- Frequent Flyer numbers for up to six airlines.
- Frequent Lodger and Car Rental Membership numbers.

AAdvantage

A feature called "BargainFinder" lets you define specific travel itineraries and search for the lowest possible fares. To use BargainFinder in terminal emulation mode:

1. Go to the Reservation menu by entering /R. Select the first option— "Flight Schedules and Availability"—to record your travel plans. You are prompted for your departure and destination cities, date, and preferred time, if any. Then you are asked whether you want to see all available flights or limit the display to a specific class of service, airline, and/or connecting city.

2. After that, available flights are displayed with options to book in specific classes or to see more flights meeting your specifications. Select the flight for which you want more information; you are prompted for the number of people traveling in your party.

3. Next, the system displays the class of service preference with an additional option to "use BargainFinder to locate the lowest discounted fare available." Select that option and the system prompts for your AAdvantage number and password, as issued when you applied for the AAdvantage service.

4. Then the system allows you either to use a personal profile already on file or to enter new specifics, including names of each passenger and phone numbers.

5. When you have verified the profile data and the flight under consideration, the system lets you select several other preferences, such as smoking/non-smoking sections, special dietary meals needed, and frequent flyer number, if any.

6. Now selecting a "Price Itinerary" option puts the BargainFinder feature to work. It locates the lowest possible fares for your specifications and prompts you to either book the flight, or cancel and exit.

To use BargainFinder with CIM, key the BargainFinder button when it pops up in the Fares window while seeking information about fares using CIM.

Option 7 from the main menu is Travelers Access, a travel club that offers the Eaasy Sabre user a variety of discounted vacation packages. The option gives instructions on how to obtain membership.

For More Help

Eaasy Sabre also operates a Help Desk for additional questions. The number is 800-331-2690. (From outside the US, call 817-355-2936.)

Worldspan Travelshopper (GO WORLDSPAN)

Travelshopper is the CompuServe connection to the Worldspan Reservation system, the third largest in the world. Worldspan is owned by TWA, Northwest Airlines, and Delta. As with Eaasy Sabre, CompuServe and Worldspan have worked together to provide a CompuServe Information Manager interface to Worldspan called Travelshopper (CIM). Unlike Eaasy Sabre, Worldspan offers information about flights and flight reservations only. Neither information about hotels and rental cars nor reservations is offered.

The CompuServe Information Manager (version 1.3 or greater for DOS, or 1.5 or greater for the Macintosh) gives you access to the same information as over 45,000 Worldspan travel agents, but the CompuServe Information Manager organizes it for you in much the same way it organizes the information in Eaasy Sabre.

Key Features

These are the main sections of Travelshopper:

- PERSONAL PROFILE Provide ticketing information, default departure city, and passport information which is stored for you on-line.
- SEARCH CRITERIA Store your flight display preference, preferred airlines, fare class, maximum stops, and connections to retrieve only those flights you want to see.
- DESTINATION INPUT SCREEN Enter departure and arrival information in a window.
- ITINERARY This screen keeps track of flights you have selected and allows you to price them as a whole. It also allows you to make reservations and lets you ticket, if you desire.
- FLIGHTS View all flights (with sold-out flights listed for the stand-by traveler) or available flights only. Access FARES from the flights screen and look at only those fares available for the flight highlighted.
- DETAILS Learn more about each flight by accessing Details from the Flights screen. Details include departure/arrival information, decoded airlines, on-time rating, meals, travel time, plane type(s), stop information, and available fare classes for the flight.
- FARES/FARE RULES Shop fares by looking at all fares for a city pair and checking rules to see how you might qualify.
- PRICING Build your itinerary and choose PRICE to see not only the lowest available fare for your personal itinerary, but also other fares that give you a more complete picture of your price options. Choose a price and reserve it or escape back to browse further.
- RESERVATIONS Reserve a flight and make ticketing arrangements quickly with ticketing information stored in your Personal Profile.

To Browse or To Book

You can use Travelshopper to book or to browse. If you want to manage your own airline reservations at a time that is convenient for you, complete the enrollment questionnaire. Enrolling enables you to BOOK or change your reservations. Even without enrolling in Travelshopper, you may look at airline availability and fares. Just select "Access to Travelshopper" from the main menu and be ready to provide city names of where in the world you want to go.

Commands

Here are the single letter code commands most frequently used in the ASCII mode of Travelshopper:

M Return to Travelshopper's main menu to enter a new command. This option is available from almost every page.

?, H or **HELP** Display a further "HELP" explanation for the current page of display.

E Exit Travelshopper and return to the CompuServe main menu from anywhere in Travelshopper. Will also accept "EXIT," "BYE," or "OFF."

A Request available flights and make your reservations.

F Request all fares and fare restrictions for one specific airline or a comparison of fares for all carriers.

R Make a reservation if the specific flight information and codes are known.

O Other services area, including airline and city codes, air mileage between cities, and local times in cities.

B Back-up. This command returns the previous screen of display.

D Done. When you have completed your itinerary, enter D and Travelshopper prompts you for passenger information such as name, telephone, etc.

I Itinerary. Displays the itinerary booked up to that point.

Low Fare Finder

Low Fare Finder allows you to find the lowest fare available on the flights you have chosen. Low Fare Finder is currently available only in the book mode which means you must be a registered user to access it.

In order to use the Low Fare Finder Feature, you must first create your itinerary. This entails entering your destination city and date. Then a flight screen is displayed. Choose the line number of the flight requested. A list of available fare classes is displayed. You should choose Y and a menu is displayed with these options:

To look at available flights to the next city.

- Return flights.
- Changes.
- Reservations.
- Open flight.
- D (done) when the itinerary is complete.

If it is a multi-leg trip, choose available flights to the next city; if it is a round-trip, choose return flights; if it is a one-way trip, choose D, Itinerary complete. If Return flights is chosen, a list of return flights will be displayed. Again choose the line number of the flight requested. A list of available fare classes will be displayed. You should choose Y class. A menu will appear with options listed as above. You should now enter D done, Itinerary Complete. Your name, fare type, day and evening phone numbers, and ticketing method will be displayed. The information is displayed from your Travelshopper enrollment information stored in your own profile. After verifying this information, the Low Fare Finder screen will appear.

Displays

The Low Fare Finder will display two fares. The top fare is the fare at Y class (usually full-fare coach). The bottom fare is the lowest fare available on the chosen flight. Press RETURN and choose to book the flight or choose option 3, FARE REQUEST ONLY — Ignore input. Travelshopper displays a price for the reservation as booked on this pricing screen. The lowest fare available for this flight is automatically selected. This includes combining two eligible fares. If the Low Fare Finder calculates a combined fare for you, it will not be listed in the fare display. Record the *Fare Basis Codes* to look up the restrictions that apply. The most restrictive rules apply to combined fare quotations.

Limitations

Travelshopper calculates the lowest fare available for the flights you have booked with certain limitations:

1. The lowest fare searched for is determined by the cabin or class of service requested. For example, if you book a seat in the first class section, the system searches for the lowest fare in First Class.
2. The lower fare must have seats available for sale. The search does not include wait-listed fares.
3. It prices only two passenger types in the same reservation.
4. It searches for the lowest fare on the flight booked. It does not search for different flights or times. However, it does include advance purchase and penalty fares which are identified in the fares display. Make a note of the last day to ticket for this fare as Travelshopper may ask you for it before completing your reservation.

Your name and phone number are required.

Additional Help

The Travelshopper Help Desk (1-800-892-1011) is available if you have any questions about using the system.

OAG Electronic Edition Travel Service (GO OAG)

The Official Airline Guides Electronic Edition Travel Service is a surcharged series of travel-related databases and bills itself as the largest of its kind. In fact, OAG says that, of the 415 airlines worldwide using automated reservation systems, 413 look to OAG for schedule data. The OAG Electronic Edition allows you to view worldwide hotel/motel information, choose the most convenient schedule, find the lowest fare, view actual seat availability, book your flight, and arrange for ticketing.

Entering Data

When seeking flight information, you are prompted for your departure city, destination, and preferred date and time. The schedule information is then displayed chronologically by departure time and fares from lowest to highest. OAG does not offer the booking capability to international users of the service.

In addition to flight information, you have access to several databases with information, such as travel news and tours, cruises, and discount travel packages to Frequent Flyer/Frequent Lodger Award Program Information.

Surcharges

The OAG Electronic Edition carries a surcharge. During standard/evening time there is a $10/hour surcharge (17 cents/minute) and during prime/daytime hours the surcharge is $28/hour (47 cents/minute).

Commands

At this writing, OAG Electronic Edition Travel Service has no special interface for CIM, so all users see the same display, whether using a general third-party communications program or CIM in ASCII terminal emulation mode. OAG has its own set of commands, which are preceded by a slash (/). Commands can be used at any prompt within the OAG Electronic Edition or from the main Travel Service menu to start a new search:

/S Begin schedules request
/M Display the OAG command menu

/F   Begin fares request

/U   Send a message to OAG

/H   Begin hotel/motel request

/E   Turn expert mode on/off

/C   Review or cancel a booking

/Q   Exit OAG Electronic Edition

/ I   Information and assistance, and return to the main menu

Navigational commands within OAG for moving within a search that are *not* preceded by a slash (/) include:

+   Next display (or use RETURN key)

-   Previous display

O   Original display

M   Fares or hotel/motel menus

CX   Display connections

DF   Display direct flights

RS   Display return flights

RF   Display return fares

MM   Return to Main Menu

OFF   Exit and return to CompuServe

Enter the actual line number of the flight or fare in the following commands, not the # symbol.

A#   Display fares/seats available

B#   Book flight or connection

S#   Display flights for your fare

F#   Display fares offered on flight

L#   Display fare restrictions

X#   Display expanded information

The help command is a question mark; ? with a code shows that code's meaning and ? with a city name will show the city code.

Moving Between Databases

The /TO command is used with the following list of Database and Group Menu Access Commands. This allows you to move directly from one database to another. The list will also give you an overview of what's in OAG.

GROUP MENUS	ACCESS COMMAND
Cruises	SAIL
General & How-to-Use	GEN
Leisure & Discount Travel	FUN
Lodging & Dining	REST
Travel Industry News	NEWS
What's New ?	WNEW
Worldwide Travel Facts	TIPS
OAG Electronic Edition	OAG
AA Rated European Hotels/Restaurants	AAG
Accu-Weather Forecasts	WFI
All Cruise Travel/Cruise Discounts	ACT
Arrival/Departure Info	ARD
City Travel Planner	SRR
CruiseStar Worldwide Cruises	CST
Currency Exchange Rates	CUR
Frequent Flyer/Lodger Award Info	FFL
InsideFLYER Magazine	FRQ
Nationwide Intelligence	NWI
TravelFile	ORG
Tours & Discount Travel	DIS
TRAVEL MANAGEMENT DAILY (R)	TMD
User Comments & Suggestions	MSG
US State Dept. Travel Advisories	USS
Vacation Florida	VFL
World of Information	WOI
World Travel Guide	WTG
Zapodel's Adventure Atlas	ZAP

More Help

OAG maintains a help desk. In the USA, phone 800/323-4000; outside the USA, phone 708-574-6414.

Other Travel Features

Besides air travel databases, there are other features for travel here and abroad.

ABC Worldwide Hotel Guide (GO ABC)

This service provides descriptions, rates, phone numbers, and facilities for 60,000 domestic and international hotels. It also lists miles to airports, local and toll-free phone numbers, Telex machine identification numbers, credit card information, and more. To search the database, simply select menu choices, using price, location, and facilities to find hotels and other resorts.

The Visa Advisors and Electronic Visaguide (GO VISA)

This is a Washington, D.C., passport and visa expediting firm that provides applications and information on travel requirements for more than 200 countries. It even offers same-day service for passports to persons able to submit copies of their round trip tickets.

US Department of State's Travel Advisory Service (GO STATE)

The advisory service is maintained by the Citizen Emergency Center as a continuously updated information service to Americans traveling abroad. The database includes advisories and warnings covering such conditions as warfare, political unrest, hotel/motel shortages, currency regulations, and other information of interest to the American traveler. To locate travel advice about a particular country, select a country from an alphabetical menu.

Lee Foster Travel Reports

As noted earlier, travel writer Lee Foster offers two on-line reports for the domestic trekker.

Adventures in Travel (GO AIT)

This is a single travel article that runs for two weeks. Earlier articles may also be reviewed. The articles aim to cover all aspects of travel. Also, you may leave a question or comment for Foster, by choosing another menu item.

West Coast Travel (GO WESTCOAST)

This is consumer guide to travel destinations in the western half of the United States, as well as in Canada and Mexico. The articles are personal travel research in the field. More than 130 major destinations now are on-line, covering the 13 western states.

Information USA Travel Data

A section of Information USA (GO IUS-4732) deals with vacation and business travel. You will find information about tourist adventures, parks and camping, boating and fishing, international travel, domestic tourism and trends, and numbers for state travel hotlines.

Zagat Restaurant Survey (GO ZAGAT)

This feature offers thousands of reviews based upon annual surveys of restaurant patrons. With the guide, you can search for old favorites or discover new ones in over 20 different cities and regions based on cuisine, price, and more.

Currently, the guide covers:

- Atlanta
- Baltimore (including Annapolis)
- Boston, including surrounding areas in New Hampshire
- Rhode Island, Maine, plus Cape Cod, Martha's Vineyard, and Nantucket
- Chicago, including surrounding areas in Indiana, Michigan, and Wisconsin (including Milwaukee)
- Connecticut (Western and Southern Parts of State)
- Dallas/Fort Worth Area, including the Mid-Cities
- Hawaiian Islands
- Houston, including Galveston
- Kansas City
- Long Island
- Los Angeles/Southern California, including Orange County, Palm Springs, San Diego, and Santa Barbara
- Miami and Southern Florida, including Ft. Lauderdale, Palm Beach, and the Keys
- New Orleans
- New York City
- New York State, north of the city
- Northern New Jersey
- Orlando and Central Florida, including Tampa, St. Petersburg and Daytona
- Philadelphia, including Bucks County, Atlantic City, South Jersey, and the Wilmington, Delaware area
- Portland, OR
- St. Louis
- San Francisco and Surrounding Area, including the Wine Country, San Jose, and the Monterey Peninsula
- Seattle
- Vancouver
- Washington, D.C.

Forums

Several forums cover travel-interested topics, especially those concerning air services.

General travel forums

Want some help with your vacation or business travel plans? At least two forums stand ready.

Travel Forum (GO TRAVSIG)

This forum is devoted to all travel questions. What tales of adventure or advice do you have to share with the other members? Have you discovered a particularly good restaurant or hotel? Do you need to know where to get a good cheeseburger in Tunisia? The forum handles these and more. Primary sysop is Jerry Schneiderman, 76702,667.

Florida Forum (GO FLORIDA)

If Florida is in your travel plans, a forum with you in mind is the Florida Forum, operated by Larry Wood, 76703,704. This forum is a place for users to get useful information in the planning of a Florida visit or vacation. The forum also provides educational assistance to schools, teachers, students, and parents in the preparation of their plans to visit Florida. Special forum emphasis is on the Orlando area and its attractions.

California Forum (GO CALFORUM)

This service, managed by Linda Woeltjen, 76711,1142, and Bill Eastburn, 70007,1657, discusses all aspects of the state that is home to more than 30 million people and the vacation destination of millions of others.

Aviation Forum and Related Services

The Aviation Forum (GO AVSIG) deals with all topics relating to airplanes and flying. This includes weather, navigation, air traffic control, safety, maintenance, legal issues, and so on. It's the oldest CompuServe forum still in existence. John B. Galipault, founder/president of the Aviation Safety Institute of Worthington, Ohio, and the founding forum sysop, died in early 1993. Assistant sysops are managing the forum at this writing.

Aviation Weather and Safety

In addition, you may find these aviation services helpful:

- NWS Aviation Weather (GO AWX-1) includes weather reports of every variety as issued by the U.S. National Weather Service. They can be used as the raw material for a self-customized weather briefing.

- EMI Flight Planning/Aviation Weather Briefings (GO EMI), is where pilots may specify a route or let EMI choose the best one. En route times are corrected for forecast winds. Weather briefings are tailored.

- Aviation Safety Institute (GO ASI), where you may read about hazards to aviation in the Aviation Safety Institute's Monitor, report hazards to the folks who will do something about them, check service difficulty reports, and more.

Chapter

11

Entertainment and Games

In this chapter...

Steve Estvanik has something most authors and artists will never know: two-way communication with his audience. Frequently, he has opportunities to brainstorm with the people who best know his work, his fans. Of course, it helps that he creates his work in a new medium that is, by nature, interactive. Estvanik is a professional games programmer with a monster hit in the on-line world.

Estvanik began designing computer games in 1979 and was still in college when he wrote his first real-time multiplayer game. The Seattle programmer hit the big time in 1983 when he joined Avalon Hill, a venerated name among serious gamers, known for its line of complex board games and simulations.

Air Traffic Controller (GO ATCONTROL) was his first CompuServe game, distinguished for nearly 10 years now as one of the first non-shoot-'em-up games in the computing set. Although that program still has a respectable following, it was Estvanik's next project that broke new ground.

Sniper! (GO SNIPER) is Estvanik's version of a popular board game from TSR, a simulation of World War II man-to-man combat. The game is played

265

on computer-generated maps filled with squads of soldiers with specific goals to accomplish. Players command six- to eight-man squads in which each member has strengths and weaknesses.

The game is also an example of the new way the creative process can work in an interactive world in which the artist/author can talk with the audience. Graphics for the original on-line version of Sniper! left a lot to be desired, because the "battlefield" was displayed as merely rows of letters and symbols (A line of o's represented a stone wall, &&&& stood for a hedge, @@@@ for a light forest, and so on.) A testimonial to the strength of Estvanik's game-creating skills is the fact that Sniper! developed a strong following, even with the obvious drawbacks of such symbolism which was required, not by his program, but by the perceived limitations of telecomputing in those days. It was with the encouragement and support of his fans that Estvanik pushed those limitations, taking Sniper! into the 1990s with a brand new look. He created a graphic interface called "Scope" to replace that "ASCII alphabet soup," as one loyalist called it, with high-resolution color pictures. Suddenly, hedges look like hedges, stone walls retain their stone wall-ness, and now the forests are green. (The IBM PC compatible EGA/VGA interface can be downloaded in a CompuServe forum, as described later in this chapter.)

Refinements like Scope are, in part, a natural evolution in an interactive community. As Estvanik told a writer in *CompuServe Magazine* recently, "With other games, my work's on the market two years after I've stopped programming it. Then, if anybody makes a suggestion, it's impossible to put it into the game." But Sniper! has been an ongoing creation, thriving on user feedback. "I find it really useful when we have an informal conference on a Saturday night and start kicking ideas around. Sometimes people won't say anything specific, but they'll spark something in my mind."

Overview

There is no doubt about it: Computers have changed forever the way we look at games and entertainment. The system that does our work also helps us relax and enjoy life. The communications aspects of the machines have only heightened interest in the games we play on them and the variety of entertainment they offer us. Perhaps there are computer curmudgeons who still scoff at the idea of using such a serious instrument as a computer information service to play games, but their small numbers are overwhelmed by those who find all sorts of on-line fun. Futurists theorize that in this age, information itself is entertainment. If so, you will find no greater concentration of entertainment anywhere than on CompuServe.

CompuServe has its own menu for entertainment and games. If you enter GO GAM-1, you see:

```
BASIC ENTERTAINMENT/GAMES
    Science Trivia Quiz
    The Grolier Whiz Quiz
    ShowBizQuiz
    Classic Adventure
    Enhanced Adventure
    CastleQuest
    BlackDragon
    Biorhythms
    Roger Ebert's Movie Reviews
    Hangman
EXTENDED ENTERTAINMENT/GAMES
    Intro to Games
    Fantasy/Role-Playing/Adventures
    War/Simulation Games
    Parlor/Trivia Games
    Modem Games and Challenge Board
    Entertainment Center
    Game Forums/News
    Entertainment Forums
    Entertainment News
    Order Merchandise/Guides
```

The Games We Play

Games have been a vital part of CompuServe since the beginning. Originally, most games were designed to pit the human computer enthusiast against the computer. Today, the more popular on-line games cast the system as a kind of game master, allowing human players from all over the world to compete with each other, joining for non-stop multiplayer games and interactive quests.

The system features many types of games:

Fantasy, role-playing, and adventure games challenge the imagination and the intellect.

War games test the ability to out-maneuver the opponent.

Simulations and sports games imitate the games of real life on the computer.

Parlor and trivia games include some of the all-time family favorites.

Modem-to-modem games in which players find opponents in their local calling area and around the world and even play their games via CompuServe.

This chapter also looks at forums that support gaming of all types. Before exploring the games, here is some background on format. At the top of many game descriptions in this chapter you will see:

- A GO address where you may read the complete instructions for playing the game. Some of these instructions are lengthy, so it is a good idea to save the instructions in a file for printing out at a later time.

- The suggested age, which gives some indication of the age group for which the game was designed. The complexity and level of challenge of the game are the determining factors.

- A "Players (min/max)" comment showing how many players may play the game at the same time. In games that are not interactive, the number represents how many may play at the user's computer.

Getting Help

Most games provide the player with help while inside the game. Usually you can find it by entering HELP at nearly any location. Sometimes you receive instant help; other times you are shown a "topic index" that lets you get help for a very specific topic. If you were at the beginning of one of the adventure games and typed HELP, you might be shown a list of help topics the system thinks you might need at this location, something like this:

```
More information is available for:

Movement       Spells        Talking
Fighting       Characters    Monsters

Topic?
```

You may choose one of the topics for a complete explanation.

Sometimes, there are subtopics listed under the main topics. Remember, though, this kind of help doesn't rule out the need to read the instructions. Attempting to learn all the ins-and-outs of a complex game while on-line is a good way to waste time and money. It is better to capture the documentation and read it before attempting any of games.

Entertainment and Games: Basic Service

CompuServe's Basic Service package offers users a variety of games and a movie review database. These features are a great introduction to the entertainment portions of CompuServe, since they are provided as part of the flat monthly fee offered in the standard pricing plan. After you have explored them, you can step up to the higher-level games in the pay-as-you-go Extended Services area.

Games for a Flat Fee

If you sign up for the standard pricing option, you can play any of the games described in this section for no extra cost. They are all part of Basic Service.

Science Trivia (GO SCITRIVIA)

Science Trivia is a collection of questions in the areas of biology, chemistry, physics, and mathematics that match the style and complexity of the questions found on the College Board's Achievement and Advanced Placement Tests.

Grolier Whiz Quiz (GO GAM-46)

(12 and up. Players (min/max) 1/4. Instructions: GO GAM-54)

The Whiz Quiz is sponsored by Grolier Electronic Publishing, Inc. and is based on the on-line Academic American Encyclopedia (covered in Chapter 9). Up to four people may compete at a time in a quiz. A total of 30 questions are asked for each quiz taken from one of nearly a dozen categories. Players receive a point for each correct answer. Game scores are calculated by subtracting the total number of questions answered incorrectly from the total number of questions answered correctly. The top 10 scores for a session are entered in the Whiz Quiz Hall of Fame.

ShowBiz Quiz (GO SBQ)

If you are a show business trivia fan, there's enough here to keep you entertained for days. Showbiz Quiz is a collection of more than 70 trivia quizzes about all aspects of show business.

Classic Adventure (GO GAM-200)

(12 and up. Players (min/max) 1/1. Instructions: GO GAM-100)

This is *the* original text adventure from which all other adventures, both micro and mainframe, evolved. The game "understands" English words and phrases. The object is to explore a cave, find treasures, and deposit the booty back in the building. A perfect score is 350 points. CompuServe suggests that if this is your first text adventure, enter HELP and INFO when the game begins.

Enhanced Adventure (GO GAM-201)

(12 and up. Players (min/max) 1/1. Instructions: GO GAM-101)

An enhanced version of the original adventure game, this was expanded from the original to provide more challenges and more dangers for the skilled player.

Castlequest (GO GAM-83)

(12 and up. Players (min/max) 1/1. Instructions: GO GAM-84)

Search the castle, find the master, and deal with him as needed, while looting the castle of its treasures. You get points for depositing the treasures in the vault. (Hint: The descriptions of treasures include an exclamation point.)

BlackDragon (GO GAM-590)

(12- adult. Players (min/max) 1/1. Instructions: GO GAM-417)

BlackDragon is a fantasy role-playing game set in a multilevel maze. You use magic and encounter strange and wondrous creatures (most of them deadly). If you survive the first level, nine more await. The object is to accumulate treasure and, by converting gold into experience points, to gain strength. To win, you must be strong enough to conquer the "Arch Demon" on the final level. Skill, experience, and some luck are required.

Biorhythms (GO GAM-218)

(12 and up. Players (min/max) 1/1. Instructions: GO GAM-118)

The program plots personalized charts for any year. You may print an individual month or several months. Enter the name of the person for whom you want a chart, then enter the date of birth, the year to chart, beginning month, and number of months to chart. The biorhythm chart also provides text for appropriate days in any given month. This program should be used with an 80-column printer.

Hangman (GO GAM-212)

(Children. Players (min/max) 1/1. Instructions: GO GAM-112)

This computer classic is one of the older games on the system. Hangman is a word-guessing game in which the computer comes up with a word and you try to learn it by picking letters. Each time you enter a correct letter, the computer shows you where it goes in the word. For each incorrect guess the computer adds a part of the body to hangman's gallows.

Roger Ebert's Reviews & Features (GO EBERT)

Not a game but definitely entertaining, Roger Ebert's Reviews & Features (GO EBERT) is also among the features in this area of the system that are accessible for the flat monthly fee.

Winner of the Pulitzer Prize for criticism, Roger Ebert has been called the most influential film critic in America. He posts reviews of new and old movies here. The first selection from the main menu provides a list of his most recent reviews which are updated each week. The second selection enables readers to search the hundreds of past Ebert reviews by title, actor, or director, mostly those released, since 1970. Each review contains the title, Ebert's rating (zero to four stars), the Motion Picture Association's rating, year released, and running time along with Ebert's review.

You will also find exclusive interviews with many stars and directors as well as special essays and features, including Ebert's popular tongue-in-cheek "Glossary of Movie Terms." If you want to discuss movies with Ebert, look for him in the ShowBiz Forum (GO SHOWBIZ).

Games in the Extended Service

CompuServe's Extended Service opens up a whole world of games and entertainment for almost any taste, including the intriguing area of multiplayer interactive games.

Fantasy/Role-Playing/Adventures

This section contains descriptions of the on-line community's adventure and role-playing games, a mainstay in any gamer's activities.

British Legends (GO GAM-153)

(12 and up. Players (min/max) 1/36. Instructions: GO GAM-166)

The multiplayer game of British Legends has rolling pastures, dense forests, misty graveyards, and evil beings lurking in the shadows. The key is that not all the creatures you encounter are computer-controlled. Some are real people who are also playing at the same time you are. You must conquer more than unknown countryside: You must also battle other players. Your goal is to progress from warrior (400 points) to a witch or a wizard (102,400 points) by solving some of the game's more than 200 puzzles. Once this is achieved, you inherit enviable powers over other players. However, the way is fraught with insidious dangers and ancient evils.

Here are some tips:

- After you name your character and start the game, you first enter an Elizabethan tea room where you can chat with the natives. Ask for help and maybe find a friend. To talk it up, enter CONVERSE; anything you enter after that is treated as a message. To cancel conversation mode, enter an asterisk.

- If you want a tour before you get down to some serious gaming, enter WISH,TOUR and a witch or a wizard will take you in hand.

- The first few times you play, don't concentrate so much on solving puzzles and earning points; instead, focus on mapping the land with pencil and paper. Your diagrams will be invaluable.

- Don't face the challenge alone. Make friends. Frequent the Multi-Player Games Forum (GO MPGAMES) described later in this chapter. A section of that board is set aside for British Legends enthusiasts to swap tips and lies. Also, the associated data library may have some useful help files.

- Beware of the Finger of Death.

The Island of Kesmai (GO GAM-26)

(12-adult. Players (min/max) 1/100. Instructions: GO GAM-76)

Here you direct your alter ego around the Island of Kesmai and through its catacombs, searching for riches and avoiding danger. You may play the game alone or enter the island with others for a group adventure. Again, the Multi-Player Games Forum (GO MPGAMES) is the place to join a group or to learn more about how to play the game. The Island of Kesmai is complex. While there is considerable on-line help, the veteran explorers on the island say it is best to order the printed Island of Kesmai manual. (Enter GO ORDER to review and order this as well as other CompuServe-related products.)

The object of Kesmai is basic: Stay alive and grow wealthy. The ticket is to buy better weapons for monster-zapping and finding treasures in musty out-of-the-way places. When you start the game, the system prompts you to create a character, giving it a gender, country of origin, name, and character class (that is, fighter, martial artist, thief, wizard, or a "thaumaturge"— a magically enhanced fighter with a few wicked spells to command). Then the system tells you your character's strength, dexterity, intelligence, wisdom, constitution, and charisma. Some of these characteristics are altered by experience and spells. Part of the fun is finding that out on your own. Then you are set down on a wood dock at the edge of town. You begin your journey by entering a direction (N for North, E for East, etc.).

Kesmai has both a basic and an advanced game. Once you have entered the advanced game, though, you can never play the basic game again.

Incidentally, Kesmai enthusiasts have been busy the last few years creating front-end graphics programs to liven up the screen display for their game. Most of the programs are available in Library 4 ("Island of Kesmai") of the Multi-Player Games Forum (GO MPGAMES). Some of the major programs available there at this writing were GKTerm for IBM and compatibles, KTerm for Apple Macintosh systems, and Aterm for Amiga computers. Playing the game via these programs automatically converts the system's rather pedestrian ASCII symbols into easier-to-read graphic displays.

Here are some tips for your travels:

- Explore the town to get familiar with the mode of transport and the lay of the land.

- Become a regular in the Multi-Player Game Forum (GO MPGAMES), where ASCII maps of the town and island have been stored in the data libraries. Associated message boards offer communication with other Kesmai gamers.

- Read the instructions. The on-line version (GO GAME-76) can be downloaded in about a minute.

- When you meet another adventurer, exchange greetings and offer to team up. Some beasties are best beaten by teamwork. Another option allows you to "page" other players elsewhere on the island.

- When you are ready to call it a night and want to type QUIT to save the game, be sure to first put your character in a safe place; when you log on again and resume the game, you'll be right where you left off. You wouldn't want that place to be, say, at lunch with a dragon . . .

War/Simulation Games

War games have a long tradition in computer play, as do computer simulations. This section has CompuServe's contributions to the medium.

Sniper (GO GAM-98)

(13 and up. Players (min/max) 1/4. Instructions: GO GAM-149)

This is Steve Estvanik's multiplayer infantry combat game set in the battlegrounds of World War II. It lets you command one squad of soldiers against another in a simulation of actual wartime conditions, recreating not only the geography and weaponry of the time and place, but also the strengths and weaknesses of individual soldiers and the squad as a group, and the uncertainty of intelligence about enemy forces. You command a squad of individual soldiers on a key tactical mission. You maneuver the squad carefully through rugged, war-torn terrain, alert for enemy ambush at every step. You might engage in brief skirmishes or full-scale firefights.

The game can still be played using the basic ASCII symbolic display with which it was introduced in 1989. However, serious Sniper! fans who use IBM PCs and compatibles have begun using the high-resolution graphic interface, "Scope," introduced in 1992. Scope requires at least 512K of RAM and an EGA or VGA display. An 80286 or faster chip works best and most users prefer to use a mouse for faster movement, though a mouse isn't required. To check out the software, enter GO SCOPE and retrieve the self-extracting program, SCOPEX.EXE, a 213K file that contains the program, documentation, a glossary, and more. Off-line, enter SCOPEX and the program automatically unpacks its files. After reading the documentation, enter SCOPE to run the program. The program costs $2.00 to download, but users aren't charged for the connect-time used in the retrieval.

Here are some tips for newcomers:

- Your first stop in this game is bootcamp, an interactive tutorial. It is an option in the Scope interface; if you are using other software, enter /BOOTCAMP.

- Also, a /RECON command allows you to watch others play, useful for the novice still learning strategy.

- When you try your first combat, get in the habit of thinking of your squad as a group of individuals, each with his own strengths. Take the initiative and move, rather than sitting and firing randomly.

- Check out the Multi-Player Games Forum (GO MPGAMES) for other Sniper players. A message section and library offer conversation and helpful files.

If you should happen to run into a player who calls himself "Yngvi," be sure to pay your respects. That is programmer Estvanik's own on-line persona.

MegaWars

Actually, there are several versions of MegaWars on-line. MegaWars I: The Galactic Conflict (GO GAM-209) and MegaWars III: The New Empire (GO GAM-105).

(12 and up. Players (min/max) 1/10. Instructions: GO GAM-109) and (for Megawars III, GO GAM-154)

MegaWars I, one of the earliest multiplayer games, proved to be so popular that a similar, more complex game called MegaWars III was added a few years ago. The games were developed by two former University of Virginia students, Kelton Flinn and John Taylor. MegaWars I is a real-time space battle to be played by one to 10 people. If no one else is around, the computer plays against you. (As noted, most multiplayer games may be played at a single-player level against the computer, although it is more fun as a group activity.)

The introduction tells you there are the Colonists (the good guys) and the Kryons (the bad guys). When you enter MegaWars, you decide whether you want to be a good guy or a bad guy. What you aren't told is that there is a third force in the galaxy called the Archerons, who don't like anyone. So, even if you wind up in a one-player game or if all the players in the game are of one army, you still have to watch out for the Archerons. As if you don't have enough to worry about, black holes, described in the instructions as "annoy-ing" exist. Indeed — if you get into one of them, you are dead. Chances are one-in-four that a black hole lurks in the game you are playing.

Your mission in MegaWars I is to destroy your enemy, capture planets for your side, stay away from black holes and Archerons, rise in rank from cadet to admiral, and avoid getting zapped by other players.

MegaWars III is even more complex. This advanced simulation involves building spaceships to seek new planets, establishing colonies on them, build-ing defenses, creating economic systems, and ruling the people.

"We like to say, 'Here's a universe,' and then sit back and watch," designer Flinn once told The Associated Press. "The players can decide where their war-ships will go and how taxes will be set on their planets."

Before you rush on-line to play either game, heed the advice of master play-ers: Buy the printed game manuals. For details, enter GO ORDER at any prompt.

Air Traffic Controller (GO GAM-236)

(12- adult. Players (min/max) 1/9. Instructions: GO GAM-237)

Steve Estvanik says his goal with Air Traffic Controller was to create a game not based on warfare and competition, but on cooperation among players. It simulates an air traffic controller's duties and you are responsible for all planes within a sector of air space. Your mission is: Guide the planes safely through your assigned sector of air space or to a nearby airport. New planes arrive from other sectors and from the airports. You can influence other sectors by delaying planes or sending them out with inadequate fuel. You may also send messages to other players to notify them of planes you send into their sectors. In other words, if everyone cooperates, you all score better. If there are no other players, you can still play, though you receive only computer-generated planes. If other people are playing, you can get additional planes from them. You have direct contact with as many as four other players, to the north, south, east, and west.

Several levels of difficulty are available; the score is kept for each ten- to twelve-minute "shift" you play.

Incidentally, if you are an IBM/compatible user, you might be interested in a program called ATScope in Library 14 ("Other Games") of the MultiPlayer Games Forum (GO MPGAMES). It provides a graphics front-end interface for the game.

Parlor/Trivia Games

The term "parlor games" conjures up an image of Victorian ladies and gentlemen whiling away Sunday afternoons playing Parcheesi. Well, there's a little more action in CompuServe's parlor. It isn't everywhere you can find an electronic quiz show. . . .

You Guessed It (GO GAM-17)

(18 and up. Players (min/max) 2/6. Instructions: GO GAM-32)

You Guessed It is an on-line quiz show built around answers to trivia questions. It allows you to watch a game in progress as part of the "studio audience." Watching others play is a good way to see how the show works. The game also offers a "lobby," where potential players may meet and form teams to play the game. By playing, you win points that can be converted into usage credits.

Astrology Calculator (GO GAM-239)

(All ages. Players (min/max) 1/1. Instructions: GO GAM-197)

This casts conventional horoscopes. It asks for your birthdate, birth time, time zone in effect, and birthplace expressed as latitude and longitude.

Stage II: The Two-Stage Trivia Game (GO TMC-8)

(12 and up. Players (min/max) 1/6. Instructions: GO TMC-10)

The object here is to earn points by first answering a series of trivia questions, then discovering what the answers have in common. You win by scoring enough points to add your name to the "Stage II Spotlight" of high scorers.

Multiple Choice (GO TMC-1)

This game gives a menu that includes trivia for kids (ages 7 to 12), trivia for teens (ages 13 to 18), relaxing games, achievement challenges, trivia for everyone, a personality profile test, and serious brain challenges.

Modem Games and Challenge Board (GO MTMGAMES)

Computer users all over the world are finding it exciting to link computer to computer via telephone for game challenges. As the hobby has grown, the number of games that can be played this way has grown as well. Today many games can be played either by a solitary human at the keyboard or by phone link to another human with a computer.

"Modem-to-modem games open up a whole new world for games," says sysop Mike Schoenbach. "Not only do you get to meet and play with people from all over the world, but playing a traditional graphics computer game with another person adds a whole new dimension to the actual game play. Since each player brings to the game his or her own personal experiences and skill, each game session becomes much more unpredictable and consequently much more challenging."

Along with Mike Schoenbach (76703,4363), primary sysops are Sara Howard (76702,543) and Linda Lindley (76702,1504).

CompuServe is the first international information system to offer special services specifically for modem gamers.

Challenge Board (GO CHALLENGE)

This is an electronic directory of modem game players. After all, the key to playing modem-to-modem is finding an opponent. In this forum, users profile themselves in the directory so other gamers can search for them as opponents for most commercial, public domain, and shareware games that support the play-by-modem feature. You can search for someone in your own dialing area for a modem game challenge, so you won't spend a bundle on long distance charges. The message board is intended for challenges, so you can use it to find an opponent who plays the game you like at your level.

MTM Gaming Lobby (GO MTMLOBBY)

Here is the latest entry into CompuServe's modem-to-modem games support services. It is a large conference area that enables players to connect their modem games to opponents through the CompuServe network. The MTM Lobby allows players to stay on-line for all aspects of modem gaming. It connects them to gamers in other states or around the world at reduced CompuServe connect rates. In addition, it offers both players anonymity since neither party needs to give out a phone number to connect. In most applications, you and your opponent make a date in the Challenge Forum for the competition, meet in the MTM Lobby to discuss the preliminaries, then, following specific software instructions for most popular modem-to-modem games (available connect-free as an option on the MTM menu, accessible by entering GO MTMGAMES), connect the game. The MTM software simulates a direct connection between the players. CompuServe doesn't intrude with any kind of error-checking, so every byte transmitted from one end of the connection is automatically received on the other end.

Modem Games Forum (GO MODEMGAMES)

The forum is intended for further discussion by those who play this form of computer game. It brings gamers together from around the world to discuss the games they play, exchange files via the libraries, or enter the forum's conference rooms for real-time discussions.

Entertainment Center (GO ECENTER)

The Entertainment Center offers multiplayer games with graphical interfaces. You must have a PC compatible computer using EGA graphics or better to play the games.

Players can start their own game, join a game already in progress, or watch a game. If you join the CB Club (described in Chapter 5), you can play at discounted connect rates (for more details, GO CBCLUB).

The graphical interfaces for these games can be downloaded from the Entertainment Center Main Menu. Your connect-time during the download is free, but each download carries a nominal transaction fee.

The games currently available in the Entertainment Center, written by William Sellers of S&S Synergy, are described in the next sections.

StarSprint

StarSprint is a simple space combat game that offers you a variety of scenarios and strategies. You are given command of a ship and your team is given ownership of one or more bases. Bases are used for refueling and arming your ship; but, if the enemy captures all of your bases, the game is over. Players earn points for shooting enemy ships and capturing enemy bases. StarSprint is available for 1200, 2400, and 9600 baud.

Backgammon

Familiar board games—backgammon, chess, and checkers—can now be played between you and an opponent anywhere in the world. If your game is not private, other players in the Entertainment Center Lobby may watch your game and chat with you and your opponent.

Entertainment Center Lobby (GO ECENTER)

The Entertainment Center Lobby allows players to get to know each other with most of the same conferencing commands now available in the CB simulator. Entering /HELP in the Lobby will give you a complete list of the commands available.

Individual game instructions are included with each game you download.

Game Forums/News

As noted, CompuServe offers much in the way of human assistance with all these computer games and help through forums that support all sorts of gaming as well as provide a place for gaming news.

The Electronic Gamer Archives (GO TEG)

This is the place to find a gold mine of information about computer gaming, whether you are a novice or a grand master. You will find:

WALKTHRUS: These are detailed, step-by-step instructions for solving many computer games. Walkthrus are full solutions to the games listed, not merely hints.

REVIEWS: Read about the features of computer games or cartridge games before you buy them. Virtually all of the reviews are based on full play-throughs.

TEG'S GAZETTE: The on-line "mini-magazine" of articles, essays, convention reports, interviews, etc.

Editor-in-chief of The Electronic Gamer Archives is Patricia Fitzgibbons (76703,657) who is somewhat of a legend herself. She was one of the earlier sysops on CompuServe and now is the primary sysop for *all* the gaming forums. On-line she is known as "Nightshift." Unlike most forums on CompuServe, users and forum administrators alike may use nicknames — and are even encouraged to do so — in this forum.

The Gamers' Forum (GO GAMERS)

The forum is an on-line special interest group devoted exclusively to computer games and simulations, including adventure, war/strategy, sports, action/arcade, cartridge, computer role-playing, game design, and gaming hardware.

Multi-Player Games Forum (GO MPGAMES)

As noted, this is the forum to see to discuss and obtain information about the various Multi-Player Games available on CompuServe, including MegaWars I, MegaWars III, Island of Kesmai, YGI!, British Legends, Sniper!, Air Traffic Controller, and the Entertainment Center.

Role-Playing Games Forum (GO RPGAMES)

If you are into role-playing games, whether they are board, paper, or text RPGs, this forum is for you. The forum hosts numerous on-line games that are played via the forum's message board or the real-time conference area.

Play-By-Mail Games Forum (GO PBMGAMES)

The play of PBM (play-by-mail) and PBEM (play-by-electronic mail) games, as well as on-line versions of board and computer games, is the topic of discussion here. The forum offers numerous on-line games for forum members. Some of the games supported and played in the forum are: Legends, Beyond the Stellar Empire, Delenda, SuperNova II, Starweb, Kings & Things*, Supremacy, Spiral Arm, Feudal Lords, Continental Rails, Illuminati, Adventurer Kings, Out Time Days, Family Wars, It's a Crime, Monster Island, Xenophobe, Diplomacy, Advanced Squad Leader, Civilization, Empire, Junta, Harpoon, Dune, Monopoly, Railway Rivals, and 1830.

Game Publishers Forums (GO GAMPUB)

Two forums host game publishers who offer support for their commercial products:

1. Game Publishers A Forum (GO GAMPUBA) offers support from Accolade, Bethesda Softworks, Electronic Arts, LucasArts, Merit Software, Origin, Sierra On-Line, SSI, SubLOGIC, and Three-Sixty Pacific.
2. Game Publishers B Forum (GO GAMPUBB) supports Disney/Buena Vista Software, Impressions, Interplay, GameTek, Konami, Maxis, MicroProse, Sir-Tech, Spectrum Holobyte, and Westwood Studios.

Flight Simulation Forum (GO FSFORUM)

Flight simulation program enthusiasts meet here to talk about their hobby. Join fellow players, pilots, designers, programmers, and journalists in exchanging tips, commentary, opinions, and product information.

Chess Forum (GO CHESSFORUM)

In this forum for chess playing and chess players, members discuss and comment on chess and chess games as well as play on-line games. For details about the forum's offerings, please read the HOWTO.TXT file in Library 1 (General/Help).

12

Shopping

What in the world is a family of New England syrup makers doing on-line? They're putting a new spin on an old business idea, then selling it to the world through computers, that's what.

Operating out of CompuServe's Electronic Mall, the business called "Rent Mother Nature" (GO RM), a fascinating intersection of old and new, allows you to lease a piece of nature and benefit from its bounty.

Proprietor Robert MacArthur notes that maple syrup has been made on the family farm for generations. The family created and introduced the concept of *leasing* a sugar maple some 15 years ago. "Folks were so pleased," relays an on-line statement, "that we added leases on beehives, lobster traps, a Yankee smokehouse and now leases on pecan, cherry, apple and peach trees."

Under these leases, the harvest—however much it may be—is divided among the participants. The Cambridge, Massachusetts company promises to deliver at least the guaranteed amounts and more than the guarantee at times of bumper crops. Buyers and recipients of this unusual gift receive the lease printed on parchment stock, embossed with a gold seal, and hand personalized. As the months roll by, the company nurtures the crops and sends out periodic newsletters on the work. At the end, the harvest is sent to the customer's door by UPS.

So, can a family from the North Country find happiness in the big digital city mall? Yes — modem technology seems made for their unusual concept. "It's not like selling socks," a store manager told *CompuServe Magazine* a few years back. "It takes explaining, but the CompuServe people get it right away."

Not all merchants in the Electronic Mall are as unusual as this one, but they all — from the flower merchants to the electronics stores to the candy and clothing boutiques, small startup companies and giants like Lands' End and JC Penney alike — face some of the same challenges, primarily the demands presented by the text-based nature of the service.

"You're selling without pictures," promotion consultant Cindy Dale told the magazine. Dale, who worked closely with many of the merchants that were the first to try the Mall, noted, "You've got to do it all with words. The things that sell best are the brand names. You know exactly what you're getting."

For some merchants, the challenges of this medium prove to be too much. It is common for merchants to come and go rapidly in the Mall area of the system.

Others, though — like Walter Knoll Florist (GO WK) — seem to find a successful formula and settle in for a long and happy on-line life. Knoll — a St. Louis family with seven generations in the flower business — came to CompuServe at the inception of the Electronic Mall in early 1985 and has been there ever since, sending flowers and other gift items all over the US and to 165 different countries. Store Manager Chuck Knoll says part of the company's secret is being able to adapt to the buying habits of the CompuServe populace, even if you don't always understand them. For instance, he is still wondering why most of his CompuServe customers place their orders between 2:00 and 4:00 in the morning. The connection between insomnia and flower purchasing has yet to be analyzed.

Shopping Overview

Since the beginning of the personal computer phenomenon, talk has been of how computers one day would enable us to buy goods and services without leaving the home or office. For CompuServe subscribers, the on-line shopping arena is already large and growing steadily. Predictions are for a steady increase in this form of on-line mail-order shopping.

Of course, shopping by computer will probably never replace the hands-on shopping experience. After all, shopping is a social activity for many people for whom going to a real mall involves more than just shopping. It is a gathering place for everyone from senior citizens to kids. It is, as some suggest, a "high touch" experience in a high-tech world. But more and more, telecomputerists are finding ways to coordinate shopping via computer with their traditional shopping and buying habits. On-line shopping can be:

- Part of a comparative shopping strategy.
- An efficient way to get the "big picture" of what is available before making purchases.
- A quick means to order or re-order merchandise with which you are already familiar.

On-line shopping has become more than a high-tech pastime or novelty. Its practical side becomes more apparent all the time as electronic merchants come up with new ways to use the medium, including contests and drawings, special on-line showings and introductions of new product lines, and discounts on connect-time to attract customers during sales.

Getting Started

The main shopping area is The Electronic Mall, a registered CompuServe trademark. Here you find merchants (many of whom you may recognize already from outside the electronic realm) offering on-line ordering and product information that matches and sometimes exceeds the services you expect in a "real" mall. In other areas, an on-line catalog contains thousands of items to compare and order, with many prices below retail; a special database lets you search out information about new cars; a menu-driven area shows you what a leading consumer magazine says about particular brands of products, and more.

To get started:

- If you are using the CompuServe Information Manager software, select the Shopping option from the Services pull-down menu.
- If you are using a general communications program, enter GO SHOPPING from any prompt.

No matter how you get there, you see a menu like this one:

```
        BASIC SHOPPING SERVICES
            The Electronic MALL (R) (FREE)
            SHOPPERS ADVANTAGE Club (FREE)
            Order From CompuServe (FREE)
            Online Inquiry (FREE)
            Consumer Reports
            CompuServe Classifieds
        EXTENDED SHOPPING SERVICES
            SOFTEX (sm) Software Catalog
            New Car Showroom
```

The first four menu items are listed as *free*; therefore, even if you are not a Basic Services subscriber, but rather pay according to the amount of time you spend on-line, you will not incur connect-charges in these areas. Of course, if you are a Basic Services subscriber, you will not incur connect-charges for these areas as well as for Consumer Reports or reading CompuServe Classifieds.

Shopping the Electronic Mall (GO MALL)

When you select the Electronic Mall from the above menu, you are taken to a menu from which you may examine an introduction to the Electronic Mall concept, which provides directions on how to place an order. Other options list the latest happenings among the mall merchants and take you to a feedback area where you may leave messages for those who manage the mall. To enter the mall and begin shopping, select the Enter the Electronic Mall option.

In day-to-day use, you are likely to see announcements about the mall while entering. If you are using CIM, all you have to do to get beyond the announcements is answer Yes when asked if you want to continue in order to get to the next display. If you are using a general non-CIM program, just press ENTER. The Mall's main menu looks like this:

```
SHOP THE MALL

Mall Directory of Merchants
    1  Shop by Department
    2  Shop by Merchant (Alphabetic Listings)
    3  Merchants Shipping Outside the US

    4  Product Category Index
    5  Directory of Catalogs
```

These options offer the following:

1. The first displays the names of mall stores by departments.

2. The second provides an alphabetical list of merchants by store name.

3. The third is a list of merchants who are willing to ship to CompuServe-users outside the USA.

4. The fourth offers an alphabetical index of products and services available in the mall, which is especially useful for first-time users.

5. The last option takes you to a special area of the mall where you may review all of the merchants that offer to send you catalogs via US mail.

In this area, you can choose the catalogs you want, and post your name and address once to receive them all.

Selecting option 1 from the above menu causes the system to display lists of product groups (such as apparel/accessories, audio equipment, automotive, books, business services, cameras/optical equipment, children's clothes/merchandise, etc.). You are prompted either to select a group or press RETURN to see more of the index. When you choose a group, subsequent menus become more specific. For instance, if you select "books" from the first menu, the system then asks what type of book you are looking for (advice/self help, biographies/history, business/finance, classics, computer/technical, and so on). The next group of menus will focus on specific bookstores and publishers with electronic kiosks in the mall from which you may choose. Codes with the listing of merchants are service names (or direct addresses) for the stores, so from anywhere in the system you may reach one of them by using the GO option followed by an address.

Just as each store in a shopping mall has different display windows, the electronic mall gives store managers a free hand to display introductory pages. Most mall merchants present visitors with a "signboard" before entering the main shopping area.

Entering a Mall Store

To enter a mall store, either select it through the menus as illustrated above, or access it directly with the GO option followed by its unique address. When you arrive, you are greeted by a welcome message that often tells you about new products or special sales which are going on in that particular mall store. That is followed by a general menu of options, which varies slightly from store to store. Most offer an introduction for an overview, followed by one or more catalogs (often searchable by keywords or topics). Many of the stores also offer to send you print catalogs from a menu choice. To receive the print catalog all you need to do is choose the option and list your name and address when prompted.

This is usually followed by ordering instructions and customer service information.

Ordering Products

When looking through on-line catalogs of products, you are usually shown descriptions, including prices, followed by a prompt that says, "Enter 'O' to order." If you want to order a product you have read about, enter O (that is, the letter "O," not a zero), and the system notes it. The O command is universal in the electronic mall — it means *order* in all the stores. Here is the rundown on ordering:

- You browse through a single store's database, ordering as many things as you like with the O command.

- As you exit the store, you are taken to an order area (the electronic version of the check-out clerk with a cash register) where you are asked for information such as name, address, phone number, and your method of payment (usually a credit card number, though the billing options vary depending on the merchant).

- There are stopping places all along the way to make corrections to the ordering information or to cancel the entire order. This means the O command *isn't* a final commitment; a slip of the fingers won't get you in trouble.

- Most mall stores later send you notification by CompuServe Mail of what you have ordered, along with an order number and other pertinent information. By retrieving and filing this mail, you have a record of the order in case you must refer to it later.

A List of Merchants

Here are the names of the mall merchants at this writing, along with a brief description of their products and services, and their service names in parentheses. (As noted, some Electronic Mall merchants come and go rapidly. Check on-line for the latest list.)

- ADVENTURES IN FOOD (GO AIF): Gourmet food items.
- AIR FRANCE (GO AF): Tour booking, information on sights and scenes.
- ALASKA PEDDLER (GO AK): Alaskan goods.
- AMERICAN EXPRESS (GO AE): Travelers cheques, gift cheques.
- AMERICANA CLOTHING (GO AC): Levi's, Dockers, Champion, etc.
- AT&T ONLINE STORE (GO DP): AT&T Dataport fax modems.
- AT&T TOLL-FREE 800 DIRECTORY (GO TFD): On-line telephone directory.
- AUTOMOBILE INFORMATION CENTER (GO AI): Wholesale and retail prices starting in 1978.
- AUTOQUOT-R (GO AQ): Vehicle price quotes.
- AUTOVANTAGE ONLINE (GO AV): New and used car information.
- BARNES & NOBLE (GO BN): Books.
- BMG COMPACT DISC CLUB (GO CD): Over 450 compact disc selections.
- BOAT XPRESS (GO BX): Nationwide boat merchandising.

- BOOKS ON TAPE (GO BOT): Audio books.

- BOSE EXPRESS MUSIC (GO BEM): Cassettes, CDs, records, etc.

- BRETON HARBOR BASKETS & GIFTS (GO BH): Gifts, gift baskets, and other items.

- BRODERBUND SOFTWARE (GO BB): Fun and educational games.

- BROOKS BROTHERS (GO BR): Men's and women's apparel.

- BUICK MAGAZINE (GO BU): Car information, customer service.

- BUSINESS INCORPORATING GUIDE (GO INC): Nationwide incorporating.

- BUYER'S MARKET FROM ZIFF (GO BMC): Information on computers and related products.

- CAREERTRACK (GO CT): Career and personal training programs.

- CATALOG STORE (GO CA): Free catalogs and information.

- CHECKFREE CORPORATION (GO CF): Electronic payment service.

- CHEF'S CATALOG, THE (GO CC): Cookware and kitchen accessories.

- COFFEE ANYONE ??? (TM) (GO COF): Gifts, 48-hour shipment of your order.

- COLUMBIA HOUSE MUSIC (GO CH): Compact discs and tapes.

- COMPUBOOKS (GO CBK): Discount computer books.

- COMPUTER EXPRESS (GO CE): Apple, IBM, Macintosh, and Amiga software.

- COMPUTER SHOPPER (GO CS): Computer goods.

- CONTACT LENS SUPPLY, INC. (GO CL): Contact lenses, supplies.

- COSMETICS EXPRESS (GO CM): Fragrance, skin care, cosmetics.

- COURT PHARMACY (GO RX): Full service pharmacy.

- CREATE-A-BOOK (GO CK): Fun books that make your child a star.

- DALCO COMPUTER ELECTRONICS (GO DA): PC components and supplies.

- DATA BASED ADVISOR (GO DB): Database management and applications development.

- DESKTOP DIRECT FROM DIGITAL (GO DD): Computer products.

- DIRECT MICRO (GO DM): Computer accessories and software.

- DOW JONES & CO. (GO DJ): Business and financial periodicals.

- DREYFUS CORPORATION (GO DR): Mutual funds.

- 800 FLOWER AND GIFT SHOPPE (GO GM): Gifts for all occasions.

- ENTREPRENEUR MAGAZINE (GO ENT):   Small business emporium.
- EXECUTIVE STAMPER (GO EX):   Rubber stamps, engraved gifts.
- FINE JEWELRY OUTLET (GO FJO):   Gems and jewelry.
- FLORIDA FRUIT SHIPPERS (GO FFS):   Oranges, tropical fruit, etc.
- FLOWER STOP (GO FS):   Flowers and gifts.
- FORD CARS & TRUCKS (GO FD):   Car and truck information, and dealer locator.
- FORD MOTOR COMPANY (GO FMC):   Car and truck information, auto accessories.
- GARRETT WADE COMPANY (GO GW):   Tools and supplies.
- GIFT SENDER (GO GS):   Gifts for all occasions.
- GIMMEE JIMMY'S COOKIES (GO GIM):   Homemade gourmet cookies.
- H&R BLOCK (GO HRB):   Income tax data, preparation.
- HAMMACHER SCHLEMMER (GO HS):   Gifts, unique and unusual products.
- HEATH COMPANY (GO HTH):   Build-it-yourself kits, etc.
- HOLABIRD SPORTS DISCOUNTERS (GO HB):   Sporting goods.
- HOMEFINDER BY AMS (GO HF):   Relocating services.
- HONEYBAKED HAMS (GO HAM):   Specialty ham and gift basket store.
- IBM LINK (GO IL):   Electronic connection to IBM information.
- INDEPENDENT INVESTORS RESEARCH, INC. (GO IIR):   Earnings and forecasting data.
- JC PENNEY ONLINE CATALOG (GO JCP):   Apparel, electronics, and merchandise.
- JDR MICRODEVICES (GO JDR):   Computers, periperals, and electronic goods.
- JUSTICE RECORDS (GO JR):   Specializing in R&B and jazz.
- K & B CAMERA (GO KB):   Photographic products.
- LANDS' END (GO LA):   Apparel.
- LASER'S EDGE, THE (GO LE):   Laserdiscs and laser disc equipment.
- LIBRARY OF SCIENCE (GO LOS):   Science data.
- LINCOLN/MERCURY SHOWROOM (GO LM):   Car information and dealer locator.
- MAC ZONE and PC ZONE (GO MZ):   PC and Macintosh equipment and software.

- MACMILLAN PUBLISHING (GO MMP): Career development and training books.
- MACUSER (GO MC): Mac computer goods.
- MACWAREHOUSE (GO MW): Macintosh hardware, software and accessories.
- MAX ULE DISCOUNT BROKERAGE (GO TKR): Brokerage and financial info.
- MCGRAW-HILL BOOK COMPANY (GO MH): Computer and business books.
- METRO SOFTWARE (GO MSI): Printer services.
- MICROSOFT PRESS (GO MSP): Windows and programming books.
- MICROWAREHOUSE (GO MCW): PC Hardware, software, etc.
- MISSION CONTROL SOFTWARE (GO MCS): Software and accessories.
- MONEY'S FINANCIAL MARKET (GO MFM): Finance tools from *Money Magazine*.
- MUSIC ALLEY ONLINE (GO MAO): Mixers, synthesizers, keyboards.
- NARADA PRODUCTIONS (GO NP): Compact discs and cassettes.
- NEWSNET (GO NN): Online news service signup.
- OMAHA STEAKS (GO OS): Gourmet food.
- OMRON (GO OM): Office automation products.
- PARSONS TECHNOLOGY (GO PA): Financial and productivity software.
- PAUL FREDRICK SHIRT CO. (GO PFS): Men's shirts.
- PC CATALOG (GO PCA): PC products.
- PC COMPUTING (GO CMP): Computer publications.
- PC MAGAZINE (GO PM): Computer publications.
- PC PUBLICATIONS (GO PCB): *PC Today* and *PC Novice* magazine subscriptions.
- PENNY WISE CUSTOM PRINT SHOP (GO PWP): Imprintable gifts, etc.
- PENNY WISE OFFICE PRODUCTS (GO PW): Office products.
- PETWORKS (GO PT): Professional pet supplies.
- PRC DATABASE PUBLISHING (GO PRC): Best of 'GO Graphics' directory.
- PEACHPIT PRESS (GO PPP): Desktop publishing.
- READ USA (GO RU): Discount best selling books.
- RELO (GO RL): The International Relocation Network.
- RENT MOTHER NATURE (GO RM): Gift leasing programs, etc.

- SAFEWARE COMPUTER INSURANCE (GO SAF): High-tech equipment insurance.
- SHAREWARE DEPOT (GO SD): Software.
- SHARON LUGGAGE AND GIFTS (GO SL): Luggage, travel accessories, etc.
- SHOPPERS ADVANTAGE CLUB (GO SAC): Discount shopping club.
- SIERRA ONLINE (GO SI): Computer games and accessories.
- SMALL COMPUTER BOOK CLUB (GO BK): Computer books.
- SOFTDISK PUBLISHING (GO SP): Software by subscription.
- TRW CREDENTIALS (GO CRE): Credit reporting.
- TWENTIETH CENTURY INVESTORS (GO TC): Investment information.
- UNIVERSITY OF PHOENIX (GO UP): Business degree programs online.
- VOLKSWAGEN (GO VW): Car information.
- WALDEN*COMPUTER*BOOKS (GO WB): Computer books and accessories.
- WALTER KNOLL FLORIST (GO WK): Plants, flowers, fruits, balloons, etc.
- WILEY PROFESSIONAL BOOKS (GO JW): Technical and professional books.
- WINDOWS SOURCES MAGAZINE (GO WS): Publication.
- Z BEST (GO ZB): Discount electronics.

Shoppers Advantage Club (GO SAC)

Shoppers Advantage, a discount shopping club formerly called Comp-U-Store, is the grand-daddy of on-line shopping services. All CompuServe subscribers may browse this feature and buy products on-line; but if you sign on as a member you receive greater discount prices than you would if you shop as a non-member. Members also receive a two-year warranty on the merchandise they order and a lowest price guarantee. The standard annual membership fee is $39, but the club often offers a trial membership for a dollar or two.

Generally, the discount prices are available because Shoppers Advantage keeps no inventory. The club arranges for shipping and delivery directly from the manufacturers and distributors, enabling members to save money.

Help and Questions

The store operates a staff hotline (1-800-843-7777) to handle members' questions and provide assistance with the system. The hotline opens at 9:00 a.m.

and operates to 11:00 p.m. Monday through Friday and to 7:00 p.m. on Saturday and Sunday.

Typical Browsing Session

Shoppers Advantage is a gateway from CompuServe to computers elsewhere. The main menu for the service looks like this:

```
Shoppers Advantage

    1  All About Us
    2  Shopping/Ordering for MEMBERS Only
    3  Shopping/Ordering for NON Members
    4  How To Join
    5  Join Our Electronic Mailing List
    6  Free "Best Buys" Catalog

       Shoppers Advantage HotLine
       (Customer Service/Help Desk)
       1-800-843-7777
```

As a non-member, you may use option 3 in that example to browse and purchase. Choosing it, you see an introductory bulletin or two, and eventually find yourself at the main directory:

```
    MAIN DIRECTORY TOP

    1     All About Us
    2     What's New
    3     Best Buys Catalog Products
    4     Department Store
    5     Shop by Model #
    6     Shop by Product Category
    7     Shop by Product Code
    8     Info/Member Feedback
    9     Other Services
    10    Researching a Product
    11    Bridal Registry
    12    Message Mailbox

    Enter choice :
```

Suppose you were in the market for a cellular phone. The shopping could be handled through menus. Choosing option 4 from the Main Menu, you are taken to the "Department Store" option. As with the Electronic Mall index illustrated in the previous section, Shoppers Advantage works by providing increasingly more specific menus. After you select the Department Store option, the system offers a menu to ask which department (bed/bath, cars/auto accessories, computers/accessories, formal living/dining, home furnishings, home/office, housewares, leisure, and so on). You could choose "Phones and Answering Machines" from the Department Store menu to see a menu of various types of phones and answering machines. When you select "cellular phones," the system prompts you to indicate the brand of phone you're thinking about, the wattage you had in mind, whether you want one with hands-free operation or whether it should be a hand-held unit. You may choose what you are looking for specifically or choose "No Preference."

Two questions the system usually asks, regardless of the product, are:

1. What is the two-letter code for the state to which the item would be shipped if you were to order on-line? This standard two-letter postal code is necessary so the system can provide the correct price quotation, but it does not obligate you to buy.

2. What is the least and most you want to spend? You don't have to answer this one, but if you do, you enter the least amount, followed by a semi-colon, followed by the highest amount: "50.00;150.00."

After all the questions, Shoppers Advantage gets down to some serious comparisons, displaying something like this:

```
Cellular phones
                                          AUTO-  HAND-  HAND-
Model                      Prices  WATTAGE DIAL  CPBL   HELD
- - - - - - - - - -        - - - - - - - - - - - - - - - - -

Manufacturer: FUJITSU TEN
  4 COMMANDERFX     List$:  open     3      NO    YES    NO
    Non-Member Price:      450.35
    Member Price:         429.95
    Title: CELLULAR PHONE

Manufacturer: GENERAL ELECTRIC
  5 TP5000          List$:  open     3      NO    YES    NO
    Non-Member Price:      574.60
    Member Price:         549.95
    Title: 3 WATTS
```

```
Manufacturer: MITSUBISHI
  6  3000              List$:   open    UNDER 3   YES    YES    NO

Enter HELP for instructions for
product comparisons

Enter choice(s) or "O" to order :
```

The list may be more than one page, with a prompt at the bottom. At the prompt, you may press RETURN to see the next page, or you may enter:

- Any of the numbers to see descriptions of the items.
- "O" (capital letter "O") to order.
- HELP for instructions on how to compare two or more products from a multipage list.
- EXIT to leave the feature.

Special SAC Commands

While Shoppers Advantage is largely menu-driven, it also provides special commands for advanced users.

- GO MAIN: To go to the Main Directory
- GO ALL: To go to All About Us
- GO NEW: To see What's New
- GO BEST: To go to Best Buys
- GO DEPT: To go to Department Store
- GO STORE: To go to Department Store
- GO MODEL: To go to Shop by Model #
- GO CAT: To go to Shop by Product Category
- GO CODE: To go to Shop by Product Code
- GO INFO: To go to Information/Feedback
- GO OTHER: To go to Other Services
- GO FIND: To go to Researching a Product
- GO BRIDE: To go to Bridal Registry
- GO MAIL: To go to Your Questions and Comments
- GO MEMBER: To go to Member Address Change

The following are primarily navigational commands:

- ADDRESS: Change Address.
- BACK: Return to previous prompt.
- CANCEL: Cancel orders already placed.
- CHANGE: Go to the top of the area you're currently in.
- CHECKOUT: Process orders currently placed.
- DISPLAY: Display orders already placed.
- ENROLL: Join or change address.
- EXIT: Exit the system.
- HELP: Gives help messages at each prompt.
- ?: Gives help messages at each prompt.
- MENU: Return to previous menu.
- p#: Go to a specific page for multiple-paged menu and text displays.
- REDISPLAY: Redisplay current display and prompt.
- SCROLL ON: Change paging to scroll.
- SCROLL OFF: Return to paging.
- SHIP: Change ship-to state.
- TOP: Go to the Main Directory.

Note   If you're at the "Model #" prompt, you must put a slash before any system command.

Ordering Directly from CompuServe (GO ORDER)

CompuServe also offers its own on-line ordering service for a variety of products, from books and manuals, to tee-shirts, coffee mugs, and posters. As with other shopping features, you may browse without ordering. Items you do order are charged to your monthly CompuServe bill. There are no connect-charges while you are in the On-line Ordering Service area. You aren't charged for connect-time while viewing descriptions or placing an order.

Anytime you are in the ordering service, you may view items chosen during that session by entering DIS (for DISplay) at a prompt. After the items are displayed, you are asked if you want to make a change in the order. If you have made a mistake, you may correct it on the spot. When you complete your order, the entire list is displayed for verification. At that point, you may change or confirm it. Then you are given an order number to jot down so you may check on the order later if necessary.

Consumer Reports (GO CSR)

Consumer Reports allows you to search reports prepared by the Consumers Union staff. The reports are similar to what you find in *Consumer Reports* magazine, modified slightly for placement in this electronic database.

Reports are listed in one of four categories — appliances, automobiles, electronics/cameras, and home — and are alphabetized within each category. The reports generally cover products and services that cost $50.00 or more, or lower-priced products and services that are typically bought frequently or in bulk.

Most reports are divided into four sections:

1. Introduction/overview
2. What to look for
3. Recommendations
4. Models tested/ratings

Occasionally, other choices, such as features/specifications or article updates, are available. A guide explains ratings symbols and a full description of each characteristic. Generally, the ratings system is:

[*****] Excellent
[****] Very Good
[***]   Good
[**]   Fair
[*]   Poor

Classified Service (GO CLASSIFIEDS)

Like your local newspaper, CompuServe has a classified ads section where you may read or browse messages from other subscribers in 12 categories. These classifications include Employment/Education, Job Search, MS-DOS Computers/ Software, Apple/Mac Computers/Software, Other Computers/Software, Business Services/Investments, Travel, Real Estate, Cars/Boats/Planes/RVs/Cycles, Electronics/Hobbies/Collectibles, Occasions/Announcements/Reunion, and Miscellaneous Info/ Merchandise.

Each category is further divided into subsections. For example, real estate is subdivided into business/commercial, residential, and vacation homes. After you select a subdivision, you see a menu of current ads with 40-character subject descriptions. A two-letter state or country code follows each title. Usually the text of the ad lists the country or province of origin.

After reading the text, you may send a reply immediately to most of the classifieds or make a note of the classified's number for responding later. Comments or questions will be sent to the poster's CompuServe Mail box. Your reply is limited to 10 lines.

The cost of listing an ad in the Classifieds area depends on the length of the message and the time length the message will be displayed. For instance, the cost per line (up to 70 characters) for:

- A seven-day (one-week) listing is $1.00 per line.

- A 14-day (two-week) listing is $1.50 per line.

- A 56-day (eight-week) listing is $5.20 per line.

- A 182-day (26-week) listing is $14.30 per line.

So, three lines of text submitted for one week cost $3.00, while the same three lines submitted for an eight-week run is $15.60.

Softex (GO SOFTEX)

Softex is CompuServe's own software catalog, with which you may purchase programs on-line and retrieve them immediately. The charges are placed on your regular CompuServe bill. A database lets you search for software by computer type, publisher, title, or Softex catalog number. You may examine descriptions of programs, including details of equipment requirements. After you indicate that you want a specific program, CompuServe tells you what, if anything, you need to do to prepare your computer to receive the file. The system then copies the software to the disk location you specify.

New Car/Truck Showroom (GO NEWCAR)

The New Car/Truck Showroom lets you view and compare features of passenger cars, vans, and trucks to help you make buying decisions. The database has information on more than 850 cars, vans, special-purpose vehicles, and light-duty trucks. The feature is surcharged; you may look at models one at a time for 90 cents or two at a time in a side-by-side comparison format for $1.20.

On-line Inquiry (GO OLI)

From the On-line Inquiry Menu, you may request general information about an ad displayed in *CompuServe Magazine*. You may leave your name and address at the prompts supplied, and further information will be sent to you. You may also add specific comments or special requests to the inquiry if you like. The requests are filed electronically and are accessible only by the advertisers you specify.

13

Personal Interests, Health, Hobbies, and Sports

In this chapter...

Food and Wine
Health and Fitness
Special Interest Forums
Hobbies
Arts, Music, Literature
Automobile Information
Pets/Animal/Fish

A forum sysop is a lot like a mayor. Part promoter, part motivator, the sysop is the defender and the advocate, the visionary and conscience of the community—in a phrase, the Truest Believer. No one fits the bill better than Neil Shapiro.

Chief sysop of MAUG—the remarkable Micronetworked Apple User Groups described in Chapter 6—for more than 10 years now, Shapiro has guided his lively and fiercely independent electronic community as it has grown from a single electronic clubhouse to a network of more than a dozen related forums covering every aspect of Appledom. It is a priceless resource for anyone using these computers, whether old Apple IIs or the latest in Macintosh.

As one of the world's most experienced sysops, Shapiro has an exceptional ability, not only to cultivate and nurture new features, but also to anticipate new interests. He is known for his instinct for having a forum set up and waiting just when the first waves of new enthusiasts are looking for a gathering place. He has demonstrated his acumen for years in the Apple corner of the system and, starting in the 1990s, Shapiro has also explored some surprising new areas. Witness his opening of The New Age Forum (GO NEWAGE) to discuss and debate topics ranging from meditation and herbal medicine to crystals and the I Ching.

"What makes a techie-minded Mac maven think that he can suddenly shift gears from the left-brain to the right?" Shapiro wrote of himself in an on-line introduction in the new forum. "Well, while I am not presumptuous enough to consider myself an expert in New Age matters, I am as curious, as investigative and, I hope, as open-minded as anyone joining us here."

Shapiro notes that he first began thinking of "New Age" ideas twenty years ago, when he was taught the Tarot cards by a popular science fiction author at a writer's workshop he attended. (Shapiro, himself, has sold and published two sci-fi novels and more than thirty short stories.) "I was fascinated by the imagery, the colors, the mythopoetic wonder of the deck and all that it seemed to whisper about. In the past twenty years my interest in Tarot has led me to study many of the myths and archetypes it is wrapped up with." His exploration of new ideas continues. For instance, experiences in the New Age Forum drew him to topics related to the Masonic Orders and, ultimately, encouraged him to open yet another feature, the Masonry Forum (GO MASONRY).

The New Age and Masonry forums are among the latest additions in one of the faster growing neighborhoods of CompuServe, the section devoted to general interest forums. More than ten years ago, when CompuServe was initially organized as a computer information service for the general public, this was one of the first areas established, called "Home Services" in those days. No accident, that name. Even then, there was a feeling that personal computers would eventually be used in homes as much as in offices. In fact, in those days, you were as likely to hear them called "home computers" as "personal computers." It isn't surprising, then, that throughout its evolution CompuServe has taken into account the need for "Home Services" of all types. In addition to unusual topics, like New Age ideas, many of the forums in this section cover health and fitness issues, hobbies of all types, help with interpersonal relationships, and more. Nowadays, you find most of these services included as "Lifestyles," sometimes presented under menus as "Personal Interests and Hobbies," accessible from the General Services menu.

Of course, not everything on the "Home" menu means "non-work." On the contrary, one of the more active forums in this part of CompuServe is Paul and Sarah Edwards' popular Working From Home Forum (GO WORK), a feature devoted to the facets of telecommuting and "worksteading." For a growing number of us, home is not only where the heart is, but also where the *job* is; the Edwards' forum provides all manner of support for the homebound labor force.

This chapter is an overview of these services and how you can use them in your own personal life.

Home and Hobby Overview

The contents of this chapter come from the Hobbies/Lifestyles/Education menu. Here is what it looks like:

```
EXTENDED HOBBIES/LIFESTYLES/EDUCATION
 1   Food/Wine
 2   Personal Finance/Banking
 3   Health/Fitness
 4   The Electronic MALL/Shopping
 5   Special Interest Forums
 6   Hobbies
 7   Arts/Music/Literature
 8   Reference
 9   Automotive Information
10   Education
11   Pets/Animals/Fish
```

The submenus under this HOME menu are daunting, but many of the offerings have already been discussed. For example, the offerings under Personal Finance and Banking were described in Chapter 8. The Electronic Mall and how to use it were described in Chapter 12. Most reference and education topics were reviewed in Chapter 9.

Why did we put them there? As you have seen, CompuServe usually lists most services on more than one menu, and often in more than one major topic. That is because it is difficult to define many areas too narrowly.

We are focusing our attention at this late point in the book on topics included under the HOME menu which have not been discussed elsewhere in the book. Remember, other services are located on the HOME submenus than are listed here, but they are described elsewhere in the book.

Food and Wine

Epicurean delights are featured in several CompuServe forums described in this section.

Cook's On-line Forum (GO COOKS)

This is a forum for everyone who has an interest in food and cooking. Members exchange their favorite recipes, cooking tips, and information on new products. The forum's libraries are filled with hundreds of recipes as well as several programs for storing and maintaining recipes. Larry Wood (76703,704) is forum administrator.

Wine Forum (GO WINEFORUM)

The Wine Forum hosts discussions on all aspects of wine, beers, and a variety of other beverages. A special feature is on-line wine tasting held in the forum's conference area. The users who participate purchase the same wines and taste them together during the planned conferences. Transcripts of these real-time gatherings are available in the forum's libraries. Administrator of the forum is Jim Kronman (76703,431) a systems engineer in the aerospace industry who also publishes a wine newsletter.

Health and Fitness

CompuServe offers various information both in forums and databases about health issues ranging from human sexuality and AIDS to thoughts on how to get fit and stay fit.

AIDS Information

Acquired Immune Deficiency Syndrome (AIDS), the most frightening and frustrating disease of our times, is part of several CompuServe forums and databases. From its own submenu (GO AIDS), you can choose several forums and databases from which to glean information.

One AIDS menu selection offers the latest news clips about AIDS from the Executive News Service. One of the primary sources of information is the Comprehensive Core Medical Library (GO CCMLAIDS). This surcharged database includes the full text of AIDS-related articles from leading medical reference books, text books, and general medical journals, such as the *New England Journal of Medicine*, *Science*, and *Nature*. Information available for an article includes author, title, publication and publication date, and references if included in the article, as well as the full text of the article. You may retrieve articles by entering subject words, author, publication, or publication year as your search criteria.

Cancer Forum (GO CANCER)

The Cancer Forum shares information as well as provides support for cancer patients, their friends, and relatives. The forum is administered by John Ross (76703,551). Support on the forum is also provided by the volunteers of the Cancer HotLine in Kansas City.

Physicians Data Query (GO PDQ-1)

This is a collection of surcharged databases copyrighted and published by the National Cancer Institute. The Consumer Cancer Information File contains material written for the layperson covering more than 80 forms of cancer, treatment alternatives, stage expectations, and general prognoses. Information is retrieved by entering the cancer name.

The Professional Cancer Information File is written for health care providers and contains current information on most major cancers. The information usually includes prognosis, stage-of-growth classifications with treatment options, and extensive bibliographies for further research. Information is retrieved by entering the cancer name.

An organization directory lists the name, address, parent, and subsidiary organizations of approximately 1,500 institutions having designated National Cancer Institute cancer centers or other career-approved programs. The physicians directory contains the name, address, and phone number of approximately 12,000 cancer specialists. Another file contains data on about 1,000 protocols for cancer treatment.

Diabetes Forum (GO DIABETES)

Diabetes was formerly discussed in a general health forum until it was discovered that it and hypoglycemia had become major topics themselves. As a result, a forum was created for the discussion of the disease in a self-help and support group setting. It was founded by diabetics with the idea that patients, their families, friends, and health care professionals should have a place to discuss the lifestyles that are crucial to their health. Forum administrator is Dave Groves (76703,4223) an insulin-dependent, Type I diabetic since 1954 at the age of nine.

Handicapped Issues

Several services address the issues and needs of the handicapped and the disabled.

The Disabilities Forum (GO DISABILITIES)

This forum is open to all people interested in disabilities, from those with handicapping conditions and their families to those who assist, train, educate, or employ the disabled. Sysops are David Manning (76703,237), Karen Mann (72527,664), Larry Orloff (70305,1173), and David Andrews (72157,3547).

IBM Special Needs Forum (GO IBMSPEC)

The IBM Special Needs Forum is aimed at finding information and IBM PC-compatible programs for primary and adult students with special education needs. It addresses education of the handicapped, literacy programs, special education, and so forth. The primary sysop is Georgia Griffith (76703,266).

The Handicapped Users' Database (GO HUD-1)

This is a collection of information specifically for those with handicaps. It includes the latest news about handicapped issues, a reference library, rehabilitation research and development, lists of self-help organizations for those with handicaps, sources of special computer software and hardware for the handicapped, and more.

General Health and Fitness

CompuServe has offered a growing number of forums and features about health in general.

The Health and Fitness Forum (GO GOODHEALTH)

This forum aims to discuss wellness-related matters, from nutrition and mental health, to child care, aging, and fitness. A variety of professionals (physicians, optometrists, pharmacists, counselors, physiologists, nurses, therapists) join interested nonprofessionals in an often free-wheeling discussion. Various self-help groups—including Alcoholics Anonymous, Overeaters Anonymous, and a Shape-Up Support Group—meet weekly in the conference area. Primary sysop is Allan Stevens (76702,562).

HealthNet (GO HNT)

HealthNet is one of the older on-line home medical reference sources for the personal computer user. The database is in three parts: the HealthNet Reference Library, the HealthNet Newsletter, and HouseCalls, in which you may submit questions to the HealthNet staff to be answered publicly and anonymously. It is one of the few offerings in this chapter that is part of the Basic Services.

Information USA/Health (GO IUS-5596)

This is part of a larger Information USA database; it lists information centers, publications, and hotline numbers you may consult for help on health matters ranging from arthritis to second opinions for surgery.

Human Sexuality (GO HUMAN)

Howard and Martha Lewis (76703,267) began years ago with a single forum devoted to the issues of human sexuality. Today there are two forums as well as a database filled with information presented in article form, including question-and-answer features and "tutorials." The Lewises call on experts in sex-related medical fields to answer questions and counsel those who make use of the very active area of CompuServe. The HSX Support Groups/Open Forum (GO HSX 100) is an open forum with sections on everything from a shyness workshop to living with AIDS, and naturist lifestyles (for social nudists). The HSX Support Groups/Adult Forum (GO HSX-200) deals with sensitive topics, each requiring an application for access. In addition, the conference areas have more than 50 scheduled conferences each week.

NORD Services/Rare Disease Database (GO NORD)

The National Organization for Rare Disorders (NORD) is a non-profit, voluntary health agency dedicated to the identification, control, and cure of rare "Orphan Diseases." This Rare Disease Database offers the latest in new scientific information about these rare diseases and may be a vital link to those trying to stay abreast of the latest medical advances.

PaperChase (GO PCH-1)

PaperChase is a surcharged database that gives you access to the world's largest biomedical database, MEDLINE. Prepared by the National Library of Medicine, MEDLINE has more than seven million references to articles from 4,000 journals. PaperChase has all the references indexed for MEDLINE since its inception in 1966. Each week, over 8,000 new medical references are added. PaperChase also has references in the Health Planning and Administration (HEALTH) database which includes references in the non-clinical literature on all aspects of healthcare planning, facilities, insurance, management, personnel, licensure, and accreditation.

Special Interest Forums

Here's a list of some of the special interest forums found on the HOME menu that were not otherwise noted previously.

Consumer Electronics Forum (GO CEFORUM)

Consumer audio, video, software, satellite systems, telephone equipment, camcorders, and even a section on movies and movie theaters are the focal points of this forum. Primary sysop is Dawn Gordon (76703,204).

Gardening Forum (GO GARDENING)

Managed by the experts at *National Gardening Magazine*, this forum is the place where gardening enthusiasts can meet and exchange ideas as well as talk to the people who know gardening inside-out. Primary sysop is Alison Mixter (76711,456).

Masonry Forum (GO MASONRY)

This is the place to discuss and learn about all aspects of Freemasonry (which may be publicly discussed), including the history, symbolism, and day-to-day concerns of brothers and lodges. Primary sysop is Neil Shapiro (76703,401).

Mensa Forum (GO MENSA)

The Mensa Forum is open to anyone, but joining Mensa, the organization, is a little more difficult. Mensa is for anyone with a score in the 98th percentile or above on an acceptable I.Q. test or equivalent. The file BROCH.TXT from forum Library 1 has general information on Mensa. Primary sysop is David L. Van Geest, business manager of Mensa of Illinois, (76711,330).

Military Forum (GO MILITARY)

Veterans of any war and those interested in the military are invited to join this forum to exchange views and information about the military, military history, veterans' issues, Civil War, and related topics. Primary sysop is Duane Goodridge (76711,217).

Earth Forum (GO EARTH)

Saving the earth and its environment is the topic of this forum. Individuals as well as environmentally-concerned organizations are on-line here to discuss the issues. Primary sysop is Joe Reynolds (76704,37).

New Age Forum (GO NEWAGE)

The forum focuses on all aspects of various beliefs and practices which are often categorized together as "New Age." Here you will find discussions about everything, including crystals, homeopathic healing, Jungian aspects of the Tarot, and such things as applications of quantum theories to cosmological models that incorporate ESP. Primary sysop is Neil Shapiro (76703,401).

Religion Forum (GO RELIGION)

The Religion Forum is a place for the free exchange of thoughts and feelings on topics connected with religion. Issues of faith, morality, spirituality, religious history or ritual, and more are all welcome topics. Primary sysop is Georgia Griffith (76703,266).

Space and Astronomy (GO SPACE)

This area offers two forums, both under the direction of Dick DeLoach (76703,303), a research scientist at NASA Langley Research Center.

- Astronomy Forum (GO ASTROFORUM) for amateurs and professionals alike who have an interest in astronomy.
- Space Forum (GO SPACEFORUM) for those interested in outer space; the exploration, development, colonization, and exploitation of it, and the technology related to it.

In addition, you can access an on-line NASA database with NASA graphics, news and archived material, a database of articles and other information from *Sky & Telescope Magazine*, and a database maintained by the American Sunspot Program which keeps track of past and future sunspot activity.

Working From Home Forum (GO WORK)

This is the forum for those who work full-time or part-time at home or who are part of the growing number of salaried telecommuters who hold jobs in businesses and industries, but who do their work at home. Regulars use it to exchange information, make contacts, share resources and solutions to problems, meet and enjoy each other's company. You can find home/office management tips, resources, laws, tax issues and benefits, and marketing approaches. The sysops are Paul and Sarah Edwards (76703,242). They are the authors of the book *Working From Home: Everything You Need To Know About Living and Working Under the Same Roof,* now in its second edition. They also co-host the national radio show "Home Office" on the Business Radio Network.

Hobbies

Hobbies form an integral part of home life. Here is a rundown of the forums devoted to hobbies.

Photography Forum (GO PHOTOFORUM)

Amateur and professional photographers meet in the Photography Forum to discuss what is a hobby for some and a livelihood for others. Mike Wilmer (76703,4400), a graduate of Brookings Institute of Photography and a professional portrait photographer, is the administrator. Photographic technology is changing rapidly and many of the members of this forum are on the cutting edge of that technology.

Outdoor Activities (GO OUTACT)

If you enjoy the outdoors, you are likely to enjoy some or all of the services offered in this area. Associated with the services here is the Outdoor News Clips (GO OUTNEWS), a surcharged database of outdoor-related news clips from Executive News Service.

Great Outdoors Forum (GO OUTDOORS)

This forum offers outdoor interests of all types, including fishing, hunting, camping, scouting activities, cycling, birding, climbing, skiing, boating, photography, and more. Primary sysop is Joe Reynolds (76704,37).

Sailing Forum (GO SAILING)

The Sailing Forum's members refer to it as an electronic yacht club where people discuss and learn about all aspects of sailing, and receive the latest information on the sport of yacht racing. John Lovell (76703,1013) is primary sysop.

Scuba Forum (GO SCUBA)

This forum is administered by experienced and professional divers. All aspects of SCUBA diving for both novice and experienced divers and snorklers are discussed. Richard C. Drew (76701,123), a SCUBA diving instructor, is primary sysop.

Sports Forum (GO FANS)

This is the place on CompuServe to talk sports as well as play sports. In addition to ongoing discussions on all types of sports at all levels, the forum conducts and sponsors contests and fantasy games based on real sporting events, including fantasy football, Rotisserie-style baseball leagues, college/pro football handicapping contests, and a Super Bowl contest. Primary sysop is Harry Conover (76701,220).

ModelNet (GO MODELNET)

If you build model airplanes, model cars, model boats, or model rockets, this is the forum where you can meet with other model hobbyists and those who provide the kits and information with which to build them. Doug Pratt (76703,3041) is the primary sysop.

TrainNet (GO TRAINNET)

Trains of all sizes are the topic here. The forum is dedicated to model railroading and railfans alike; it has things to offer anyone interested in anything that runs on flanged wheels, from Amtrak to Z Scale. Dorr Altizer (76702,402) is the primary sysop.

HamNet (Ham Radio) Forum (GO HAMNET)

One of the older forums on CompuServe, HamNet is devoted to amateur radio and related subjects, including on-the-air operating, advanced techniques, short wave listening, satellite television, and packet radio. Primary sysops are Scott Loftesness W3VS (76703,4070), Dan Ferguson (SWL) (76702,771), Ken Hoehn N8NYO (Scanning) (70007,2374), and Bill Everett K7RIE (NARA) (76702,753).

Comics and Animation Forum (GO COMICS)

Whether collecting comics is your passion or just learning more about the world of comic books, comic strips, sequential art of all kinds, and animation, you'll find kindred spirits here. In addition to comics and animation fans, there are more than two dozen professionals in the forum. Doug Pratt (76703,3041) is primary sysop and a Pogo fanatic.

Genealogy Forum (GO ROOTS)

This successful forum is dedicated to genealogy, family history, and related subjects, particularly the use of personal computers in maintaining genealogy files. It also focuses on helping adopted people find their birth parents. Forum members list the surnames in which they are interested in the member directory, thereby creating a quick reference guide for those seeking others working on the same family tree. Dick Eastman (76701,263) is primary sysop.

Collectibles Forum (GO COLLECTIBLES)

The Collectibles Forum began as a coin and stamp collecting forum. But soon it became a forum for all sorts of collectibles, including baseball cards, autographs, dolls, figurines, and more. Stamp dealer Dave Cunningham (76702,453) is primary sysop.

Crafts Forum (GO CRAFTS)

The Crafts Forum is designed to be a meeting place for craftspeople to congregate and share ideas, techniques, and experiences. A broad range of crafts is covered and the list is growing every day. Susan Lazear (76702,1664) and Kathy Morgret (76702,1665) are primary sysops.

Arts, Music, Literature

These three topics are found in many of the forums in HOME as well as forums elsewhere on CompuServe. Forums of special interest in this area are:

Science Fiction & Fantasy Forum (GO SCIFI)

Up-to-date news from the science fiction and fantasy fields, reviews and discussions of books and movies, and more fans of Star Trek (in its several incarnations) and Dr. No than you find anyplace else on-line are the features of this forum. Regulars include a number of published science fiction and fantasy authors. Administrator of the forum is Wilma Meier (76701,274).

Music/Arts Forum (GO MUSICARTS)

The forum features discussions of a wide variety of music, schedules of upcoming performing arts events, and more. You'll also find many members knowledgable in many subjects, who are happy to share their expertise with other members. Jim Maki (76701,33) and Paul Miller (76702,756) are primary sysops.

RockNet (GO ROCKNET)

The RockNet Forum features live discussions of the latest rock 'n roll music and is part of a forum-database area set aside for modern music. Administrator of the area is Les Tracy (76703,1061). He is assisted by a group of reviewers who spend their time at rock concerts and report back on the latest happenings. The database (GO ROCK) contains late-breaking ROCKNET news, reviews and commentary, as well as rumors, the top charts and lists, and reports on rock radio and video.

ShowBiz Forum (GO SHOWBIZ)

This forum discusses films and television programs, record albums, celebrity gossip, and nightly news shows. The forum is administered by Eliot Stein (76703,305), longtime editor of the entertainment news and features service "Hollywood Hotline."

ShowBiz invites visitors to air views and reviews of the latest film and music releases and TV shows. It also has message sections on cable viewing, radio programming, theater, the regular and "infotainment" media, and show-business collecting.

Automobile Information

Several forums provide information about cars.

Automobile Forum (GO CARS)

The Automobile Forum contains a wide range of questions, answers, news reports, and comments on automotive topics, such as questions about buying, selling, and leasing cars, automobile performance, and where to get parts and accessories. Shel Hall (76701,103) is the forum's primary sysop.

Motor Sports Forum (GO RACING)

Motor sports of all kinds are discussed in this forum, a service of Racing Information Systems. Many races are covered live and on-line on the Motor Sports Forum. Primary sysop is Michael F. Hollander (76703,771).

Worldwide Car Network Forum (GO WCN)

This is a joint venture of European and American concerns where car enthusiasts can share their knowledge and love of automobiles. The forum accommodates virtually every type of car and truck ever made, from pre-1950 vehicles to modern, sports, and exotic cars. The forum's message sections and libraries also cover such topics as motorcycles, car clubs, and model cars. Also offered in the forum is the Worldwide Car Network's Gold Book of car values. Running the show is editor Liz Stallworth-Allen (76702,1637).

Pets/Animal/Fish

Animal lovers can find the following forums on CompuServe to meet their needs:

Aquaria/Fish Forums

Two forums are for the use of amateur and professional fish breeders. Both are under the direction of John R. Benn (76703,4256).

Aquaria/Fish Forum (GO AQUAFORUM)

This forum offers a communication service to the widely diverse interests that center around aquariums and tropical fish. Included in this group are public aquarium administrators, aquarium product manufacturers, fish farmers and breeders, and, especially, the general aquarium hobbyists.

Fishnet—ADC Forum (GO AQUADATA)

In Fishnet, the primary features are several database-like segments that serve as a primary reference resource for aquarists, hobbyists, aquaculturists, fishery scientists, and other professionals.

Humane Society Forum (GO HSUS)

Sponsored by the Humane Society of the United States, this forum is the place to discuss issues important to the society including animal experiments, wildlife rehabilitation, legislation, and animal ethics. Primary sysop is P.E. Preston (76702,2013).

Pets/Animal Forum (GO PETS)

Dogs, cats, birds, snakes, horses, cows, and pets of all kinds take the main stage in this forum where pet lovers and professionals mingle to discuss pets and how to care for them. Primary sysop is John Benn (76703,4256).

Miscellaneous

Finally, here are some notable recent additions.

Seniors Forum (GO SENIORS)

Betty Knight, 76703,4037, manages this forum devoted to information, discussions and references on senior citizen issues. It is open to visitors of all ages.

Politics

Georgia Griffith, 76703,266, manages two new forums that focus on politics. The White House Forum (GO WHITEHOUSE) is your link to the Clinton White House; the Political Debate Forum (GO POLITICS) takes on more general political issues.

Chapter

14

Automated Software Alternatives

In this chapter...

Typical features of automated software
Programs for IBM and compatibles
Apple Software
Commodore Amiga Automation
Atari Software
Programs for Other Systems

Steve Sneed has spent many hours trying to make CompuServe easier for the rest of us. Now he has committed his thoughts to software, creating OzCIS, one of the exciting new breeds of automated terminal programs. Is it hot? It was downloaded nearly 10,000 times in the first five months it was available in the IBM Network (GO IBMNET) data libraries. That qualifies the bright, fast, colorful public domain program as a major hit on-line.

"I didn't push it or anything," Sneed told a writer with *CompuServe Magazine* recently. "It's just developed its own life. I'm still somewhat amazed."

OzCIS began evolving two years ago, when Sneed was an assistant sysop in IBMNET. "When I began maintaining the library catalogs for the forums, I realized I needed some tools to assist me." A professional programmer with TurboPower Software, Sneed, who lives in Colorado Springs, Colorado, opted to write his own tools. Later he added features as he thought of them — such as a message board manager — until the software started looking like a full-fledged navigation program.

Sneed had not planned to release his program publicly, but word spread on-line from friends and co-workers about how the software combined a friendly interface with the speed and flexibility of legendary existing automated programs like TapCIS and Autosig. More and more, Sneed was being urged to "cut it loose" and release OzCIS for public use. Some suggested he make it a commercial venture. However, Sneed said he had neither the time nor the inclination to start a company or to run a shareware operation, so — to many people's surprise — he released OzCIS for free. He uploaded it to the libraries of the IBM Communications Forum (GO IBMCOM) and sat back to watch the world beat a path to the door. Within weeks, OzCIS was already an international program, being shared by CompuServe users in Australia, Germany, and throughout Europe.

Many may have been first attracted by the software's name. Was the reference to "Oz," as in "The Wizard of . . ."? (No, actually — technically — it probably ought to be "ohhhs," as in the Ozark Mountains of north central Arkansas, where Sneed grew up.) Then rave reviews by the program's first wave of users attracted even more fans.

These days, it is a big job supporting a major system like OzCIS — Sneed spends several hours a day answering questions on the IBMCOM message board. But a group of volunteers, calling themselves Team Oz, has assembled around him to help out with fielding questions (some 400 questions a week are posted) and with future developments.

"This is what makes it worthwhile to me," Sneed told the magazine, "how the users are coming in, spending their time, effort and connect dollars to help other users. That's really made CompuServe what it is today, that spirit of people helping people."

Software Overview

Whether you start out using the CompuServe Information Manager or a general third-party communications program, chances are once you have used CompuServe for a while you will notice you have settled into a routine, visiting the same key forums and features and pushing some of the same buttons in the same sequence each time you log on. Computers are masters at performing routines that are tedious to humans. So, why couldn't you tell your computer where to go on CompuServe and what to do *before* you log on, then send it on its merry way?

Well, the fact is, you can.

If you are using CIM, you already have an introduction to such automation in how the program handles CompuServe Mail, for instance, enabling you to write messages, place them in your Out-Basket, then go on-line and deliver them all at once. This handy feature is just the tip of the iceberg when it comes to what is available in automated terminal programs these days. The software alternatives this chapter describes can be customized to automate large portions of your CompuServe use. Automated programs are available for most platforms; some are commercial, some are shareware, and some are freeware (public domain). Most are available for downloading on CompuServe or can be ordered through the system.

Typical Features

A fundamental characteristic of most automated programs is that they are intended to work *only* with CompuServe. They are customized to work intimately with the system; the automation works by anticipating CompuServe prompts. So in most cases, the program will not work with your local computer bulletin board system or another information service.

What can automated programs do? Here are some typical features basic to almost all of them:

- Capture messages to read and compose replies off-line.
- Capture mail to read and compose replies off-line.
- Save messages and mail, with a searching mechanism.
- Keep an address book of other users and their IDs.
- Build forum library directories for browsing off-line.
- Store preferences for several forums so that several may be visited during a single logon.

In Addition...

Many of these programs also have:

- Scripts to help you automatically join a forum.
- Multiple session configuration files. This feature is helpful if you have more than one CompuServe ID, want to specify different download paths for different sessions, or regularly visit certain collections of forums.
- Support for gateway services, such as ZiffNet.
- Support for the CompuServe B+ protocol for uploading and downloading.
- A viewer or decoder for Graphics Interchange Format (GIF), the standard for platform-independent graphic image exchange.
- Support non-English languages (German, French, Spanish, etc.).

Since some automated programs do not have all these features, you should shop for the right program to meet your needs. This chapter is the place to begin. After you have read these sections, visit forums that support your specific hardware and talk to other subscribers to see what they are using to communicate. When a new program comes on-line, many forum users become the first test audience.

Following is an overview of some commonly used automated packages, but probably not all of them. Some are in beta test at this writing, which means they are not yet bug-free to the satisfaction of the developer. Others may have been developed since this book was published.

For IBM PCs and Compatibles

The IBM PC has been the most popular platform for experimentation in the field of automated terminal programs. This section describes the major programs operating today.

Autosig

Autosig, a free communications program, is the granddaddy of this style of software, the oldest continuously updated automated terminal program around. When it was designed in the mid-1980s, it was created in the spirit of the medium: by a group of volunteers ("a community hack," someone called it). The program was developed by a project group of sysops in the IBMCOM forum, including Vernon Buerg (70007,1212), Jim McKeown (76702,1102), and Don Watkins (76703,750). You can find the latest version of the program and support for it in the IBM Communications Forum (GO IBMCOM). Messages about Autosig can be found in Message Section 1 ("Autosig") and the program and related files can be found in Library 1.

Autosig (sometimes known as ATO for short) automates the processing of forum and CompuServe mail messages quickly and economically. You can also use Autosig to upload/download program and data files to CompuServe, and as a terminal emulator for CompuServe's other services.

The key to the speed is Autosig's "grouping" (or batching) of messages in all of your forums (and your replies to them) for transmission to and from CompuServe. The key to the economy is Autosig's frugal use of on-line connection time. The developers say you may find your bills drop by 10 times what you pay if you use the system through the manual menus. (Or you may find that your bills don't drop at all, but you get 10 times the productivity out of CompuServe.)

Hardware Requirements

Autosig's hardware, software, and network requirements are detailed in the file ATO63A.REQ in IBMCOM's Library 1 (or from the Software Access Area of CompuServe (GO ACCSOFT). Here is a summary of what hardware is needed:

- An IBM PC, XT, AT, PS/2 (not the 50Z) or close compatible and at least 256K — more often 320K — of available memory.
- A minimum of 250K of disk space.

- A Hayes command set compatible modem that is auto-dial capable.

Optional are a hard disk (recommended for speed) and a mouse (MS and Logitech compatible are supported). Any monitor will work; graphics are not used.

Software Requirements

You will need the following software for Autosig:

- DOS 3.0 or later is recommended. DOS 2.x will work, but may cause problems.
- DESQview and Double DOS environments are supported. Autosig does not work with Novell NetWare loaded.

The Files You Will Need

All files needed can be downloaded from the "Autosig" Library (Library 1) of the IBM Communications Forum (GO IBMCOM). You will need:

- ATOSIG.REQ A complete description of the hardware and software requirements. Download and read this before going further (an ASCII file).
- ATOSIG.EXE The executable program itself and a script (an automation tool) for setting your forum parameters to get started (a self-extracting archive).
- ATODOC.EXE The user's manual, containing everything you want to know about the program (a self-extracting archive).

You may also download the program in the Software Access area of CompuServe (GO ACCSOFT).

Advanced Uses

Other optional files in the IBM Communications Forum will enhance your use of Autosig, including:

- ACL313.EXE, a program that allows you to find out how much you are spending while you are using Autosig.
- ATOBRO.EXE, a program that allows you to create scripts for downloading files from the Libraries (Libs) — (a self-extracting archive).
- ATOADV.EXE, a manual that documents Autosig's advanced functions (a self-extracting archive).
- DLSCAN.ARC, a program which builds a catalog of files in the CompuServe Libraries of your choice, and automatically downloads the ones you pick (through Autosig).

TapCIS

TapCIS, selected by *PC World* magazine in 1990 as one of the top shareware communications products, is the masterpiece of the late Howard Benner, a Wilmington, Delaware, public relations and marketing specialist who first popularized the idea of automated terminal software. Benner wrote his first automated program for the Tandy Corp. Model 100 laptop in the early 1980s, then was involved in the creation of the public domain Autosig for the early IBM systems. After that, he created more powerful commercial versions of the program, first a system called "ZapCIS," then the greatly improved TapCIS.

Benner passed away in June 1990 at age 44, after a long bout with malignant melanoma, but the program he launched continues, supported in The TapCIS Forum (GO TapCIS) by a band of Howard's friends.

Through TapCIS, Howard made many friends. For instance, Andrew Tobias, author of a number of national business books and creator of the Managing Your Money financial software, was frustrated with his early attempts to use CompuServe, not having the time to study the system's commands and structure. "Then I got TapCIS," he said, "and became CompuServe's biggest fan. I now log on painlessly once or twice a day by pressing just two keys when I turn on my computer. I read the paper for a couple of minutes while TapCIS gets everything that might interest me, logs off and beeps. Then I mark the items that do interest me, press one more key and go back to the newspaper. Three minutes later, it has logged on, retrieved the full text of the messages I've marked, logged off and beeped. I then take my time answering the messages that require it, with TapCIS' very adequate word processor, and press one final key. Three minutes later, it has logged on, sent my messages and logged off."

System Requirements

TapCIS requires an IBM PC / XT / AT / PS/2 or close compatible. It runs in 384K of RAM and will operate as a DOS application under Windows, DESQview, and OS/2. A hard disk is recommended for desktop use, and twin 720K 3.5-inch floppies for portable operation. TapCIS can be run on a single 720K floppy, but the user will need to manage remaining disk space very carefully.

A modem using the standard Hayes AT command set is recommended, although users have configured TapCIS with a wide variety of non-AT modems and hardwired configurations. 2400 bps is best for the most economical performance, but TapCIS will work at any rate from 300 to 9600 bps. TapCIS has been thoroughly tested with CompuServe at 9600 bps and will offer full speed performance when CompuServe opens 9600 dial-in lines to the public.

The Files You Will Need

TapCIS is stored in Library 1 of the TapCIS Forum (GO TapCIS) as TAP.EXE (the program) and TAPDOC.EXE (documentation).

As noted, the program is supported by its own forum. The people you will find there are the developers of the program and the people who use it daily. In addition, the libraries are filled with add-on programs and ideas.

You can also download TapCIS from the Software Access area of Compu-Serve (GO ACCSOFT). TapCIS is also available by mail if you wish to save the downloading time and the time to print the complete manual.

Key Features

Among TapCIS's features are:

- A split-screen text editor for preparing messages off-line with WordPerfect-like cursor, editing, and word wrap. Many WordStar editing commands are included for those used to that interface.

- Address book, which you can compile as you read messages, that allows you to send messages to other users based on their names without having to remember user IDs. Search by name, user ID, user name, or comments.

- Skip forward/backward by message or thread, jump to a message, read messages that contain a search string, skip through the messages by on-line session, or view messages previously saved.

- Options to allow forums to be defined as "Read all new threads," "Quick scan subjects for thread selection off-line," "Read messages to me only."

- A data library management system lets you do keyword searches of the files in a forum's libraries, browse them off-line, and subsequently do batch, unattended B+ protocol downloads on-line (including the ability to restart a transfer if aborted by you or by CompuServe).

- Auto or manual dialing from a selection of six phone numbers.

- Integral time and charges log, and recap to help you keep track of expenses. Month-to-date charges are listed by forum. Cumulative charges, a projection for the month, and a daily usage graph are included.

- Universal, context-sensitive help.

- User scripts including comments and text capture for simplifying access to other parts of the CompuServe service, such as stock quotations, news, weather, and so on.

Shareware Trial

Unlike Autosig, TapCIS is a commercial program, currently priced at $79.00. It is marketed as shareware, which means you may download it and try it out before buying it. TapCIS goes a step further than most shareware with a trial period. If you decide to stop using TapCIS within 90 days of paying for it, the company promises to refund the full purchase price.

You can register TapCIS by electronic mail using a MasterCard, Visa, or American Express number to user ID 74020,10, or by simply answering "Yes" to the registration option when you start the program. The printed documentation and your permanent registration number will be sent by mail.

TapCIS is published by Support Group, Inc., Lake Technology Park, McHenry, Maryland 21541; Phone:(800) USA-GROUP. CompuServe ID 74020,10.

OzCIS

Steve Sneed's offering to the IBM/compatibles community is, like TapCIS, a feature-packed system and, like Autosig, is free. But OzCIS is far more than a "me-too" program. Its own special niche is that it is the first major automated program designed specifically for the higher-end computers. While Autosig and TapCIS will both run on virtually *any* IBM or compatible, OzCIS is intended for machines built around an 80286 or higher chip.

Sneed set out to create a product that would offer the features he would demand of such a program if he went out to buy one. So he did it; he offers it free of charge to individual users, though if you intend to make commercial use of the program, a registration fee is required.

System Requirements

Hardware and software requirements for OzCIS include:

- An IBM AT-compatible computer (80286 or better processor, 10mhz or faster) or IBM PS/2 MicroChannel computer with a 286 or better processor, and at least one megabyte of RAM.

- A minimum of 486K of free conventional memory must be available when OzCIS loads; 520K to 550K or more is strongly recommended. OzCIS simply won't run on XT-class machines (8086/8088).

- At least a megabyte of EMS/XMS memory is recommended. OzCIS makes heavy use of overlays, and having EMS available for overlay storage will improve response times. Also, OzCIS uses virtual memory to EMS or XMS for indexing the message and catalog files, so making EMS or XMS available will dramatically increase the capacity of these areas. OzCIS can make use of up to two megabytes of EMS.

- A hard disk with at least 1.5 megabytes free. This is a bare minimum. If you maintain a large number of forums, you will need more.

- A mouse is not required, but using one can make several features more convenient to use. If you use a mouse, the mouse driver must be recent enough to support the "Save-State" and "Restore-State" services. MS V6.0

or later; LogiTech 4.01 or later. Ports 1 through 4 are supported for AT-class machines, and ports 1 through 8 for PS/2 machines.

- The modem must be a fully Hayes-compatible model, including most high-speed modems such as US Robotics' HST/V.32/Dual Standard models or the Microcom MNP series models. A "direct-connect" option is available for those connecting through modem servers or pools, but no support for network comm servers is provided. An error-correcting modem (MNP or V.42) is recommended.

- OzCIS can be run under Windows, DESQview, and OS/2. For Windows and DV, you will need to define a PIF (program information file) for OzCIS. In Windows or DESQview, it is best to run in Full-Screen mode, as opposed to windowing, due to the dramatic increase in demand for memory, though it will run without incident when sufficient resources and processor power are available. It is not recommended to run OzCIS in windowed mode on a 386-SX or slow DX type of computer. PIFs in Library section 12.

- While DOS 3.1 or later will work, DOS 5.0 is recommended. The program has not been thoroughly tested under alternative OS shells such as 4DOS, but preliminary observations show no conflicts.

- While any PC color video system will work for text or graphics in the program, a SuperVGA system is recommended to take full advantage of the program's graphics capabilities. If your SVGA card has an available VESA driver, use it. OzCIS does not at this time support Hercules Graphics Workstation or other TIGA or Targa type cards other than in SVGA emulation mode. The program supports UltraVision and all high-resolution text modes, such as 132-column and/or 43/50-line display modes.

Key Features

Typically, the OzCIS user has the program make automated passes to favorite forums to get a QuickScan list of message headers (topics), then selects those of interest while off-line. Once the selections have been made, new messages composed, or messages replied to, the user sends OzCIS back for a follow-up second pass to perform the tasks of posting messages, picking up messages tagged for download, or any other tasks you may have wanted performed, such as library scans, file uploads or downloads, and other functions.

Here are some of the other OzCIS features:

- Automated handling and management of CompuServe Mail. This includes uploads of files as mail, auto-downloading of mail files, and sending and receiving messages. Lost message retrieval allows you to "undelete" mail received and discarded within 48 hours. Full support for alternate routing such as >FAX, >INTERNET, >POSTAL, and >NMH.

- Automated address book with the ability to extract addresses from received messages, etc.
- General text, message reply, and review editors. The reply editor has a split screen feature which allows you to see and scroll the original message in the upper half of the screen while composing your reply in the lower half. Quoting text from the original to the reply can be performed with a fast-paste feature. Many WordStar commands are used in all the editors.
- On-line display of GIF graphics and weather maps.
- A configuration menu for each forum to give you individual control over the functions and tasks performed on each pass in each forum. These include selecting which sections to visit, retrieving all messages and/or only those addressed to you, message header QuickScans, library updates, file uploads and downloads, etc.
- A scripting language, with variables, conditionals, and branching allows exceptional flexibility in customized on-line processing.
- Thread tracking, and message storage and management, featuring the ability to call up a thread map of all messages relating to the current message being viewed, and the capability to scroll to and view any message in the tree.
- User configurable message and CompuServe Mail purging system.
- Forum library tools. You can perform automated long or short library scans by individual forum and library section.
- Support for 43/50-line display modes.

The Files You Will Need

OzCIS is available for downloading in the "OzCIS" data library (Section 12) of the IBM Communications Forum (GO IBMCOM). A total of four files is required for the program. They are OZCIS1.EXE, OZCIS2.EXE, OZCIS3.EXE, and OZCIS4.EXE.

These are self-extracting archive files, which means they are in compressed format, but require no decompression utility in order to make them usable. The files total about 700K and take about an hour to download at 2400 bps under normal CompuServe conditions.

In addition, you may download the program files from the Software Access area of CompuServe (GO ACCSOFT).

Support

OzCIS maintains Section 12 of the IBM Communications Forum (GO IBMCOM) message board for technical support for its users. In addition, the forum's Library 12 contains files with tools which can be adapted to OzCIS' use. Some are user-contributed scripts for accessing various networks around the world, while others are scripts that are ready-made and tested for various purposes within CompuServe, such as downloading ENS stories, AP News stories, ACCU-Weather maps, etc. You will also find pre-written PIF files, Windows icons, and threads of discussions of merit which may be helpful in configuring OzCIS for your system.

Golden CommPass for OS/2

Golden CommPass is a commercial automated program for an OS/2 link with CompuServe. As with most automated programs in this chapter, Golden CommPass allows you to make all decisions and compose new messages off-line, at your own convenience. It is enhanced by descriptive icons, windows, and prompts which guide the user in the proper direction for the next steps. The program is published by Creative Systems Programming Corp., a Mount Laurel, New Jersey firm operated by Larry B. Finkelstein, an assistant sysop in the IBM OS/2 Users Forum (GO IBMOS2).

System Requirements

Golden CommPass operates on IBM PC 286, 386, 386sx, 486, 486sx, or other machines capable of running OS/2. Three to four megabytes of RAM are the minimum advised. It needs 1.5 megabytes of hard disk space.

A Hayes-compatible modem is recommended, but it is possible to configure Golden CommPass for use with other modems. It needs OS/2 1.21, OS/2 1.3, or OS/2 2.0 to operate.

Features

The program offers an OS/2 communications engine to automate access to CompuServe. It is packaged as a separate Dynamic Link Library (DLL) package, so it is easily replaceable and extendable. All CompuServe scripting logic is contained in a single Dynamic Link Library (DLL) package, so changes to the CompuServe interface can be implemented without disruption of the rest of the Golden CommPass installation.

Other features include:

- The program uses OS/2's multitasking and multithreading capabilities and provides a graphical user interface (GUI) for accessing CompuServe. It supports the OS/2 system clipboard to cut and paste text between other OS/2 applications and Golden CommPass.

- All message-indexing operations are processed in the background using multiple threads. Presentation Manager windows are used to display the message threads index, to mark message headers, and to display the data library catalog.

- Icons indicate actions that need to be performed, either off-line or on-line.

- Context-sensitive help is built in and is available to the user at any time by selecting the HELP push button.

- Off-line, the program allows processing of multiple message files, message header files, or library catalogs concurrently. It allows the user to work with the different files in the order that the user selects.

- The text of individual forum messages is displayed in separate windows for each forum. When replying to a forum message, the message window is split horizontally, so you can continue viewing the original message.

- It provides navigation of the forum message threads by locating the parent message or any children messages. A "Bookmark" option allows you to mark selected messages so you can easily find them. Bookmarks are preserved between sessions.

- Macros can be created for signing messages, or other frequently used text.

- The user can select any OS/2 supported font, has complete control of colors and window sizes, and can selectively overwrite or append messages to message file on a forum-by-forum basis.

- Communication takes place in the background, so other activities can be performed while the communications session is active.

Support

Technical support for the program is available on CompuServe on the IBM OS/2 Information Exchange (GO IBMOS2). Free technical support is also available via telephone for the first 90 days after purchase.

Getting the Program

Golden CommPass is available on a single 3.5" low-density (720K) or 5.25" high-density (1.2 megabyte) diskette. It's available directly from Creative Systems Programming Corporation for $99.00 (as of this writing), or it can be downloaded from the Software Access Area of CompuServe (GO ACCSOFT). Orders within the continental United States will be shipped via UPS ground delivery at no additional charge. The program can also be shipped UPS Red (overnight) or UPS Blue (two-day), but shipping costs will be added to the purchase price. Orders within Canada, Alaska, and Hawaii will be sent via US Air mail unless other instructions are received at the time of purchase. All other orders will be charged an additional $15.00 for shipping and handling. These packages will be shipped via US Air mail unless other instructions are received at the time of purchase.

Checks or money orders (in US funds) may be mailed to: Creative Systems Programming Corporation, Post Office Box 961, Mount Laurel, NJ 08054-0961. VISA and MasterCard are also accepted, and may be used to order via telephone, mail, or electronically via CompuServe Mail.

To contact the firm, phone (609) 234-1500 or write CompuServe Mail to 71511,151.

For Apple Computers

Apple computers have also seen interesting experiments in automating CompuServe.

Navigator for the Macintosh

Mike O'Connor is a programmer with a message: Computing ought to be easy. Ever since he began programming the IBM System 38 and DecSystem 20 in the mid-1970s, he has believed that the technology should be accessible to all of us. His philosophy brought him to the Apple Macintosh when it was introduced 10 years ago. That attitude ultimately inspired him to write the best known automated terminal program in the Mac community, the highly praised CompuServe Navigator.

About the time he was learning about his new Mac in 1984, O'Connor was also discovering the then-new Macintosh Forum that Neil Shapiro had opened as the latest part of MAUG (the Micronetworked Apple Users Group).

"What a fantastic resource that turned out to be," O'Connor, who lives in Long Island, New York, told a reporter with CompuServe's electronic *Online Today* publication a few years ago. "Not only were the discussions lively, but many developers and even Apple employees were there sharing their knowledge of the new machine."

It was while browsing the message board in the original Mac forum in April 1986 that O'Connor came across a public note that would change his life. It was a simple, wistful message for a fellow forum member. "He dreamed of being able to automatically visit several forums, pick up mail, save it all in a file and then leisurely review and compose responses off-line," O'Connor recalled. "It sounded like a super idea, and I took on the challenge."

A few months later, Navigator appeared in its first incarnation, as a $40.00 shareware program. Quickly, CompuServe itself also realized the potential of O'Connor's efforts and the company agreed to begin distributing the program through the on-line CompuServe Store (GO ORDER) merchandise area. Now Navigator has its own support forum and an army of satisfied customers.

Features

Navigator users can predefine their entire CompuServe session prior to the time they actually connect. Once the session is set up, Navigator will go on-line and retrieve the information the user requested.

The software can be used to access the forums, CompuServe Mail, Quick Quotes, most of the menus and articles, and the CompuServe Phones Database. Once the information is retrieved from CompuServe, Navigator allows users to review the information (and respond to forum and CompuServe Mail messages) off-line.

Users can access areas not supported by Navigator's "auto-mode" by setting up a "terminal mode" session tile, which tells the program to pause part of the way through its session and let the user take over control.

Navigator version 3 supports CompuServe's Host-Micro Interface protocol, the same protocol that CompuServe Information Manager uses. The protocol allows most of the information that is sent to and from CompuServe (forum messages, CompuServe Mail messages, and files) to be transferred to the Macintosh under CompuServe's error-correcting "B" protocol.

Navigator, which is MultiFinder and System 7 compatible, can also transfer and display GIF-formatted images found in numerous forums and in the Accu-Weather Maps (GO MAPS) database, send fax and Internet messages, and operate sophisticated forum library searches.

Support

The CompuServe Navigator is supported by CompuServe's Customer Service support team as well as by experts in the Navigator Support Forum (GO NAVSUP), which can be accessed free of connect-time. You can also find help in the Macintosh Communications Forum (GO MACCOM).

The Navigator Support Forum's Library 4, "Manual Mode/Scripts," offers many scripts that further expand Navigator's functionality. For example, the library includes APVSCR.TTX for reading the Associated Press' hourly news update, ENSVAR.TXT, which facilitates the forwarding of stories from an Executive News Service clipping folder to CompuServe Mail, and WEATHR.SCR, a tool that simplifies the retrieval of local weather forecasts.

System Requirements

The program requires:

- Two double-sided 800K disk drives or one double-sided 800K disk drive and a hard disk.
- System 4.1 for a minimum system required, although System 6.0.1 or higher is needed to use some of the features.
- A total of 650K of available memory.

Although most modems will work, a Hayes-compatible modem is recommended.

Ordering the Program

You can order Navigator through the CompuServe On-line Ordering area (GO ORDER). If you have a Canadian or American mailing address and you ordered the program through the on-line ordering area, you will be a registered user from the time you order. If you purchased your copy of The CompuServe Navigator through a retail outlet (regardless of your mailing address), you need to follow the instructions on the registration card that is enclosed with the manual and disk.

Copilot for IIgs

Copilot for Apple IIgs computers was written by Kenneth I. Gluckman (73250,2572). It is intended to automate access to the forums and permit off-line reading and writing of messages, and selection of files to download.

At this writing, the latest on-line is an evaluation copy of version 2.0.2 which has some non-essential features disabled. On payment of a $25.00 fee you will be told how to activate all features. (Update costs $10.00 for registered users of 1.x.) Users have contributed supporting scripts and programs.

To find the latest Copilot and supporting files, search for COPILOT in Library 12 ("Telecommunications") in the Apple II/III Users Forum (GO APPUSER).

For Commodore Amiga Systems

For Commodore's colorful Amiga systems, CompuServe has provided a challenge for automation.

AutoPilot

AutoPilot, a shareware program for the Amiga, was created by veteran sysop Steve Ahlstrom of Denver, Colorado, (76703,2006) who has been an administrator in the Amiga forums for several years now. His goal, he says, was to incorporate features specifically requested by his forum members, including multitasking, an integral message reader/editor, and an interactive on-line mode.

Features

The software manages most on-line tasks automatically, with a single click of the mouse. It can collect your mail, forum messages, and downloads of text and binary files. It has its own editor and message viewer in which you compose messages or replies to be uploaded. All reading and composing are done off-line. AutoPilot can collect catalogs of the libraries, then display the file descriptions individually for you to make your selections off-line. When you sign on again, the files you selected will be automatically downloaded to your computer.

System Requirements

To run properly and easily, AutoPilot requires that you have, in addition to OS 2.04 or later, at least two megabytes of memory and at least five megabytes of free space on a hard drive. The disk font library you must have is version 37 or later. You must not use PowerPacker or other programs on AutoPilot which would alter the code in any way.

Where to Get It

A demo version of AutoPilot found in Library 9 of the Amiga Vendor Forum (GO AMIGAVENDOR) is fully functional for basic work on the CompuServe Amiga Forums and CompuServe Mail, but many of its special features are disabled. These will be turned on after you have the program working and have sent your registration fee which is $69.95, at this writing.

After registration, your program will be changed from a working demo to a fully registered version by a binary CompuServe Mail message which you will receive from the publisher, AForums Ltd. This will happen within 24 hours if you register on-line through the CompuServe Software Registration Program (GO SWREG).

To find the Demo version of AutoPilot, search Library 9 of the Amiga Vendor Forum with the keyword AUTOPILOT. (At this writing, the file was called AP.LHA.)

Support

The Amiga Vendor Forum (GO AMIGAVENDOR), in addition to the demo program, also provides auxiliary programs to enhance AutoPilot for specific uses. For instance, the file APSCPT.LZH has two scripts, one for capturing the CompuServe on-line and the other for tapping headlines from The Associated Press.

Whap!

Whap! is an older automated program written by Jim Nangano in partnership with Amiga forums sysop Steve Ahlstrom. Initially released in July 1988, the software also illustrates how telecommuting enables new kinds of teamwork.

Thousands of miles separate the two programmers—Nangano in Newark, Delaware and Ahlstrom in Colorado—yet they were able to work together on a common project.

This is actually two programs that work together. "I wrote a program called 'View,'" Ahlstrom told *CompuServe Magazine* a few years ago, "and Jim wrote 'Whap!' so we were each able to concentrate primarily on the software we were personally developing. We had to decide on how the two programs should talk to each other. Eventually we designed a way for Whap! to call and talk to View and for View to do the same with Whap!"

As the first major automated program for the Amiga community, the combined software quickly garnered a following, with thousands of users in the United States and Canada as well as in Europe and Australia.

Features

With Whap!, you can call CompuServe, collect your CompuServe Mail and the messages from as many as 10 forums, upload your answers to the previous session's mail and messages, download or upload any software you have selected, and sign-off, all by clicking the Whap! icon.

Once off-line, you can read and answer the mail and messages in View!, the Whap! editor. You can read the message in an upper window while answering it in the bottom one, using the scroll bar to move through the entire message. Messages may be saved to a file, if you like. The program multitasks, so you can play your favorite game or write letters while Whap! does the on-line work for you.

On Whap!'s initial visit to a forum, it collects a list of the available message board section names. Then it asks you to choose any or all to read routinely in whole, quick-scan message headers, or just retrieve those messages specifically addressed to you. After reading the downloaded messages off-line, compose your replies for posting upon your next logon.

Whap! permits similar control of a forum's libraries. At your request, the program obtains any forum library's catalog and allows you to mark files of interest. File transfers are done via CompuServe's Quick 'B' Protocol guaranteeing error-free downloads and uploads in the shortest time possible.

System Requirements

It is possible to use Whap! on a 512K Amiga, but it will perform much better if you have 1 megabyte of memory. Hard disks are not necessary, but the system should have two disk drives.

Where to Find the Files and Support

You'll find Whap! in Library 9 of Amiga Vendor Forum (GO AMIGAVENDOR). Search with the keyword WHAP to get the latest version. This is a demo version, but is fully working. You can use the demo as much as you wish before you register. Registration costs $39.95.

In addition, Library 9 has a number of programs to make the program more efficient.

For Atari Systems

Atari computer users can also automate their CompuServe travels.

QuickCIS

We personal computer enthusiasts are an independent lot. Just because the magazines and newspapers tell us that PC selection comes down to choosing between IBM/compatibles and Macintoshes these days, it ain't necessarily so. There still are *alternative* computers if you want to go your own way. And the going gets easier if you are on CompuServe and can link up with some fellow techno-rebels. If you need proof, just look into Ron Luks' amazingly active Atari Network forums, described in Chapter 6.

Also, simply because everyone seems to be using TapCIS or OzCIS or Navigator or some other IBM or Mac automated terminal program doesn't mean there aren't alternatives there too. Witness the public domain QuickCIS written to automate CompuServe access on Atari ST computers.

Programmer Jim Ness (74415,1727) says the Atari community has the same needs for automation as those in the larger IBM and Apple world. "It enables folks to download more information in less time, cutting on-line charges to an absolute minimum," he told a reporter with CompuServe electronic *Online Today* publication. "Moreover, as you use on-line time more effectively, you are likely to broaden your horizons by visiting more forums, reviewing more messages and exploring additional libraries."

What Does It Do?

QuickCIS easily configures to logon, checks your CompuServe Mail area, and travels to as many as six forums. While in each forum, QuickCIS reads messages (and there are ways to control exactly what is captured), checks as many as seven libraries for new uploads, and downloads requested files. Once done, you are automatically signed off, enabling you to read everything at your leisure, without an eye on the on-line charge clock.

Also, a built-in editor facilitates responding to mail and messages as well as starting new threads. After each forum's message sections have been read, the file descriptions from visited libraries are shown. If you come across something of interest, mark it for download on your next forum session.

Ness also points out several special features. "QuickCIS," he explains, "can make a delayed call at a time you specify, taking advantage of lower phone rates. It also can create a library of previous messages and store them for future reference."

Getting the Files and Support

The files for the program are contained in the Atari Productivity Forum (GO ATARIPRO) Telecommunications Library (Library 2). To find the latest version, Search with the keyword QUICKCIS. At this writing, the latest version, 1.71, was in QWKCIS.PRG. However, a beta file of version 1.72 was being tested.

For Other Systems

Other non-IBM and non-Mac systems also have automated software alternatives.

XC for Unix

XC is an automated communications program for Unix and Xenix. It supports shell escapes, and has BREAK capability, a dialing directory, and a script language that includes shell command and variable support.

XC includes built-in Xmodem and CompuServe B+ Protocol support as well as access to external Ymodem and Zmodem transfer programs.

You'll find the source code for XC in two files in the Library 4 of the Unix Forum (GO UNIXFORUM). XC.TAZ is the compressed source code for XC. XC.SHK is the self-extracting ASCII file for the XC source code.

ARCTIC for British Visitors

ARCTIC (ARChimedes Terminal Interface to CompuServe) is an off-line reader and CompuServe access program for the Acorn Archimedes, created by Richard Proctor (100031,604) of Waveney Games in Dorset, England. A shareware program, it supports messaging, mail, conferencing, and libraries.

Features

Arctic allows users to take their time when looking at messages, composing replies at their leisure without incurring any charges. You can look through the messages in many ways using keys, menus, or mouse clicks. An embedded editor is familiar to all Arc users as it is a derivative of !edit.

Arctic switches to on-line operation with a simple mouse click; you do not have to do any actions while Arctic is on-line (unless you want to). On the other hand, should you wish to operate on-line either within conferences or other parts of CompuServe, Arctic supports a split screen on-line operation allowing you to type in one window while conferencing takes place in the other window. You can also program a set of context-sensitive hot keys to perform actions you may wish to perform often or quickly without having to remember complete CompuServe instructions. The software also provides an address book for captured user IDs from messages, with comments and user histories if wanted.

In forum libraries, it maintains an off-line support system for catalog browsing, uploads and downloads, and a log to relate library files with files you have downloaded.

In its default setting, the program is prepared to support up to 20 forums (the setting can be changed), with options for setting sections to read on the individual message boards and libraries. It also provides features for handling private messages and navigation of gateways to non-CompuServe forums.

System Requirements

The program is fully Risc-OS compliant and can run on any machine with at least 2MB of RAM and a floppy disk drive. The software will run on any Acorn Archimedes Computer running Risc-OS, including A4, A310, A410, A440, A3000, A3010, A3020, A4000, A5000, and A540.

The developers say Arctic may run on a 1B machine if nothing else is loaded, but 2B is more realistic. A hard disk is not required, although it will make the program run smoother and faster. Arctic also needs Clib version 3.75 (or higher), which is available in the UK Computing Forum (GO UKCOMP). It should work with all Hayes-compatible modems and may work with some others; it supports operation at 1200, 2400, and 9600 baud.

Where to Download It

The program can be obtained in Section 5, "Archie/Beeb/Z88," in the UK Computing Forum (GO UKCOMP). To find the latest version and supporting files, search the library with the keyword ARTICC. At this writing, the primary files were ARCTIC.ARC and RUNIMG.ARC.

Support

Arctic is a shareware program. The version in the UK Computing Forum (GO UKCOMP) library will perform all functions, but if you don't register it, it will remind you (frequently) that your copy is unregistered. Registration may be made by sending a check for 15 pounds to Waveney Games, 28 Diprose Road, Corfe Mullen, Wimborne, Dorset BH21 3QY.

Email8 for Tandy 100 and 102

Email8 — also called EM8SIG — for Tandy Model 100 and 102 was written by Marvin M. Miller, who supported it and constantly upgraded it until his death in late 1987. Miller had told associates in the Model 100 Forum (GO M100SIG) of his plans for further improvements to the program. In 1988, when it was determined that because of changes in CompuServe, particularly as they related to the Forums, EM8SIG would no longer be useable, a campaign began to upgrade the beloved program to work with the new format. Stan Wong undertook the work, with George Sherman writing the documentation.

Features

EM8SIG is menu-driven and can perform many of its functions with the press of a single function key. It aids in preparing CompuServe Mail and forum messages off-line, supports multiple addressee CompuServe Mail, and keeps a record of CompuServe charges. It also allows unattended operation: auto-log onto C60-4Serve at preset times when phone rates are low, send/receive messages, auto-logoff, and redial if a busy signal is encountered. The program supports a variety of Model 100 peripheral devices, such as the Chipmunk disk drive, RAM banks, cassette tape, and printer.

Where to Get It

This public domain program can be retrieved from Library 3 ("Telecom") of the Model 100 Forum (GO M100SIG). For the latest version, search the keyword EM8SIG.

Also Consider Script Files

Finally, in addition to these programs, you also can find scripts specifically developed for use with CompuServe for some general purpose communication programs.

Now why, with all these automated programs, would anyone want to tackle the problem of CompuServe automation from inside a general communications program? One reason is that nowadays telecomputerists are likely to visit more than one on-line service. While they may like the features of a dedicated program (such as CIM, TapCIS, Navigator, or AutoPilot), it could be a source of irritation to have to change communications programs when logging on to something other than CompuServe. For some users, a better approach seems to be to use the same general communications software for visiting all services and use sophisticated script files inside the program to extensively automate.

In your exploration, you can find scripts for major communications programs such as Microphone (MAILS.BIN), ProComm (CISTER.ZIP, PCPCIS.ARC, FDOC20.CMD), Telix (CIS2.SLT), and other products in related vendor support forums.

CISOP for Crosstalk

A major entry in this area of script file collections — and an excellent example of the concept — is CISOP for the Crosstalk software. CISOP stands for CompuServe Information Service OPerations and is a series of script files developed to work in conjunction with Crosstalk Mk.4, well known in IBM computing circles.

CISOP author Dean Ammons has been a fan of automated navigation for some time. As he told a writer with CompuServe's *Online Today*, "I started with Autosig before switching to ZAPCIS/TapCIS, not because I did not like ATO, but because TapCIS offered library catalog processing. Soon, I realized that I desired more library functions than the basic set TapCIS offered. So, being a programmer, I wrote a series of Crosstalk scripts called CISDL (CIS Data Libraries). CISDL did for library processing what TapCIS did for message handling. These turned out to be fairly popular with members of the Crosstalk Forum (GO XTALK), except everyone wanted both in a single package."

Ammons did not stop with automating the forums. Incorporated is the ability to search and capture descriptions from the File Finders based on single or multiple criteria. As you review the descriptions, mark those files of interest for retrieval during your next on-line session.

CISOP is also capable of taking advantage of CompuServe Mail enhancements, such as fax, Internet, MCI Mail, and postal delivery options. Batch file processing, invaluable for those employing database programs with the mail merge feature, is permitted. A carbon copy function is built in, automatically generating distribution lists shown at the message's bottom.

CISOP does not require navigating CompuServe menus or familiarity with any system commands. To facilitate unattended operations, safeguards are included to ensure a computer will not be left hanging on-line, running up phone and connect-time charges if something unexpected occurs in your absence.

The set of needed files can be found in Library 4 ("Crosstalk Mark 4") and Library 7 ("Crosstalk Communicator") of the Crosstalk Forum (GO XTALK). Introductory information is contained in CISOP.TXT in Library 7. To find it and related files, search the libraries with a keyword of CISOP.

15

Carry It On

In this chapter...

The You Factor
You're Now an Electronic Citizen
This, Above All...
Reaching Fellow Citizens

The journey isn't over. While the end of our time together is nearing and we are packing up to take our leave, your real exploration of the remarkable world on the other side of your computer screen is just starting. You won't be left empty-handed. Following this chapter is the On-Line Survival Kit, a section full of lists and tips to sustain you in your electronic travels. Having come this far, you have camped on CompuServe turf long enough to consider yourself a patron of the on-line arts and have learned important facts about Compu-Serve's style of electronic communication, among them:

- What may at first appear to be a system held together with baling wire and black magic is actually a logical network of related features. If services appear unrelated, it is only because of their diversity.
- The way features appear on your screen depends largely on the kind of communications software you are using. If you employ the CompuServe Information Manager, you find the system that intimately interacts with the pull-down menus and cursor bars on your screen. If you use a third-party automated program, you find you can do as much of your Compu-Serving off-line as on, allowing the software to make judicious decisions about how and when to log on to do your bidding. If you use a general terminal program, a go-everywhere program that can log on as easily to other systems as CompuServe, you can travel the system in real-time using ASCII menus and prompts.

- Several ways exist for navigating. The simplest is slow, through menus; faster is by direct (GO) commands at markers known as prompts. Methods of moving about the system are interchangeable and available to all, no matter what your level of expertise; you can progress from one approach to the next at your own pace.

- Once you learn commands in one area of the system you can use them in similar services elsewhere. Commands used in a computing-related forum also work across the system in a forum devoted to gardening. Moreover, similar *concepts* are also at work in entirely different parts of the system. A compelling similarity, for instance, exists between commands for message-writing in the forums and those in CompuServe Mail and elsewhere.

- Fears of getting lost, though natural because of the system's sheer size, are groundless. No matter where you are, a simple command or two takes you back to the system's front door or gets you out of the system entirely. Help files abound on all features.

- You can't "break" CompuServe. Many a new user has feared that by entering a wrong command or hitting the wrong key at the wrong time, CompuServe will come to a grinding halt, bells and whistles will sound, and the CompuServe cops will be dispatched. The system has withstood the arrival and experimentation of hundreds of thousands of computer enthusiasts and is still humming along quite nicely, thank you.

- Things change often, with new services coming on-line almost weekly. However, commands for operating them—and basic concepts behind those commands—seldom are drastically different from those in existing features.

The *You* Factor

There is much emphasis on software around CompuServe these days. There is the CompuServe Information Manager software and the exciting area of third-party terminal programs, surveyed in the previous chapter. From the user interface perspective, this is the beginning of The Glory Days.

It would be a mistake, though, to think that CIM or any other innovative software or hardware will be the primary influence on how this extraordinary system evolves in the years to come. That key role will be played by a much more sophisticated system, one that operates as fast as imagination and uses only two interactive components:

- You.
- And all the rest of us.

The more you are on-line, the more you realize that CompuServe is not a network of computers, but a network of *people*. Powerful software is important because it makes computers increasingly incidental to the network (or at least far less interesting than all that data being exchanged up there at the human-to-human level of the system).

We all know that machines can't do it all — if circuitry were all it took, we could become computer experts simply by buying the equipment — but sometimes, in our rush to travel the system faster and faster and with more software automation, we forget the essential human connection. The importance of electronic camaraderie is easy to overlook, but it doesn't have to be that way. As the software simplifies the basic navigation of the system, you have more time (not to mention all that saved connect-time money) to occasionally explore unfamiliar areas of the system, to find your own Next Big Thing among CompuServe's hundreds of features. And, since software itself can be assigned to handle the routine information gathering (retrieving files, browsing messages, sending and receiving letters), you have more opportunity to stop and talk with old friends on-line, to develop new relationships, and to reopen electronic mail correspondence perhaps too long neglected.

Keeping open the people-to-people network taps a resource that is broader than technology alone, a human resource that is, as they say in our part of the world, as old as the hills. Our homes are in West Virginia, a region in which relatively few people have even heard of CompuServe. But there is a resonance here in the way people communicate, an old-fashioned resonance that we have also found on-line in the first decade of this amazing international computer experience. In both these worlds, we find friendliness mixed with straightforwardness, honesty along with good humor. In both there is as much time given to nonsense as no-nonsense. It is what has held our mountain communities together during the good times and the bad. And, we suspect, this same essential humanity, as a constant during the years of rapid change, will also sustain this ever-growing electronic medium, no matter where it takes us, because it is what compels us to reach out to one another.

You're Now an Electronic Citizen

Anyone who spends time on-line learns, like any good citizen, that you get more out of a system if you also put something into it. You will find you can enrich your on-line time if you enhance the system. If you simply prowl as a nameless subscriber with nothing to say, you will likely become dissatisfied, impatient, frustrated. The genius of CompuServe is its two-way communication on a human, personal level.

So, now that you know the way, *participate*. Get to know the forums. Take a look at the list in Appendix J of the On-Line Survival Kit and choose a few you think you might be interested in. Set aside time to explore each one on your personal list. Check the section names, choose some messages, and read their threads. If someone asks a question publicly and you know the answer, jump in. Leave an introductory message to the sysop just to say hello. If you want some specific information and don't see it, leave a message to ask. Questions and answers are the life's blood of the forums. Be sure to return in a day or two to read the responses, and don't wait too long, since your replies may scroll off the message board.

Be *self-reliant*. Don't ask the sysop to explain what the forum is all about. Read the announcements and files in the libraries. Also please don't ask a sysop to go above and beyond what he or she already is doing for the forum. You would be surprised how often we see messages to sysops that say, "Please call me on the phone and tell me…" Now, that isn't necessary. Your computer has put you in touch with one of the most amazing communications tools of our time, so let's allow the harried sysop to work in that environment.

Try to *contribute*. If you have a special program you have written and you think someone else might be interested in it, leave it in a forum library. If you find someone else's public program that you really like, write a CompuServe Mail message to its creator expressing thanks. Always be thinking of new features you would like to see. CompuServe isn't exactly flying by the seat of its pants, but employees acknowledge that, since no one has ever given birth to an animal quite like this before, no one is sure just what it should look like. The company looks to its subscribers for suggestions and provides the Feedback area (GO FEEDBACK) for communications. Feedback is so special, the company doesn't charge you for the time you spend there. Extensive changes in the system have been made because one subscriber had a better idea.

Be *responsible*. Report wrongdoing. Did someone try to trick you into divulging your password? Is someone leaving messages that smack of false advertising? Have you run across a program on-line that you know is copyrighted rather than in the public domain or shareware? Report it through Feedback.

And *protect* yourself. Change your password regularly. If someday you try to log on and find out that your password no longer works with your user ID, report it immediately to customer service. Your number and password may have been stolen. Unless you report it, you might be charged for the time the thief spent on-line with your number.

There are very few hard-and-fast rules laid down by CompuServe. Those that are can be viewed on-line by entering GO RULES at any prompt or read in the back of the book (Appendix G). You will find it is a short list and the reason is simple. The company seems to have the philosophy that rules shouldn't be made until they are necessary—an enlightened attitude, in our opinion. The fact is that the majority of people who use CompuServe regulate themselves and thereby regulate the system, rewarding kindnesses and friendship with more kindness and friendship.

This, Above All...

We want to leave you with this message: Have *fun* on CompuServe, however you define fun, whether it's playing a game, chatting with the world on CB, talking technical matters in a forum, or retrieving financial information that will just set the office on its ear. Don't feel guilty if you start seeing yourself as a child with a new toy. There is nothing wrong with a little wide-eyed enthusiasm. We hope the excitement never fades for you, although your priorities for using CompuServe are likely to change with your experience, moods, and needs. That's all right, too. As you grow, CompuServe grows too.

Prophets of the new age say information services and telecomputing are likely to play a major role in what all of us do. Winners will be those who keep abreast of both the technology and the information it brings to the home, the business, and the marketplace. No one can predict what CompuServe will be like tomorrow, next week, or next year. "We don't make predictions. They make us nervous," one CompuServe official said. In this slightly wacky world of developing computer technology, nothing is forever. But those who don't keep informed can easily fall behind. We feel that, while it isn't the ultimate computer service yet, CompuServe is the best training ground around for those who want to keep on top of what's happening with computer communications.

Reaching Fellow Citizens

One of the joys of writing and updating this book over the past decade has been that staying in touch with our readers is so simple. The same service we write about also provides you with a way to reach us.

Charlie can be reached by sending CompuServe Mail to 71635,1025, while Dave's user ID is 70475,1165. We invite your comments about the book. Your opinions are valuable to us. We are especially interested in tips you may have for helping others learn this remarkable system.

Good luck. See you around the system!

On-Line Survival Kit

A

Getting Started: Tips for CIM and Non-CIM Users

In this appendix ...

Guidelines for CIM Users
Guidelines for Non-CIM Users

Most newcomers these days use the CompuServe Information Manager software at least for their initial visits to the system, which means they can take advantage of the software's automatic signup feature and its easy logon procedures. Appendix B provides a general overview of CIM; this section focuses on the signup and logon procedures.

Meanwhile, if you are not a CIM user, you can use third-party software to visit CompuServe; in your initial visit, ASCII menus present options very much like those presented in the CIM automatic signup. The later part of this appendix has signup and logon tips for non-CIM users.

Guidelines for CIM Users

This section offers an overview on signup and logon using the CompuServe Information Manager.

Automatic Signup

Your CIM distribution disk offers an opportunity in its installation procedures to copy signup software to your disk along with other files. At the end of the installation, you are invited by the program to sign up for CompuServe membership. You may accept the invitation at that point or you may sign up later from a disk or directory that contains the signup software.

The distribution disk package provides details on running the signup software. Here is an overview of the procedure, starting with the introductory pull-down menu shown in Figure A.1.

The menu provides some text articles for background on various features. CompuServe advises you to read the items called "Regular Account Terms," "Operating Rules," and "the Executive Option Description." Another item on the menu, "Modem Settings" is relevant only if your communications specifications cannot be determined automatically by the Information Manager software. (The program automatically notifies you if there is a problem and refers you to the installation guide.) After you have reviewed the articles, select the "Sign Me Up" option, which produces a form (dialog box) such as the one in Figure A.2.

Here are some important specifics about the lines to be completed in the form:

- **Serial number** refers to a number that is provided along the edge of a specific page in the Membership Booklet that came with your distribution disk.

- **Agreement number** is provided in the Membership Booklet on the same page.

- **Country** you live in may be designated in the check box. (If you mark "Other" you will be asked to enter the country's name.)

- **Account type** means either personal or business accounts. Most subscribers have personal accounts. (Business accounts are available within

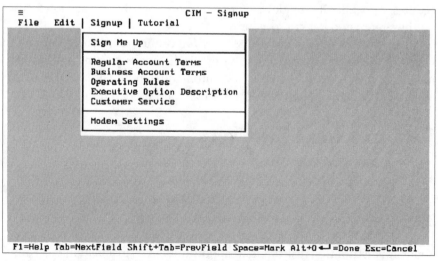

Figure A.1 Signup Introduction

```
≡                            CIM - Signup
 File    Edit    Signup    Tutorial

        ┌──────────────────────────────────────────────────────┐
        │  Serial No. _____      Agreement No. _____  │
        │                                                        │
        │  ┌─Country───────┐      ┌─Payment Method─────────────┐ │
        │  │ (♦) USA        │      │ (♦) VISA                   │ │
        │  │ ( ) Canada     │      │ ( ) MasterCard             │ │
        │  │ ( ) Japan      │      │ ( ) American Express       │ │
        │  │ ( ) Other      │      │ ( ) Electronic Funds Transfer│
        │  └───────────────┘      │ ( ) Corporate Billing      │ │
        │  Country Name (if other):└────────────────────────────┘ │
        │  _____                            │
        │                                                        │
        │  ┌─Account Usage─┐      ┌──────────┐   ┌──────────┐    │
        │  │ (♦) Personal   │      │ Proceed  │   │  Quit    │    │
        │  │ ( ) Business   │      └──────────┘   └──────────┘    │
        │  └───────────────┘                                     │
        └──────────────────────────────────────────────────────┘

 F1=Help Tab=NextField Shift+Tab=PrevField Space=Mark Alt+O ◄┘=Done Esc=Cancel
```

Figure A.2 Signup Form

the United States and Canada to organizations that have established credit. A single monthly invoice is sent that lists total charges for each user ID assigned to the account. If you select the business account options, CompuServe will verify the credit information; they send you a password via US Mail. There is a $10.00 fee and a $10.00 monthly minimum for each user ID associated with this billing option.)

- **Payment method:** The check box allows you to mark a choice for how to pay the monthly bill.

After you have reviewed and approved the information, you may move on to a new form (dialog box) that collects your member information. The form is designed for you to supply your name, address, and phone number (with area code), as well as other information depending on your account type and chosen billing method. Use standard punctuation and be sure to fill in the expiration date for your credit card as it appears on the plastic (in the mm/yy format).

The form also lets you select other options available to all subscribers, including:

- *CompuServe Magazine*, a monthly sent free to all members.
- The Member Directory, an on-line database of CompuServe users.
- Promotional Mail, automatically sent by CompuServe to explain new services, special orders, and so on.
- External Mailings, that is, letters from organizations other than Compu-Serve, telling about their products and services.

As first displayed, all the options are in effect, but you may "un-select" any of them (using the SPACE BAR or the mouse as described above). Later, if you change your mind about membership options, you may modify them on-line.

Once you have supplied all the requested information, the signup software displays a dialog box asking whether you also want the "Executive Option," which gives you access to additional CompuServe features for an extra charge.

When you have made this selection, the signup software displays Compu-Serve's terms and rules. Then the program connects to CompuServe to deliver your signup information automatically. The program also saves all necessary information in the data file on your disk; if it finds errors, it will ask you to correct them. Next you see a dialog box that asks you to agree to the terms and rules of CompuServe membership. To do so, enter the word AGREE.

The software then disconnects from CompuServe and displays (1) your user ID, (2) your password, and (3) the local telephone number you may use to dial up the information service, along with some hints to help you prevent un-authorized use of your account.

As the final step, the software displays a dialog box in which you should fill in the user ID number and password you have just received. The program verifies that information and notifies you.

Making the Connection

CIM is designed to operate off-line until you request a feature that requires a connection.

Connecting

As needed, the software automatically dials up CompuServe, using the phone number(s) you have recorded on the Setup Screen. Consider the following details about logging on:

- While the connection is being made, the program flashes "WORKING" in the upper-right corner of the screen. (This same WORKING message appears at other times during the running of the program as you request certain actions that require the program to retrieve new data.)

- The Cancel action button is automatically highlighted, so you may stop the connection by pressing RETURN.

- When the phone connection is made, the program automatically sends to CompuServe your user ID number and your password (as saved in the Setup Screen), then enters the system and takes you to the service you have selected or prompts for additional information.

- A CONNECTED clock appears in the upper-right corner to keep track of the cumulative connect-time. It automatically stops whenever you disconnect from the system and resumes whenever you reconnect. That way, at the end of a session with the Information Manager, you have a report of the total *on-line time*, not counting the time the program is off-line.

- A MAIL icon sometimes appears in the lower portion of the screen when you log on. This reports if you have new messages waiting in your electronic mailbox.

- A What's New list menu appears on the system twice weekly which you will automatically see. It provides information on service-related developments on the system.

For many on-line features (mail, forums, real-time conferencing, weather, stocks, etc.), the Information Manager uses the built-in desktops with pull-down menus, windows, and so forth. However, to access some services, the computer must act like a *terminal*, automatically using the Terminal Emulator mentioned above.

Disconnecting

At any point, you may disconnect from CompuServe this way:

- **IBM users** should press CONTROL-D.
- **Macintosh users**, press COMMAND-D.
- In terminal emulation in either version (that is, outside the usual windowed interface), enter the command OFF at a CompuServe prompt.

This logs you off the system but allows you to remain in the Information Manager program.

Guidelines for Non-CIM Users

If you are signing up for CompuServe using a communications program *other than* the CompuServe Information Manager software, you will need to take care of some technical matters on your own. You will need to set the software's communications parameters to those CompuServe anticipates and you will need to handle the logon yourself. The manual that came with your software no doubt has some discussion on this; this section provides further assistance.

Two Preliminaries

Before you make the modem call to CompuServe, there are a couple of things you need to check in your software.

- Your program should be communicating in *full duplex*. This means that after you are connected to CompuServe, the letters and numbers you type on your keyboard are transmitted to Columbus, then echo (or "bounce back") to you and are displayed on your screen. When you are on-line, what you see on the screen is *not* coming directly from your keyboard but rather is an echo of what the system "thinks" you have typed.

- The terminal software should also be set to seven-bit ASCII, even parity. The stop bit should be set at one. (As an alternate setting, CompuServe also recognizes eight-bit words, one stop bit, no parity. However, we *don't* recommend that setting for this first logon because it generally results in some garbled characters and that is likely to confuse you.) If none of these terms are familiar, check the documentation for your terminal software. If that doesn't help, call the dealer who sold you the program and ask about setting terminal parameters. You might want to read this parameter to the technician.

Dialing the Number

The material that came with your signup kit included a list of CompuServe connection numbers. Call the connection number for your area, either Compu-Serve, or an alternative network. If you use an auto-dial modem, type in the number you want called. A note to those with old-fashioned manual modems: Wait until you hear the high-pitched modem tone on the other end of the phone line, then switch your modem to the "originate" mode.

The best way to connect to CompuServe is through one of its own local phone numbers. Most metropolitan areas in the contiguous United States now have them. There is a 30-cent surcharge if you connect directly through a CompuServe number. Most other connections carry a surcharge of $2.00 an hour. For details on specific rates, enter GO RATES at any prompt.

Logging On through CompuServe's Own Network

To log on directly to CompuServe:

1. Dial the CompuServe network phone number and make the modem connection.
2. Press CONTROL C (that is, hold down the control key and the letter C together).
3. The system displays "Host Name:" Enter CIS <RETURN>.
4. At the next prompt — "User ID:" — enter your ID number and press RETURN.
5. At the subsequent Password: prompt, type your password and press RETURN.

Logging On through the Tymnet Network

To reach CompuServe through Tymnet, follow these steps:

1. Dial your Tymnet number. The system responds with "PLEASE TYPE YOUR TERMINAL IDENTIFIER." (If you are logging on at any speed other than 300 baud, this message is garbled. But don't let that throw you; just continue to step 2 and everything will work out.)

2. Press the letter A (upper- or lowercase), but *don't* follow it with the RETURN key. The system responds with PLEASE LOG IN:.

3. Enter CML05 and press RETURN. If you make a typo but catch it *before* you press the RETURN key, press the ESCAPE key instead. Next, just re-enter the host name, CML05.

4. When the system displays "Host Name:" enter CIS <RETURN>.

5. At the next prompt — "User ID:" — enter your ID number and press RETURN.

6. At the subsequent Password: prompt, type your password and press RETURN.

Logging On through the SprintNet Network

To reach CompuServe through SprintNet, follow these steps:

1. Connect with your SprintNet number. If you are:

   • Connecting at 300 or 1200 bps, press the RETURN key twice.

   • Connecting at 2400 to 9600 bps, enter the @ sign and press RETURN.

2. Your screen then displays the following:

```
SprintNet
202 08C

Terminal=
```

3. Enter D1 and press RETURN. Now Telenet displays the symbol @.

4. Enter C 202202E.

5. When the system displays "Host Name:" enter CIS <RETURN>.

6. At the next prompt — "User ID:" — enter your ID number and press RETURN.

7. At the subsequent Password: prompt, type your password and press RETURN.

Logging On through Canadian DataPac

Canadian subscribers to CompuServe often connect through DataPac, a network provided by Bell of Canada, to connect to Tymnet or Telenet in the United States. To log on through DataPac:

1. Dial the DataPac number and make the modem connection.

2. Type the appropriate service request signal, that is:

   • If you are connecting at 300 baud, enter a period (.) and press RETURN.

   • If you are connecting at 1200 baud, press two periods (..) and press RETURN.

   • If you are connecting at 2400 baud, press three periods (...) and press RETURN.

3. The periods won't print on your screen. DataPac will display a message like "DATAPAC: 9999 9999." The numbers are a port address.

4. CompuServe has two addresses available on DataPac. Enter one of these addresses: 29400138 or 90100057, and press RETURN.

5. When the system displays "Host Name:" enter CIS <RETURN>.

6. At the next prompt — "User ID:"— enter your ID number and press RETURN.

7. At the subsequent Password: prompt, type your password and press RETURN.

Logging On through AlaskaNet

To reach CompuServe through AlaskaNet, follow these steps:

1. Establish a connection by dialing your local AlaskaNet access number.

2. When your screen shows, "PLEASE ENTER YOUR TERMINAL IDENTIFIER," enter the letter A (with no RETURN).

3. The system then displays, "Welcome to AlaskaNet, Please Log In:".

4. Enter COMPUSERVE <RETURN>.

5. When the system displays "Host Name:" enter CIS <RETURN>.

6. At the next prompt — "User ID:"— enter your ID number and press RETURN.

7. At the subsequent Password: prompt, type your password and press RETURN.

Logging On by Local Access Transport Area (LATA) Networks

Some regional Bell phone companies now offer access to CompuServe through local access transport area (LATA) networks with surcharges that often are lower than those of other networks, except a direct connection to a CompuServe line. To see where LATA service is available, enter GO PHONES at a Compu-Serve prompt and look for the networks by area code or by city and state. LATA connections differ slightly from network to network. To find information on a specific LATA network, enter GO LOG at any prompt and see option 2, Log-on/Log-off instructions. In general, here are the logon steps for a LATA:

1. Dial the LATA network telephone access number and make the connection.

2. Press RETURN and the screen displays a message welcoming you to that particular LATA.

3. Enter .CPS and press RETURN. CPS *must* be typed in uppercase, that is, capitalized.

4. When the system displays "Host Name:" enter CIS <RETURN>.

5. At the next prompt — "User ID:"— enter your ID number and press RETURN.

6. At the subsequent Password: prompt, type your password and press RETURN.

Entering User ID and Password

Many modern third-party terminal programs automate the logon procedure. They do this by storing your user ID and password in a file on the disk and automatically providing them to CompuServe when asked at logon. Check the manual that came with your terminal program to see if and how the software handles this.

If your software doesn't automate logon (or if you just like to do these things for yourself), you can enter the information manually. When the screen displays "Host Name:" enter CIS and press RETURN. When it then displays "User ID:" type in the *signup user ID number* exactly as it appears in your signup information envelope, comma and all, and press RETURN, such as:

```
User ID: 71635,1025<RETURN>
```

Note there is *no space* between the comma and the numbers.

Next you are prompted with "Password:". Here you should enter the two words that make up the *signup password*. Enter them exactly as they came in the starter kit, complete with the character or space that separates them, such as:

```
BOAT/TOUCH <RETURN>
```

Unlike the user ID number, the letters of the password *do not* appear on the screen as you type them. That is for your protection; if someone were looking over your shoulder right now, that person would be unable to see and memorize your all-important secret password.

Note At this point, if you get a message saying something about an "invalid entry," it is likely the password was entered incorrectly. Try again when prompted. If you get another "invalid entry," recheck the user number you entered above. Perhaps *it* was entered incorrectly. If so, enter a CONTROL-C by pressing the control and "c" keys together; you get another "User ID:" prompt, and you can start again.

Signup Procedure

When you are logging on for the first time with a new account number, CompuServe will seek some additional information from you.

More Numbers

After the user ID number and password are accepted, you are asked for two more pieces of information from your starter kit: your *agreement number* and the *serial number*. When prompted, type them in exactly as they appear in the signup information envelope and press RETURN. Finally, the door opens for you. When you are officially on-line, you see a welcome message, then a note about the amount of your usage credit with this starter kit.

Billing/Mailing Data

After a few pages of introduction, the system wants to know your billing address, with a menu like this:

Will Your Billing/Mailing
Address be from

1   United States
2   Canada
3   Japan
4   Other
5   Exit Subscription Process

Enter choice:

Notice, the menu includes an option to exit the subscription process (option 5). This option appears on subsequent menus as well, so you can abort the signup process at any point. If there is some reason you can't finish the signup now, use the exit option, then log on again later and start all over.

At the colon prompt, enter the number of the mailing address chosen and press RETURN. After that, you are shown this menu from which you are to select a billing method:

```
Please Select the Desired
Billing Method

    1   VISA
    2   MasterCard
    3   American Express
    4   Checkfree
    5   Explanation of Charge Card
    6   Explanation of Checkfree
    7   Exit Subscription Process

Enter Choice:
```

Service Agreement

Next, the Service Agreement is displayed for you to read. You will be asked to indicate that you understand and agree to the terms.

More Options

After the agreement, CompuServe presents you with a few more choices:

```
Do You Wish to

    1   Select the Executive Option
    2   See a Description of the
            Executive Option
    3   Proceed with the Standard
            CompuServe Subscription
    4   Exit Subscription Process

Enter choice:
```

As noted elsewhere, The Executive Option offers additional services, particularly business-oriented features, that, in time, you may find useful. They are "value-added" — that is, extra-cost — services.

Collecting the Personal Data

After this, CompuServe gets down to collecting some basic billing information, including last name, first name and middle initial, address, ZIP code, phone numbers, Social Security number, and so forth. After you have filled in the blanks, the system gives you a chance to review the information. If any changes are necessary, just enter the number of the incorrect item and, when prompted, enter the new information. When everything is okay, enter OK at the colon prompt.

Next we come to the data for the credit card or the Checkfree banking method. In entering the information, just refer to notes you jotted before we logged on. After the data has been entered and verified, the system has three more questions for you:

1. Would you like to be on the mailing list for *CompuServe Magazine*, the system's monthly magazine? It is free.

2. Would you like your name, city, and state included in CompuServe's on-line Subscriber Directory? That is up to you, of course, but we suggest you give the system the go-ahead on this item as well. The directory is a kind of electronic phone book that makes it easier for on-line friends to write to you via electronic mail. In a few minutes we shall stop by the area where this directory is located. If, in the future, you decide you want your name removed from the directory, CompuServe will comply.

3. What kind of computer equipment are you using? CompuServe displays a menu of computer types and asks you to select the number that describes your machine. CompuServe later uses this information to help format the text it sends to your screen in various features.

Generating the User ID and Temporary Password

After that, CompuServe generates two very important pieces of information: your new *permanent user ID* (usually a seven- to nine-digit number beginning with a 7 such as 71735,1025 or 70475,1165), and another *temporary password* (again, two unrelated words connected by a symbol). As we pointed out before you logged on, the ID number and password provided in the starter kit were intended to be replaced at this point by the system; they are no longer needed. Write down the *new* ID and password on two separate sheets of paper (and be sure to obliterate this information from your printout if your printer is on). No one else should ever have this information.

If anyone else obtains your account number and password, that individual has the keys to your on-line account and can log on under your name. Before you know it, the intruder has perhaps run up a horrendous bill on your behalf.

After the system produces your new permanent ID and temporary password, it gives you a little test to make sure you know them, prompting:

Please verify that you have
copied the User ID number and
password down correctly by
entering them at the following
prompts.

User ID Number:
Password:

A new permanent password will be sent to you in the mail once your signup information has been verified and processed. When it is sent, you will be told the date when the temporary password is discontinued and your new password becomes effective.

Notes:

1. Until that second, permanent password becomes effective, a few services on CompuServe will not be open to you. Generally, you cannot contribute material on-line, such as public messages, until the permanent password is implemented. During our tours, we shall point out those times when a permanent password is needed to use a particular feature.

2. Once the permanent password has been mailed to you, you will probably receive an electronic message from CompuServe that officially welcomes you to the neighborhood. More on that later.

B

CompuServe Information Manager and Other CompuServe Software

In this appendix...

Software Overview
CompuServe Information Manager
CompuServe Navigator (for Apple Macintosh)
Professional Connection

CompuServe itself publishes communications software that can be used with the system. The programs can be retrieved (downloaded) from CompuServe and charged to your regular bill. In addition, the system offers free on-line support forums to help users of the programs. For many subscribers, CompuServe wouldn't be CompuServe unless it were viewed through one of these specific programs. For on-line details about the software and new versions, enter GO CISSOFT.

Software Overview

CompuServe's software comes in two styles:

- System-specific communication software (most notably, its well-known CompuServe Information Manager, or CIM, programs), and
- General communication software (generally older communications programs that can be easily used with other systems besides CompuServe).

CompuServe Specific Software

Four programs CompuServe has designed specifically for use on this system are:

1. CompuServe Information Manager for DOS computers.
2. CompuServe Information Manager for Windows.
3. CompuServe Information Manager for Apple Macintosh.
4. CompuServe Navigator for Macintosh.

All four, developed to simplify the user interface to CompuServe, take advantage of CompuServe's Host Micro Interface protocol, which allows most of the information that is sent to and from CompuServe (such as forum messages, CompuServe Mail messages, and files) to be transferred to the Macintosh under CompuServe's error-correcting "B" protocol. HMI is a method to speed delivery of data from the system to your screen and ensures that these programs can avoid problems caused by phoneline static.

General Communications Software

In addition, the system produces general programs, such as Professional Connection 3, available for use on the IBM PC/XT/AT/PS 2 and compatibles. PC3 was created in the years before CIM, but still has its followers, particularly among those who want a "go-everywhere" program that can be used on CompuServe and other systems as well. However, its design seems to run counter to the popular enthusiasm for system-specific programs that can work more closely to specific features on-line. Note that the general software does *not* operate with the new Host Micro Interface protocol; instead, they deal with the software in its original ASCII state.

CompuServe Information Manager

This section offers a quick rundown on the CompuServe Information Manager software.

Environments

CIM supports a modem of 300 baud or higher (ideally, a Hayes-compatible) and an optional printer. All versions are distributed by CompuServe with instructions for installing the program on your system, including creation of necessary subdirectories. We assume you will follow those instructions for configuring your system and making secure backup copies.

During installation, the program offers you an opportunity to copy signup software to your disk along with other Information Manager files. If you are not already a CompuServe subscriber (or if you want to obtain an additional CompuServe account), copy the signup software. At the end of the installation, you are invited by the program to sign up for CompuServe membership. You may accept the invitation at that point, or you may sign up later from a disk or directory that contains the signup software.

IBM and Compatibles

The IBM CIM comes in three versions:

- For the minimum configuration, there is CIM version 1 (actually, version 1.36 at this writing) which will work on an IBM or compatible with at least 640K of random access memory and at least 470K free when the program is started. MS-DOS 3.1 or higher is required. The program is compatible with color and monochrome monitors, and a variety of video adapters (Hercules, EGA, MCGA, VGA, and so on). The version will work on a system without hard disk; the minimum disk configuration is two low-density (360K) 5.25-inch floppy drives, though a hard disk with at least 500K of free space is recommended. Mouse is optional.

- For advanced DOS systems, there is CIM version 2 (version 2.1.1 at this writing). It is recommended for a system with an 80286 or faster processor, a hard disk drive with at least 1.5M available, at least 500K of available RAM, and either a color or monochrome monitor. Mouse is optional.

- The Windows version for IBM or compatibles with an 80386SX processor or higher requires at least 2MB of RAM memory, Microsoft Windows Version 3.0 or higher (though Version 3.1 or higher is recommended), an IBM EGA or higher resolution monitor compatible with the Microsoft Windows graphical environment, a hard disk with 4MB of space available with Windows installed, a high-density floppy drive and a mouse (or other pointing device) that is compatible with Microsoft Windows.

Apple Macintosh

The Apple Macintosh version (2.1.1) is compatible with a Macintosh Plus or later model with at least one megabyte of RAM, Mac System 6.0.4 or later, a hard disk, and at least one 800K floppy disk drive. (CompuServe recommends either two drives or a hard disk and one floppy drive.)

Using a Mouse

Apple Macintosh users: You will use a mouse pointing device, of course, as you do with all Macintosh software.

IBM PC/compatible users: With the DOS version of the software you may also use a mouse as an *optional* peripheral. Just be sure to do all setup procedures as specified in the mouse documentation *before* starting up the CIM program. The Windows version requires a mouse.

Running the CIM on IBM PCs

The new Windows version of CIM appears on the Windows screen as an icon. Run the program as you would any other Windows application, clicking on it with the mouse pointer.

To run the DOS program, the command is CIM entered at DOS level (on the subdirectory where the program resides). In addition, three optional switches may be appended to the command, separated by a space:

1. You may run the program by entering CIM -NOEMM if you do not want the CIM program to automatically use 64K of expanded memory. (That is, if you do *not* specify -NOEMM, up to 64K of expanded memory will be used if available.)

2. CIM can also operate in special monochrome/grey scale modes for those with monochrome monitors (and color graphics cards). If you are using a monochrome monitor with a CGA card and find the highlighted characters on the program's menus hard to read, you may want to start CIM with the -MONO switch by entering CIM -MONO at the DOS prompt.

3. Users of laptops with LCD screens may want to start the program with CIM -LCD at DOS.

Note If more than one switch is used, separate each with a space, as in CIM -MONO -NOEMM.

Finally, if you have a high-resolution graphics adapter, you may use the SETMODE function to establish a screen size of 43 lines (for EGA) or 50 lines (for VGA). SETMODE must be used *before* you run CIM. After you exit the program, you may return to a normal screen by re-entering the SETMODE command.

Running CIM on Apple Macintosh

To run the program on a Macintosh system, open the folder that contains CIM software, then double-click on the CIM icon. This should display the "About Box" discussed in the next section.

The About Box

After the program is run, the screen displays an introductory banner called the "About Box."

- In the IBM version, a cursor appears on the OK button; when you are ready to continue, press RETURN.
- In the Macintosh version, the About Box stays on the screen until you click on it.

In both versions of the software, the subsequent display is CIM's initial desktop, discussed below.

Setup Screen

The first time you run CIM, the screen displays a form that lets you record the particulars for your CompuServe account (your name, password, access number, and so on) as well as the specifics for your hardware (baud rate and dialing type of your modem, port number, etc.) as shown in Figure B.1.

The program creates a special file on your disk to save the configuration data you supply in the form. (If you are not already a CompuServe subscriber, you may use the signup software on the distribution disk to obtain a membership.

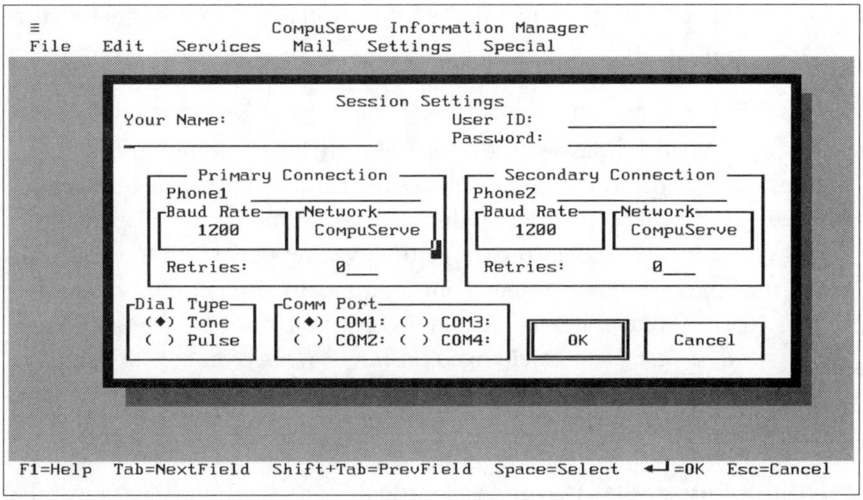

```
  ≡                     CompuServe Information Manager
  File    Edit    Services    Mail    Settings    Special

                         Session Settings
       Your Name:                   User ID:      _____
       _____         Password:     _____

       ┌── Primary Connection ──┐    ┌── Secondary Connection ──┐
       │ Phone1 _____    │    │ Phone2 _____      │
       │ ┌Baud Rate┐ ┌Network─┐ │    │ ┌Baud Rate┐ ┌Network─┐   │
       │ │  1200   │ │CompuServe│    │ │  1200   │ │CompuServe│  │
       │ Retries:      0___     │    │ Retries:      0___       │
       └────────────────────────┘    └──────────────────────────┘
       ┌Dial Type┐ ┌Comm Port──────────┐
       │ (♦) Tone │ │ (♦) COM1: ( ) COM3: │  ┌────────┐  ┌────────┐
       │ ( ) Pulse│ │ ( ) COM2: ( ) COM4: │  │   OK   │  │ Cancel │
       └──────────┘ └────────────────────┘  └────────┘  └────────┘

  F1=Help   Tab=NextField   Shift+Tab=PrevField   Space=Select   ◄┘=OK   Esc=Cancel
```

Figure B.1 Setup Screen

See Appendix A, "Getting Started," for details on the **Automatic Signup** procedures.)

To fill out this form on your screen:

1. Enter your name in the first line ("field") and move to the next line (User ID:) either by pressing the TAB or by using your mouse. (If you don't have a mouse, note that in all forms like this one, the TAB key always takes you to the next field or blank line, while SHIFT-TAB always moves you back a field.)

2. To correct a typographical error, backspace, and retype.

3. When you are satisfied with all the settings, move the cursor (with TAB or mouse) to the OK box at the bottom of the screen (by pressing RETURN or clicking on with the mouse). Or you may move to the **Cancel** box to wipe out all the entries on the screen. Once OK is selected, the program automatically saves the data in the configuration file. On MS-DOS systems, this file is **CIM.CFG**; on Apple Macintosh systems, the file is **CIM Prefs**. The information may be revised at any time by selecting the "Session settings" option from the Special pull-down menu. (Or if you want to eliminate your pre-recorded settings and start fresh, you may delete this file from the disk and complete the setup form again the next time you run the program.)

Here is some background to help you fill out the form:

Your name and **User ID** are required.

Your Password is optional. By including it now, you save time later when CIM logs on to the system, because you are allowing it to supply the information automatically. If you leave this field blank, then you are prompted to manually enter your password each time you log in. Also, once a password is entered, the software *masks* it on the screen so that it is not displayed.

Note To *change* a password that has already been entered in the Settings screen, position the cursor on the field and enter the *first four characters* of the existing password (which causes the program to display the rest of it). Press DELETE to remove the existing password, then enter the new password, which may contain up to 14 letters, numbers, and punctuation marks. Remember, though, if you want to change your password, it first must be changed on-line — while you are connected to the system — *before* you change it in this form.

Telephone numbers may use the standard punctuation. If you must dial 9 to get an outside line, include the "9," as a prefix. Note the comma.

It means that there will be a brief pause before the rest of the number is dialed. A number in the Primary Connection box is required; the Secondary Connection is optional. If you define a secondary connection, CIM will use that number if repeated busy signals occur on the Primary Connection number.

> **Note** Appendix A of this book includes information on getting numbers for accessing the system.

Baud rates, the speed at which your modem sends and receives data. The initial setting is 1200 baud; other possible settings can be automatically displayed. IBM users, move the cursor to the field, then use the up/down arrow keys to display others, and highlight the one you want. Macintosh users, click and hold on the Baud Rate box and you will see a menu of alternative settings.

The **Network** field refers to the communications network you use to reach CompuServe. While it is initially set to CompuServe's own network, you may review and select other networks, such as BT/Tymnet and Telenet (Sprintnet), if the CompuServe network cannot be reached with a local call in your area. The field works like the baud rates item above. **IBM users**: Move the cursor to the field, then use the up/down arrow keys to view additional networks besides CompuServe, and highlight the one you want. **Macintosh users**: Click and hold on the Network box, and you will see a menu of alternative settings.

> **Note** One of the alternative settings is Direct, but this should be used only if your computer is *hard-wired* to a CompuServe network node. In almost all cases, this applies only to CompuServe employees, not subscribers.

Retries allows you to tell the system how many times to try re-dialing when a busy signal is reached on a connection.

Dial type refers to how your modem dials the phone, either *pulse* or *tone* dialing. The *manual* option is selected if you have a non-dialing modem (or you are hard-wired to another system that connects to CompuServe for you).

Comm port refers to the serial port on your computer through which it communicates with CompuServe.

Modem displays the control strings currently used by your modem. TAB into the field and, if you need to make changes, refer to the users' manual with your modem. CIM defaults to the standard Hayes computer "AT" command set. Ordinarily you will not have to change these control settings. However, if you use a modem that uses different control strings, consult your manuals.

Components of CIM

Those familiar with *windowed* application software will quickly recognize CIM's basic components, the popular "desktop metaphors," in screens like the one shown in Figure B.2.

The Parts

The program uses:

- **Menu bars** along the top of the screen that provide a quick overview of the broad group of features and commands currently available. The menu bars link to:

- **Pull-down menus**, which identify individual functions within a group of commands. For instance, the main menu bar names "Mail" as one of its command groups. Its pull-down menu lists specific "Mail" options available. For some of the major menus, see the section below called, "Desktop menus." Such pull-down menus frequently connect with:

- **Dialog boxes**, various windows that the program displays usually to get information from you, such as criteria for file searches, options for

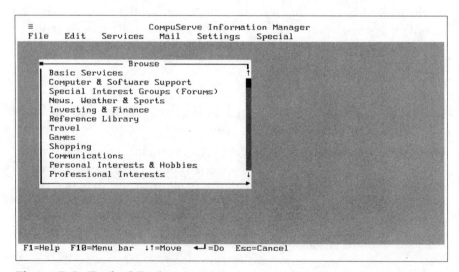

Figure B.2   Typical Desktop

message delivery, selections from lists of alternatives, and so on. Dialog boxes may contain *fields* (or blank lines) to be filled in, *text boxes* for longer information, *lists* and *option groups*, *action buttons* to start and stop specific on-line operations, and *check boxes* for you to specify whether the system should implement certain options. Also featured are:

- **List menus**, which tell you the major groups of services or features available on-line from CompuServe. (So, pull-down menus generally relate to built-in Information Manager options; list menus relate to services on-line.)

Navigating the Parts

For mouse device users, navigating the components of the Information Manager is simply a matter of positioning the cursor and clicking, as with other mouse-supported programs. To pick an item from a pull-down menu, (1) display the menu by clicking on the menu bar choice, (2) highlight the choice by moving the mouse with the button held down, then, (3) when the choice is highlighted, release the button.

For keyboard-oriented users, navigate with *action keys*, one- and two-key keyboard combinations that move the cursor, highlight choices, mark alternatives, retrieve files, and so on. Here are the most important keys to get you started:

- Up/down arrow keys. They move the bar cursor up and down on pull-down menus, dialog boxes, and so on.
- RETURN. It selects the highlighted choice or choices on a pull-down menu, list menu, and so on. RETURN also signals that all the fields in a form (that is, a dialog box) are filled in as you want and you are ready to move on.
- SPACE BAR. It marks or unmarks a check box or a list box choice.
- ESC. This key cancels the current operation or activity.
- TAB. This moves forward in a dialog box (except inside a text box). SHIFT-TAB moves back to the previous field.

Other action keys operate in connection with the program's built-in text writing/editing feature and as *accelerator keys* that are alternatives to selecting pull-down menus. These special key sequences are described on the menus themselves. The IBM PC/compatible version of the software usually lists these alternatives as function keys or as a combination of the CONTROL or ALT key and a letter key; the Macintosh version often uses the COMMAND, CONTROL or OPTION key, and a letter.

Getting Help

CIM also provides quick help, organized into topics that may be selected from a menu or by an index that includes all available help topics. To reach it:

IBM users should press the F1 function key.

Macintosh users with an extended keyboard may press the HELP key, while those with a standard keyboard should press COMMAND-? (that is, hold down the COMMAND key and press the question mark).

Main Desktop Menus

As noted, CIM's functions may be accessed from a series of menus that can be pulled down from a main menu bar. This section includes the menus used with the initial desktop setup.

THE SERVICES MENU is shown in Figure B.3.

The options on the Services Menu are:

- **Favorite Places** maintains a personal menu of favorite services on CompuServe for quick access. (With CIM 2.x, you can adjust the order of the services listed in several ways. Auto Tracking automatically arranges your favorite services in order of most recent usage; alphabetic arranges your favorite services in alphabetical order; manual allows you to arrange your favorite services in whatever order you like, by manually positioning them in the menu.)

- **Find . . .** allows you to locate services on-line related to a specified topic.

- **Browse** lets you access on-line features through menus.

- **Go . . .** to go to a specific on-line feature.

- **What's New** lets you see news of recent CompuServe events.

- **Special Events** reviews special CompuServe promotions.

- **Quotes** gives you quick access to current stock quotations.

- **Weather** gives you quick access to current weather information.

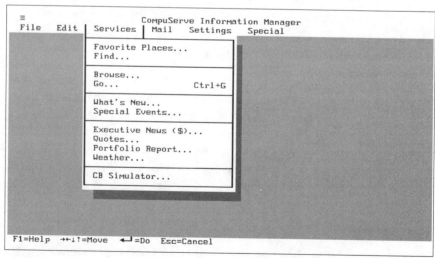

Figure B.3   Services Menu

- **CB Simulator** takes you to the real-time conferencing service called the "CB Simulator."

- **Executive News Service**, added with CIM version 2.x, takes you to the Executive News Service, where you can review the news, create clipping folders, etc.

- **Stock Portfolio**, also added in version 2.x, lets you create and maintain a record of securities you purchase. It produces an up-to-date report to analyze their market performance at any time.

THE MAIL MENU is shown in Figure B.4.
The options on the Mail Menu are:

- **Get New Mail** retrieves messages from your New Mail mailbox to either read them immediately or place them in the In-Basket for later when you are off-line.

- **Create Mail** composes a message with the built-in text feature to either send immediately or place in the Out-Basket for later posting.

- **Send Mail in Out-Basket** delivers one or more messages that you have placed in the Out-Basket.

- **Send/Receive All Mail** combines two functions. First, it sends all messages currently in your Out-Basket, then retrieves all new messages and places them in the In-Basket for later reading.

- **Send File** lets you post a disk file, such as a program in binary form.

- **In-Basket** accesses messages currently in the In-Basket.

- **Filing Cabinet** lets you access the messages in your electronic Filing Cabinet.

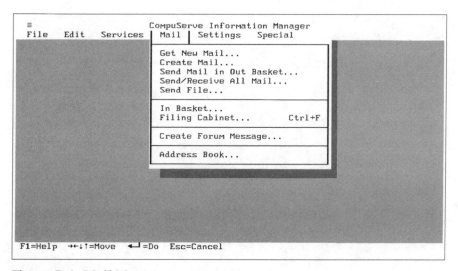

Figure B.4 Mail Menu

- **Create Forum Message** is used for composing messages for delivery to discussion forums.

- **Address Book** lets you see and modify the items listed in your Address Book.

THE SPECIAL MENU is shown in Figure B.5.

The options for the Special Menu are:

- **Session settings**, which lets you change the communications settings for the program's connection with CompuServe.

- **Preferences**, which records your selections of specific displays in CIM.

- **Terminal Emulator**, which lets your computer leave the Information Manager interface temporarily and act like a computer terminal.

The IBM PC-compatible version of the software also uses two other menus, Files and Edit.

THE FILE MENU is shown in Figure B.6.

The options on the File Menu are:

- **New** lets you create a new file.

- **Open** opens an existing file.

- **Save** updates a current file.

- **Save As** lets you update a file you specify.

- **Print** prints the current file.

- **Disconnect** can disconnect you from the on-line system.

- **Exit** takes you out of the CIM program.

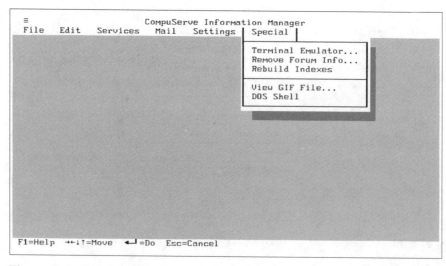

Figure B.5 Special Menu

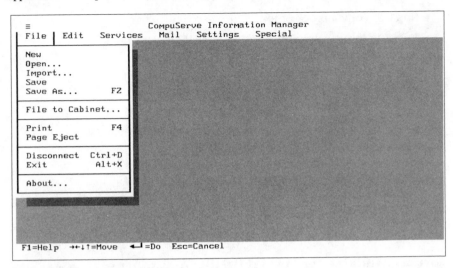

Figure B.6   File Menu

- **About CIM** takes you to the "About Box," an introductory screen that also automatically appears when you first run the program.
- **Credenza**, added in version 2.x, allows you to access the Filing Cabinet, In-Basket, Out-Basket, and Address Book from almost anywhere on the Information Service.

THE EDIT MENU is shown in Figure B.7.
The options on the Edit Menu are:

- **Undo** to reverse the previous editing change.
- **Cut** to remove a block of text.

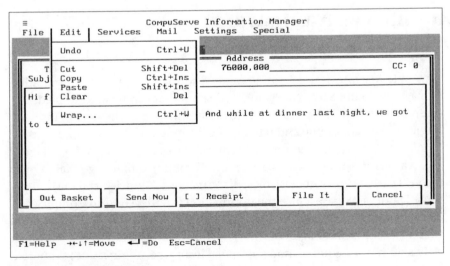

Figure B.7   Edit Menu

- **Copy** to copy a block of text.
- **Paste** to insert a previously cut or copied block of text.
- **Clear** to delete a block of text.

Other Desktop Menus

Besides the main pull-down menus illustrated in the previous section, other desktops are used by CIM, including those for:

- The forums
- The CB Simulator
- Terminal Emulation

Forums Available for Special On-line Assistance

Several forums have been set up on-line to support users of the new Information Manager software.

- **IBM DOS users**, select the Go ... option and specify the address CIMSUPPORT.
- **IBM Windows users**, select the Go ... option and specify the address WCIMSUPPORT.
- **Macintosh users**, select the Go ... option and specify the address MACCIM.

If you are already familiar with CompuServe forums, you will be able to use these support facilities now, because they operate as all other forums do.

CompuServe Navigator (for Apple Macintosh)

For Apple Macintosh users, an alternative to the CompuServe Information Manager is CompuServe Navigator, a program that can be used to predefine an entire CompuServe session prior to connecting. Once the session is set up, Navigator will go on-line and retrieve the information the user requested.

Like other so-called "automated terminal programs" (covered in Chapter 14), Navigator can be used to access the Forums, CompuServe Mail, Quick Quotes Database (stock quotes), most of the menus and articles, and the CompuServe Phones Database. Once the information is retrieved from CompuServe, Navigator allows you to review the information (and respond to Forum and CompuServe Mail messages) off-line — while the billing clock is not running.

In addition, a "terminal mode" is available for accessing areas not supported by Navigator's "auto-mode."

Environment

Navigator works on any system from the Mac Plus on up. It requires two double-sided 800K disk drives or one double-sided 800K disk drive and a hard disk, System 4.1 (the minimum system required), or System 6.0.1 or higher to use some of the additional features of Navigator. The software is MultiFinder and System 7 compatible. The program requires 650K of available memory.

Support Forums

Users of Navigator can get free on-line help with the software in the Navigator Support Forum (GO NAVSUP).

Professional Connection

The Professional Connection 3.2 — also called PC3.2 — was developed by CompuServe in the days before the CompuServe Information Manager program for use with the IBM PC, XT, AT, and compatible PCs. Its major purpose is to enable you to use your microcomputer to communicate with other computer systems.

Its Main Menu lists a number of the most popular services on the CompuServe Information Service, allowing you to access them by simply selecting a numbered option. The software then automatically logs on and takes you to the selected service. The software can also be customized with your own menu choices and provides several methods of automatically recording your dialogue with another computer system. You can redisplay previous parts of this dialogue while you're still on-line, or save it to a file at your microcomputer for later review or use.

PC 3.2 also allows you to customize access to other computer systems, enabling you to modify the information, so you can automatically access as many systems as you like.

Appendix

C

Finding Phone Numbers

In this appendix...
On-line Phone Database
Toll-free 800-number Assistance

Access numbers for CompuServe can be found off-line and on-line.

On-line Phone Database

A searchable database of telephone access numbers across the country is available on-line to help you locate direct CompuServe lines, as well as indirect connections through services like BT/Tymnet and SprintNet. The database, which you can reach by entering Go... PHONE at any prompt, also reports any recently changed network number or planned additions, and where the nearest 300-, 1200-, 2400-, and 9600-baud access numbers are for you. A menu gives you options to look specifically for CompuServe numbers or for all network numbers, and to search by area code or by city and state. The resulting lists identify with a code (in parentheses) whether the lines are operated by CompuServe, BT/Tymnet, SprintNet, DataPac, local access transport areas, or others.

Toll-free 800-number Assistance

In addition, CompuServe has set up a free network that can find various access numbers around the world. The CompuServe Network Services Assistance area can be reached on any CompuServe access number or by dialing 1-800-848-4480.

After dialing the number, enter CPS at the host prompt. When asked for a User ID, enter 74,74 with the password NETWORK.

The system, a completely menu-driven database, permits you to list and search for CompuServe direct access phone numbers and other network gateways by state or area code.

Appendix

D

Password Protection

It is wise to change your password regularly. Enter GO PASSWORD (or select the Go... option in the CIM software and specify PASSWORD). This takes you to the TERMINAL/OPTIONS area of the system where you are asked to confirm your present password, then type in your new password. Most passwords are two unrelated words connected with a symbol. After you have typed in the new password, the system confirms that the change has been made.

If you ever forget your password or think it has been stolen, contact the customer service people immediately (800-848-8990 or in Ohio, 614-457-8650). The representative there won't be able to give you a new password over the phone, but can mail it to you at the address on file with your account number.

E

The Costs

In this appendix...

CompuServe offers several ways to pay for the goods. The standard plan offers monthly access to a number of features for a flat fee, with metered charges for access to features beyond this homebase of services. Or as an alternative, you can opt to have a pay-as-you-go billing on *all* features. In addition, CompuServe provides the Executive Option for special billing discounts for some features, especially financial services.

The Billing Options

This section provides the rundown on the billing plans and the prices as of this writing. (Of course, prices are subject to change, but then, you figured that, huh?) Here is an overview of the entries in this section:

- Standard Pricing Plan
- Alternative Pricing Plan
- Hourly Connect Rates
- What is *Always* Free? Member Support Services
- How to Change from One Plan to Another
- Considering the Executive Service Option

Standard Pricing Plan

The standard pricing plan includes unlimited connect-time to use assorted features for a membership of $8.95 per month. New members are not charged the membership fee until the second month. When you are using Compu-Serve's US and Canadian networks, these services are free of communication (network) charges. Supplemental network charges still apply outside of the US and Canada. Enter GO RATES for more information.

Use of features outside this core group (that is, in the "Extended Services") is billed by connect-time minute. These services are indicated by a "+" or "$" next to the menu choice.

- Services marked with a "+" are charged at the CompuServe charge depending on the modem speed.
- Services marked with a "$" are charged at an additional rate.

For additional information on premium surcharges, see the article elsewhere in this appendix or enter GO TRANSACTION on-line.

The services included in the unlimited-access, basic services area are:

- In News, Sports and Weather:
  Associated Press Online (Hourly News Summaries, Sports, Entertainment, Business News, Today in History)
  Accu-Weather Maps
  National Weather Service

- In the Reference Library:
  Grolier's Academic American Encyclopedia
  Consumer Reports
  Peterson's College Database
  Healthnet

- In Shopping:
  The Electronic Mall
  Shopper's Advantage

- In Money Talks:
  Basic Current Stock Quotes
  Issue/Symbol Reference
  Mortgage Calculator
  FundWatch On-line

- Games and Entertainment:

    Science Trivia Quiz

    The Grolier Whiz Quiz

    ShowBizQuiz

    CastleQuest

    Black Dragon

    Classic Adventure

    Enhanced Adventure

    Hangman

    Ebert's Movie Reviews

- In Communications Exchange:

    CompuServe Mail (Enter GO MAILRATES for additional details)

    Classified Ads (to read; placement costs extra)

    DOS CIM, MAC CIM, and WIN CIM Support Forum

    Practice Forum

    Navigator Support Forum

    Directory of Members

    Ask Customer Service

- In Travel and Leisure:

    Travelshopper (airline, hotel, rental car information and reservations) plus other travel information

    Department of State Advisories

    Visa Advisors

    Eaasy Sabre

    Zagat Restaurant Survey

CompuServe's billing period runs Sunday through Saturday. The billing month ends on the last Saturday of each month, so your $8.95 charge will be applied to your CompuServe account on the last Saturday of each month.

You may access the basic services at any baud rate, from 300 to 9600. Access to extended services, as well as all usage (except FREE areas) for members on the Alternative Pricing Plan, will be billed at an hourly rate based on the speed at which you access.

Alternative Pricing Plan

If the standard basic plan, with its unlimited access area, does not appeal to you, you can opt for the alternative pricing plan. Under this plan, you are charged a $2.50 monthly membership support fee which supports unlimited use of the on-line Membership Support services free of connect-time charges (see the section below entitled "What is *Always* Free? Member Support Services" or enter GO FREE on-line). All other usage is billed at the hourly connect rates based on baud rate, plus any applicable network charges, and premium surcharges. Hourly connect-time charges are billed in one-minute increments, with a one minute minimum charge per session.

How to Change from One Plan to Another

You select a billing option when you sign up as a CompuServe member. Later, if you would like to change from one to the other (from the standard option to the alternative and back again), enter GO CHOICES. This provides a menu with details of the plans, commonly asked questions, and so on, as well as options to change the billing.

There is no fee to change from one pricing plan to the other. However, keep in mind that the billing month ends the last Saturday of the month. Also note:

- When you change from the Alternative Pricing Plan to the Standard Pricing Plan, the change will take place at the beginning of the following billing month. For example, if you request to change to the Standard Pricing Plan on January 6, the Standard Pricing Plan would be effective in the February billing month.

- When you change from the Standard Pricing Plan to the Alternative Pricing Plan, the change will be effective and the last $8.95 charge will be applied at the end of the billing month. For example, if you request to change to the Alternative Pricing Plan on January 6, the Standard Pricing Plan will be effective through the end of the January billing month. The Alternative Pricing Plan will begin on the first day of the February billing month.

Hourly Connect Rates

Hourly connect-time charges apply for all usage of extended services for members on the Standard Pricing Plan. For members on the Alternative Pricing Plan, hourly connect-time charges are in effect at all times except in the Free services (GO FREE).

As of this writing, the rates, based on modem speed, are:

For connection at:	Standard Pricing	Alternate Pricing
300bps	$ 6.00 an hour	$ 6.30 an hour
1200 or 2400bps	$ 8.00 an hour	$12.80 an hour
9600bps	$16.00 an hour	$22.80 an hour

Connect-time is billed in one minute increments, with a minimum of one minute per session. Connect-time rates do not include communications (network) charges or premium surcharges, which are billed in addition to hourly connect-time charges. (For details on network surcharges, enter GO BIL-74.)

What Is *Always* Free?
Member Support Services

Whether you are signed up for the standard or alternative billing method, some CompuServe services are always free. In other words, these features, called the Member Support Services, are part of basic services and are also free of connect-time charges to members on the Alternative Pricing Plan. Applicable network charges are still effective in these areas for all members. (GO RATES for current information on network rates.) If you are on the Alternative Pricing Plan, the free areas are identified by a "FREE" banner on each menu page.

The free services are:

• The Electronic Mall	(GO MALL)
• What's New Articles	(GO NEW)
• Access Phone Numbers	(GO PHONES)
• Logon Instructions	(GO LOGON)
• Billing Information	(GO BILLING)
• Review Charges	(GO CHARGES)
• Electronic Funds Transfer (EFT) Amount	(GO BILL)
• Change Your Password	(GO PASSWORD)
• Change Your Billing	(GO BILLING)
• Change Your Phone or Address	(GO ADDRESS)
• Service Terms and Rules	(GO RULES)
• On-line Settings	(GO PROFILE)
• Subject Index	(GO INDEX)
• On-line Questions and Answers	(GO QUESTIONS)
• On-line Ordering	(GO ORDER)
• Summary of Commands	(GO COMMAND)
• Practice Forum	(GO PRACTICE)
• CompuServe Help Forum	(GO HELPFORUM)
• Rates Information	(GO RATES)
• On-line Tour of CompuServe	(GO TOUR)

- Membership Directory   (GO DIRECTORY)
- Feedback   (GO FEEDBACK)

Also, Member Support Services for European Members (in addition to the services already listed) include:

- Access Phone Numbers   (GO EUROPHONES)
- Logon Instructions   (GO EUROLOGON)
- On-line Questions and Answers   (GO EUROQUESTIONS)

The Executive Service Option

Also affecting your billing is whether you opt for the Executive Service Option, which allows you to receive access to exclusive databases (most of them financial in nature), merchandise offers, and discounts. Executive Option users have:

- Access to exclusive databases, including Company Analyzer, Disclosure II, Executive News Service, SuperSite, Institutional Broker's Estimate System, Securities Screening, Return Analysis and Company Screening. Many of these reports are designed to take full advantage of 80 character screens.
- Volume discounts on information retrieval from selected transaction price financial databases.
- A six-month storage period for personal files without charge (30 days is standard).
- A 10 percent discount on the purchase of most CompuServe products. This does not include sale items.
- A 50 percent increase in the amount of on-line storage available in your Personal File Area, along with an opportunity to purchase additional storage space at a reduced weekly rate.

Executive Option users are subject to a $10.00 monthly minimum usage level. Your monthly $8.95 CompuServe basic membership on the Standard Pricing Plan, or the $2.50 membership support fee under the Alternative Pricing Plan is applied to this minimum.

Seeing Your Charges On-line

You can review your current charges on-line in the billing area (free of access connect charges). To do that, enter GO CHARGES which takes you to a menu where you can choose from:

1. Explanation, which explains what information is offered in each report and defines the billing processes.

2. Account Balance, providing the most current billing information available. This information is usually 48 hours old.

3. Billing History. Each Sunday your charges for that week are compiled and the sum then becomes part of billing history. The billing history option allows you to examine charges, payments, and adjustment details on your account for up to 90 days (excluding current activity).

4. Current Activity, which includes the activity on your account before charges are compiled each week. You will see a series of chronologically ordered items describing your usage activity. This includes the date you logged on, a description of your activity (baud rate, network, premium programs accessed, etc.), the time you logged on, the number of minutes you were on-line and the amount of charges you accrued for that session.

5. Previous Activity, including all activity for up to 90 days excluding Current Activity (above). The report is identical in format to Current Activity as described above (option 4). You will be provided with a list of the weeks available and their totals. You should then select the desired week that you wish to see by entering the number that appears to the left of that week-ending date. You will then be able to see the date, time, and description of your logons within that week.

6. Mail Hardcopy. You are provided with the opportunity to mail detailed hardcopy of your charges to your account address. There is a $3.50 fee associated with that service. For rate information, enter GO RATES at any ! prompt.

Premium Charges

Some CompuServe services carry extra, "premium" surcharges. The actual costs vary from feature to feature. The surcharges generally are based on the number of minutes of connect-time used in accessing them, the amount of data retrieved from them, or both. You are billed the surcharge in addition to the connect-time charges and applicable network charges.

This section contains information on the major premium surcharges.

Aviation Flight Plannings and Weather Briefings (GO EMI)

Flight plans are surcharged at $.015 per nautical mile (a minimum of $2.50 and a maximum of $6.00). An additional 50 cents is charged for each plan using registered aircraft data, although the maximum remains $6.00. Basic Aerolog Flight Plan is $1.50.

Demographic Data

CompuServe offers several surcharged demographic features.

Neighborhood (ZIP) Report (GO NEIGHBOR)

The Neighborhood Report carries a $10.00 surcharge for each ZIP code you request.

US/State/County Reports (GO USSTCN)

The US/State/County Reports carry a $10.00 surcharge for each report you request.

SUPERSITE (GO SUPERSITE)

Each SUPERSITE report is surcharged as follows:

- Demographic Reports — 1980 Housing, 1980 Hispanic, 1980 Education, 1980 Energy, 1980 Income, Housing, Component Area
  $20.00/report
- Demographic Reports — Forecast Summary
  $25.00/report
- Demographic Reports — Demographic Forecast, Income, Age by Sex, Age by Income, Housing Value by Age, Combined Income + Demographic, Net Worth + Disposable Income, Age 55 Plus, Year 2000, Demographic
  $50.00/report
- Sales Potential Reports — Health Insurance
  $25.00/report
- Sales Potential Reports — Ice Cream Store
  $50.00/report
- Sales Potential Reports — Apparel Store, Drug Store, Grocery Store, Department Store, Shopping Center, Home Improvement
  $75.00/report
- Sales Potential Reports — Financial Services, Investment Services, Automotive Aftermarket, Consumer Electronics, Restaurant Market, Media
  $100.00/report
- ACORN Target Marketing Reports — Profiles + Forecasts, Population Profile, Household Profile, Population Forecast, Household Forecast
  $75.00/report
- ACORN Target Marketing Reports — Potential Market, Convenience Store, Shopping Center, Retail, Media Analysis
  $100.00/report

Business Demographics (GO BUSDEM)

Each Business Demographic report by Market Statistics carries a $10.00 surcharge for each market that you request.

Education

Costs for the surcharged education features are detailed in this section.

Dissertation Abstracts (GO DISSERTATION)

Dissertation Abstracts is surcharged as follows:

- A search with no hits (that is, no titles found), $1.00.
- A standard search which retrieves up to 10 titles, $5.00.
- Additional titles (in groups of 10), $5.00.
- Full reference, with abstract where available (selected from the titles), $5.00 each.

A running total of transaction charges is displayed on Dissertation Abstract menu pages, but note that connect-time charges are *not* included in the displayed total.

Educational Resources Information Center (GO ERIC)

Educational Resources Information Center (ERIC) carries these transaction charges:

- A search with no hits (that is, no titles found), $1.00.
- A standard search which retrieves up to 10 titles, $2.00.
- Additional titles (in groups of 10), $2.00.
- Full reference, with abstract where available (selected from the titles), $2.00 each.
- Reprints, normal delivery, $18.00 each.
- Reprints, express delivery, $42.00 each.

A running total of transaction charges is displayed on Dissertation Abstract menu pages, but note that connect-time charges are *not* included in the displayed total.

CompuServe Mail

If you use the basic Standard Pricing Plan, your monthly $8.95 membership fee includes an electronic mail allowance of $9.00. With this allowance you can send up to the equivalent of 60 three-page messages per month with no additional charge. (Each 2,500 characters is about one double-spaced page.) This monthly allowance applies to both ASCII and binary messages. Your remaining message allowance expires at the end of each month. Here is what is included in your monthly allowance:

- Send Mail (per message):

    First 7,500 characters, 15 cents.

    Additional 2,500 characters, 5 cents.

- Receipt Requested: 15 cents per recipient.

- Read/Download Internet Messages:

    First 7,500 characters, 15 cents.

    Additional 2,500 characters, 5 cents.

> **Notes** Regarding the Send Mail allowance, note that the charge per message is multiplied by the number of recipients you have chosen to receive your message. Surcharged messages, such as Congressgrams, fax, telex, and postal are not included in the $9.00 monthly allowance.
>
> If Internet messages are deleted without reading or automatically deleted by the system after 30 days, no charges are incurred.

These special mail items are *not* included in your monthly allowance:

- Congressgrams ($1.00), CandidateGrams ($1.50), SantaGrams ($2.00), and CupidGrams ($2.00).
- 500 characters to MCI MAIL (45 cents).
- 500 to 7,500 characters to MCI MAIL ($1.00).
- Additional 7,500 characters to MCI MAIL ($1.00).
- Postal letter with a US destination (first page, $1.50; additional page, 20 cents).
- Postal letter outside the US (first page, $2.50; additional page, 20 cents).
- TELEX and TWX messages with US destination ($1.15 per 300 characters sent).
- FAX messages (cost varies depending upon the destination).

Alternative Pricing Plan

If you are using the Alternative Pricing Plan, your CompuServe Mail usage is billed an hourly connect-time charge, as described earlier in this appendix. In addition to connect-time charges, the following items have additional premium charges:

- Receipt Requested (15 cents per recipient).
- Multiple send feature (10 cents for each after the first recipient, up to 10 per message).
- Congressgrams ($1.00), CandidateGrams ($1.50), SantaGrams ($2.00), and CupidGrams ($2.00).
- 500 characters to MCI MAIL (45 cents).
- 500 to 7,500 characters to MCI MAIL ($1.00).
- Additional 7,500 characters to MCI MAIL ($1.00).
- Postal letter with a US destination (first page, $1.50; additional page, 20 cents).
- Postal letter outside the US (first page, $2.50; additional page, 20 cents).
- TELEX and TWX messages with US destination ($1.15 per 300 characters sent).
- FAX messages (cost varies depending upon the destination).

Games and Entertainment

Only a few of the features in this section are surcharged. Here are the details.

Modem-to-Modem Gaming (GO CHALLENGE)

The actual modem-to-modem game-playing is surcharged at $6.00 per connect hour. However, there is no surcharge for access to the MTM Lobby, Challenge Board, and MTM-related forums.

Soap Opera Summaries (GO SOAPS)

The Soap Opera Summaries are surcharged at $6.00 an hour.

Magill's Survey of Cinema (GO MAGILL)

This movie database is surcharged as follows:

- A search with no hits (that is, no titles found), $1.00.
- A standard search which retrieves up to 10 titles, $2.00.
- Additional titles (in groups of 10), $2.00.
- Complete text of movie information (selected from the titles), $2.00.

Legal

Here are the surcharges for several law-related features.

Trademark Research Center (GO TRADERE)

The Trademark Research Center is surcharged as follows:

- Search and display results, $1.00.
- Select database from results menu (retrieves up to five titles), $5.00.
- Additional titles (in groups of five), $5.00.
- Full article (selected from the titles), $5.00 each.
- Reprints, normal delivery, $18.00 each.
- Reprints, express delivery, $42.00 each.

There is a $1.00 charge for a search that retrieves no titles, plus any connect-time and applicable network charges.

Patent Research Center (GO PATENT)

The Patent Research Center is surcharged as follows:

- Search and display results, $1.00.
- Select database from results menu (retrieves up to five titles), $5.00.
- Additional titles (in groups of five), $5.00.
- Full article (selected from the titles), $5.00 each.

There is a $1.00 charge for a search that retrieves no titles, plus any connect-time and applicable network charges.

Legal Research Center (GO LEGALRC)

The Legal Research Center is surcharged as follows:

- Search and display results, $1.00.
- Select database from results menu (retrieves up to five titles), $5.00.
- Additional titles (in groups of five), $5.00.
- Full article (selected from the titles), $5.00 each.
- Reprints, normal delivery, $18.00 each.
- Reprints, express delivery, $42.00 each.

There is a $1.00 charge for a search that retrieves no titles, plus any connect-time and applicable network charges.

Medical

These are the surcharges for some of CompuServe's medical features.

PaperChase (GO PAPERCHASE)

PaperChase is surcharged as follows:

- $18.00 an hour when accessed between 7:00 p.m. and 8:00 a.m. local time on weekdays and any time on weekends.
- $24.00 an hour when accessed between 8:00 a.m. and 7:00 p.m. local time on weekdays.

CCML AIDS Articles (GO AIDSNEWS)

Comprehensive Core Medical Library AIDS Articles carry these surcharges:

- A standard search which retrieves up to 10 titles, $5.00.
- Additional titles (in groups of 10), $5.00.
- Full reference, with abstract where available (selected from the titles), $5.00 each.

Physicians Data Query

The Physicians Data Query is surcharged as follows:

- A search with no hits, $1.00.
- A standard search which retrieves up to 10 titles, $5.00.
- Additional titles (in groups of 10), $5.00.
- Full reference, with abstract where available (selected from the titles), $5.00 each.

PsycINFO Abstracts (GO PSYCINFO)

PsycINFO Abstracts is surcharged as follows:

- A search with no hits, $1.00.
- A standard search which retrieves up to 10 titles, $5.00.
- Additional titles (in groups of 10), $5.00.
- Full reference, with abstract where available (selected from the titles), $5.00 each.
- Reprints, normal delivery, $18.00 each.
- Reprints, express delivery, $42.00 each.

Health Database Plus (GO HLTDB)

The Health Database Plus is surcharged as follows:

- $1.50 per full-text article retrieved.
- $1.00 per summarized article retrieved.

The Article Citation menu indicates if an article has full text; you will be charged only once for each article you display or download during your session. (If you choose to scroll more than one article, you won't be charged for the second or subsequent articles until you actually begin to display each one.)

IQuest Medical InfoCenter (GO IQMEDICINE)

IQuest Medical Info Center has the following surcharges:

- Search, $9.00.
- SmartSCAN, $5.00.
- Database search surcharges, $2.00 to $25.00.
- Abstract, $3.00 each.
- No hit charge, $1.00.
- Hard copy delivery (regular service and delivery), $18.00 per article.
- Hard copy delivery (express), $42.00 per article.

In a bibliographic database a Search is defined as retrieval of up to 10 bibliographic references; in a full-text database a Search is the retrieval of up to 15 titles plus one full article selected from those 15 titles.

News/AP Sports Wire

Here are the surcharges for some of the CompuServe news features:

Executive News Service (GO ENS)

This service is surcharged at $15.00 an hour.

AP Sports Wire (GO APN-1)

The AP Sports report is surcharged at $15.00 an hour.

US Newspaper Library (GO NPL)

The US Newspaper Library has the following surcharges:

- A search with no hits (that is, no titles found), $1.00.
- A standard search which retrieves up to five titles, $4.00.
- Additional titles (in groups of five), $4.00.
- Full reference, with abstract where available (selected from the titles), $3.00 each.

UK Newspaper Library (GO UKPAPERS)

The UK Newspaper Library is surcharged as follows:

- A search with no hits (that is, no titles found), $1.00.
- A standard search which retrieves up to five titles, $5.00.
- Additional titles (in groups of five), $5.00.
- Full reference, with abstract where available (selected from the titles), $7.50 each.

Reference

The surcharges are listed for some of CompuServe reference features.

New Car Showroom (GO NEWCAR)

The New Car Showroom is surcharged as follows:

- Comparison Search: $1.20/comparison.
- Price/One Model: $ .90/price.
- Auto Selector: $ .40.

IQuest (GO IQUEST)

IQuest is surcharged as follows:

- Search, $9.00.
- SmartSCAN, $5.00.
- Database search surcharges, $2.00 to $75.00.
- Abstract, $3.00 each.
- No hit charge, $1.00.
- Hard copy delivery (regular service and delivery), $18.00 per article.
- Hard copy delivery (express), $42.00 per article.

In a bibliographic database a Search is defined as retrieval of up to 10 bibliographic references; in a full-text database a Search is the retrieval of up to 15 titles plus one full article selected from those 15 titles.

Computer Database Plus (GO COMPDB)

The Computer Database Plus has the following surcharges:

- 25 cents per minute ($15.00 per hour) connect surcharge.
- $2.50 per article retrieved (displayed or downloaded, $1.50 if abstract is not available).
- $1.00 per article abstract retrieved (displayed or downloaded).

Computer Directory (GO COMPDIR)

The Computer Directory is surcharged as follows:

- $15.00 per hour connect surcharge (25 cents per minute).
- $1.00 per menu of matching products, regardless of the number of entries.
- $1.00 per menu of matching manufacturers of products, regardless of the number of entries.
- 25 cents per full product listing displayed.
- 25 cents per full manufacturer of products listing displayed.
- The $1.00 for displaying a menu of matching products or matching product manufacturers is a flat rate. You will be charged a dollar whether there are two matching entries or 200.

Magazine Database Plus (GO MDP)

The surcharge is $1.50 per article retrieved (displayed or downloaded). All articles contain the full text.

Books in Print (GO BOOKS)

Books in Print is surcharged as follows:

- A search with no hits (that is, no titles found), $1.00.
- A standard search which retrieves up to 10 titles, $2.00.
- Additional titles (in groups of 10), $2.00.
- Full reference, with abstract where available (selected from the titles), $2.00 each.

Book Review Digest (GO BRD)

Book Review Digest is surcharged as follows:

- A search with no hits (that is, no titles found), $1.00.

- A standard search which retrieves up to 10 titles, $2.00.
- Additional titles (in groups of 10), $2.00.
- Full reference, with abstract where available (selected from the titles), $2.00 each.

Marquis Who's Who (GO BIOGRAPHY)

Marquis Who's Who is surcharged as follows:

- A search with no hits (that is, no titles found), $1.00.
- A standard search which retrieves up to five titles, $5.00.
- Additional titles (in groups of five), $5.00.
- Full biography (selected from the names), $5.00 each.

Biz*File (GO BIZFILE)

The surcharge is $15.00 per hour (25 cents per minute).

Phone*File (GO PHONEFILE)

The surcharge is $15.00 per hour (25 cents per minute).

UK Marketing Library (GO UKMARKETING)

The UK Marketing Library is surcharged as follows:

- A search with no hits (that is, no titles found), $1.00.
- Search (retrieves up to 10 abbreviated records), up to $5.00.
- Additional titles (in groups of 10), up to $5.00.
- Full Record (selected from the abbreviated records), up to $11.00.

UK Trademark Library (GO UKTRADEMARK)

The UK Trademark Library is surcharged as follows:

- A search with no hits (that is, no titles found), $1.00.
- Search (retrieves up to 10 abbreviated records), up to $5.00.
- Additional titles (in groups of 10), up to $5.00.
- Full Record (selected from the abbreviated records), $7.50 each.

Media Newsletters (GO MEDIANEWS)

Media Newsletters is surcharged as follows:

- A search with no hits (that is, no titles found), $1.00.
- Search (retrieves up to 10 titles), up to $5.00.
- Additional titles (in groups of 10), up to $5.00.
- Full Record (selected from the titles), $5.00 each.

Compendex (GO COMPEN)

Compendex is surcharged as follows:

- A search with no hits (that is, no titles found), $1.00.
- Search (retrieves up to 10 titles), $5.00.
- Additional titles (in groups of 10), $5.00.
- Full Record (selected from the titles), $5.00 each.
- Reprints, normal delivery, $18.00 each.
- Reprints, express delivery, $42.00 each.

National Technical Info Service (GO NTIS)

This service is surcharged as follows:

- A search with no hits (that is, no titles found), $1.00.
- Search (retrieves up to 10 titles), $2.00.
- Additional titles (in groups of 10), $2.00.
- Full Record (selected from the titles), $2.00 each.

DP Newsletters (GO DPNEWS)

DP Newsletters is surcharged as follows:

- A search with no hits (that is, no titles found), $1.00.
- Search (retrieves up to 10 titles), $5.00.
- Additional titles (in groups of 10), $5.00.
- Full Record (selected from the titles), $5.00 each.

Support On Site (GO ONSITE)

Surcharges are 25 cents per minute ($15.00 per hour).

Money Matters/Markets

Many of CompuServe's business features are surcharged. Here are the details.

Current Market Quotes

Users of the CompuServe Information Manager also receive free quotes when using either the Quotes option on the Services pull-down menu or when entering the QUOTE command on-line. This applies in both basic and extended Services.

For other users, the surcharge depends on whether you are using the Standard or Alternative Pricing Plan.

Standard Pricing Plan surcharges are:

While in CompuServe's basic service, you may use the Basic Quote program (GO BASICQUOTE) to retrieve free current and end-of-day quotes. The QUOTE command is also available for your use at $.015/quote.

The following rates apply while in extended services:

Current and end-of-day quotes:	$.015/quote
Portfolio Valuation:	$1.00/report + quote surcharges
Current Market Snapshot (E):	$.10/report

News:

The surcharge while in Company News (/CONEWS) is $15.00 per hour.

Alternative Pricing Plan surcharges are:

Current and end-of-day quotes:	$.015/quote
Portfolio Valuation:	$1.00/report + quote surcharges
Current Market Snapshot (E):	$.10/report

News:

The surcharge while in Company News (/CONEWS) is $15.00 per hour.

Microquote (GO MICROQUOTE)

The surcharges for Microquote are:

Most recent closing quote:	$.015/quote/day
Historical quote (can be downloaded):	$.05/quote/day
Most recent closing commodities quote:	$.02/quote/day
Commodities quote (can be downloaded):	$ .05/quote/day
Dividends, splits, distrib. and interest payments:	$.15/item displayed
Detailed issue examination:	$1.25/day
Issue price movement statistics:	$1.25/day
Portfolio evaluation:	$1.00/per report plus quote surcharges
Return analysis (E):	$.50/report $.15/issue
Stock market highlights (for previous day):	$15.00/hour
Bonds listing:	$.05/bond
Options Profile:	$1.25/report

The surcharge is waived for retrieving H&R Block data (ticker symbol = HRB) through this area. You are encouraged to use the HRB ticker symbol to try this area.

Security Screening (GO SCREEN)

Security Screening is surcharged as follows:

Disclosure Company Screening	$5.00/screen $ .50/company displayed

Securities
Screening $5.00/screen
$ .25/issue displayed

You are only billed if you decide to produce a report or save a file of output. If you had performed a search along several criteria, but never selected a report or file to be produced, then you can exit the program without incurring any additional surcharges.

Note The feature will allow a report to be produced, or a file to be saved, only up to a surcharge of $50.00. If your reports would amount to more than that, the program will tell you that too many companies are available to be reported and it will prompt you to continue the search.

Security Charting

The service is surcharged as:

Price/Volume Chart: $1.00/chart

On-line Brokerage

These are the surcharges for the on-line brokers:

- Quick Way (GO QWK)

    During Daytime/Prime hours, $14.00 an hour.

    Evening/Standard hours, $4.00 an hour.
- Spear Rees & Company (GO SPEAR)

    Daytime/Prime hours, $14.00 an hour.

    Evening/Standard hours, $4.00 an hour.
- Max Ule (GO TKR)

    Tickerscreen, 2 cents per issue.

Company Analyzer (GO ANALYZER)

Automatically displayed is a current quote that costs $.015, and a menu from which you can choose one or more of the following:

- Descriptive company information from S&P Online at $1.00, Disclosure's "Company Name and Address" at no surcharge, or Disclosure's "Company Profile" at $5.00.
- Daily, weekly, or monthly pricing history at 5 cents per quote displayed.

- Dividend history at 15 cents per dividend displayed.
- A pricing Statistics report for the last 52 weeks at $1.25.
- A detailed Issue Description at $1.25.
- A report of the available bonds for 5 cents per bond displayed.
- An Options Profile report at $1.25.
- A Return on $1,000 Invested report at 15 cents.
- A Management Discussion report from Disclosure at $5.00.
- Disclosure's "Officers, Directors, and Salaries" report at $5.00.
- Ownership reports from Disclosure ranging in price from $5.00 to $10.00.
- Price Volume Graphs for $1.00 each.
- Any current news at $15.00 per hour.
- Earnings/Growth Forecasts including Value Line's forecast at $1.60, an I/B/E/S "Detailed Earnings Report" at $2.00, and an I/B/E/S "Summary Earnings Discussion" at 50 cents.
- Financial Reports from Value Line at 40 cents per year displayed, or all Disclosure financial reports on a company for $10.00.

Disclosure II (GO DISCLOSURE)

The following are surcharges for Disclosure II:

COMPANY REPORTS

Company Name and Address	No surcharge
Company Profile	$5.00
Financial Statements	$10.00
Management Discussion	$5.00
Officers and Directors	$5.00
All of the Above	$15.00

(Prices above are the prices of the reports if requested separately. All five documents can be generated as one report for $15.00.)

OWNERSHIP REPORTS

Ownership and Subsidiary	
Summary	$5.00
Five Percent Owners	$10.00
Insider Holdings	$10.00

Institutional Holdings	$10.00
All of the Above	$25.00

(Prices above are the prices of the reports if requested separately. All four documents can be generated as one report for $25.00.)

Standard and Poor's Online (GO S&P)

The Standard and Poor's Online surcharges are:

Company Information access:	$1.00
Master List menu:	$2.00
Investment Ideas:	$2.00

RateGram

RateGram Reports are surcharged as follows:

Liquid Money Market Account Report	$1.00/report
Certificates of Deposit(CDs)/Small Minimum Balance	$1.00/report
Jumbo Certificates of Deposit	$1.00/report
Money Market Mutual Funds	$1.00/report
Yield Summary This Week: Top CDs/Treasuries	$1.00/report
Rate Almanac	$1.00/report

Institutional Brokers Earnings Estimate (GO IBES)

This service is surcharged as follows:

Summary Earnings Discussion:	$ .50/company
Detailed Earnings Report:	$2.00/company

MMS International

This service is surcharged as follows:

Calendar of Economic Events	No surcharge
Daily Equity Market Report	$5.00/report
Daily Currency Market Report	$5.00/report
Daily Debt Market Report	$5.00/report
MMS Monthly Forecasts	No surcharge
MMS Quarterly Forecasts	No surcharge
FEDWATCH	$5.00/report
MMS Weekly Economic Survey	$5.00/report
Economic Briefings	No surcharge

Commodity Markets

The Commodity Markets are surcharged as follows:

Commodity Quotes (GO CPRICE)

Most recent closing commodity quote:	$.02/quote/contract/day
Historical commodity quotes:	$.05/quote/contract/day

News-A-Tron (GO NAT)

Commodity Market reports:	$1.25/set of reports
Stock Indexes Analysis and News Report:	$1.25/set of reports

Futures Focus

During Prime/Daytime hours:	$20.00/connect hour
During Standard/Evening hours:	$15.00/connect hour

MQINT/IQINT

MQINT/IQINT are downloading interfaces that access data on stocks and commodities.

MQINT surcharges are:

Current and most-recent-closing quotes:	$.015/quote

Commodities:	$.02/quote
Historical quotes:	$.05/quote

IQINT surcharges are:

MicroQuote (MQUOTE):	$.05/quote
Disclosure (ADISC):	$.16/item
Institutional Brokers Estimate System (MIBES):	$.50/item

Company News (CONEWS)

This service is surcharged at $15.00 per hour.

Commerce Business Daily (GO COMBUS)

Commerce Business Daily is surcharged as follows:

- A search with no hits (that is, no titles found), $1.00.
- A standard search which retrieves up to 10 titles, $2.00.
- Additional titles (in groups of 10), $2.00.
- Full reference, (selected from the titles), $2.00 each.

Business Dateline (GO BUSDATE)

Business Dateline is surcharged as follows:

- A search with no hits, $1.00.
- A standard search which retrieves up to five titles, $7.50.
- Additional titles (in groups of five), $7.50.
- Full reference, (selected from the titles), $6.00 each.

Corporate Affiliations (GO AFFILIATIONS)

This service is surcharged as follows:

- A search with no hits, $1.00.
- A standard search which retrieves up to five titles, $7.50.
- Additional titles (in groups of five), $7.50.
- Full reference, (selected from the titles), $6.00 each.

TRW Business Credit Profiles (GO TRWREPORTS)

This service is surcharged as follows:

- A search with no hits, $1.00.
- A standard search which retrieves up to 24 company locations, $9.00.
- First full report (selected from the locations), $34.00.
- Up to four more full reports (selected from the locations), $9.00 each.

To view more than five full reports you must re-enter the search and pay an additional $9.00 search charge plus applicable full-report charges, including another $29.00 "First full-report" charge.

Thomas Companies and Products (GO THOMAS)

The surcharges for this service are:

- A search with no hits, $1.00.
- A standard search which retrieves up to 10 titles, $5.00.
- Additional titles (in groups of 10), $5.00.
- Full abstract, (selected from the titles), $5.00 each.

Marketing/Mgmt Research Center (GO MKTGRC)

This service is surcharged as follows:

Search and Display Results Menu	$1.00
Search — no hits	$1.00
Select database from Results Menu (retrieves up to 10 titles)	$4.00
Additional titles (in groups of 10)	$4.00
Full entry (selected from the titles)	$4.00 each
Reprints, normal delivery	$18.00 each
Reprints, express delivery	$42.00 each

InvesText (GO INVTEXT)

This service is surcharged as follows:

Access Company or Industry Reports

Report Title Search — no hits	$1.00
Search (retrieves up to 10 report titles)	$4.00
Additional Report Titles (in groups of 10)	$4.00
Page Citations (selected from Report Titles)	No transaction charge
Additional Page Citations	No transaction charge
Full Page (selected from the Page Citations)	$11.00 each

Access by Topic or Report Number

Search — no hits	$1.00
Search (retrieves up to 10 Page Citations)	$4.00
Additional Page Citations (in groups of 10)	$4.00
Full Page (selected from the Page Citations)	$11.00 each

Return Analysis (GO RETURN)

Each Return Analysis costs $0.50 per report plus $0.15 for each return that is calculated.

Portfolio Valuation (GO PORT)

Each Portfolio Valuation costs $1.00 per report plus quote surcharges. Quotes can be drawn from either the current quotes or historical quotes databases. Quote surcharges are $.05 each if historical quotes are requested, and $.015 each for current and most recent closing quotes.

Historical Quotes (GO PRICES)

You are charged $.05 for each historical quote displayed and $.015 for the most recent closing quote. Requests for weekly and monthly prices are similarly surcharged at $.05 per quote displayed.

Multiple Issue Pricing—1 Day (GO QSHEET)

This feature is surcharged at $.05 per quote unless the requested date is the most recent trading date (i.e. a <CR> is entered at the "Pricing date:" prompt). The most recent data is surcharged at $.015 per quote.

Dividends (GO DIVIDENDS)

Each dividend displayed costs 15 cents.

Detailed Issue Examination (GO EXAMINE)

Each issue examination report costs $1.25, whether the request is for an option, equity, debt, warrant, or mutual fund issue.

Option Profiles (GO OPRICE)

Each Option Profile report costs $1.25 for any specified date range.

IQuest Business Management (GO IQBUSINESS)

IQuest Business Management InfoCenter transaction charges are:

Search	$9.00
SmartSCAN	$5.00
Database search surcharges	$2.00 to $25.00
Abstract	$2.00 each
No hit charge (first no hit)	Free
No hit charge (after first)	$1.00
Hard copy delivery (regular service and delivery)	$16.00 per article
Hard copy delivery (express service and delivery)	$39.00 per article

D&B Dun's Market Identifiers (GO DMI)

This service is surcharged as follows:

- A search with no hits, $1.00.
- A standard search which retrieves up to five names, $7.50.
- Additional names (in groups of five), $7.50.
- Full reference, selected from the names, $7.50 each.

D&B Canadian Dun's Market Identifiers (GO DBCAN)

This service is surcharged as follows:

- A search with no hits, $1.00.
- A standard search which retrieves up to five names, $7.50.
- Additional names (in groups of five), $7.50.
- Full reference, selected from the names, $7.50 each.

D&B International Dun's Market Identifiers (GO DBINT)

This service is surcharged as follows:

- A search with no hits, $1.00.
- A standard search which retrieves up to five names, $7.50.
- Additional names (in groups of five), $7.50.
- Full reference, selected from the names, $7.50 each.

Dun's Electronic Business Directory (GO DYP)

The surcharges for this service are:

- A search with no hits, $1.00.
- A standard search which retrieves up to five names, $5.00.
- Additional names (in groups of five), $5.00.
- Full reference, selected from the names, $2.00 each.

European Company Library (GO EUROLIB)

The surcharges for this service are:

- Search — no hits, $1.00.
- Search (retrieves up to five names), up to $7.50.
- Additional names (in groups of five), up to $7.50.
- Full reference (selected from the names), from $5.00 to $7.50.

German Company Library (GO GERLIB)

This service is surcharged as follows:

- Search — no hits, $1.00.
- Search (retrieves up to five names), up to $7.50.
- Additional names (in groups of five), up to $7.50.
- Full reference (selected from Page Citations), from $5.00 to $30.00 each.

Australian/New Zealand Company Library (GO ANZCOLIB)

The surcharges for this service are:

- *D&B-Australian Dun's Market Identifiers*

  $7.50 per search (five references).

  $7.50 for each additional five.

  $7.50 per article searched.

- *D&B-New Zealand Dun's Market Identifiers*

  $7.50 per search (five references).

  $7.50 for each additional five.

  $7.50 per article searched.

- *Asia-Pacific*

  $5.00 per search (10 references).

  $5.00 for each additional 10.

  $5.00 per abstract.

- *Reuter's Textline*

  $5.00 per search (10 references).

  $5.00 for each additional 10.

  $5.00 per article.

UK Company Library (GO UKLIB)

UK Company Library is surcharged as follows:

- Search — no hits, $1.00.
- Search (retrieves up to five citations), up to $7.50.
- Additional Page Citations (in groups of five), up to $7.50.
- Full reference (selected from Page Citations), from $5.00 to $75.00 each.

Business Database Plus (GO BUSDB)

This service charges:

- 25 cents per minute ($15.00 per hour) connect surcharge.
- $1.50 per article retrieved (displayed or downloaded).

Official Airline Guide (GO OAG)

The Official Airline Guide charges:

- During Daytime/Prime hours:

  $28.00/connect-hour surcharge
- During Evening/Standard hours:

  $10.00/connect-hour surcharge

Classifieds (GO CLASSIFIEDS)

The cost of listing an ad in the Classifieds area depends on the length of the message and the time length the message will be displayed. The cost per *line* (70 characters) for:

- A 7-day listing is $1.00.
- A 14-day listing is $1.50.
- A 56-day (8 week) listing is $5.20.
- A 182-day (26 week) listing is $14.30.

Appendix

F

Troubleshooting and Getting Help

In this appendix...

Feedback
CompuServe Magazine
Forums

From time to time you might run into a problem not already addressed in this book. This section suggests places to go for answers.

Feedback

Feedback is a special area of CompuServe where you can leave your comments and questions, a kind of on-line letter to the editor. You are invited to write a message to the Customer Service representatives, just as you might in CompuServe Mail. To reach the area, enter GO FEEDBACK. The time you spend in Feedback is not billed and you receive answers to your questions either through CompuServe Mail or direct contact.

Also, you may order written documentation for most of the services from Feedback. If the documentation you want isn't listed, ask about it in a message in Feedback directed to Customer Service.

Finally, Feedback has added a section for answers to common questions. It is a menu-driven area accessible from the main Feedback menu. So far the area has discussions on topics such as billing, logon, CompuServe Mail, forums, the Personal File Area, setting up first services, creating Personal Menus, using on-line ordering, navigating the CB Simulator, the market quotes features, and more.

411

CompuServe Magazine

You receive the monthly *CompuServe Magazine* as part of your CompuServe membership. As noted earlier, operated in conjunction with the magazine is *Online Today*, a daily electronic publication, which includes an active letters-to-the-editor department. To read or write letters to OLT, enter GO OLT-30.

Forums

CompuServe offers a number of free forums for questions and answers about the system in general as well as software specifics. Here are the helpful free forums:

- The CompuServe Help Forum (GO HELPFORUM).
- The Practice Forum (GO PRACTICE) for practicing the forum commands.
- The CIM Support Forums (GO CIMSUPPORT, GO MACCIMSUP, and GO WCIMSUPPORT).

Customer Service

When all else fails, talk to a human being. Customer Service can be reached by a toll-free line. The number (outside Ohio) is 800-848-8990. Inside Ohio, call 614-457-8650. The Customer Service office is open from 8:00 a.m. to midnight Eastern Time Monday through Friday, and noon to 10:00 p.m. on weekends.

G

CompuServe Operating Rules

In this appendix...

Operating Rules
CompuServe Information Service Agreement Terms
More on Copyright

As a CompuServe subscriber, you signed an agreement to abide by the system's rules and regulations. For the record, here is that agreement (which may also be read on-line by entering GO RULES or, if you are using the CompuServe Information Manager, selecting the Go... option and specifying RULES at the prompt).

Operating Rules

The operating rules are designed to protect the data and communications offered by CompuServe Incorporated, information providers, and members. The rules are also provided to make on-line information usage and communications a positive and secure experience for members.

Members agree during the on-line signup procedure to the terms and conditions outlined in the operating rules.

Introduction

These operating rules are part of the terms of your service Agreement with CompuServe, and you are bound by them. CompuServe may modify these rules at any time by publishing the modified rule(s) over the service.

Copyright

The entire contents of the service are copyrighted as a collective work under the United States copyright laws. The copying, reproduction, or publication of any part of the service is prohibited, unless expressly authorized by CompuServe.

Each member who places data, materials, or other information, including communications, in the public areas of the service grants CompuServe the right to edit, copy, republish, and distribute such data, materials, and other information to its members and other persons. Subject to this grant, each member who places data, materials or other information on the service retains any rights that member may have in such data, materials, or other information.

Copyrighted Material

Copyrighted material must not be placed on the service without the author's permission. Only the owner(s) or persons they specifically authorize may upload copyrighted material to the service.

Members may download copyrighted material for their own use. Any member may also non-commercially redistribute a copyrighted program with the expressed permission of the owner or authorized person. Permission must be specified in the document, on the service, or must be obtained directly from the author.

Public Domain Material

Any member may upload public domain programs to the service. Any member may download public domain programs for their own use or non-commercially redistribute a public domain program. Member assumes all risks regarding the determination of whether a program is in the public domain.

Information Content and Uses of the Service

Member agrees not to publish on or over the service any information which violates or infringes upon the rights of any other person or any information which would be abusive, profane, or sexually offensive to an average person, or which, without the approval of CompuServe, contains any advertising or any solicitation of other members to use goods or services. This paragraph, however, shall not be interpreted to restrict a member from utilizing Compu-Serve Mail in the conduct of a legitimate business except that member may not, without the approval of CompuServe, send unsolicited advertising or promotional material to other CompuServe members.

Member agrees not to use the facilities and capabilities of the service to conduct any business or activity, or solicit the performance of any activity which is prohibited by law, or to solicit CompuServe members to become members of other competitive information services.

Editing of Public Information

CompuServe reserves the right in its sole discretion to edit any public information appearing on the service, regardless of whether it violates the standards for information content.

Service Termination

CompuServe reserves the right in its sole discretion to suspend or terminate service to any member at any time.

Indemnification

Member agrees to indemnify and hold CompuServe harmless from any claims and expenses, including reasonable attorney's fees, related to member's violation of the service agreement, including these rules.

Standard Pricing Plan

Multiple members of the same household may share a single User ID Number. However, only one person is authorized to access the service at any given time on one User ID number.

CompuServe Information Service Agreement Terms

The following are CompuServe's agreement terms:

1. The CompuServe Information Service (the "service") consists of the computing and communications services, software, databases, data, information, and all other material (collectively "Information") available through CompuServe Incorporated ("CompuServe"). These terms and any operating rules published over the service constitute the entire agreement (collectively "Agreement") between CompuServe and Customer with respect to the service and supersede all other communications.

2. Upon notice published over the service, CompuServe may modify this agreement, the operating rules, or prices. CompuServe may discontinue or revise any or all other aspects of the service at its sole discretion and without prior notice.

3. Unless otherwise agreed, Customer's right to use the service or to designate Users is not transferable and is subject to any limits established by CompuServe, or by Customer's credit card company if billing is through a credit card.

4. Customer agrees to indemnify CompuServe against liability for any and all use of Customer's account.

5. Customer is responsible for and must provide all telephone and other equipment and services necessary to access the service.

6. Customer shall pay, in accordance with the provisions of the Billing Option selected by Customer, any registration or monthly fees, connect-time charges, minimum charges, and other charges incurred by Customer or its designated Users at the rates in effect for the billing period in which those charges are incurred, including but not limited to, charges for any purchases made through the service and any surcharges incurred while using any supplemental networks or services other than the service. The Customer shall pay all applicable sales and use taxes relating to its and the Users' use of the service. The Customer shall be responsible for all use of the service accessed through Customer's or its designated Users' password(s).

7. CUSTOMER EXPRESSLY AGREES THAT USE OF THE SERVICE, WHICH INCLUDES THE CONTENTS THEREOF AND ANY STORAGE OR USE OF INFORMATION, IS AT CUSTOMER'S SOLE RISK. NEITHER COMPUSERVE NOR ANY OF ITS INFORMATION PROVIDERS, LICENSORS, EMPLOYEES, OR AGENTS WARRANT THAT THE SERVICE WILL BE UNINTERRUPTED OR ERROR FREE; NOR DOES COMPUSERVE OR ANY OF ITS INFORMATION PROVIDERS, LICENSORS, EMPLOYEES, OR AGENTS MAKE ANY WARRANTY AS TO THE RESULTS TO BE OBTAINED FROM USE OF THE SERVICE. THE SERVICE IS DISTRIBUTED ON AN "AS IS" BASIS WITHOUT WARRANTIES OF ANY KIND, EITHER EXPRESS OR IMPLIED INCLUDING BUT NOT LIMITED TO WARRANTIES OF TITLE OR IMPLIED WARRANTIES OF MERCHANTABILITY OR FITNESS FOR A PARTICULAR PURPOSE OR USE WITH RESPECT TO THE SERVICE OR INFORMATION. NEITHER COMPUSERVE NOR ANYONE ELSE INVOLVED IN CREATING, PRODUCING, OR DELIVERING THE SERVICE SHALL BE LIABLE FOR ANY DIRECT, INDIRECT, INCIDENTAL, SPECIAL, OR CONSEQUENTIAL DAMAGES ARISING OUT OF USE OF THE SERVICE OR INABILITY TO USE THE SERVICE OR OUT OF ANY BREACH OF ANY WARRANTY. THE PROVISIONS OF THIS SECTION 7 WILL SURVIVE ANY TERMINATION OF THIS AGREEMENT.

8. Except as expressly permitted in the operating rules, neither Customer nor its designated Users may reproduce, redistribute, retransmit, publish or otherwise transfer, or commercially exploit, any Information which they receive through the service.

9. The provisions of paragraphs 7 and 8 are for the benefit of CompuServe and its Information Providers, Licensors, Employees, and Agents; and each shall have the right to assert and enforce such provisions directly on its own behalf.

10. This agreement is, and shall be governed by and construed in accordance with the law of the State of Ohio applicable to agreements, made and performed in Ohio. Any cause of action of Customer or its designated Users with respect to the service must be instituted within one year after the claim or cause of action has arisen or be barred.

11. If Customer's account is a qualified business account and approved by CompuServe for corporate billing, charges for the services provided under this agreement will be accumulated and identified by User ID number and will normally be invoiced following the end of the month in which the service is provided. Terms of payment on all charges are net, ten (10) days in the currency in which billed. If any payment due hereunder is not made by the Customer within thirty (30) days after the invoice date, late charges of one and one-half percent (1½%) per month shall be due and payable with respect to such payment, and CompuServe may, in addition, at its sole discretion and without notice to the Customer, (a) suspend its performance under this agreement and the Customer's and its Users' access to and use of the service, or (b) terminate this Agreement and Customer's and its Users' access to and the use of the service. For accounts not approved by CompuServe for corporate billing, Customer must provide payment by credit card or electronic funds transfer.

12. This Agreement contains the full understanding of the parties with respect to the subject matter hereof, and no waiver, alteration, or modification of any of the provisions hereof shall be binding on either party unless in writing and signed by duly authorized representatives of the parties. Neither the course of conduct between parties nor trade practice shall act to modify the provisions of this Agreement.

More on Copyright

In the mid-1980s, much discussion occurred on-line about what the copyright clause in the operating rules means to those who upload and download files in the forums.

Here is how CompuServe has elaborated on its copyright policy in a statement posted on the system. (For more on the company's copyright position, enter GO COPYRIGHT.)

Introduction

The CompuServe Information Service provides access to more than 1,700 products covering thousands of subject areas to our members worldwide. Material offered on the CompuServe Information Service originates with a wide variety of sources, ranging from creative public domain software programs uploaded by members to multifaceted databases provided by large corporations.

Answers to Frequently Asked Questions

The following information will address some commonly asked questions about copyright and ownership of material, particularly as it relates to public domain information and shareware programs.

What is a compilation copyright?

CompuServe has copyrighted the contents of the CompuServe Information Service as a compilation copyright, just as many magazines and newspapers reserve such a copyright on the contents of their publications. This copyright is held in accordance with the 1976 Copyright Act of the United States.

A compilation copyright is granted when an organization collects information in a lawful way, adds value to it, and offers it to others. In this case, the CompuServe Information Service is a value-added product; CompuServe Incorporated has committed substantial financial resources to collecting more than 1,700 areas of the service and offering them in an organized, structured way to a defined user base through a nationwide telecommunications network. The compilation copyright is intended to protect that substantial investment from unauthorized exploitation. This does *not* mean that CompuServe assumes ownership of individual programs and databases provided to the system by members or information providers.

If I upload a software program I have developed to CompuServe, do I still retain ownership of the program?

Yes, you do. CompuServe's compilation copyright does *not* supercede individual ownership rights or copyrights to any of the material furnished to the service by members or information providers.

For example, a member who creates a program and uploads it to a CompuServe forum data library *still owns* that program, and may upload it to other information services and bulletin board systems.

It should be noted, however, that CompuServe cannot grant any redistribution rights for materials copyrighted by the author, unless specifically authorized to do so; CompuServe does not own the material or the copyright. These rights must be obtained directly from the author.

What is CompuServe's stance toward copyrighted, public domain, and shareware programs?

Each of these types of property has special characteristics, and deserves separate explanation:

1. **Copyrighted material**. CompuServe does not allow copyrighted material to be placed on the CompuServe Information Service without the author's permission. Only the owner(s) or persons they specifically

authorize may upload copyrighted material to the service. Any member may download copyrighted material for (his or her) own use. Any member may also non-commercially redistribute a copyrighted program with the expressed permission of the owner or authorized person. Permission must be specified in the document, on the service, or must be obtained directly from the author.

2. **Public domain**. Any member may upload public domain programs to the service. Any member may download public domain programs for personal use or non-commercially redistribute a public domain program.

3. **Shareware**. Only the owner or an authorized person may upload shareware programs. Any member may download shareware programs for personal use, subject to the terms provided by the owner. Any member may non-commercially redistribute a shareware program subject to the provided terms explicitly displayed in the software itself, or with permission of the owner or authorized person.

As a CompuServe member, can I download public domain information and shareware programs for my own use from CompuServe forum data libraries?

Yes, you can. Public domain information and shareware programs are uploaded to CompuServe data libraries by their authors for use by other CompuServe members.

May I download programs from CompuServe forum data libraries and share them with a friend, or upload them to another bulletin board system?

In keeping with the spirit of the development of public domain information and shareware, it is not CompuServe's current policy to prevent casual redistribution of this type of information — this is low volume and low frequency use or redistribution of information where no commercialism is involved. This means that a customer may download a file and share it with others for no commercial gain — either via a bulletin board service, diskette, or other means.

A member may not, however, download a large number of files for redistribution via any means, nor is it acceptable for a member to update another bulletin board regularly with files obtained from CompuServe.

It is important to note that CompuServe cannot grant redistribution rights for programs clearly copyrighted by the author, unless specifically authorized to do so. Such permission must be obtained directly from the author of the program.

May I download and resell a program from a CompuServe forum data library?

Commercial exploitation of material contained on the CompuServe Information Service is specifically prohibited by the CompuServe service agreement, to which each member agrees before being permitted to access the service.

Therefore, members cannot lawfully download and redistribute public information or shareware programs for personal gain.

In addition, mass redistribution of public domain information or shareware is also prohibited. Mass distribution is defined as high frequency and/or high volume transfers.

What are the penalties for violating the compilation copyright or service agreement provisions?

When a situation involving exploitation is brought to CompuServe's attention, we investigate and, if warranted, remind the violator of the terms of the service agreement. If subsequent violations are reported, access to the CompuServe Information Service may be terminated for the violator and, in extreme cases, a letter is sent from our legal counsel asking that he or she cease and desist, or risk further legal action.

This is done as a positive step to protect the value and use of the material for CompuServe Information Service members, and to discourage unauthorized redistribution of that material.

Appendix

Writing On-Line

In this appendix...

Writing with CompuServe Information Manager
Writing with Non-CIM Software

It used to be that nearly everything you wrote on CompuServe — electronic mail, notes in forums, replies, and all the rest — was composed on-line with the connect-time "money meter" constantly running. After a while, though, subscribers began experimenting with how to write their letters off-line for later delivery. While the procedure they devised worked well, it was a little technical. CompuServe's on-line editing commands had never been simple but, for many, the *off-line* procedures were even more complex. Letters written off-line had to be saved in ASCII format in the user's own word processor, then transmitted to CompuServe through a communications program that incorporated either an ASCII transfer or an error-checking file protocol. This was difficult to explain in a general way because of all the variables: different kinds of computers using different word processors and different communications programs. And, as if that weren't confusing enough for the uninitiated, even the terms differed from program to program. What one word processor referred to as "ASCII" was called a "DOS file" by another; what one communication program's manual called an "error-free transfer" was termed a "binary file protocol" by another.

Writing with CompuServe Information Manager

The CompuServe Information Manager sidesteps these problems by building into the software a full-screen editor that you may call into service whether you are currently on-line or off-line. The same editing system may be used to write and edit:

- **Letters** for delivery through CompuServe Mail.

- **Messages** to be posted in the assorted discussion forums.

- **Rough drafts** of messages and letters in progress that may be held in the electronic Filing Cabinet or in your disk's Out-Basket.

- **Comments** for the Address Book's entries.

- **Miscellaneous text** written and stored through CIM's File section.

CIM automatically summons its text feature whenever you have an option to compose or edit a file, such as in the handling of electronic mail or the writing and editing of forum messages.

Wrapping and Scrolling

Once the cursor appears in the text box, you may begin composing your message by just typing. The text feature is designed to automatically *word wrap*; that is, when you reach the end of each line, the text wraps after the last word that fits and the cursor moves to the next line, taking with it any leftover word. Also, you may start a new line (such as at the beginning of new paragraphs) by pressing the RETURN key. (The "wrap" of lines in the text box can be changed. You may set your lines up to 132 characters long. When you type more characters than the screen is able to show, the characters at the left scroll off so you can always see what you are typing. Other commands let you move your field of viewing.)

Most text boxes display ten lines at a time which is considered a *page*. When you complete the typing of the last visible line and continue typing, the display automatically *scrolls* (the top line disappears as the lines move up to make room for the additional text).

The specifics for editing text depend on whether you are using the Apple Macintosh or the IBM PC/compatible versions of CIM:

- Apple Macintosh users, note that you may use the standard Macintosh editing functions. CIM recognizes them all; this aspect of CIM is probably already familiar to you, including functions for cutting, copying, and pasting text.

- IBM PC/compatible (with and without the optional mouse attachment), please continue with the next section, which covers cursor position and editing commands.

Editing on the IBM PC/Compatible

The keys for getting in and out of the editing feature and for getting help with the editing commands are:

- **TAB** which lets you move the cursor into the text box to begin writing new text or editing an existing file.

- **F3** which lets you exit the text box. F3 always takes you to an action button for your next set of options.

Navigating

To make changes in the text, position the cursor where you want to start editing. Obviously, with a mouse, this is simply a matter of moving the cursor to the specific character position in the text box and clicking on the position. If you are using keyboard commands, assorted keys control the positioning of the cursor:

- **Arrow keys** move the cursor one space either left, right, up, or down to the next or previous row or column.
- **CONTROL-left** and **CONTROL-right** arrows move the length of one word to the left or the right.
- **HOME** and **END** move to the beginning and the end of the line, respectively.
- **PgUp** and **PgDn** move the cursor to the previous or next "page" (group of 10 screen lines), respectively.
- **CONTROL-HOME** and **CONTROL-END** move to the beginning and the end of the text, respectively.

Inserting and Deleting

To *insert* text, position the cursor in the line where you want to add material and type. The inserted letters and words will go in at that spot and the rest of the text will wrap accordingly.

To *delete* text requires a few other keys and key sequences, including:

- **DELETE** key deletes the character currently under the cursor. (DELETE is also used to remove a marked block of text, as discussed below.)
- **BACKSPACE** deletes the first character to the left of the current cursor position.
- **CONTROL-DELETE** removes either the first word to the right of the cursor or the current character and all the characters to the right in the current word.
- **CONTROL-BACKSPACE** deletes either the first word to the left of the cursor or all the characters to the left of the cursor in the current word.

Blocking Text for Changes

You may also manipulate *blocks* of lines in the text box. CIM uses an invisible "scratchpad" that temporarily holds the blocks as you move, copy, or delete them. A text block you put on the scratchpad replaces any earlier contents and remains on the pad until you replace it with another block or until you exit CIM. This means the scratchpad may be used to move or copy blocks of text into different messages as well as the current one.

With appropriate action buttons, the program lets you mark a block of lines, then:

1. **Cut** (that is, delete) it from the current position, removing it from the document.

2. **Paste** it into a new position in the text box (removing it from the original spot, then inserting it into the new location).

3. **Copy** it into a new position, thus having it in more than one place in the document, in the new spot as well as in the original location.

To *mark* a text block:

- **Mouse users** should move the cursor to the first or last character and press the button. Holding down the button, move the cursor to the other end of the block. When you release the button, the text you have traversed is marked (highlighted). To change (that is, to expand or reduce) the marked block, hold down the SHIFT key while using the mouse to either (1) mark additional text or (2) unmark a portion of the marked block.

- **Keyboard command users** should use the SHIFT key. Hold down SHIFT while moving the cursor with the cursor movement keys to mark lines, words, and individual letters. As you move, the text is highlighted. If you move farther than you intended, move the cursor back over the highlighted area to unmark the text. Release the SHIFT key when the text is highlighted as you want it.

Note   By the way, you may not make other editing changes while you are blocking the text.

Changing Marked Blocks

After a block of text is marked, you may cut, copy, or paste the material. CIM provides two ways to do that:

1. Multiple key sequences, similar to the cursor movement sequences discussed above.

2. An alternative pull-down menu. Available in the program whenever the composing and changing of text is an option, the Edit function produces a menu with a bar cursor to highlight options.

To move text in a document:

- *STEP 1* Block the text, then **Cut** or **Copy** the block by either selecting the option from the pull-down menu or using the key sequences:

  SHIFT-DELETE to cut the block that is marked.

  CONTROL-INSERT to copy the marked block.

  Cut and Copy are similar in that they both make a copy of the marked block of text on the scratchpad. The functions are different because cutting deletes the block from the original document while copying leaves the original in the document.

- *STEP 2* Move with the cursor-positioning commands to the place in the original where you want to put the blocked text.

- *STEP 3* Use the **Paste** command to insert the material from the scratchpad. When the pasting is done, the cursor is positioned at the end of the inserted block. To use the Paste function, either select the option from the pull-down menu or use the key sequence **SHIFT-INSERT**, which pastes the material that is on the scratchpad into the place in the document currently marked by the cursor.

Besides these functions, you may also simply delete a block of text, (a function called **Clear** on the pull-down menu). To do that, mark the text with the SHIFT key as described above, then, when the text is blocked, press the DELETE key.

"Undoing" Editing; Changing Word Wrap

CIM also enables you to *undo* an editing operation and restore the previous text. This lets you reverse a change, restore deleted material, eliminate added lines, and so on. The command is **CONTROL-U**, which undoes the *most recent* change, putting it back in the condition it was in the last time you pressed the RETURN key.

In addition, the software also allows you to change the size of the lines in the text box, effectively altering the right margin. To use this option, select either **Wrap** from the pull-down Edit menu or enter **CONTROL-W**. Either way, you are shown a dialog box that reports the current right margin and lets you set a new number from 20 to 132. The dialog box also has a **Word Wrap** option that you may mark or unmark to indicate whether you want words to be automatically wrapped at the end of screen lines. Any changes you make in the right margin and word wrap setting apply only to the current text box window; they will be reset when the window is closed or cancelled.

Finally, two special cursor-positioning commands are available for when the word wrap has been set in such a way that the lines are too wide to be shown on the screen. The commands, which move the cursor horizontally on a line, are:

- **CONTROL-PgDn** moves the screen's field of vision to the right.
- **CONTROL-PgUp** moves the field of vision to the left.

Using CIM'S File Command Group

CIM also supports a third, probably lesser-used option for the writing feature called the **File** section, which is available for file-handling capabilities that are occasionally outside the uses of the Filing Cabinet and In- and Out-Baskets described in this appendix.

Accessible from the program's main pull-down menu, File provides a variety of options, including several for creating and maintaining disk files beyond those incorporated in CIM itself. It operates from the pull-down menu with these options:

- **New** may be used for composing text in a new file. Selecting it causes the program to display and empty the text box for your work.

- **Open** lets you edit an existing file, displaying a dialog box. Initially, the program includes the name of the current file in the "Name: " field, but you can identify a different file by either typing it in or moving the bar cursor up or down to highlight other files in the menu list. In addition, if you want a file on a different subdirectory of your disk, you can select other options from the menu. When you have identified a file to open, CIM displays the first lines in a text box.

Later versions of CIM (2.0 and beyond) add several more File functions options:

1. Credenza Menu allows you to access the Filing Cabinet, In-Basket, Out-Basket, and Address Book from almost anywhere on the Information Service.

2. You can now bring an ASCII text file into a message you create in Compu-Serve Mail or a CompuServe forum, or into any text box, at the current cursor position using the Import command on the File menu. You can also edit the 'imported' text with the CIM text editor.

3. You can access menus and functions from your Filing Cabinet without having to close it. In earlier CIM versions, you had to select Cancel or press Escape to close your Filing Cabinet before you could access other menus or functions.

The File commands should be used only with files that have been saved in ASCII format (sometimes called "DOS text files").

When you are finished composing or editing a file, you may exit the text box (IBM PC/compatible users, press F3 or ESCAPE; Macintosh users, position the cursor on an action icon). The File area offers two choices for saving the text:

- **Save**, which saves the same file you've opened, replacing the earlier version. If you select it, you are prompted with a dialog box asking you to confirm that the earlier version of the file is to be replaced.

- **Save As**, which allows you to save the file with a different name. If the name you enter is a file that already exists, you will be prompted to confirm that you want to replace it with the current file.

The **File** options can be useful if you have an ASCII-format file elsewhere on your disk (such as one created by another word processor) that you want to call into CIM to perhaps send by CompuServe Mail. To do that:

1. Use the **Open** function on the File menu to open a text window on your screen that contains the text of the file you want to send. Then mark the portions of the file you want to send (using the shifted cursor keys or the mouse).

2. Choose the **Copy** function of the text feature as discussed in Chapter 3 to make a copy of this text in CIM's "scratchpad" memory.

3. Select **Create Mail** from the Mail pull-down menu and enter the Address and Subject information.

4. When the cursor enters the text file itself, choose the **Paste** edit function as discussed in Chapter 3. The text you copied from the file will be pasted in as the text of your message, which you can then send.

Generic Editor

If you don't want to use CIM's built-in editor, Version 2.x of the software incorporates a Generic Editor feature that allows you to use a text editor or word processor of *your choice* when editing messages.

Once in the message text box, select the "User Editor" option under the Edit pull-down menu (or use the Ctrl+E hotkey) to invoke the editor specified in your CIS.INI file. If you wish to use a word processor as your generic editor, remember to always save the contents of a message as ASCII text. (Most word processors default to use binary formatting characters and fonts which will not appear correctly in a text message.)

To modify your CIS.INI file to use a generic editor, select Open from the File pull-down menu or use any text editor. Insert the following line after the [DOSCim] line in CIS.INI:

```
Editor=(Full path name for editor executable)
```

as in Editor=C:\DOS\EDIT.COM.

Literal Editing

Editors in later CIM versions also now include support for literal or unformatted editing. This allows you to include items which you do not wish to be wrapped (such as columns or lists) by CIM's editor. The literal option may be selected or deselected by choosing the "Enable Literal" option from the Edit pull-down menu, or by using the F7 key.

Writing with Non-CIM Software

If you don't use the CompuServe Information Manager or another program that has a built-in text editor, you may use one of CompuServe's own word processors on-line. Two text editors are in use throughout the system:

- LINEDIT, a line-numbered editor.
- EDIT, an unnumbered editor.

In many features—such as the forums and CompuServe Mail—you may choose which editor you want to use. In the forums, a preference can be specified in the OPTIONS area of individual forums. In Mail, you may choose an editor with the SET options on the main menu.

Here are characteristics that both editors share:

- You must press the RETURN key at the end of each screen line.
- You cannot use your computer's cursor-positioning arrow keys to edit the document.
- To close a document and leave the editor, use the command /EXIT.

The next sections describe things that are unique to each editor.

LINEDIT, the Line-numbered Editor

For newcomers, LINEDIT is the easier of the two editors because it prompts for each line with a new line number and it uses menus for editing changes. The menus list options, like this:

```
Edit Menu

  1    CHANGE characters in line
  2    REPLACE line
  3    DELETE line
  4    INSERT new line(s)
  5    TYPE all lines
  6    POST message on board

Enter choice !
```

Note that the numbered menu options enable you to change characters in a line, replace a line, delete a line, insert new lines, among other things. One option, TYPE, is recommended as your first step, because it lets you see the numbered lines of your message; thereafter, all the other commands, such as REPLACE and DELETE, will ask for line-number references.

EDIT, the Unnumbered Editor

By contrast, the EDIT editor works without a menu. Commands are entered on the lines of text. Every command begins with a forward slash. (If a line does not begin with a slash, the computer assumes it is text.)

In using EDIT, it is helpful to think in terms of an invisible pointer that marks the position of the current line. You can direct the line pointer to move up or down your file. The pointer can be directed to move downward line-by-line from the first line of your text file searching for information to be displayed, changed, or erased.

- /EX is used to exit the writing/editing service and return to Command Mode. Incidentally, you don't have to be at the bottom of the file to close with this command.

- /T positions the line pointer at an imaginary line just before the first line of the file. This allows you to insert new lines above the current first line of the file.

- /P *n* displays a specified number (*n*) of lines in the file. If *n* is omitted, only the current line will be displayed. For example, a "/P3" will display three lines starting with the current line.

Tip /T followed by carriage return and a "/P1000" will display the entire contents of the file, unless it is more than 1,000 lines long.

- /L/*string* scans the lines following the current line one-by-one until the first occurrence of the specified string is located. To display the line located, give the /P command. (If you terminate the /L/*string* command with an ESCAPE key, the located line will be displayed immediately.) Your pointer must be on a line *above* the line you are searching for in order to use /L/. It always searches downward in the file.

Tip If you give the "/T" command just before the "/L/ string" command, you will be able to locate a string above the current line.

- /C/*oldstring*/*newstring*. This command replaces any specified string in the current line with a new string where: *oldstring* = the string to be replaced and *newstring* = the replacement string. If omitted, then *oldstring* will be erased.

- /GC/*oldstring*/*newstring*, meaning "global change," is the same as the /C command, except that all occurrences of the old text are changed to the specified new text. If *newstring* isn't specified, then the command removes all occurrences of *oldstring*.

- /A/*string* adds the specified string to the end of the current line. The line pointer will remain on that line after the command is executed.

- /D*n* deletes the number of lines (*n*) specified, starting with the current line. The pointer will be positioned at the line following the last line erased. If omitted, only the current line is erased.

- /B moves the line pointer to the last line of your file.

- /N *n*, meaning Next, moves your line pointer down the file a specified number of lines from its current position: If you enter *n* as a positive number (/N2), the line pointer advances down your file *n* (2) lines. If you enter *n* as a negative number (/N-3), the line pointer retreats up the file *n* (-3) lines.

- /TYPE displays the contents of the workspace.

- /HELP gives more information about editing commands.

I

File Transfer

In this appendix...

Protocols
Retrieval (Downloading)
Uploading

Tens of thousands of files—text articles as well as public domain and share-ware programs—can be retrieved, saved on your disk, and used when you are off-line. In addition, you may contribute text and original programs to the growing on-line resources, sending them from your disk directly to Compu-Serve so others may retrieve them. Similarly, you may transfer electronic letters between your disk and your on-line electronic mailbox. This process of file trans-fer is also called *downloading* (receiving) and *uploading* (sending).

Transfer with CIM and Automated Software

If you're using the CompuServe Information Manager software, retrieving and sending files is easy, because pull-down menus direct you throughout the proc-ess. To retrieve a forum file with CIM, just visit the library and browse or search the files with the pull-down menu options. When you find something inter-esting, select the "Retrieve" option on the display and the program takes care of the rest. Or you may mark a file to add it to a group for retrieval later.

Similarly, if you are using automated software, such as TapCIS, OzCIS, and others described in Chapter 14, you generally don't have to sweat the details in downloading, because the program itself will handle it. Check the manual that came with your program.

Transfer with General Communications Software

If you use a general, third-party communications program to log on to Compu-Serve, file transfer is a little trickier. That's because you need to know something about transfer *protocols* and how to choose one that both CompuServe and your software can use.

Protocols

A protocol is a set of rules that allows computers to send data back and forth without errors caused by static on the phone lines. With a protocol, computers carry on a clever little conversation during the file transfer, periodically checking to see if the data received is identical to what was sent.

With CompuServe Information Manager and most automated programs, the software itself selects a protocol for your data transfer; with a third-party general communications program, you must make that selection yourself. CompuServe offers several different transfer protocols, so check the manual to see if your terminal software also supports any of those described in the following sections.

B and Quick B Protocol

CompuServe's B Protocol and QB ("Quick B") Protocol were developed specifically for CompuServe. (This is the protocol automatically supported by the CompuServe Information Manager; it is also included in a number of other communications programs.)

Xmodem

Xmodem is a well-known public domain protocol developed in the late 1970s by Ward Christensen of Chicago. If your third-party communications program supports only one transfer protocol, it probably is Xmodem. However, each program may support a slightly different version. In some parts of Compu-Serve a "Macintosh Xmodem" is listed on protocol menus, indicating an Xmodem installation for the Apple Macintosh computer.

Ymodem

Ymodem is a similar protocol that sends and receives a larger block of data for verification during that electronic conversation between the computers.

Kermit

Kermit is a protocol developed at Columbia University for file transfer that is becoming increasingly popular in communications software.

Retrieval (Downloading)

When you are retrieving files using communications software other than the CompuServe Information Manager, you are shown a menu from which to select a protocol. It is up to you to have done your homework by studying your software's manual. If the manual tells you that your program supports the Xmodem protocol, you could select that option from the menu, then, when prompted, initiate the download with whatever command sequences your software requires for an Xmodem transfer.

Most communications programs also pause before the transfer begins to prompt you for the name you want to assign the file as it arrives on your disk. This does not have to be the same name as exists on-line. The on-line file may be called BBALL.BAS, but you might have it saved on your disk as BASE-BALL.BAS. Just be sure to specify a legal filename for your computer. Also, if you have a hard disk and use directories and subdirectories to organize it, be sure to enter the full pathway name when specifying the filename.

After this, the actual download begins. CompuServe sends data and your machine captures it, comparing blocks of data to verify what is received, then saving it on your disk.

After the transfer is done — the file has been transmitted from CompuServe, confirmed, and saved on your disk under the name you specified — the system notifies you. If you download a second file at this point, the system does not prompt you to choose a transfer protocol; it skips that menu, assuming you are using the same protocol you used on the first transfer.

One more note about the file transfer menu. "DC4/DC2 (Capture)," listed on most CompuServe file transfer menus, is *not* an error-checking protocol; it does not compare data blocks like B and Quick B Protocol, Xmodem, and others. Instead, DC4/DC2, sometimes called an "ASCII" transfer, is simply an ASCII display of the file. Some communications programs have an option called "ASCII dump" or "buffer capture." You can use this option for such capturing. But DC4/DC2 should be used only for capturing *text files* where occasional static on the phone line usually can do no more than garble a few characters. In other words, *program files* should always be downloaded only with an error-checking protocol to protect against noisy phone lines.

Uploading

Uploading can be used in a number of CompuServe features, and the procedure is about the same in each. Once you select the upload option, you are prompted, then asked for a filename.

Consider the following points about filenames. Various parts of CompuServe — especially the data libraries of forums — use names to identify files. A name can always be one to six characters with an optional extension (a period and up to three characters), as in NEWONE.TXT. You may use alphabetic or numeric characters and/or hyphens in the name, but the first character must be a letter of the alphabet. When the system prompts for a filename, it means the name under which the data will be stored on CompuServe; what you enter does *not* have to be the same name that exists on your disk. So you might have a file called PROPOSAL.DAT on your disk and upload it to Compu-Serve to be saved there as NEWONE.TXT.

After you have specified a filename, the system wants to know which transfer protocol you want to use and will display its menu of available protocols (such as B Protocol, Xmodem, Kermit) as in downloading. (See above for the list of protocols.) After the protocol is specified, the system needs one other piece of information: the file *type*. To get this information, it displays a menu asking if the file is in ASCII, binary, or graphics. File type means the format in which the file should be *saved* on CompuServe. Here are some additional notes:

- ASCII (the "American Standard Code for Information Interchange") usually means text, including letters, documents, or source code of programs.
- Binary means computer programs, primarily, or files saved in a specific program's unique format, such as some spreadsheet data.

Remember to specify the same file type as is used for the file currently stored on your disk. If the file you are uploading is binary (a program, for instance), you should specify that it should be saved in binary format on CompuServe's end of the connection; if it is an ASCII text (perhaps an article or letter), it should be saved in ASCII on the receiving end.

(A confusion about text files sometimes arises because many commercial word processors routinely store documents, not in ASCII, but in a binary for-mat to save space on your disk and to embed commands for printers and so on. It is a mistake to upload one of these *compressed* binary files and have it saved as ASCII on CompuServe. Since it is not ASCII, it will not be readable by those who download it. Fortunately, your word processor itself usually offers the solution. A good word processor usually has an option for saving files in a plain vanilla ASCII rather than its own compressed format. Check the users' manual of your word processor and use that option to save your text files in true ASCII before uploading them.)

After the file type has been specified, the system prompts you to begin the transmission. Your communications program's manual should outline its command sequence for uploading. Usually, the terminal software prompts for the name of the file on your disk that you want to upload.

In a forum library, after the upload is completed, the system will ask you to enter keywords and a description of the file.

Here are a few more points:

1. As in downloading, if you were to upload a second file, the system wouldn't prompt again for a file transfer protocol; it would assume you

were using the same protocol you used for the first upload.

2. If for any reason you need to stop an upload (or a download) before it is finished, press Control C or the Escape key several times. Usually, Compu-Serve displays a message reporting the transfer is aborted and allows you to return to a menu.

3. Uploading is also possible to the CompuServe Mail service.

Finally, as noted in the discussion of downloading, DC4/DC2 CAPTURE, listed on most upload menus on the system, is *not* an error-checking protocol, which means it does not compare checksums the way B and Quick B Protocol, Xmodem, and Kermit do. Instead, DC4/DC2, sometimes called an "ASCII" transfer, is simply an ASCII display of the file; if phone line static occurs during the transfer, it *will* cause garble in the file as it is received. For that reason, it should be used sparingly for uploading material. When you select the DC4/DC2 option from the protocol menu for uploading, the system displays, "This protocol supports ASCII file transfer only. Is this an ASCII file (Y or N)?" In other words, the system is reminding you that an error-checking protocol, rather than DC4/DC2, should be used for uploading binary files. If you answer this prompt with Y for yes, meaning your file is indeed ASCII, the system then prompts with, "No error detection protocol in use. Do you wish to be prompted for each line (Y or N)?"

If you answer this question with:

- Y, the system asks you to enter the prompt character to use. (For instance, if you enter a question mark, the system will prompt with a ? at the beginning of each new line.)

- N, the system will not prompt you at the beginning of each new line.

After that, the system reports, "Begin sending your data. Use a control-Z (1A hex, 032 octal) to indicate the end of your data." Now you may tell your software to begin its ASCII transmission. (Also with the DC4/DC2 option, you can even type in your file directly from your keyboard.) When you are finished, inform CompuServe by pressing Control-Z.

But again, while DC4/DC2 is fine for transmitting text files, it cannot be used for binary files, such as programs. Use a file transfer protocol for binary files.

Appendix

J

Current List of Forums and Addresses

Here is a list of some of the forums offered on CompuServe with their "GO" addresses. For an up-to-date list on-line, enter FIND FORUMS (or, in the Compu-Serve Information Manager, select the Go… option on the Service menu and enter FORUMS).

All forums in this list are charged by the minute except those identified as "(FREE)."

ACI US Forum	GO ACIUS
AI EXPERT Forum	GO AIEXPERT
APPC Info Exchange Forum	GO APPCFORUM
ASP/Shareware Forum	GO ASPFORUM
Adobe Forum	GO ADOBE
Aldus Customer Service Forum	GO ALDSVC
Aldus/Silicon Beach Forum	GO SBSALDFORUM
Amiga Arts Forum	GO AMIGAARTS
Amiga Tech Forum	GO AMIGATECH
Amiga User's Forum	GO AMIGAUSER
Amiga Vendor Forum	GO AMIGAVENDOR
Apple II Prog. Forum	GO APPROG
Apple II Users Forum	GO APPUSER
Apple II Vendor Forum	GO APIIVEN
Aquaria/Fish Forum	GO FISHNET
Artisoft Forum	GO ARTISOFT
Ask3Com Forum	GO ASKFORUM

Astronomy Forum	GO ASTROFORUM
Atari 8-Bit Forum	GO ATARI8
Atari Portfolio Forum	GO APORTFOLIO
Atari ST Arts Forum	GO ATARIARTS
Atari ST Prod. Forum	GO ATARIPRO
Atari Vendor Forum	GO ATARIVEN
Autodesk AutoCAD Forum	GO ACAD
Autodesk Retail Products Forum	GO ARETAIL
Autodesk Software Forum	GO ASOFT
Automobile Forum	GO CARS
Aviation Forum (AVSIG)	GO AVSIG
BASIS International Forum	GO BASIS
Bacchus Wine Forum	GO WINEFORUM
Banyan Forum	GO BANFORUM
Blyth Forum	GO BLYTH
Borland	GO BORLAND
Borland Appl. Forum	GO BORAPP
Borland C+/DOS Forum +	GO BCPPDOS
Borland C+/Windows Forum +	GO BCPPWIN
Borland DB Products Forum	GO BORDB
Borland Developer Tool Forum	GO BDEVTOOLS
Borland GmbH Forum	GO BORGMBH
Borland Pascal Forum	GO BPASCAL
Borland Quattro Pro Forum	GO QUATTROPRO
Borland dBASE Forum	GO DBASE
Broadcast Pro Forum	GO BPFORUM
CA App. Development Forum	GO CAIDEV
CA Pro Solutions Forum	GO CAIPRO
CA VAX/Unix Forum	GO CAIMINI
CA–Clipper Germany Forum	GO CLIPGER
CADD/CAM/CAE Vendor Forum	GO CADDVEN
CASE DCI Forum	GO CASEFORUM
CB Forum	GO CBFORUM
CDROM Forum	GO CDROM
CIM Support Forum (FREE)	GO CIMSUPPORT
CP/M Users Group Forum	GO CPMFORUM
Cabletron Systems, Inc.	GO CTRON
Cabletron Systems Forum	GO CTRONFORUM
Cancer Forum	GO CANCER
Canon Support	GO CANON
Canopus Forum	GO CANOPUS

Central Point DOS Forum	GO CPSDOS
Central Point Win/Mac Forum	GO CPSWIN
Chess Forum	GO CHESSFORUM
Clarion Software Forum	GO CLARION
Claris Forum	GO CLARIS
Client Server Computing Forum	GO MSNETWORKS
Clipper Forum	GO CLIPPER
Coin/Stamp Collect. Forum	GO COLLECT
Color Computer Forum	GO COCO
Comics/Animation Forum	GO COMIC
Commodore Applications Forum	GO CBMAPP
Commodore Arts/Games Forum	GO CBMART
Commodore Service Forum	GO CBMSERVICE
Compaq Connection	GO CPQFORUM
CompuAdd Forum	GO COMPUADD
CompuServe Help Forum(FREE)	GO HELPFORUM
CompuServe Navigator	GO NAVIGATOR
CompuServe Pacific Forum	GO PACFORUM
Computer Art Forum	GO COMART
Computer Associates Forums	GO CAI
Computer Club Forum	GO CLUB
Computer Consult. Forum	GO CONSULT
Computer Language Forum	GO CLMFORUM
Computer Shopper (UK) Forum	GO UKSHOPPER
Computer Training Forum	GO DPTRAIN
Consumer Elect. Forum	GO CEFORUM
Cooks Online Forum	GO COOKS
Corel Forum	GO COREL
Court Reporters Forum	GO CRFORUM
Crafts Forum	GO CRAFTS
Creative Solutions/Forth Forum	GO FORTH
Crosstalk Forum	GO XTALK
DATASTORM Forum	GO DATASTORM
DBMS Magazine Forum	GO DBMSFORUM
DEC PC Forum	GO DECPC
DECPCI Forum	GO DECPCI
DTP Vendors Forum	GO DTPVENDOR
Data Access Corp. Forum	GO DACCESS
Data Based Advisor Forum	GO DBADVISOR
DataEase International Forum	GO DATAEASE
Dell Forum	GO DELL
Desktop Publishing Forum	GO DTPFORUM

Deutsches Computer Forum	GO GERNET
Developer Relations Forum	GO MSDR
Developers Contest Forum	GO DEVCONTEST
Diabetes Forum	GO DIABETES
Digitalk Forum	GO DIGITALK
Disabilities Forum	GO DISABILITIES
Download and Support Forum	GO DOWNTECH
Dr. Dobb's Forum	GO DDJFORUM
Dr. Neuhaus Forum	GO NEUHAUS
Earth Forum	GO EARTH
Education Forum	GO EDFORUM
Educational Res. Forum	GO EDRESEARCH
Eicon Technology Forum	GO EICON
Electronic Frontier Foundation	GO EFFSIG
Engineering Automation Forum	GO LEAP
Epson Forum	GO EPSON
Fed. Of Int'l Distributors	GO FEDERATION
Fifth Generation Systems Forum	GO FIFTHGEN
Financial Forums	GO FINFORUM
Fine Arts Forum	GO FINEARTS
Flight Simulator Forum	GO FSFORUM
Florida Forum	GO FLORIDA
FocServices Forum	GO FOCSERVICES
FocWizard Forum	GO FOCWIZARD
Foreign Language Forum	GO FLEFO
Fox Software Forum	GO FOXFORUM
Game Publishers A Forum	GO GAMAPUB
Game Publishers B Forum	GO GAMBPUB
Gamers Forum	GO GAMERS
Gardening Forum	GO GARDENING
Genealogy Forum	GO ROOTS
Global Crises Forum	GO CRISIS
Graphics B Vendor Forum	GO GRAPHBVEN
Graphics Corner Forum	GO CORNER
Graphics Developers Forum	GO GRAPHDEV
Graphics Forums	GO GRAPHICS
Graphics Gallery Forum	GO GALLERY
Graphics Plus Forum	GO GRAPHPLUS
Graphics Support Forum	GO GRAPHSUPPORT
Graphics Vendor Forum	GO GRAPHVEN

HP Handheld Forum	GO HPHAND
HP Peripherals Forum	GO HPPER
HP Systems Forum	GO HPSYS
HSX Adult Forum	GO HSX200
HSX Open Forum	GO HSX100
Hamnet Forum	GO HAMNET
Hayes Forum	GO HAYFORUM
Health and Fitness Forum	GO GOODHEALTH
Humane Society Forum	GO HSUS
IBM Applications Forum	GO IBMAPP
IBM Bulletin Board Forum	GO IBMBBS
IBM Communications Forum	GO IBMCOM
IBM Desktop Soft. Forum	GO IBMDESK
IBM European Users Forum	GO IBMEUROPE
IBM Hardware Forum	GO IBMHW
IBM LMU2 Forum	GO LMU2FORUM
IBM New Users Forum	GO IBMNEW
IBM OS/2 Developer 1 Forum	GO OS2DF1
IBM OS/2 Developer 2 Forum	GO OS2DF2
IBM OS/2 Support Forum	GO OS2SUPPORT
IBM OS/2 Users Forum	GO OS2USER
IBM Programming Forum	GO IBMPRO
IBM Special Needs Forum	GO IBMSPEC
IBM Systems/Util. Forum	GO IBMSYS
IBM ThinkPad Forum	GO THINKPAD
Intel Access/iRUG Forum	GO INTELACCESS
Investors Forum	GO INVFORUM
Issues Forum	GO ISSUESFORUM
Javelin/EXPRESS Forum	GO IRIFORUM
Journalism Forum	GO JFORUM
LDC Spreadsheets Forum	GO LOTUSA
LDC Word Processing Forum	GO LOTUSWP
LDC Words and Pixels Forum	GO LOTUSB
LDOS/TRSDOS6 Users Forum	GO LDOS
LOGO Forum	GO LOGOFORUM
Lan Magazine Forum	GO LANMAG
Lan Technology Forum	GO LANTECH
Legal Forum	GO LAWSIG
Literary Forum	GO LITFORUM
Logitech Forum	GO LOGITECH

MECA Software Forum	GO MECA
MIDI A Vendor Forum	GO MIDIAVEN
MIDI B Vendor Forum	GO MIDIBVEN
MIDI/Music Forum	GO MIDIFORUM
MS Applications Forum	GO MSAPP
MS Benelux Forum	GO MSBF
MS DOS 5.0 Forum	GO MSDOS
MS SQL Server Forum	GO MSSQL
MS Windows Advanced Forum	GO WINADV
MS Windows Extensions Forum	GO WINEXT
MS Windows SDK Forum	GO WINSDK
Mac A Vendor Forum	GO MACAVEN
Mac Applications Forum	GO MACAP
Mac B Vendor Forum	GO MACBVEN
Mac C Vendor Forum	GO MACCVEN
Mac CIM Support Forum(FREE)	GO MCIMSUP
Mac Communications Forum	GO MACCOMM
Mac Community/Club Forum	GO MACCLUB
Mac Developers Forum	GO MACDEV
Mac Entertainment Forum	GO MACFUN
Mac Hypertext Forum	GO MACHYPER
Mac New Users Help Forum	GO MACNEW
MacUser	GO MACUSER
MacUser Forum	GO MACUSER
MacWEEK	GO MACWEEK
MacWEEK Forum	GO MACWEEK
Macintosh Hardware Forum	GO MACHW
Macintosh Systems Forum	GO MACSYS
Macromedia Forum	GO MACROMEDIA
Markt and Technik Deutschland	GO MUT
Masonry Forum	GO MASONRY
McAfee Virus Forum	GO VIRUSFORUM
Medsig Forum	GO MEDSIG
Mensa Forum	GO MENSA
Microsoft Access Forum	GO MSACCESS
Microsoft BASIC Forum	GO MSBASIC
Microsoft CE Systems Forum	GO MSCESYSTEM
Microsoft Central Europe Forum	GO MSCE
Microsoft Connection	GO MICROSOFT
Microsoft Excel Forum	GO MSEXCEL
Microsoft Languages Forum	GO MSLANG
Microsoft WIN32 Forum	GO MSWIN32
Microsoft Word Forum	GO MSWORD

Military Forum	GO MILITARY
Model Aviation Forum	GO MODELNET
Modem Games Forum	GO MODEMGAMES
Modem Vendor Forum	GO MODEMVENDOR
Money Mag. Fin'l Info	GO MONEYMAG
Motor Sports Forum	GO RACING
MultiPlayer Games Forum	GO MPGAMES
Multimedia Conference Forum	GO MULTICON
Multimedia Forum	GO MULTIMEDIA
Multimedia Vendor Forum	GO MULTIVEN
Music/Arts Forum	GO MUSICARTS
NAIC Invest. Ed. Forum	GO NAIC
NeXT Forum	GO NEXTFORUM
New Age Forum	GO NEWAGE
Novell DSG Forum	GO DRFORUM
Novell Forum A	GO NOVA
Novell Forum B	GO NOVB
Novell Forum C	GO NOVC
Novell Library Forum	GO NOVLIB
Novell NetWare 2.X Forum	GO NETW2X
Novell NetWare 3.X Forum	GO NETW3X
Novell Vendor Forum	GO NOVVEN
OS-9 Forum	GO OS9
Oracle Forum	GO ORACLE
Outdoor Forum	GO OUTDOORFORUM
PBS Applications Forum	GO PBSAPPS
PBS Arcade Forum	GO PBSARCADE
PC Contact Forum	GO PCCONTACT
PC MagNet	GO PCMAGNET
PC MagNet After Hours Forum	GO AFTERHOURS
PC MagNet Editorial Forum	GO EDITORIAL
PC MagNet Programming Forum	GO PROGRAMMING
PC MagNet Utilities/Tips Forum	GO TIPS
PC Plus / PC Answers	GO PCPLUS
PC Vendor A Forum	GO PCVENA
PC Vendor B Forum	GO PCVENB
PC Vendor C Forum	GO PCVENC
PC Vendor D Forum	GO PCVEND
PC Vendor E Forum	GO PCVENE
PC Vendor F Forum	GO PCVENF

PC Vendor G Forum	GO PCVENG
PC Week Extra Forum	GO PCWEEK
PDP-11 Forum	GO PDP11
PR and Marketing Forum	GO PRSIG
Packard Bell Forum	GO PACKARDBELL
Palmtop Forum	GO PALMTOP
Pen Technology Forum	GO PENFORUM
Pets/Animal Forum	GO PETS
Photography Forum	GO PHOTOFORUM
Play-By-Mail Games Forum	GO PBMGAMES
Portable Prog. Forum	GO CODEPORT
Practical Periph. Forum	GO PPIFORUM
Practice Forum(FREE)	GO PRACTICE
Prisma Deutschland Forum	GO PRISMA
Quarterdeck Forum	GO QUARTERDEC
Quick Picture Forum	GO QPICS
Religion Forum	GO RELIGION
Revelation Tech Forum	GO REVELATION
Rocknet Forum	GO ROCKNET
Role-Playing Games Forum	GO RPGAMES
Safetynet Forum	GO SAFETYNET
Sailing Forum	GO SAILING
Santa Cruz Operation Forum	GO SCOFORUM
Science Fiction Forum	GO SCI-FI
Science/Math Ed. Forum	GO SCIENCE
Scuba Forum	GO DIVING
ShowBiz Forum	GO SHOWBIZ
Siemens Automatisierungs Forum	GO AUTFORUM
Software Pub. Assoc. Forum	GO SPAFORUM
Software Publishing Forum	GO SPCFORUM
Solutions Australia Forum	GO SOLUTIONS
Space/Astronomy Forum	GO SPACE
Spinnaker Software Forum	GO SPINNAKER
Sports Forum	GO FANS
Stac Electronics Forum	GO STACKER
Standard Microsystems Forum	GO SMC
Students' Forum	GO STUFO
Symantec Apps Forum	GO SYMFORUM
Symantec/Norton Forum	GO NORUTL

TAPCIS Forum	GO TAPCIS
Tandy Model 100 Forum	GO M100SIG
Tandy Professional Forum	GO TRS80PRO
Telecommunications Forum	GO TELECOM
Texas Instruments Forum	GO TIFORUM
Texas Instruments News	GO TINEWS
The Entrepreneur's Forum	GO USEN
The Intel Forum	GO INTELFORUM
Thomas–Conrad Forum	GO TCCFORUM
Toshiba Forum	GO TOSHIBA
Toshiba GmbH Forum	GO TOSHGER
TrainNet Forum	GO TRAINNET
Travel Forum	GO TRAVSIG
UK Computing Forum	GO UKCOMP
UK Forum	GO UKFORUM
UKSHARE Forum	GO UKSHARE
UNIX Forum	GO UNIXFORUM
Ultimedia Tools Series A Forum	GO ULTIATOOLS
Ultimedia Tools Series B Forum	GO ULTIBTOOLS
UserLand Forum	GO USERLAND
VAX Forum	GO VAXFORUM
Ventura Software Forum	GO VENTURA
WP Customer Support Forum	GO WPCS
WPMA Forum	GO WPMA
WinCIM Support Forum	GO WCIMSUPPORT
WinNT Pre-Release Forum	GO WINNT
Windows 3rd Party A Forum	GO WINAPA
Windows 3rd Party App. D Forum	GO WINAPD
Windows 3rd Party B Forum	GO WINAPB
Windows 3rd Party C Forum	GO WINAPC
Windows New Users Forum	GO WINNEW
Wolfram Research Forum	GO WOLFRAM
WordPerfect Corporation	GO WORDPERFECT
WordPerfect Users Forum	GO WPUSER
WordStar Forum	GO WORDSTAR
Working-From-Home Forum	GO WORK
Worldwide Car Network	GO WWCAR
Zenith Data Systems Forum	GO ZENITH
Ziff Cobb Applications Forum	GO COBBAPP

Ziff Cobb Programming Forum	GO COBBPR
Ziff Computer Shopper Forum	GO COMPSHOPPER
Ziff Corporate Computing Forum	GO CORPORATE
Ziff Executives Online Forum	GO EXECUTIVES
Ziff PC Sources Forum	GO SOURCES
ZiffNet	GO ZIFFNET
ZiffNet Support Forum	GO SUPPORT
ZiffNet/Mac	GO ZMAC

Appendix

Terminal Settings (For Non-CIM Users)

In this appendix...

Defaults
SET Command for Temporary Settings

Defaults

Defaults—that is, the settings for all your screen appearances, what on-line editing program and file transfer protocol you use, and so forth—are controlled in the Terminal Type area (GO TERMINAL). You *need not* visit this area if you are using the CompuServe Information Manager, because that software regulates all your terminal settings automatically. But, if you are using a third-party general program to communicate with CompuServe, you may need to visit Terminal Settings to coordinate your program with the system. Consult your software users' manual.

Some 25 options, discussed in this appendix, are controlled in this part of the system.

Logon/Service Options

The Logon/service options include:

- First Service, can be set to either MAIN menu (Normal setting), a designated first service (you specify which one), personal MENU (a menu you

447

have constructed), or COMMAND mode in the personal file area (PER).

- CompuServe Mail Waiting, can be set to Go to CompuServe Mail (takes you to Mail when you have messages waiting) or notify only (notifies you that you have messages waiting, then takes you to your first service).

- Personal Menu Established, can be set to YES (which you select to *create* or *change* your personal menu) or NO (when you haven't created a personal menu or what to delete on an existing personal menu). See Personal Menu.

- TOP Goes To, can be set to MAIN menu, a designated top page, a Personal MENU you have constructed, or COMMAND mode in the personal file area.

- On-line Editor Preference determines the word editor you will normally use. You may change this for a specific forum via the forum options or for CompuServe Mail via the Mail options. The possible settings here are EDIT (which doesn't use line numbers), LINEDIT (which uses line numbers), or DEFAULT (no preference). See Writing.

- Forum Presentation Mode determines the type of presentation you normally receive in each forum you visit. You may change this for a specific forum via the forum options. The settings are MENU mode (novice/intermediate), COMMAND mode (expert), or DEFAULT (no preference).

Display Options

The Display options are:

- Paged Display, can be set to YES (Output is presented in pages; you are asked to enter <CR> after each page) or NO (Output is scrolled continuously to the end of the article).

- Brief Prompts, can be YES for expert mode (You receive abbreviated prompts such as ! or More!) or NO for novice/intermediate mode (You receive full prompts such as Enter choice! or Enter <CR> for more!).

- Clear Screen Between Pages, can be either YES or NO. The latter suppresses screen clear and use of cursor positioning.

- Blank Lines Sent, can be YES (the normal mode) or NO.

> **Note** Not sending blank lines can save space but may make output more difficult to read.

- Line Feeds Sent, with which the normal setting is YES. Choose NO *only* if your terminal or software always adds a line feed to a carriage return. Not sending line feeds may result in text writing over itself.

Terminal Type/Parameters

Terminal Type/Parameters include:

- Terminal Type, can be either VIDTEX (Professional Connection and related CompuServe software products, but not CIM), ANSI, VT100, VT52, Heath (Zenith), ADM, CRT, or other.
- Screen Width determines the number of characters per line on your screen.
- Lines Per Page determines the number of lines per screen for your system.
- Form Feeds, can be either REAL (uses your micro control to do new page form feeds) or SIMULATED (prints out eight blank lines between pages).
- Horizontal Tabs, can also be either REAL (uses your micro control to move to tab stops across the page) or SIMULATED (uses spaces to simulate tabs).
- Characters Received (CAPS), can be set to U/L, the normal mode (the output to you is in upper- or lowercase depending on how it is sent by Compu-Serve), UPPER only (You receive only uppercase output) or LOWER only (You receive only lowercase output).
- Characters Sent in CAPS, can be NO, the normal mode (meaning that whatever you input is in the case you send it) or YES (whatever you input is always in CAPS regardless of how you send it).
- Parity can be either EVEN, ODD, or ZERO.
- Output Delays, normally is set to 1, but can be increased if your printer operates at a slower speed than your modem and characters are lost at the beginning of each line. (Delays aren't recognized, however, if you are accessing through a supplemental network such as Tymnet or Datapak).
- Backspace Erase, can be set to YES, the normal setting (when a backspace is received, CompuServe sends a space and another backspace which has the effect of erasing the last character typed) or NO (with no special processing when a backspace is received).
- Send Micro Inquiry Sequence at Logon, should be set to YES if your software is *The Professional Connection* or another of CompuServe's own communications programs.

Transfer Protocols/Graphics Support

Transfer protocols/graphics support options are:

- File Transfer Protocol Preference, can be set to record a preferred transfer protocol — B Protocol, Quick B protocol, Xmodem, Ymodem, Kermit — or set to SHOW MENU (which causes the system to present a menu of available protocols when you request a file transfer).

- GIF Support, should be set to YES only if your communication software supports CompuServe's Graphic Interchange Facility.
- NAPLPS Support, should be YES if your terminal software supports NAPLPS, the North American Presentation Level Protocol Syntax.
- RLE Support, should be YES if your terminal software supports RLE, that is, Run-Length Encoded graphics.

SET Command for Temporary Settings

CompuServe also supports a powerful SET command that lets you make quick adjustments to your screen display without having to go into the Terminal Settings area. At nearly any prompt on the system, you may enter SET and the system prompts you with "SET sub-command:" The changes are in effect *during that session only*. After you log off and back on again, all defaults automatically reset to the values saved in the Terminal Settings area.

Several options may be temporarily adjusted with the SET command, including:

- WIDth, to adjust the screen width default to a number between 16 and 255 characters.
- LINe, to change the number of lines the system thinks your screen can accommodate. You can use the SET command to quickly change that. With SET LIN you can enter a number between zero and 63. Entering SET LIN 16 at a ! prompt would tell the system you want pages of no more than 16 lines at a time.
- PAGe, to turn on or off paging. If you decide that you temporarily don't want your text interrupted by the messages like "Press <CR> for more !" you can enter SET PAG OFF. That means for the current session, the system would avoid paging, no matter how your defaults were set in the TERMINAL/OPTIONS area. To turn paging back on — you got it, SET PAG ON.
- BRIef, to turn on and off brief mode. New subscribers automatically receive full menus (or "verbose" prompts) at all features. However, at any ! prompt, you may enter SET BRI ON to turn off the menu for the current session. SET BRI OFF turns the menus back on.

Also controlled by SET are:

- BLANK (YES/NO) to send blank lines.
- CAPS (YES/NO) to send characters in CAPS.
- DELAY (0-255) to output delay.
- ERASE (YES/NO) to set erase when backspacing.

- FEEDS (YES/NO) to set automatic line feeds.
- FORM (REAL/SIM) to set form feeds, either real or simulated.
- PARITY (EVEN/ODD/ONE/ZERO) to change the parity setting.
- TABS (REAL/SIM) to set horizontal tabs, either real or simulated.

L

Graphics

In this appendix...

The Forums
How to See the Pictures
Where to Find a Viewer
Graphics File Finder

Graphics are one of the hot new topics on CompuServe. The system has a number of facilities for displaying high-quality pictures on your screen, including a network of a half dozen forums that specialize in them. Most on-line pictures these days are GIF (Graphics Interchange Format) images. GIF (pronounced "jiff") images can be created and viewed with nearly any type of computer system, making them ideal for the exchange of images among users of differing hardware.

The Forums

At this writing, the graphics forums are:

- The Graphics Support Forum (GO GRAPHSUP) contains all programs/utilities necessary for viewing graphics.

- The Fine Art Forum (GO FINEART) focuses on high-resolution computer reproductions of world-class art.

- The Graphics Corner Forum (GO CORNER) has high-resolution, scanned or digitized images.

- The Quick Picture Forum (GO QPIC) contains 32-color or less, scanned or digitized images.

- The Graphics Gallery Forum (GO GALLERY) has image collections from such organizations as NASA, USDA, and the Smithsonian.

- The Graphics Developers Forum (GO GRAPHDEV) is the home of the Stone Soup workgroups for fractals, raytracing, and virtual reality.
- The Graphics Plus Forum (GO GRAPHPLUS) is for GIF images that are at least 800 x 600 in size.
- Graphics A Vendor Forum (GO GRAPHVEN) and Graphics B Vendor Forum (GO GRAPHBVEN).

How to See the Pictures

A GIF is a graphic file in which the data has been compressed to allow faster downloads. The GIF image can be displayed on nearly any kind of computer. Some communications software—notably the CompuServe Information Manager — has built-in facilities for viewing GIF pictures on-line and off-line. Others need to retrieve a decoder or viewer program designed to decompress the data in the file. GIF pictures files then can be downloaded (retrieved) and, with the viewer, looked at off-line. (Even some CIM users like to use such decoders, saying they prefer the picture quality in the viewer software to CIM's graphics facilities.)

Where to Find a Viewer

In Library 1 ("Forum Information") of the Graphics Support Forum (GO GRAPHSUP) are files that list viewer/decoder programs for different kinds of computers. You'll find:

- PROGS.IBM (IBM and compatibles).
- PROGS.MAC (Macintosh).
- PROGS.AMG (Amiga).
- PROGS.TXT (other types).

Download the program that is right for you, then read it with any word processor or text editor to see what viewers are available, the configurations supported, and any special features offered. Once you have found a viewer to try, go to Library 3 of the Graphics Support Forum (GO GRAPHSUP) and download the decoder you have chosen.

Testing It Out

Once you have retrieved the decoder and checked out the users' manual, you can give it a test drive. In Library 3 ("Hall of Fame") of the Computer Art Forum (GO COMART) you will find XMASTR.GIF, a simple, small-sized GIF; it is a good choice for testing your decoder program.

Finding Pictures

Once you are satisfied with your choice of viewers, you're ready for more pictures. A catalog, or listing, of the files in our libraries is available in each library. A catalog, or listing, of the files in the graphics forum libraries is available in each. Using the Library number in place of the ## in the following filenames, look for:

- QPIC##.CAT for The Quick Picture Forum (GO QPIC).
- ART##.CAT for The Graphics Gallery Forum (GO GALLERY).
- CA##.CAT for Computer Art Forum (GO COMART).
- GC##.CAT for The Graphics Corner Forum (GO CORNER).

For faster downloading, each catalog is also available as an archived (compressed) data file; just look for *.ARC instead of *.CAT.

Also, a master catalog of all files in all the libraries of each forum is available. You can find these master catalogs in Library 1 of each forum; the filenames are QPICS.ARC, ARTGAL.ARC, COMART.ARC, CORNER.ARC, and PICS.ARC.

Keywords

Using keywords is another way of finding files. If you don't know the name of a file, keywords can help you locate it. When you enter a Library, choose BROWSE (the first choice on your options menu), then enter the keyword to use in the search. You might use CATs, for example, to search for programs or GIFs that pertain to cats. You can also specify a particular resolution, entering 320 x 200 to search for files that have a resolution of 320 x 200 (note, though, that the spaces *are* required).

Graphics File Finder

Finally, with the Graphics File Finder (GO GRAPHFF), file searches can easily be conducted in any or all of the forums, without having to visit each forum separately. GRAPHFF allows you to search by filename, file type, keyword, file submitter, or file extension, and these specifications can be combined to further narrow the search.

Index